GLOBAL ISSUES OF OUR TIME

Edited by John Lidstone

CAMBRIDGE
UNIVERSITY PRESS

Published by the Press Syndicate of the University of Cambridge
The Pitt Building, Trumpington Street, Cambridge CB2 1RP, UK
40 West 20th Street, New York, NY 10011–4211, USA
10 Stamford Road, Oakleigh, Melbourne 3166, Australia

© Cambridge University Press 1995
First published 1995

Printed in Hong Kong by Colorcraft

National Library of Australia cataloguing in publication data
Global issues of our time.
Includes index.
1. Human ecology. 2. Human ecology – Problems, exercises, etc. 3. Human geography. 4. Human geography – Problems, exercises, etc. 5. Social ecology. 6. Social ecology – Problems, exercises, etc. I.
Lidstone, John, 1947– .
363.7076

Library of Congress cataloguing in publication data
Global issues of our time/edited by John Lidstone.
    p.   cm.
Includes index.
1. Geography—Juvenile literature. [1. Geography.]
I. Lidstone, John, 1947–
G133.G56 1994
910—dc20   93–34256
                                                    CIP
                                                    AC

A catalogue record for this book is available from the British Library.

ISBN 0 521 421632   Paperback

CONTENTS

	Foreword	vi
1	Looking at the world—positively	1
2	Amazonia: The view from Brazil	10
3	Rich and poor in Nigeria: Bridging the gap	19
4	China's population	27
5	Fighting the war against hunger in India	36
6	Urbanisation in Bangladesh	47
7	Urbanisation in Brazil	52
8	Development in Bhutan: Good or bad?	60
9	Saving Australia's soils	71
10	Dams: The environmental hazard	81
11	A new airport for Hong Kong	91
12	Industrial pollution in Taiwan	99
13	Bulgaria: At a geographical crossroads	104
14	The diamond trade: Rich world–poor world	111
15	Defending Finland from acid rain	118
16	Controlling road traffic in Singapore	128
17	Past floods: Understanding the greenhouse effect	137
18	The Netherlands and global warming	144
19	Energy: A persistent global issue	149
20	Changing lifestyles in Europe: The coal and steel industries	159
	Index	168

UNITED KINGDOM
David Wright, Lecturer, Geographical Education, University of East Anglia, Norwich
Rising sea levels
Chapter 17

NETHERLANDS (NEDERLAND)
Drs Marga Terwindt, Lecturer in Geographical Education, Geografisch Instituut, Universiteit-Utrecht
Rising sea levels
Chapter 18

GERMANY (DEUTSCHE DEMOKRATISCHE REPUBLIK/ BUNDESREPUBLIK DEUTSCHLAND)
Dr Hartmut Volkmann, Professor of Geography, Ruhr-Universität, Bochum
Unemployment
Chapter 20

FINLAND (SUOMI)
Dr Lea Houtsonen, Lecturer in Geography, University of Helsinki
Acid rain
Chapter 15

CANADA
Patricia Green-Milberg, Lecturer in Geography, CEGEP, John Abbott College, Québec
Water management and indigenous people
Chapter 10

UNITED STATES OF AMERICA
Dr Joseph P. Stoltman, Professor of Geographical Education, Western Michigan University, Kalamazoo, Michigan
Energy conservation
Chapter 19

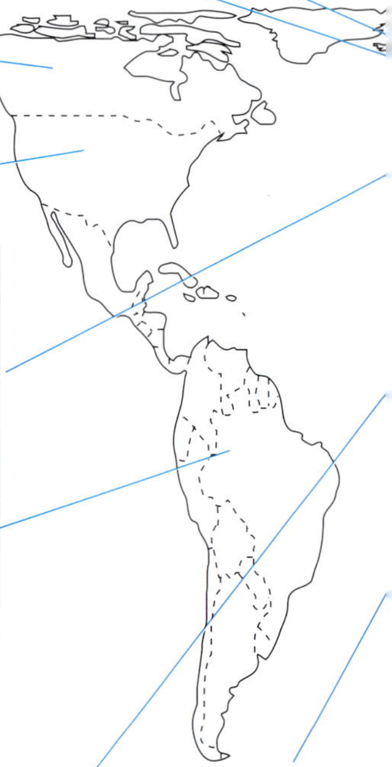

BELGIUM (BELGIQUE/ BELGIË)
Dr Ann Verhetsel, Lecturer in Economic Geography, Faculty of Applied Economics, Universiteit-Antwerpen
The diamond trade
Chapter 14

BRAZIL (BRASIL)
David Marcio S. Rodrigues, Lecturer in Geography, Universidade Federal de Minas, Gerais,
Rainforest management
Chapter 2

Sônia Maria Marchiorato Carneiro, Adjunct Teacher, Departamento de Métodos e Técnicas da Educação, Setor de Educação da Universidade Federal do Paraná, Curitiba; **Antônio Lineu Carneiro**, Adjunct Teacher,

Departamento de Métodos e Técnicas da Educação, Setor de Educação da Universidade Federal do Paraná, Curitiba; **Zeno Soares Crocetti**, Teacher, Departamento de Educação da Prefeitura Municipal, Curitiba
Urban development
Chapter 7

BULGARIA (BÂLGARIJA)
Dr Dimitar Kanchev, Senior Lecturer, Geographical Education, University of Sofia
Nationhood
Chapter 13

NIGERIA
Dr Julie Okpala, Senior Lecturer, Geographical Education, University of Nigeria
Poverty
Chapter 3

This world map shows each of the contributors to the book, their location throughout the world and the topic of their contribution with corresponding chapter numbers (local names are given in brackets)

BHUTAN (DRUK-YUL)

Jagar Dorji, Curriculum Officer, Ministry of Education, Royal Kingdom of Bhutan
Development and conservation
Chapter 8

CHINA (ZHONGGUO)

Dr Lee Chun-Fen, Professor of Geography, East China Normal University, Shanghai; **Dr Yan Zheng-Yuang**, Associate Professor of Geography, East China Normal University, Shanghai
Population
Chapter 4

BANGLADESH

Dr Mesbah-us-Saleheen, Professor of Geography, Department of Geography, Jahangirnagar University, Savar, Dhaka; **Dr A. H. M. Raihan Sharif**, Associate Professor of Geography, Department of Geography, Jahangirnagar University, Savar, Dhaka; **Sheikh Md Mozurul Huq**, Associate Professor of Geography, Department of Geography, Jahangirnagar University, Savar, Dhaka; **Dr A. K. M. Abul Kalam**, Assistant Professor of Geography, Department of Geography, Jahangirnagar University, Savar, Dhaka
Urbanisation
Chapter 6

TAIWAN (T'AIWAN)*

Dr Linda Chung-Ling Ouyang, Lecturer, Department of Geography, Taiwan Normal University, Taipei
Industrial pollution
Chapter 12

HONG KONG

Tammy Yim Lin Kwan, formerly Lecturer in Geographical Education, University of Hong Kong, currently Lecturer, Queensland University of Technology, Brisbane
Economic development
Chapter 11

INDIA (BHARAT)

Dr Savita Sinha, Professor of Geography, National Council of Education Research and Training, New Delhi
Hunger
Chapter 5

AUSTRALIA

Dr John Lidstone, Senior Lecturer in Education, Queensland University of Technology, Brisbane
Book editor
Chapter 1

Marilyn Wiber, Head, Geography Department, Mentone Girls' Grammar School, Melbourne, Victoria
Soil erosion
Chapter 9

SINGAPORE

Yee Sze Onn, Senior Lecturer, Geographical Education, National Institute of Education, Nanyang Technological University, Singapore
Traffic and congestion
Chapter 16

* The status of Taiwan as an independent nation state is not universally recognised

FOREWORD

On behalf of the global community of geographical educators, I welcome the publication of this book, which supports all aspects of the 'International Charter on Geographical Education'.

The charter, which was developed and proclaimed by the Commission on Geographical Education of the International Geographical Union in Washington, DC, 1992, begins with a chapter on global issues, challenges and responses of our time. It states

> The resolution of major issues and problems facing our world requires the full commitment of people of all generations. All of the following issues have a strong geographical dimension:
>
> population dynamics, food and hunger, urbanisation, socio-economic disparities, illiteracy, poverty, unemployment, refugees and stateless persons, violation of human rights, disease, crime, gender inequalities, migration, extinction of plants and animals, deforestation, soil erosion, desertification, natural disasters, toxic and nuclear waste, climatic change, atmospheric pollution, ozone holes, limits of resource, limits to growth, land use, ethnic conflict, war, regionalism, nationalism and globalisation on 'Spaceship Earth'.
>
> The conflicts created by these problems and issues present a challenge to geographical educators, who are committed to giving all people the hope, confidence and ability to work for a better world.

In the face of the current global challenges, it is encouraging to see how John Lidstone has succeeded in finding authors from around the world who share the readiness, ability and commitment, not just to analyse and criticise current and future issues on our 'Spaceship Earth', but also to offer ideas, visions and strategies to meet the many dilemmas confronting our 'global village'. These authors, representing all the continents of the world, are internationally recognised. They offer our young people an opportunity to increase their international knowledge and competence, to cooperate on a broad range of economic, political, cultural and environmental issues in a shrinking world, and to face the future with confidence and hope.

May this publication lead to more understanding and peace among people on the one hand and between human beings and our natural environment on the other!

Hartwig Haubrich
Chair of the Commission on Geographical Education of the International Geographical Union

IGU Commission on
Geographical Education

CHAPTER 1

LOOKING AT THE WORLD—POSITIVELY

John Lidstone

GLOBAL ISSUES

Some of the global issues of our time are summarised in Figure 1.1. Some of them affect some countries more than others and some are more visible than others. However, they are all serious and demand attention. Much of the evidence presented to us in newspapers or on television seems to indicate that the world is in a mess. Many people respond to the flood of information about social and environmental problems by asking if there is a future at all.

While all the issues listed in Figure 1.1 are of major importance and should not be ignored, there is much that is good in the world and much that is getting better. Here are some examples.

- **Disease control:** Smallpox was once a major killer in the world, but in 1979 the World Health Organisation declared that it had been totally eradicated. Few people today die of influenza, but in 1918 twenty million people died in *one* influenza epidemic.
- **Wealth:** While it is true that about 750 million people, which is 20 per cent of the world's population, are living in poverty, the same number were living in poverty 200 years ago, which represented well over 90 per cent of the world's population. Today there are 3.6 billion people, including most of those who are reading this book, who are *not* living in poverty.
- **Life expectancy:** In almost all countries of the world life expectancy has increased greatly in recent years. Figure 1.2 shows that life expectancy has increased since 1965, especially in low income countries. It also shows that in 1900 life expectancy in the United States was about the same as in developing countries in 1965. Similarly, the percentage of infants surviving the first year of life has increased since 1965, especially in the developing countries. It is true that a child in the developed world has a better chance of surviving the first year of life than a child in the developing world, but great progress is being made and will continue to be made.
- **Resources:** Finally, the world is not running out of resources. Between 1950 and 1970 there was a forty-fold increase in the known material reserves of the world. It has been claimed that there has never been a time in history of greater abundance of resources, nor has there been a time when we are less likely to run out of resources than today. The world is becoming better at both creating resources by new discoveries and conserving existing resources.

Despite this good news, we must not pretend that all is right with the world. Figure 1.3 shows where the people are in the world and where the world's income goes. The amount of wealth shared between the fifty wealthiest countries is much greater than that shared between the forty-five poorest countries.

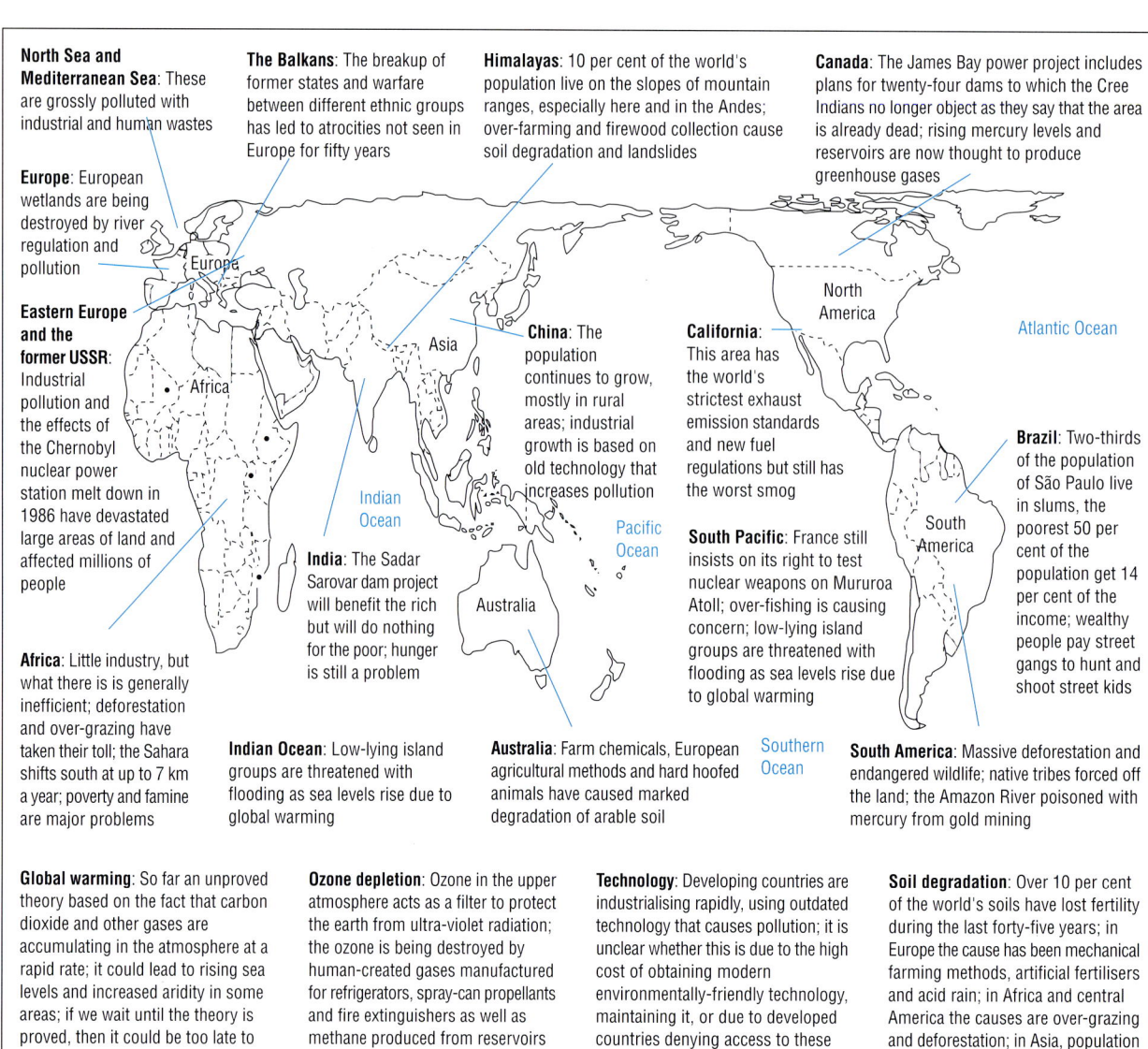

Figure 1.1 Some of the global issues of our time

LOOKING AT THE WORLD—POSITIVELY

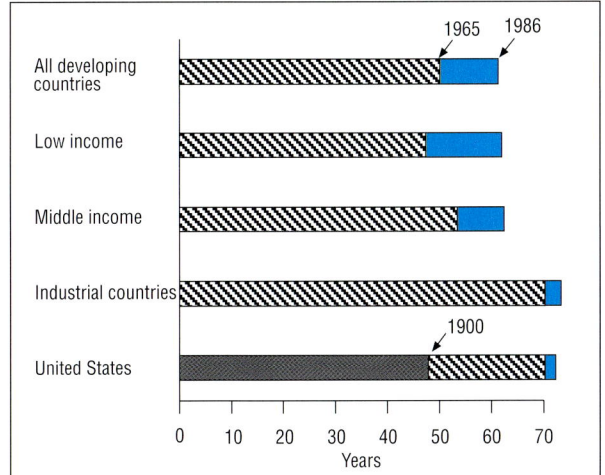

Figure 1.2a Life expectancy at birth

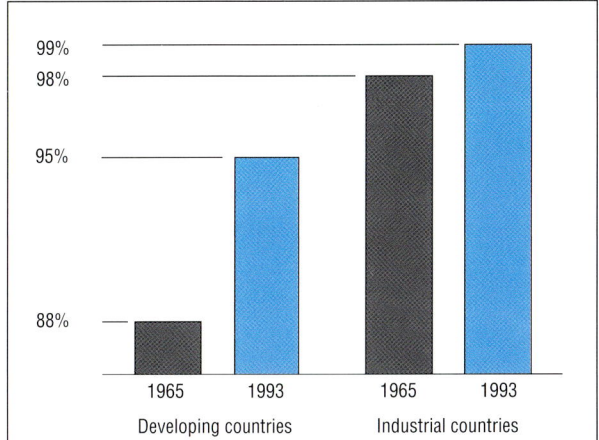

Figure 1.2b Infants surviving the first year of life

1. Discuss the differences between the changes in life expectancies in the groups of countries shown in Figure 1.2a. What do you think will happen in the next twenty years?
2. Discuss the information contained in Figures 1.2 and 1.3. In your opinion, what appears to be the main cause of poverty?

Life expectancy at birth is one of the main factors that controls the future size of the population. If life expectancy increases, then the population will also increase, unless the number of births decreases. Look at Figure 1.4.

3. For each of the sixteen countries, compare the changes in life expectancy and total fertility between 1970 and 1990. What conclusions can you draw about future population growth?
4. Compare your conclusions to the previous activities with those of others in your class. Make a list of the various points of view that emerge.

So far, this chapter has included some facts that, to the best of our knowledge, are correct. It has also included some conclusions that either the writer or the reader has drawn from those facts. We have a choice about the way we interpret the information that is before us, and the way we choose to interpret it will probably decide what actions we will take.

Psychologists have now proved that what we expect to happen affects how we understand events and often also affects the events themselves. This finding is important for two reasons. First, people who are *optimists* when they are

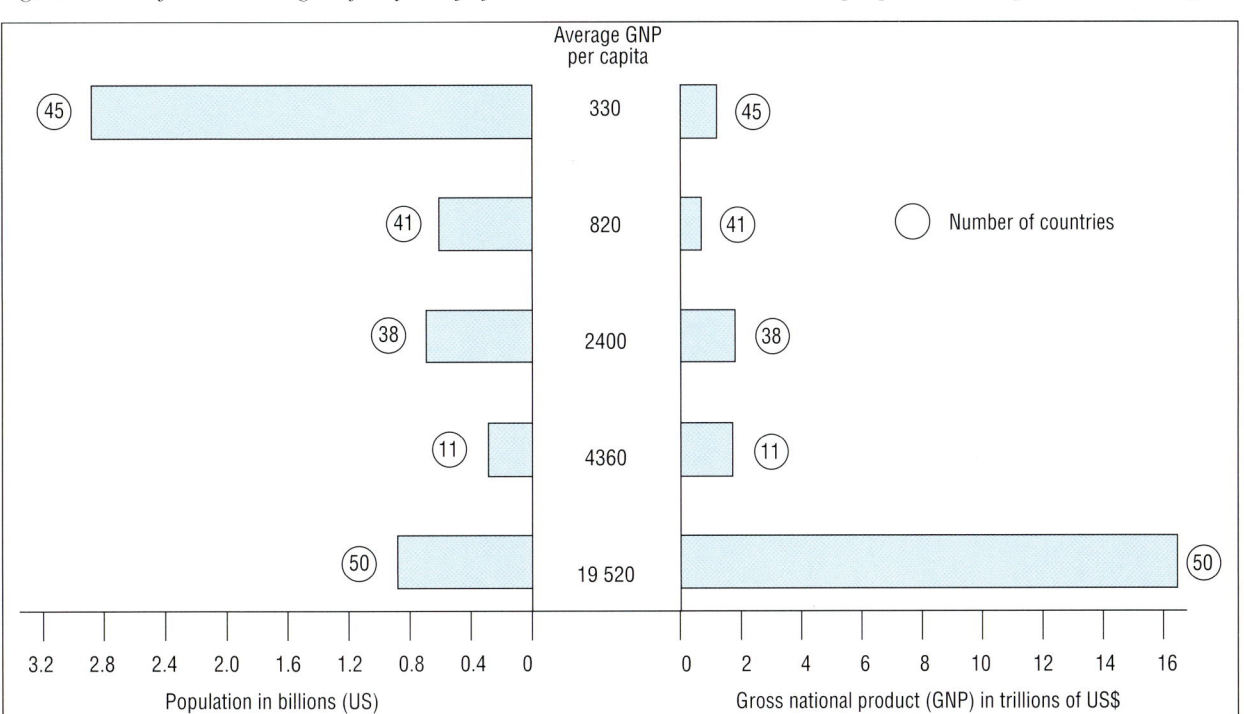

Figure 1.3 Where the people are and where the income goes

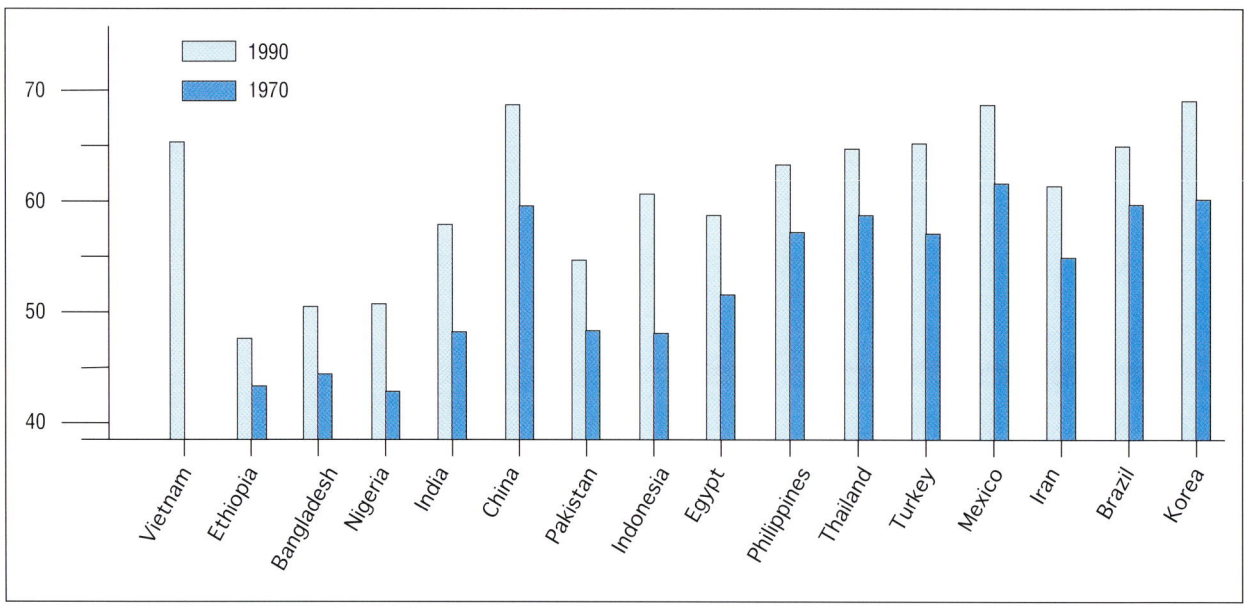

Figure 1.4a   Life expectancy at birth for the sixteen largest developing countries

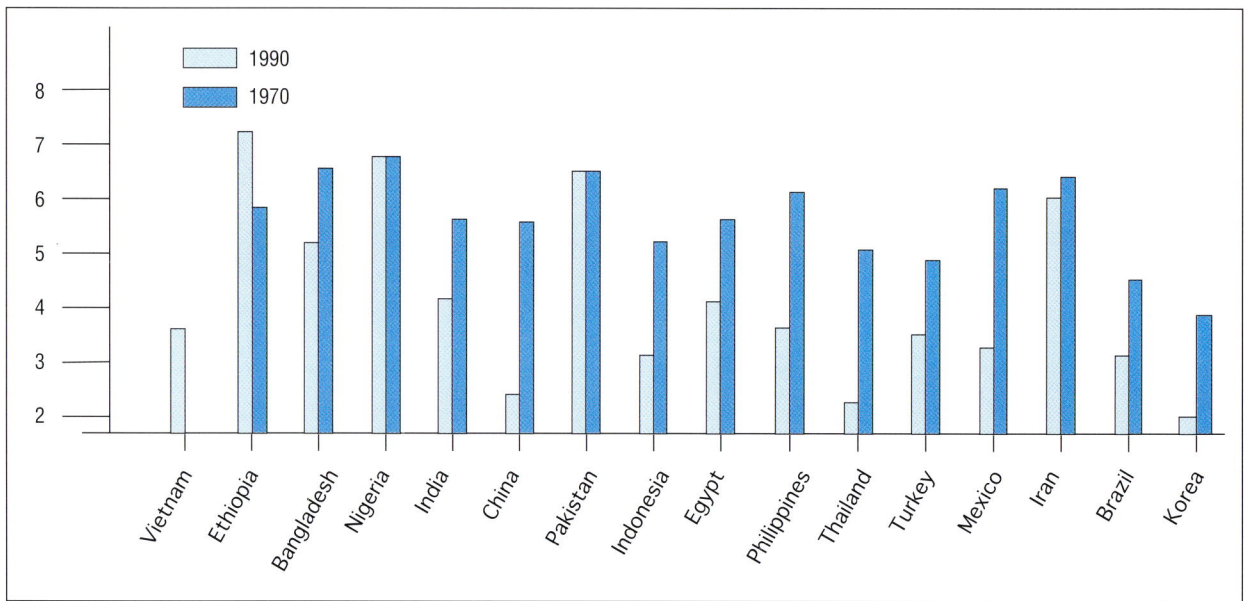

Figure 1.4b   The total fertility rate (births per woman) for the sixteen largest developing countries

young appear to be healthier and happier in later life, and are often more willing to try to achieve improvements than those who are *pessimists*. Second, if we convince ourselves that we cannot do something to make the world a better place, then we will probably stop trying.

WHAT SHOULD WE BE DOING?

The information we receive about the social and environmental problems facing the world comes from two main sources—**scientists** and **lobby groups**. Sometimes these two groups include the same people, but they are acting in different ways.

Lobby groups are generally political, which means that they seek to achieve reforms through government action. To do this, lobby groups must persuade politicians of the need for the changes they desire, and they must show that voters or the people will support politicians who support those reforms.

Both these aims need the issues to be presented in sensational form. They must be clear, simple enough to be understood quickly and the consequences of ignoring them must seem to be very serious. This can cause problems because in most issues the facts are sometimes disputed, are rarely as simple as they are made to seem and are often difficult to interpret. The facts may also lead to more than one possible conclusion.

Scientists are not just scientists. They are also people who may have strong opinions. But when they are acting as scientists, they are not concerned with right and wrong or politics. Often advertisers and lobbyists claim that something 'has not been scientifically proved'. However, scientists do not establish either proof or truth. They are concerned with how useful a theory or a law is in describing, explaining or predicting what happens either in society or in nature.

Someone once described scientists as professional sceptics. Scientists challenge any idea about how nature or society works and insist that the idea be checked by observation and experiment. Albert Einstein, the great physicist, once commented that 'imagination is more important than knowledge, and there is no completely logical way to a new scientific idea'.

Most lobby groups contain very sincere people who have interpreted the facts as they see them and believe that reform is needed. As a result of their work, scientists may support one lobby group or another. However, when we make decisions regarding issues, we should at first be sceptical—like scientists. We should listen to both sides of any discussion and arm ourselves with facts, not opinions, before coming to any conclusions.

In dealing with social and environmental problems, the facts may be interpreted in a range of ways. Table 1.1 shows two opposite ways of looking at the world. We may not agree entirely with either of the extremes, but feel that the truth lies somewhere in between. However, most of us will have views that fall towards one end or the other on each aspect of life on earth.

> 5 *a* Table 1.1 lists a number of opposing statements about the future of the world. On a copy of the table place a tick in the boxes to show how much you agree with each statement. (A tick in box 1 means that you agree strongly with the statement on the left. A tick in box 5 means that you agree strongly with the statement on the right. A tick in box 3 means that you agree with both statements.) Add up the value of all your ticks and compare your total with others in your class.
> *b* Debate your current views on some of the statements made in Table 1.1.

If you scored less than 35 you tend to agree with the statements in Group A. People who agree strongly with these statements are sometimes described as Cornucopians. The name means 'horn of plenty' and these people believe that if present trends continue, economic growth and technological advances will produce a less crowded, healthier world with less pollution and more resources.

If you scored over 49, you tend to agree with the statements in Group B. These people are referred to as Neo-Malthusians. Thomas Malthus was an eighteenth century economist who believed that population would eventually outgrow food supplies and would be brought back into balance only by starvation, war and disease. These people believe that if present trends continue, the world will become more crowded and polluted, and many resources will become exhausted. This will lead to greater social and political turmoil as the rich get richer and the poor get poorer.

People who scored between 35 and 49 are neutral between the two extremes and will probably examine each issue on its merits.

Cornucopians think that Neo-Malthusians are 'doom and gloom pessimists'. Neo-Malthusians call Cornucopians 'unrealistic technological optimists'. People of either view can

Table 1.1 How to manage the world in the future

Group A	1	2	3	4	5	Group B
Human beings should use nature to increase economic growth						Human beings should work with nature so that economic growth is gained which sustains the earth's life-support system
Environmental problems are exaggerated and can be cured by new inventions and economic growth						Environmental problems are serious now and could become more serious unless we shift towards sustainable forms of economic growth
Population should not be controlled since only people can solve the world's problems						Population should be controlled in order to prevent disruption of local, regional and global life support systems
People should have as many children as they want						People should be free to have as many children as they want only if this freedom does not infringe on the rights of others to survive

May be copied for classroom use. © Cambridge University Press 1995

Group A	1	2	3	4	5	Group B
We will not run out of renewable resources because we will learn to manage them better or find substitutes						In many areas potentially renewable resources are already seriously degraded; there are no substitutes for the earth's topsoils, grasslands, forests, fisheries and wildlife
We will not run out of non-renewable resources because we can find more, mine less concentrated deposits or find substitutes						We may not find substitutes for some non-renewable resources and substitutes may take too long to phase in without causing economic hardship
Economic growth and new technologies can reduce resource depletion, pollution and environmental degradation to acceptable levels						Because of high rates of resource use and unnecessary waste, more developed countries are causing unacceptable regional and global resource depletion, pollution and environmental degradation
Economic growth can be achieved by nuclear power, oil, coal and natural gas						Economic growth can be achieved through energy conservation (perpetual solar, wind and flowing water) and sustainable use of potentially renewable biomass such as wood and crop wastes
Recycling, reuse and reducing unnecessary resource wastes are good ideas, but should not limit economic growth						Reducing unnecessary resource waste is essential for the health of the earth and long term economic productivity; non-renewable resources will last longer, renewable resource stocks can recover and the environmental impact of resource exploitation can be minimised
The earth's plants and animals exist to serve our needs						The earth's plants and animals are potentially renewable resources that should be used only on a sustainable basis to meet vital needs, not frivolous wants
Pollution control should not interfere with economic growth, which provides funds for pollution control						Inadequate pollution control damages people and other forms of life and reduces long term economic productivity
Polluters should be given government subsidies and tax breaks to install pollution control equipment						Polluters should pay for reducing pollution to acceptable levels; goods and services should include the costs of pollution control so that consumers will know the effects of what they buy and use
We should emphasise reducing pollution in the environment						We should emphasise preventing pollution from entering the environment
Waste materials should be burned, dumped or buried						Waste materials should be regarded as resources to be recycled or reused

May be copied for classroom use. © Cambridge University Press 1995

be either optimistic or pessimistic. Optimistic Neo-Malthusians work hard towards encouraging people to change their lifestyles to reduce pressure on the natural environment and to achieve greater social justice at a global scale. Optimistic Cornucopians work hard towards developing new technological solutions to global issues. Pessimists on both sides probably sit back and do nothing!

> 6 Consider whether you tend towards a Cornucopian or a Neo-Malthusian approach to global issues. Decide what you personally are prepared to do to assist in reaching a solution to the problems that face the world now.

WHAT IS HAPPENING IN THE WORLD TODAY?

> 7 This book contains nineteen case studies covering eighteen different countries. Before you examine these case studies, discuss your image of life in each of the eighteen countries. What problems and advantages do you associate with each country? In which countries do you think that people have the best lives? (Use the map on pages iv and v.)

Table 1.2 presents a series of measures of life in each of these eighteen countries on a scale from 0 to 10 in terms of human misery or happiness. (Zero means that a particular aspect of life is unlikely to cause particular misery to people in that country and 10 means that a particular aspect of life in a country causes its people great misery.) The final two columns give a human suffering index for life in that country and indicate where the country comes in a rank order for human suffering. This measurement scale has been devised by the Population Crisis Committee in Washington and covers 141 countries in total.

According to this scale, of the countries discussed in this book, Belgium and the Netherlands, with a score of 2 each, are the countries with the least human suffering. Bhutan, with a score of 73, has the most human misery. (Overall, within the world position of 141 nations, Denmark has a score of 1—the least human suffering—and Mozambique has a score of 93—the most human suffering.)

Figure 1.5 shows the pattern of human misery and quality of life over the whole world.

Table 1.2 Measures of human suffering and quality of life

Country	Life expectancy	Daily kJ supply	Clean drinking water	Infant immunisation	Secondary school enrolment	GNP per head	Rate of inflation	Communications technology	Political freedom	Civil rights	Human suffering index	World position—141 nations
Australia	0	0	0	0	0	1	2	1	0	0	4	6
Bangladesh	10	5	2	8	10	10	6	10	2	5	68	100
Belgium	1	0	0	0	0	0	0	1	0	0	2	2
Bhutan	10	-	7	1	10	10	6	10	8	4	73	111
Brazil	4	0	0	5	10	6	10	6	3	6	50	59
Bulgaria	2	0	0	0	4	6	10	3	2	5	32	34
Canada	0	0	0	0	0	0	1	0	1	1	3	4
China	3	0	2	0	10	9	7	10	10	10	61	78
Finland	1	3	0	0	0	0	1	1	2	0	8	15
Germany	1	0	0	0	1	0	0	1	0	3	6	9
Hong Kong	0	1	0	5	5	2	5	1	5	5	29	30
India	8	4	2	2	10	9	6	10	4	8	63	84
Netherlands	0	1	0	0	0	0	0	1	0	0	2	2
Nigeria	10	5	5	8	10	10	0	10	6	6	70	105
Singapore	1	1	0	4	6	2	0	1	6	7	28	28
Taiwan	1	0	1	4	1	5	1	3	4	5	25	25
UK	1	0	0	0	3	1	5	1	1	4	16	22
USA	1	0	0	0	0	0	2	0	1	1	5	8

Source: Population Crisis Committee, Washington DC, 1992

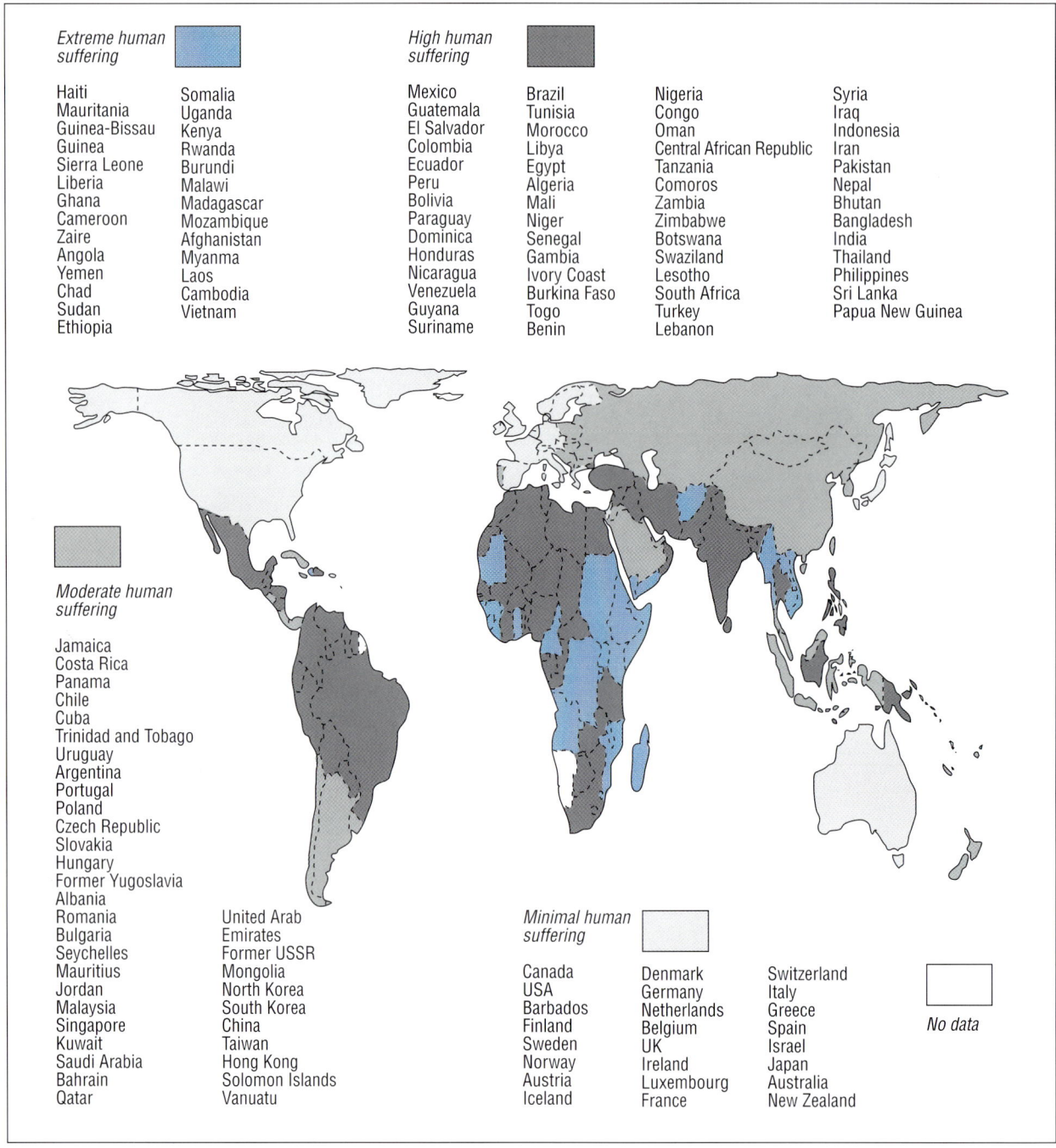

Figure 1.5 *The extent of human suffering in the world*

8 Discuss the ten aspects of life that have been identified as representing important contributors to human misery. For each, decide how important you regard that aspect in your own life. Are some aspects more important to you than others?

9 If your own country appears on the list, do you agree with the ratings that have been given?

10 Examine the details for each country in the list. Identify any figures that you find surprising. How do they match your previous impressions of each country?

11 Using an atlas draw an outline map of the world. Using different colours for each category shown in Figure 1.5, shade your map to show the distribution of human misery. Examine the pattern your shading has created. Compare this pattern with that on other maps in your atlas or other books which discuss the differences between countries. What similarities/differences do you notice?

HOW SHOULD WE VIEW GLOBAL ISSUES?

If an absence of the aspects of life listed in Table 1.2 represents measures of human misery, then we can assume that their presence represents human happiness. However, if we start at the other end and consider the things that bring happiness, then frequently the list will include many material things.

> 12 Make a list of items that are currently regarded as status symbols that could be regarded in other ways. (For example, a brand new, large car could be regarded as a status symbol, but the pollution it creates could mean that it is considered in other ways too.)

When we try to decide how the earth should be managed, there is one basic rule. Each generation should meet its own needs without damaging the chances of future generations meeting theirs. This seems simple, but how to achieve it is very complex. Both Cornucopians and Neo-Malthusians would agree with the general principle, although they would disagree about what to do. One thing that all deep thinkers have agreed upon down the ages is that the constant search for material wealth will eventually lead to disaster. Table 1.3 lists some of the statements that have been made throughout history by leaders of major world religions.

These teachings do not mean that we must all give up the good things in life that we enjoy. It may be that many of us would actually be happier with a simpler lifestyle. A contributor writing in the *Worldwatch Institute Report on Progress Towards a Sustainable Lifestyle* wrote

> How much of the packaging that we throw out with the household trash every year—78 kilograms apiece in the Netherlands—would we rather never see? How many of the unsolicited sales pitches each of us receives daily—37% of the mail in the United States—are nothing but bothersome junk? How many of the 18 kilograms of non-refillable drinks bottles each Japanese throws out each year could not just as easily be refilled? How much of the advertising in our morning newspapers—65% of the print area—would we not gladly see left out? How many of the kilometres we drive—6160 a year apiece in the former West Germany—would we not gladly give up if livable neighbourhoods were closer to work, a variety of shops closer to home, streets safe to walk and bike and public transport easier and faster? In many ways we may be happier with less.

The chapters of this book have been selected to show some of the ways in which different countries have started to address the global issues of our time. As you read the book and respond to the suggested activities, ask yourself what you and your country can learn from these experiences and what you can offer to others to help them. Compare the problems experienced in one country with the solutions suggested for another. In particular, you could consider the following questions.

Table 1.3 The teachings of world religions or cultures on consumption

Religion or culture	Teaching and source
American Indian	'Miserable as we seem in thy eyes, we consider ourselves ... much happier than thou, in that we are very content with the little that we have.' *Micmac Chief*
Buddhist	'Whoever in this world overcomes his selfish cravings, his sorrows fall away from him, like drops of water from a lotus flower.' *Dhammapada, 336*
Christian	'What shall it profit a man if he shall gain the whole world and lose his own soul?' *Luke, 9:25*
Confucian	'Excess and deficiency are equally at fault.' *Confucius, XI.15*
Ancient Greek	'Nothing in excess.' *Inscription at Oracle, Delphi*
Hindu	'That person who lives completely free from desires, without longing ... attains peace.' *Bhagavad-Gita, II.71*
Islamic	'Poverty is my pride.' *Muhammad*
Jewish	'Give me neither poverty nor riches.' *Proverbs, 30:8*
Taoist	'He who knows he has enough is rich.' *Tao Te Ching*

> 13 What are the links between the urban problems of Singapore and those of Dhaka?
> 14 What has the experience of hunger in India to offer those facing the current urban problems in Bangladesh?
> 15 What are the connections between the problems of energy in the United States, unemployment in Germany and acid rain in Finland? Is there a solution to all these problems?
> 16 'Energy' is a recurring theme in several chapters. Discuss the links you observe between each country as you study the text.
> 17 Colonialism is mentioned in several chapters. What have been the results of colonialism in various countries in the world? Are there any colonial relationships between countries today?
> 18 Discuss how you could change your life to be more environmentally friendly without any inconvenience to yourself.

CHAPTER 2

AMAZONIA: THE VIEW FROM BRAZIL

● ● ● ● ● ● ● ● ●

David Marcio S. Rodrigues

The Amazon River is the largest river in the world and its basin covers more than 40 per cent of the total land area of South America. At any one time, the Amazon, and its more than 1000 tributaries, contain two-thirds of all the river water in the world. Seventeen of its tributaries are over 1600 kilometres long.

The map, Figure 2.2, which illustrates the northern portion of South America, shows that more than half the area of Brazil (60 per cent in fact) lies within the basin of the Amazon River, and by far the greatest part of the Amazon Basin lies within Brazilian territory.

BRAZIL'S PROBLEM WITH THE AMAZON

Brazil's intended future use of the Amazon forests has been heavily criticised, especially the destruction of the forests, the pollution of the rivers and the gradual disappearance of the native population.

This criticism is partly due to a realisation by many world leaders that past mistakes in the use of natural resources in their own countries have led to environmental problems. And, having failed to care for natural resources in their own countries, many people want to influence others who do still have large reserves of natural resources.

For over a hundred years, many people in underdeveloped countries have been living without adequate food, housing or hygiene. At the same time, people in the more developed world have been using natural resources unwisely in an effort to develop their own economies. Today, many renewable flora and fauna resources are becoming extinct while non-renewable mineral reserves are increasing due to the development of more sophisticated technology.

The need to conserve natural resources is now well known and undeniable, but at the same time the Brazilian government has a duty to meet the needs of its own people. There are many poor people in Brazil living in overcrowded conditions. These people often look towards the vast areas of the Amazon for a chance to improve their own lives. The 'forest people' (workers whose living is made from the mining and collection of minerals, vegetation and animals in the Amazon) are also concerned that preserva-

Figure 2.1   The Negro River near the city of Manaus, one tributary of the Amazon River

AMAZONIA: THE VIEW FROM BRAZIL

Figure 2.2 The Amazon Basin covers a huge area of South America, including half the land area of Brazil

tion of the forests and the native Indian population may destroy their own livelihoods. Brazil must develop its own economy if it is to give all its people the standard of living that they desire. To do this, Brazil must make use of the natural resources that are available—including those that exist within the Amazon Basin.

Realising the importance of the Amazon region, both to the world and to its own future, the Brazilian government has designated the Brazilian part of the Amazon Basin the 'Legal Amazon'. This area includes the states of Acre, Amazonas, Para and Rondonia, the federal territories of Amapa and Roraima, and the northern parts of the states of Mato Grosso and Goias.

If we are to judge how Amazonia should be managed, we need to understand the nature of this huge area and its place within the independent nation of Brazil as well as its contribution to the welfare of the planet we all share.

> 1   a   Use an atlas map and compare the size of Brazil with that of your own country and continent. What other countries and cities lie at a similar distance from your nearest city as Brasilia (the capital of Brazil) to Manaus (in the Amazon Basin)?
>   b   Discuss the problems that may occur in governing and caring for a country as large as Brazil.
> 2   Some people have said that Brazil should stop all development in the Amazon. Look at a map of your own country and imagine that you have been asked to stop development in 60 per cent of your country's area. What problems would this cause for your country?

THE PLACE OF AMAZONIA IN BRAZIL

Although Brazil occupies such a large part of South America, it has traditionally been oriented eastwards over the Atlantic Ocean rather than westward towards the rest of South America. Almost 95 per cent of the total population of Brazil is concentrated in an area 500 kilometres along the coast of the Atlantic Ocean. All the large Brazilian seaport cities are located in this area. An atlas map of South America shows that the borders with neighbouring countries coincide with those parts of Brazil that have low population density.

> 3   Make a list of the seven countries of South America that share borders with Brazil's Amazon region. How many of them have capital cities closer to Manaus than Brazil's capital? Why is the Brazilian government particularly conscious of this?

WHAT THE AMAZON REGION HAS TO OFFER

The Amazon Basin is undulating with flat areas along the river beds, with the Guiana plateau to the north, and the Central plateau to the south. This region is crossed by the rivers that make up the Amazon Basin—including the Amazon itself which is 6577 kilometres long.

Much of the region has an equatorial climate where both the humidity and temperatures are high. Temperatures average between 25°C and 27°C each month. In the northern and south-eastern parts of the region the climate is tropical with less rainfall and a clearly marked dry season.

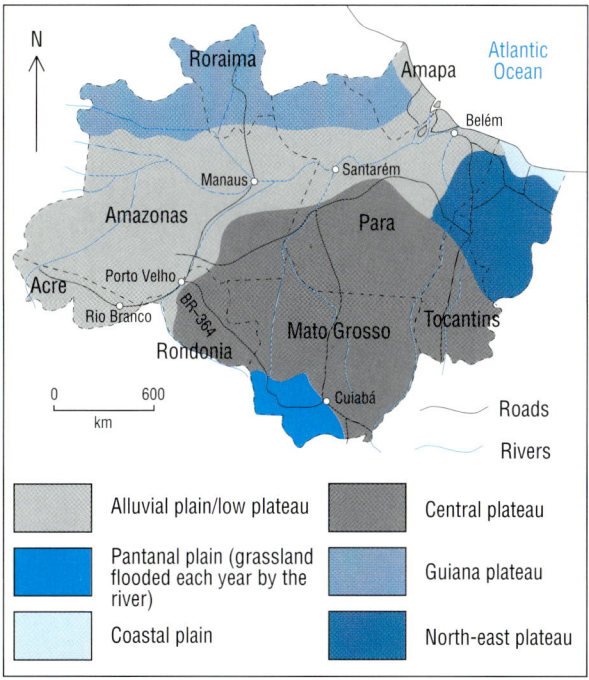

Figure 2.3 The landscapes of Amazonia

Figure 2.4 An area of igapo forest growing on land permanently saturated by river water

Figure 2.5b A typical dwelling of a forest person who travels vast distances by boat to collect rubber and other products

The landforms and the climate help to explain the natural vegetation of the region and also explain why it is described as the kingdom of the waters and the forest.

The Amazon rainforests are the largest in the world (2 500 000 square kilometres) and some of the oldest. There are thousands of different species of trees, liana climbers (cipos) and flowering plants. Some of the trees best known outside Brazil are the Brazil nut tree, the rubber tree (*Hevea brasiliensis*) and the palm trees, but the Amazon Basin is one of the few places left on earth where new species of plants and animals remain to be discovered.

The real richness of the forest lies in its genetic diversity (that is, the great variety of different plants and animals to be found). Of every ten species of living things on earth, six are to be found in the tropical forests and only three will be known to scientists. In the Amazon area, there are known to be more than 1500 species of fish, many of them still not classified by scientists. Almost half of all bird species on earth are found here. There are 319 different sorts of humming bird alone. One-quarter of all pharmaceutical substances have come from tropical forests.

The Amazon Basin contains a variety of forest types, depending on the relief and hydrography (the flow of water). Much of the lower land is covered with rainforest. In lower areas where the land is always covered with water, there are the so-called **igapo forests**, with smaller trees and some palm trees. Running through these igapo forests there is an intricate network of channels called **igarapes**. These channels are very important locally because they provide a transport network for the people who live on the river banks.

On slightly higher areas where the ground is not covered in water, and on the hills of the north and south of the region, there is **'firm land' forest**. The trees are often 60 metres tall and their tops are so close that they do not allow the sun's rays through. This creates a shady environment which is ideal for the development of the micro-organisms that are so important in the nutrient cycles of the forest.

Between these two forest types is the **holm forest** where rubber trees are very common.

As well as the plant and water resources of the Amazon, the area contains vast reserves of gold and other mineral resources that are needed by Brazil and other countries around the world.

The system of rivers, tributaries and channels makes water travel possible and this has been vital in influencing the settlement of the region. Rivers are also important sources of food. However, both the rivers and the forests have made road building very difficult.

Figure 2.5a Small boats such as these have great social, political and economic importance in the lives of the forest people of the Amazon

> 4 Research the origins of decorative plants in your country and discover how many have their origins in the tropical forests of the Amazon.
> 5 Research the uses of native plants from the Amazon in the pharmaceutical industry. Make a list of the medicines that have helped your family that were first discovered in forest plants and trees.

Figure 2.6 A small settlement on the banks of the Tocantins River illustrates the simple conditions in which many of the people of the region live

PEOPLE IN THE AMAZON

Sometimes it is suggested that we have the option of leaving Amazonia in its natural state. In fact, development began four hundred years ago, and has continued ever since. The speed of that development has increased in the past quarter of a century, so the problem the Brazilian government faces is how to manage the development rather than to decide whether or not it should take place.

Settlement in the Amazon has always depended on the navigability of the rivers. Even today, settlement stops where navigation ends, often at waterfalls. Small boats are used for transport between the cities, villages and isolated dwellings of the Amazon. Typical forest people dwellings are simple in construction. Forest people sail great distances into the forest to reach areas where rubber or other products may be collected.

Even government sponsored programs to enlarge the road network has had little overall effect on settlement. Only along the Belém–Brasilia Highway and at some places in the states of Acre and Rondonia has the road network led to increases in population. The roads that have been built join the main towns, all of which lie on rivers.

The current population of the Brazilian Amazon is 7 million. It has the lowest density of population in the country, with fewer than three inhabitants per square kilometre. Half its population is under twenty years of age. The people in this region are generally illiterate and have insufficient health care. Most have had no training and live very modestly from fishing, subsistence agriculture or collecting. Many of the people of the Amazon live in poverty.

The most populated areas of Amazonia are the six major urban areas: Belém, Manaus, Santarém, Cuiabá, Porto Velho and Rio Branco, and the areas along the Belém–Brasilia Highway. These areas have experienced particularly rapid population growth in the last fifteen years.

However, after the area of the Belém–Brasilia Highway, the highest rates of population growth have occurred in the extreme south-eastern part of Amazonia. This area, which used to be called the 'Lost Eldorado', has more recently become known as one of the most devastated areas of Amazonia—Rondonia.

Attracted by the fertility of the soil, the migrants who arrived in Rondonia soon discovered that only 18 per cent of the state's area was suitable for agriculture. Its population, which was hardly 100 000 in 1970, reached 1 million in 1990. In the beginning, the migrants who came from the south along the BR–364 highway (Cuiabá–Porto Velho), produced cocoa and coffee.

Their adventure along this 1400 kilometre road inspired many others and after the road was paved in 1984, migration increased greatly.

In recent years, attempts at farming in the Amazon have failed more and more frequently, particularly in the states of Rondonia and Acre. This has pushed the people towards mining activities which are precarious and frequently illegal. As a result, Amazonia now has a large number of unemployed workers and slum areas have expanded around the few existing towns.

The further result of unemployment and the growth of slums is that infant mortality is high and the crime rate is rising. When people are struggling to gain a livelihood, destruction of the forests and increasing exploitation of the natural environment are inevitable. Figures 2.7 and 2.8 were

Figure 2.7 A crab seller with his catch in jacás (baskets made from natural fibres used to transport food) in the market at Belém

Figure 2.8 Food is transported to the towns and cities of the Amazon in small boats like these seen at Belém

taken in the city of Belém, but similar sights would be seen in all the towns and cities of the Amazon.

Despite the problems of Amazonia mentioned above, people are still moving into the area in search of a living. Furthermore, if Brazil does not allow her own people to develop the vast spaces of Amazonia, then those of neighbouring countries may do so. For the economic future of its own people, as a matter of national security, and for the sake of the Amazon environment itself, the Brazilian government must control developments in Amazonia.

> 6 Why do you think the state of Rondonia has been described as both 'the Lost Eldorado' and one of the areas of greatest devastation of the Amazon forest?
> 7 Make a list of the problems facing the Brazilian government in deciding how to manage the Amazon region.

The fate of the Indian people

It is estimated that when Pedro Alvares Cabral, the Portuguese explorer, arrived in Brazil in 1500, there were approximately 5 million indigenous people living in the area that we now call Brazil.

Thinking that they had reached India, the Portuguese called these inhabitants Indians. As the conquerors reached the interior of the continent, the native people died in large numbers from European diseases—whooping cough and measles in particular. Many Indians were also enslaved or exterminated, just like the natives of the English colonies in Australia and the United States.

Today, the Brazilian Amazon region is the home of the remaining 138 000 native people. They represent less than 10 per cent of the natives who lived here four hundred years ago and 65 per cent of all Indians in Brazil.

As Brazil was developed by the European invaders, many Indians were driven inland from the coast. However, some Indians have integrated into modern Brazilian society. They go to college, have liberal professions, have spouses from outside the Indian community, join the army and enter religious orders. Others want to continue to live their traditional lifestyle. And in the Amazon, while many Indians try to continue living their traditional lifestyle, others have adopted aspects of European culture and some have gone into partnership with foresters and prospectors looking for gold and cassiterite (tin ore), or they collect forest products for international cosmetic firms (such as the Body Shop). Many of the people in Amazonia today are of mixed race.

In the 1980s, an Indian chief called Mario Juruna was elected to Congress and questioned the sincerity of European Brazilians' intentions towards the Indians. However, other people have also taken up the cause of the Amazon Indians. A typical case was that of the rock singer Sting, who paraded with Chief Raoni of the Kayapo tribe through several capitals of the developed world, suggesting that, after four hundred years, Europeans continue to admire the exotic look of the South American 'savage'.

After they were received by Pope John Paul II and by President Mitterrand of France, the sincerity of the cause was questioned. Later however, another story emerged. In 1991, it looked as if Sting had achieved something when the Brazilian government agreed to give protected area status to the homeland of the Kayapo Indians, an area two-thirds the size of Italy. However, recent investigations have shown that the Kayapo Indians earn about US$10 million a year from selling mahogany to Europe to be made into furniture and lavatory seats. The tribespeople have tried to persuade Brazil's president to allow them to carry out deforestation of their lands. This is the very thing that ecological groups want to prevent.

> 8 Do you think that rock singers such as Sting perform a useful function by drawing the attention of the world to the problems faced by the Indians, or do they oversimplify the problems faced by the Brazilian government in trying to care for all its citizens?

Despite their cultural assimilation and growing racial mixing with other Brazilians, the Indians of the Amazon region still face many problems with the government. Small areas have been set aside as Indian reservations. However, their precise boundaries have yet to be defined and the government has yet to find ways to prevent farmers, foresters and prospectors from invading Indian land.

Of all the remaining tribes of the Amazon, the one that appears to be most at risk is the Ianomami people. The Ianomamis may be regarded as some of the most primitive people on earth. They still use stone tools and live by collecting forest products. They grow tobacco, manioc roots, bananas and sugar cane. They have never developed the idea of trading their goods. They wear no clothes and live in collective huts or **malocas**, which house from eighty to a hundred people.

Figure 2.9   An Ianomami maloca

Unfortunately for the Ianomamis, their traditional lands coincide with some of the richest deposits of gold, cassiterite and other minerals. The gold rush reached their territory in 1987 and since then more than 20 000 prospectors have moved in. The gold mines have produced an average of 2 tonnes per month, an enormous quantity of gold, but while this has been good news for the prospectors, a high price has been paid by the Indians: 15 per cent of the population has died as a result of disease and conflict.

The new arrivals in the area have built more than eighty clandestine airstrips for smuggling precious minerals. The mercury used for extracting the gold from its ore often escapes into the rivers and pollutes them, poisoning the fish and the people who eat them. The mines and the airstrips lead to devastation of the forest. The prospectors bring in European diseases and either destroy or deny the Ianomamis' natural sources of food. The result is that the 10 000 surviving members of the Ianomami people are being systematically destroyed.

This has caused great concern in Brazil and important magazines such as *Veja* have devoted whole issues to discussing the disaster. The Brazilian government is faced with the problem of making decisions that are in the interests of the Brazilian economy and people as a whole, in the interests of indigenous people such as the Ianomami, as well as the protection of the forests that are so important to the planet.

In spite of the opinion of many people in other countries that the Indians should be isolated and protected as if they are rare animals in a large zoo, the authorities in charge of Brazilian Indians believe that they should be treated like human beings, and deserve to take part in the evolution achieved by the rest of humanity. In fact, what Brazilians defend is the preservation of Indian culture.

9 Research the history of any other group of indigenous peoples whose lands have been subject to a colonial power. You could choose the Indians of North America, the Aborigines of Australia, the Maori of New Zealand or other Indian tribes of the South American continent. To what extent have the indigenous peoples gained and lost by the encounter?

10 Discuss the costs and benefits to the Ianomami of preserving their traditional tribal lifestyle or adopting a 'modern Western lifestyle'. Is it possible for them to adopt or maintain some aspects of each?

11 In your class, discuss the plight of the Indians in the Amazon. Given the present situation in Brazil, what do you think the government should do?

12 Discuss the problems of enforcing the laws about Indian reservations in the forests of the Amazon, between Indians who are still living traditional lifestyles and migrants who are often illiterate and desperate to support their families.

COLLECTING, MINING AND CATTLE RANCHING IN AMAZONIA

Various land uses have been introduced into Amazonia since colonial times in an attempt to gain economic benefits from the region for the whole of Brazil. These have included collecting, mining, farming and cattle ranching. Some of these have been shown to be environmentally sustainable, some have been successful in earning money but environmentally damaging, while others have failed on both counts.

Collecting

The economic history of the Amazon region reveals a close relationship between **strativism** and human settlement. Strativism is the classical form of a colonial economy, based on the simple exploitation of natural resources. It is an activity characterised by collecting the natural products of the forest and occupies many of the forest people of Amazonia.

Collecting the products of the forest is made difficult both by the huge areas involved and by the way in which particular trees and other plants are distributed. With so many different species, collectors have to travel large distances between one rubber tree and the next. Problems of size and distance have led to the present situation of economic underdevelopment in the Amazon—and led to the conditions of near slavery in which many of the workers were kept up until the 1960s. Many workers engaged in collecting forest products such as rubber or Brazil nuts were not paid for their labour in money but with clothes and food. This trapped them in a difficult type of labour relationship. Since the 1960s, the growth of towns, transport networks and an increased range of jobs in industry have reduced the number of people who live in this way. Nevertheless, rubber, forestry products and nuts remain the main products.

Fishing is another way in which the renewable natural resources of the area are used. It is, however, usually carried out informally by people who live near the rivers for their own use. The only exceptions are the pirarucu (a type of codfish native to the Amazon) and the peixe-boi. Both are fished commercially and run the risk of extinction.

Some other creatures are hunted for their leather and fur. Among these are the lontra, the alligator and the onca which also run the risk of total extinction because of excessive and uncontrolled hunting.

Often when trees are cut down for agriculture they are not even used for their timber but are merely burned. The removal of the trees deprives the forest people of their livelihood, and the soils that are exposed when the trees are gone are often quickly eroded.

In recent years there has been an increased awareness worldwide of the need to avoid the destruction of our natural heritage. Despite this, we still live in a world where 10 per cent of all species of birds and 15 per cent of all plants and trees run the risk of extinction.

Early attempts at regulating the landuse of the Amazon

were based on the ideas of economists and groups who lived far away from the forests and their people. As a result, policies were often imposed which rarely took into consideration the views of the individuals who were most affected.

More recently, local communities have had a greater say in matters concerning their future. For example, the first national conference of latex collectors took place in Brasilia in October 1985. It was agreed that special strativist reservations should be created and that farming should be discontinued in areas where rubber and nuts are extracted. This proposal was also approved by the Indian leaders, who, in turn, received the support of latex collectors for the establishment of Indian reservations.

Mining

Since colonial times mining in Amazonia has concentrated on gold and diamonds. In the 1970s, the Radambrasil Project used aerial photography, radar and satellite surveys, as well as surveys on the ground, to prepare maps of the natural resources of the whole Amazon region and provided the basis for later selection of new areas for economic development. Today, mining generates US$1.5 billion annually from iron ore, limestone, bauxite, cassiterite, niobium, lignite, petroleum, gas, potassium, gold, diamond and manganese. Amazonia contains the world's largest deposits of bauxite, the ore from which aluminium is made.

One of the major prospecting projects developed in the Amazon region is the Carajas Project, which involves an area of about 120 000 square kilometres between the Xingu and Araguaia rivers, in the southern part of the state of Para. Mining, the building of the Tucurui hydro-electric dam, the Transamazon Highway, the huge Serra Pelada gold mine, and the recent completion of the 887 kilometre Carajas–Itaqui railway to the coast at Maranhao have attracted more than 50 000 workers from all parts of the country.

Many mining companies are environmentally aware. Others, however, cause great damage, particularly where gold is extracted as river waters become polluted by the mercury used to separate the precious metal from the rock. And as already mentioned, there is the problem that mining causes many indigenous peoples.

13 Research the uses the minerals named in Figure 2.10 are put to in the modern world. From which other areas may they be obtained?

14 In your class, discuss the effects on your lifestyle if these minerals ceased to be readily available or if the price rose dramatically.

15 List the problems that face the Brazilian government in deciding how to manage the extraction of minerals from within the Amazon region. You may think about the problems from the point of view of international consumers of the minerals, the people of Brazil as a whole, indigenous people, ecologists, or multinational mining corporations.

Cattle ranching

In the 1950s and 1960s, the Brazilian government hoped to develop the Amazon by distributing small plots of land to poor people for farming. By the early 1970s, it was thought

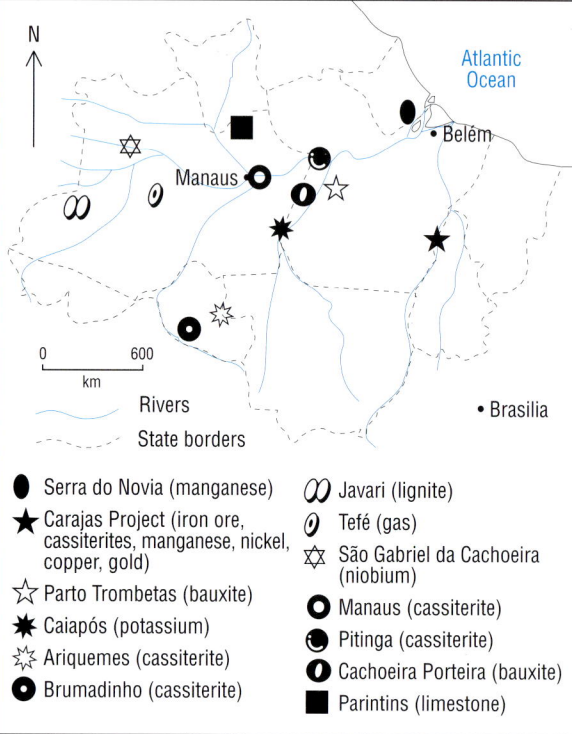

Figure 2.10 The distribution of the largest mining undertakings in the Amazon and some aspects of the gold mining operations of the Carajas Project

Figure 2.11 An area of extensive cattle raising along the Belém–Brasilia Highway, where the soil, no longer protected by the forest, is rapidly eroded

by many that it would be more successful if areas of the Amazon forests could be developed for large scale cattle ranching. The plan was first to cut down or burn the forest, then plant grass for pasture. However, the process of developing the Amazon for cattle ranching also proved to be a disaster for a number of reasons.

During the first stage of the project, poor people were brought to Amazonia from other parts of Brazil to work at forest clearing. However, these workers were poorly paid and often badly treated. Furthermore, they were generally fired soon after the initial stages of the project. Abandoned, and often unable to return to their previous homes (usually in the north-east or the southern parts of the country), they were forced to move on to private and government land. There, in order to grow subsistence crops, they destroyed more of the forest.

The most common breed of cattle introduced to the newly developed pastures in the Amazon region was the Nelore, which originates in India. Although it is the best suited for the region, the Nelore requires one hundred times more grazing land in the Amazon area than it does in the south of the country. According to some estimates, in order to produce 125 grams of beef in Amazonia (about the amount needed for a single hamburger), 6.5 square metres of forest is destroyed.

Many of the ranches in the Amazon were created by foreign multinational companies—the sheer size of the undertakings often causing great problems. One of the best known failures was the Rio Cristalino Project, started by the Volkswagen company (headquartered in Germany) on an area of 14 000 hectares. This was later sold to the Matsubara group of Japan.

After studying the problems created by large scale cattle raising in the Amazon region, Professor Orlando Valverde, a leading Brazilian specialist on the Amazon, wrote

> Besides causing a senseless devastation, the cattle raising projects formed a network of extremely large properties, which made the problem of land distribution in Brazil even worse. Besides, it constitutes a serious case of denationalisation and has unpredictable consequences of both a political and a military nature.

Many research projects carried out in the last ten years have demonstrated that cattle raising in the Amazon region has been a complete disaster from economic, environmental and social points of view.

16 Discuss the reasons why cattle ranching has been such a disaster in the Amazon. Make a list of the problems and beside each one explain why that problem occurred.
17 Discuss what Professor Valverde may have meant by 'denationalisation and has unpredictable consequences of both a political and a military nature'.

18 Discover which multinational companies have their headquarters in your country and which multinational companies own land in your country. What are the advantages of such companies and what problems do they cause for the countries in which they operate?

It now appears that the future of the Amazon lies in mining and collecting the products of the forest. Cattle raising has proved to be non-viable, and only in more fertile lands and in areas covered with savanna vegetation will agriculture be successfully developed.

THE CHALLENGE OF THE FUTURE

In the past few decades, many mistakes have been made in the development of Amazonia, but also much has been learned. There are still more problems to be faced in the future, especially in the far west.

Until the 1970s, the western part of the Amazon region was isolated from the rest of the country. The building of the BR–364 highway resulted in much of the forest alongside it being destroyed. The devastation became even worse when local district roads were also built. By 1990, between 10 and 12 per cent of the forest had been destroyed.

The lack of information on soil fertility in an area that appears to be so productive has turned the area into a 'non-existent Eldorado'. The people of Acre state, in the far west of Brazil, who are major producers of grain, are pressing for the construction of a road linking their region to the Pacific Ocean. The 4000 kilometre highway will start in Cuiabá (Brazil) and finish in Porto Ilo (Peru). It will reduce the sea voyage of ships taking grain to Japan by nineteen days. The

Figure 2.12 This area along the BR–364 highway near Cruzeiro do Sul in Acre state has been cleared of forest by farmers who have now left the land

completion of this 'highway of integration' is opposed both by Brazilian ecologists and international interests who do not want Brazil to expand its trade with Asian countries.

In fact, the greatest impact of the highway on the environment has already occurred. In the Cuiabá–Rio Branco section, it has caused the destruction of countless hectares of forest and has crossed land belonging to sixteen different Indian tribes.

> 19 List and discuss the advantages to the Brazilian economy, and to the environment as a whole, of reducing the journey of grain to Japan by nineteen days. Which groups outside Brazil may not want the road to be built?
> 20 List and discuss the disadvantages to the Brazilian economy and to the environment of such a development.

Eco-catastrophe: A political question

The early stages in the colonisation of Brazil were characterised by a long period of violent destruction of the natural resources. In the second half of this century, a new wave of destruction has swept the country—the rush to occupy the mid-west region, the poorly planned industrialisation of the north-east, and the discovery of the new economic potential of the Amazon region.

For many years, it was believed that the Amazon region was the key to Brazil's national problems. The present occupation of eastern Amazonia, however, is showing that in the near future all non-renewable natural resources may be exhausted.

In the last fifteen years there have been many fundamental changes in the form of occupation. Large corporations have moved in and are introducing the same methods that have been used in the more developed south-eastern region of Brazil—advanced technology and salaried work.

Such changes can strengthen the economy of the country if they are controlled and are geared to the gradual and careful exploitation of natural resources. In many cases, however, development may be allowed which benefits the economic aims of a few who are not necessarily concerned with the possibilities of ecological catastrophe.

This chapter has considered many of the problems that have occurred in the past and some that are continuing. However, according to many indications, the feared and well-publicised Amazonian eco-catastrophe will not take place. Brazilians are now very conscious that poor economic development is violence against the environment. There is much support for the preservation of natural resources. The Amazon region constitutes a political rather than an economic problem. It is up to the Brazilian people to choose the best way to occupy and settle the region while preserving the ecological balance which is necessary for future generations. Good decisions can only be made, however, when people understand the issues.

Brazil is fighting both the hunger of the people and the protection of the environment. Brazil, like all nations, needs to confront the reality of environmental change and the need to contribute to the extermination of the most devastating pollution of the planet—human misery.

> 21 Make a list of all the factors that the Brazilian government must consider in deciding how to manage the Amazon. For each factor, discuss the possible decisions that could be taken. Can you suggest a way of achieving acceptable social, economic and environmental aims in the Amazon?
> 22 Discuss the ways in which your country has problems with an environmentally sensitive area. For each problem that you can identify, decide whether your country has found some answers that may help the people of Brazil, or whether your country can learn from the Brazilian experience.
> 23 To what extent do you believe that forecasts of an Amazonian eco-catastrophe are still valid and to what extent do you believe that the major problems of the Amazon are now well on the way to being solved?

CHAPTER 3

RICH AND POOR IN NIGERIA: BRIDGING THE GAP

Julie Okpala

Wherever you live, your basic needs are food, clothing, shelter and security. The first three needs are easily understood and recognised. The fourth need, security, means feeling secure about your life, your property and your future. Everyone needs to feel that they have access to work and to services such as health care and education.

While we all have the same basic needs, we do not all enjoy the same access to these essentials of life. In all societies throughout the world some people can meet their needs better than others. This is called **social stratification**.

Rich people are able to acquire all of the basic necessities—for the present and for the future. They can also afford luxuries that they do not necessarily *need* to survive, but which they *want* to possess. Poor people, on the other hand, cannot afford to satisfy even their basic daily needs. In all countries there are people in both of these categories, as well as others who lie somewhere in between.

Problems may arise in a country if the social ladder is further extended so that there are some people who are *extremely rich* and there are others who are so *very poor* that they have literally nothing. The precise ways in which we recognise people who are rich or very rich varies from one culture to another. The very poor in any culture, however, are those who have difficulty in obtaining the basic needs of life.

The limits of this ladder at each end depend on the extent to which the country checks the rich from accumulating too much wealth and helps the poor to improve their lives and survive. For example, in some countries, the poor receive some form of subsistence allowance to enable them to buy food, clothing and shelter. Their children may not pay school fees or may have their fees subsidised. They may also receive free medical care and other allowances for books and clothing.

Figure 3.1   The social ladder

1 *a* Sketch the social ladder in your country as a series of boxes with headings. In each box, make a list of the ways in which you would recognise people in your country who would be described under each heading.
b How far does the social ladder in your country extend? How many people would you describe as 'very rich' and how many as 'very poor'? Does the government of your country make any attempt to limit the length of the ladder? Make lists of the methods that are used to do this under the headings of 'controlling the rich' and 'helping the poor'.

The issue of the gap between the rich and the poor is of global concern because all people have a fundamental human right to a useful existence. Furthermore, poor people are a *wasted human resource* to their own country as well as to the world community. After all, the philosophies of Asia, the technologies of Europe and the art and rhythms of Africa are appreciated all over the world. When people in any culture are too poor to be able to contribute their skills and thoughts, the whole world loses a valuable human resource.

The problem of poverty is more than wasting human resources on a global scale. Poverty is the inevitable result of some people becoming richer. Both the rich and the poor buy things from the same market. As the rich get richer, their purchases drive market prices higher to the disadvantage of the poor. Eventually, some families become so poor that they cannot feed their children properly, much less send them to school or get them adequate medical attention. Such children quickly become victims of diseases such as kwashiorkor, which is caused by a lack of protein in the diet. The symptoms of this horrible disease include a swollen belly, thinning hair, very pale skin and deterioration of the brain. The result is that the children are not only socially and physically poor but will remain illiterate for life.

If the gap between the rich and the poor becomes very wide, it can lead to greater disorder in the society. Some people, particularly the young, seek ways to get rich quickly. Sometimes this leads to criminal activities which reduce the overall health of a nation further. Negative effects quickly spread beyond borders and affect other nations.

The countries of Africa have more than their share of poverty. Figure 3.2 shows the daily kilojoule supply per head available in the countries of the world. The figures used to create this map were obtained by calculating the kilojoule content of all the food produced and imported for domestic consumption, dividing it by each country's population and expressing it as a daily amount. In general, countries with more than 10 900 kilojoules per person per day available are able to feed their people adequately. Those with less than 10 900 kilojoules will have many malnourished people.

2 Describe the pattern of countries shown in Figure 3.2. In which continent do most of the countries with low food availability lie?

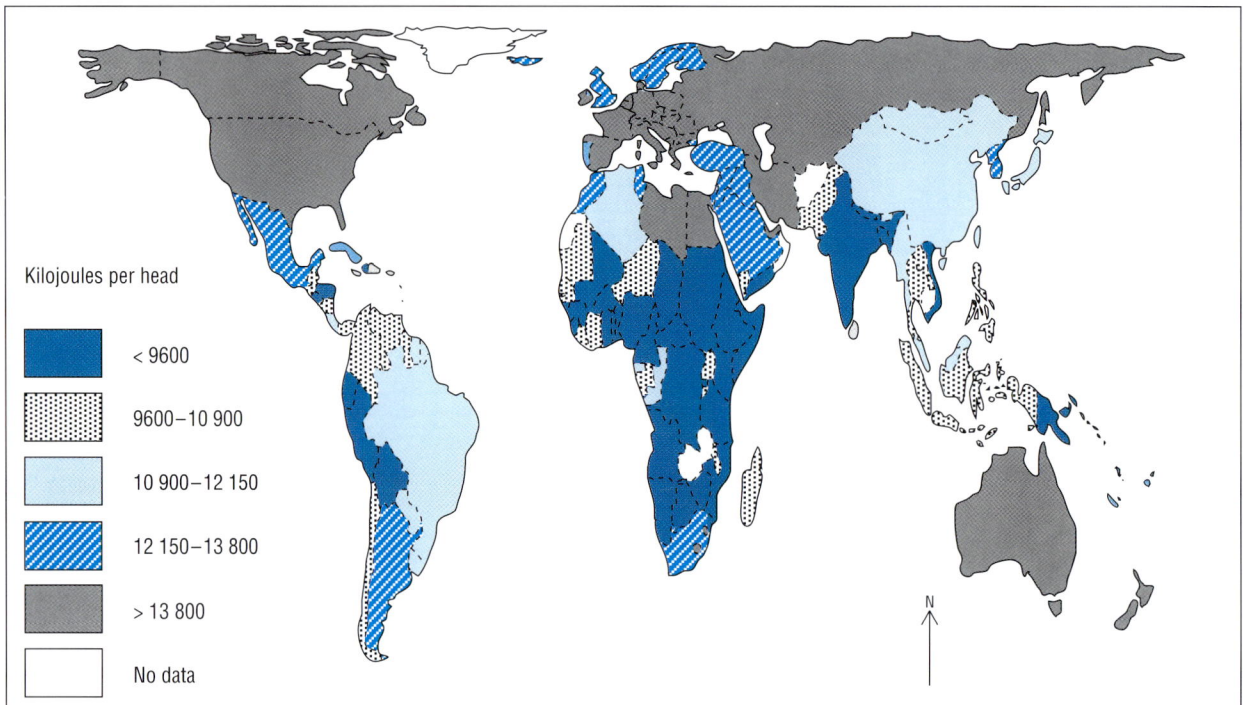

Figure 3.2 The daily kilojoule supply per head available worldwide

RICH AND POOR IN NIGERIA

Nigeria lies in west Africa, just north of the equator. It is a large country with a 1991 population of 88.5 million. The country stretches from the dense tropical forests of the coast through the savanna grasslands into the desert.

Nigeria was once a colony of Britain and obtained independence in 1960. At independence, Nigeria was a great agricultural country. It was one of the world's greatest producers and exporters of palm oil, cotton and cocoa, although petroleum had just been discovered and was being exploited. In 1962 agricultural products contributed over 80 per cent of the foreign exchange earnings of Nigeria and petroleum contributed only about 10 per cent. As Nigeria exploited more crude oil and got more money from oil, the agricultural sector was neglected. By 1973, crude oil provided 82.7 per cent of the foreign exchange, by 1976 it was about 93 per cent. By 1980, Nigeria was producing 2.05 million barrels of oil per day. The country started numerous construction, industrial, agricultural and commercial projects with the money made from oil.

As the country got richer, individuals in government and those who had links with them became richer too. Contractors engaged in the many construction projects often inflated the value of the contracts, sometimes with the help of government agents. Those in authority often received 'kickbacks' from the contractors and some stole government money. This was not seen as stealing but as taking one's share of 'the national cake'.

In these ways, the rich became richer. Before exploitation of oil in Nigeria, the social stratification could be said to be: rich, average and poor. With the oil boom, there emerged a super rich class, a bourgeoisie. The race to accumulate riches, to have more cars and houses, to travel abroad more often, to more exotic locations, had started in Nigeria. As some people became richer, things became more expensive for everyone.

One of the results of the increased emphasis on oil was that there was a declining interest in agriculture. Even subsistence agriculture was neglected. The tastes of Nigerians became increasingly sharpened towards buying foreign goods, including foods. School leavers from rural areas trooped to the towns in search of government white collar jobs. Nigeria, which had been a major exporter of agricultural products, started importing food. In 1971, Nigeria imported food valued at US$4.4 million. This represented 8.2 per cent of total imports. By 1981, food valued at US$9 million was imported. This represented 14.4 per cent of total imports.

When Nigeria's wealth increased in the 1970s, the government began various development projects to help the

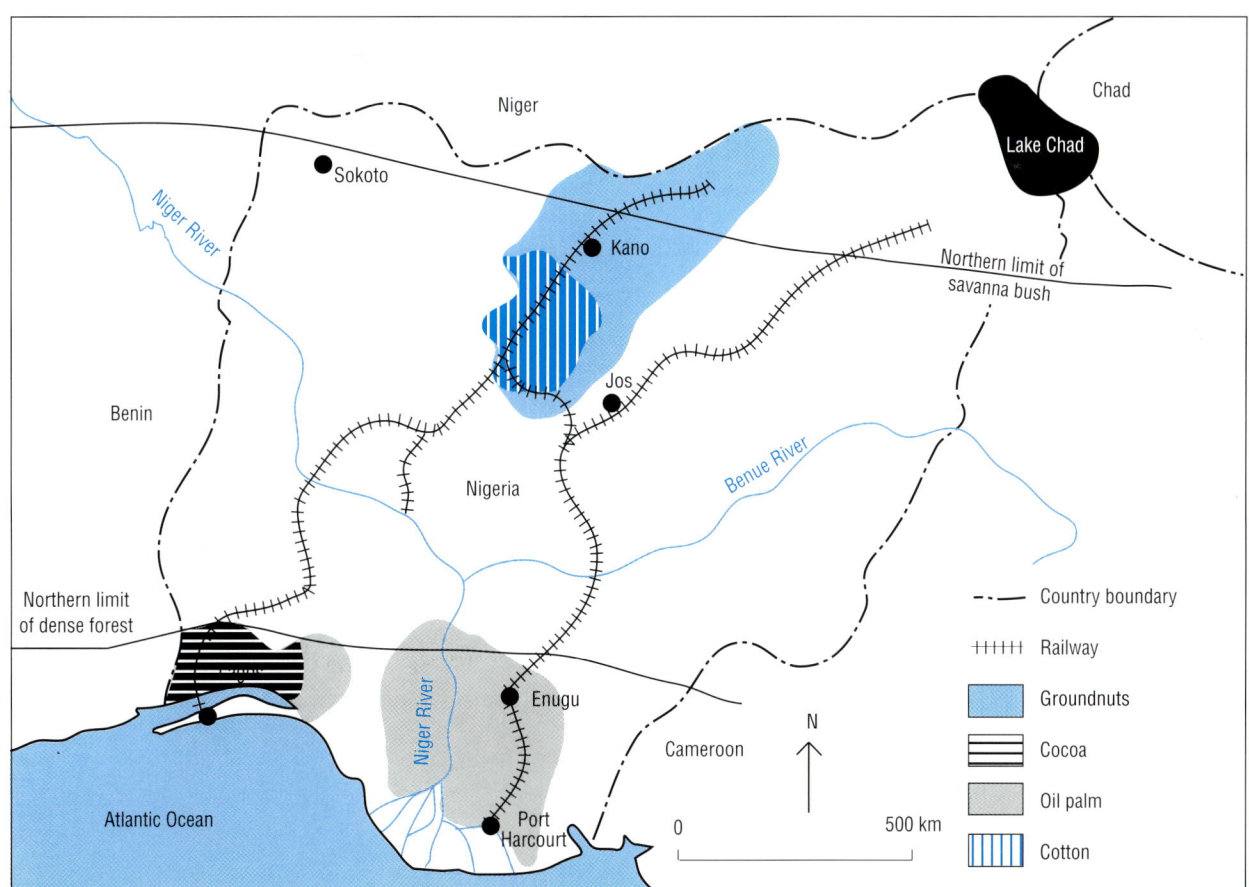

Figure 3.3   The main cities and crops of Nigeria

poorer people. For example the Universal Primary Education Project (UPE), which began in 1976, and Agricultural Development Projects.

The Universal Primary Education Project was designed to give all Nigerian citizens of school age free primary education and then, if possible, three further years of junior secondary education. The junior secondary education was to be basic vocational training to equip learners with skills to enable them to earn a living. Students or their parents still had to pay for senior secondary education—which leads to university or other forms of higher education.

The Agricultural Development Projects were to help farmers to produce more yields and to lighten their task by providing them with tractors for tilling the fields, fertilisers and high producing species of crops, and animals at subsidised rates.

Unfortunately, before these projects could really help poor people, there was fluctuation and crisis in the world petroleum market. Table 3.1 shows how the world price of oil at the end of each calendar year varied from 1970 to 1990. The actual price received by Nigeria also varied from day to day throughout each year.

> 3 Draw a line graph to show the variations in the world price of oil from 1970 to 1990. Write a sentence or two to describe how the price changed during that period.
> 4 In 1978, Nigeria, like other oil producing countries, began to reduce the production of oil from 2.10 million barrels a day to 1.57 million barrels a day. Use your graph to help you suggest why Nigeria might have done this. What effects did this have on Nigeria's earnings in the short term and in the longer term?

The rapid fall in oil prices from 1980 to 1987 caused an economic crisis in Nigeria. There was a lack of foreign exchange to import raw materials for many of the industries that had been started. There was also an acute shortage of manufactured goods and items as importers could not bring commodities in. There was great inflation as prices rose and many factories and other companies closed down. Thousands of workers lost their jobs when their employers were unable to pay their wages. The Manufacturers Association of Nigeria reported that a total of 101 companies dismissed 200 000 workers between July 1982 and July 1983.

The effects of the oil crisis on people

Nigeria started borrowing money from the International Monetary Fund. There were restrictions on the import of many goods and foods. The shortages caused by these restrictions caused prices to rise. The government cut back on many of the social services it had started in the 1970s, particularly education, health, transport and provision of water supply. Free primary education was ended and parents had to pay education and other development levies. The result was that the poor became even poorer.

Table 3.1 World price of oil, 1970 to 1990

Year	Price in US$ per barrel
1970	7
1971	7
1972	7
1973	13
1974	29
1975	29
1976	28
1977	28
1978	27
1979	43
1980	51
1981	47
1982	40
1983	34
1984	31
1985	27
1986	16
1987	16
1988	14
1989	18
1990	30

> 5 Describe the way in which the changes in the price of oil affected
>   a the Nigerian economy
>   b the 'average' people of Nigeria
>   c the poor people of Nigeria.
> 6 Figure 3.4 shows two classrooms in Nigeria. One classroom is in a school for relatively wealthy students, the other is for poorer students.
>   a Decide which photograph shows which classroom.
>   b Study the photographs and imagine yourself as much younger and as a pupil in each school. Describe your day, at home, at school, after school. You should consider how you travel to school, the school buildings and facilities, the number of children in your class.
> 7 Figure 3.5 shows two other aspects of life in Nigeria. For each photograph, describe what the people are doing. Why may this behaviour be necessary? What are the dangers involved in these activities?

The poor are struggling to provide basic needs which have become very expensive as the Naira (N) (the Nigerian currency) is devalued against other currencies in the world. For example the value of N to US$1 was about N 2 in 1984, N 3 in 1987, N 5 in 1989, N 7 in 1990 and N 18 in 1992. The cost of 250 grams of milk was N 0.5 in 1985, N 1.0 in 1989, N 2.5 in 1990 and N 7.0 in 1992. As costs of everyday items like this have risen, the suffering of the poor has increased.

Figure 3.4   Two classrooms in Nigeria

Low paid workers and the poor suffer from these high prices. The lowest paid worker in government earns less than N 400 a month. This amount is not sufficient to live adequately when a loaf of bread costs N 10; a bar of soap, N 9; 250 mL liquid milk, N 7; 4.5 litres of oil, N 40; 18 litres of water N 2 (in some places); and a cup of rice, N 3. More social services must be provided to help the poor.

> 8 Calculate the percentage of the average low paid worker's income in your country that would be needed to buy each of the items listed above. How does this compare with the costs of the items in Nigeria as percentages of N 400—an average low paid worker's salary?

While the poor are struggling to satisfy basic needs, the rich use the situation to attain luxury. This is demonstrated in the ways in which people have taken advantage of the poor economic situation to earn themselves a great deal of money. For example
- there are numerous reports of robberies of equipment from secondary schools—the robberies are usually committed by young, unemployed school leavers, often with the support of older people
- there are constant accusations that commodities such as fertilisers are being sold illegally, on the 'black market', at highly inflated prices—the farmers who need and want these fertilisers are often unable to obtain them
- smuggling has been detected, with secret airfields or secret routes across borders being uncovered in some regions
- a professional kidnapper was recently arrested—it is claimed that he sold children: boys for N 6000 and girls for N 5000
- drug trafficking is rife with many Nigerians in European prisons, arrested for drug offences—often they are the couriers or 'mules', not the sellers; it is the sellers who make the real money.

> 9 In what ways are the problems of Nigeria part of an international problem? Which of the criminal activities described above are to be found in your country? What are the penalties in your country?
> 10 List some suggestions for the government of Nigeria to consider of what you think should be done to reduce the incidence of such offences.

THE IMPLICATIONS OF THE CURRENT SITUATION

A class of very rich people, both educated and uneducated, who are benefiting from the economic situation, has emerged in Nigeria. They constantly look for ways to get richer while the poor get poorer. While many poor people cannot provide for their own and their family's basic needs, including education for their children, the children of the rich attend

Figure 3.5   Aspects of life in Nigeria

private schools that charge very high fees, considering the state schools unsuitable for their children.

Nigeria is not a welfare country, so the state does not take care of the basic needs of its citizens. There is no dole, as in some developed countries, no allowance for one parent families, and no school meals.

What the government is doing

The federal government of Nigeria has been trying its best to limit the acquisition of riches through foul means and has been helping the poor to survive. Agencies and programs have been established to achieve these ends, including the Asset Declaration Bureau and the National Drug Law Enforcement Agency.

The Asset Declaration Bureau makes it mandatory for all senior civil servants to declare their possessions. The purpose of this is to check fraud and embezzlement among public officers—if they appear to own more than they can buy with their salaries, it may be that it has been gained dishonestly.

In 1987 the National Drug Law Enforcement Agency was formed. This agency helps to track down on drug pushers, investigate cases of drug trafficking, penalises offenders and tries to trace the 'barons' through the 'mules' who are caught. In 1985 three people who were found guilty of drug offences were executed, although the death penalty has been abolished since that date. At present there are long gaol terms—up to twenty years—for drug offences. The names of Nigerians caught for drug offences outside Nigeria are published in Nigerian newspapers.

On the positive side, the government has encouraged the rich to be involved in rural development projects. In several places, the rich have donated money for building school blocks, equipping science laboratories, building rural roads, awarding scholarships to school children, providing bore holes for water supplies, and setting up industries in rural areas.

All these activities have contributed to improving the lives of poor people.

The federal government has also tried to help the poor to improve their own situation. The strategies for improving the lives of the poor and underprivileged include improving their economic production, increasing employment opportunities, improving the lives of rural women, and public enlightenment.

The Directorate for Foods, Roads and Rural Infrastructure (DFRRI), formed in 1987, has encouraged people with the finance to locate industries in rural areas to create job opportunities and attract people to stay in rural areas rather than rush to congested cities. DFRRI has also constructed link roads to rural areas that were once inaccessible. These areas are now developing markets so that people can get to them and buy their farm products. People living in many rural areas can now transport their goods more easily to markets in bigger towns too.

DAILY CHAMPION, Monday, December 30, 1991

NDE creates 1.5 million jobs

THE National Directorate of Employment (NDE), the nation's job creation factory, says it has licked the hitherto intractable huge unemployment problem which has reduced a sizeable number of Nigerian youths to a state of near helplessness.

Latest figures emerging from the office of the director-general of the NDE, Chief Chukwu Wachukwu, indicated that over 1.5 million employment opportunities have been created by the agency since inception.

Under the agricultural programme of the agency alone, no fewer than 500,000 jobs had been created nationwide.

At least 8,140 graduates and 5,819 school leavers were granted loans under the agricultural programme while a total of 57,700 hectres of land were cleared.

Following the opportunities in the agricultural sector, at least 115,400 metric tonnes of food was produced under the programme.

Chief Wachuku also announced that no fewer than 210,750 youths were trained in 80 different trades.

A total of 20,000 businesses were injected into the economy with the disbursement of loans ranging from ₦12,000 to ₦25,000 to 20,000 resettled persons.

The NDE trained 55,000 youths through its school-on-wheels scheme while about 5,000 persons were trained under the waste-to-wealth scheme. A total of 2,332 of them were granted loans to establish businesses.

Under the entrepreneurship programme, 240,000 persons were trained.

About 2,375 graduates were granted loans to set up their own businesses and the beneficiaries created over 20,000 jobs nationwide, the NDE stated.

It also stated that 2,281 retired persons were trained under the EDP, 72 of them were granted loans under the Matured Peoples Scheme.

The NDE had also engaged 35,600 persons under the special public works programme while it established 300 new small scale enterprises this December alone.

Figure 3.6 The achievements of the National Directorate of Employment

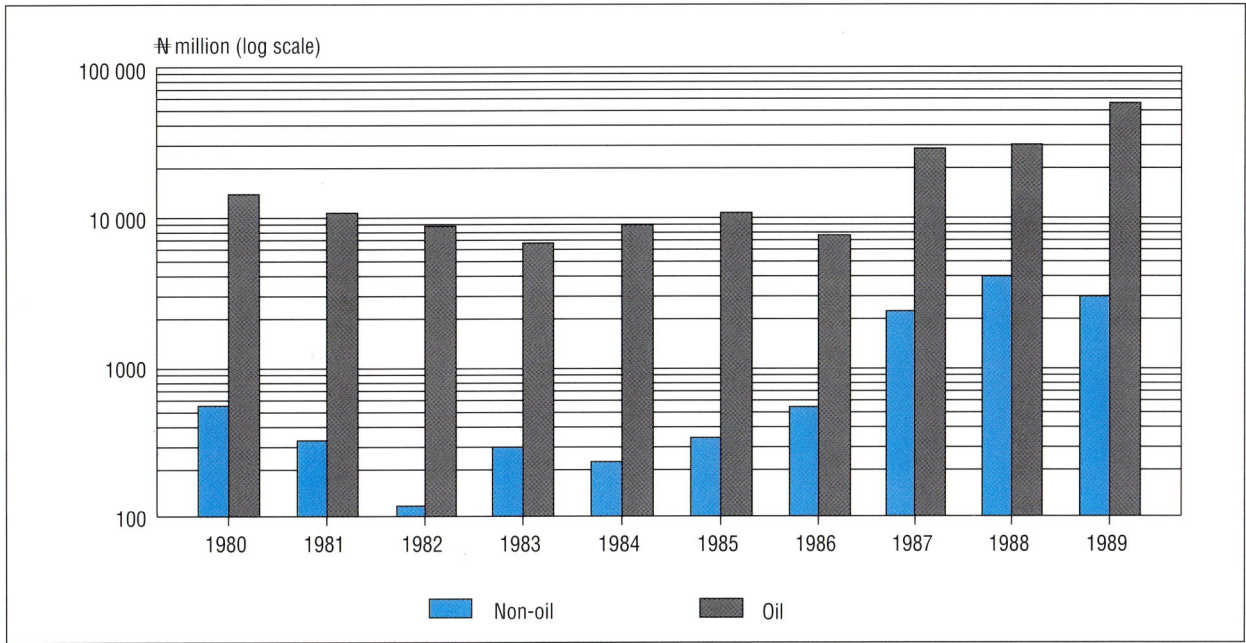

Figure 3.7 The relative value of Nigeria's oil and non-oil exports, 1980–89

Farmers have been greatly encouraged to produce more food in order to make more money. The government subsidises fertilisers which are sold to farmers. For example, in 1988 the cost of fertiliser was ₦120 per bag, but the government sold it to farmers for ₦15 per bag. The government has been combating the practice of 'black market' selling of fertiliser by encouraging farmers to join or form cooperative societies. These cooperative societies and young farmers' clubs are able to obtain consignments of fertilisers and other scarce commodities straight from the government to be distributed to their members.

The unemployment problem is being tackled by providing job opportunities for school leavers through the National Directorate of Employment (NDE). This body was set up in 1987 to create employment with emphasis on self reliance and entrepreneurship. One of the functions of NDE was to promote direct labour, promote self-employment, organise artisans into cooperatives and encourage a culture of maintenance and repair.

The NDE has an Open Apprenticeship Scheme directed at unemployed youth. Unemployed secondary school graduates are attached to private workshops to learn skills—such as mechanics, plumbing, hair dressing, welding, typing and electronics—after which they are given a 'soft loan' to establish their own businesses. Unemployed university graduates are also given loans to start their own businesses, particularly in the agricultural industry. When the loans are paid back, the money is recycled. The beneficiaries of these loans have guarantors from their towns or local government. They also use their degree certificates as collateral for the loans. The Waste to Wealth scheme for school drop outs is another project of the NDE. (See Figure 3.6, which details some of the NDE's achievements.)

The government has also tried to encourage lower income groups, particularly farmers. In 1977 the government established marketing boards to negotiate between farmers and foreign buyers of agricultural products such as cotton, palm oil, cocoa, and groundnuts. The farmers sold their products to the marketing board who, in turn, sold the products to foreign buyers. In 1986, the marketing boards were abolished. Farmers of export crops now directly export their products thus getting better deals in the form of higher prices. For example in 1989 farmers received about ₦24 000 for a tonne of cocoa compared with ₦3000 per tonne which the Cocoa Marketing Board would have paid them. In order to encourage local production, the government banned the import of some agricultural commodities such as wheat and rice.

Farmers have also been helped by the government to produce more by the construction of bore holes, dams for irrigation, silos for storage, reservoirs, irrigation pumps and by the provision of improved seeds and machinery at cheap rates. Figure 3.7 shows the relative value of Nigeria's oil and non-oil exports from 1980 to 1989. The vertical axis of this bar chart is a logarithmic scale. This means that each line in the bottom scale represents 100 Naira, each line in the second scale represents 1000 Naira and each line in the upper scale represents 10 000 Naira.

> 11 Study the earnings of Nigeria in Figure 3.7 (amounts in million Naira). Remember that the vertical axis is drawn to a logarithmic scale. Describe the changes in oil and non-oil exports that have occurred during the 1980s.

In addition to encouraging both farming and marketing, the Nigerian government has introduced other programs

designed to improve the conditions of poorer people. These have included work in the areas of
- public transport
- local government
- the role of women
- education of young people, and
- public enlightenment.

Each is discussed below.

The government is working to provide cheaper transport for poorer people by providing each of the thirty states in the country with a number of buses for public transport under the Federal Urban Mass Transit Programme. It also checks the fares charged by individual bus operators to ensure that they remain affordable.

More states and more local government areas have been created to bring development and government facilities closer to people in remote areas. At independence, Nigeria was governed under three regions. This increased to four regions in 1961, twelve states in 1967, nineteen states in 1976, twenty-one states in 1987 to the present thirty states (by 1991). The creation of these states has resulted in more jobs and better living standards for the people. Rural people now find it easier to contact their leaders and make their demands known to them.

The wife of the President of Nigeria, Mrs Maryam Babangida, has tried to help rural Nigerian women to improve their lives. In 1987, she initiated the Better Life for Rural Women Programme. She encouraged rural women to form cooperatives and to learn crafts and trades. Women are encouraged to attend adult education schools where they learn health care and home management. Nigerian women's cooperatives have opened shopping centres and have farms throughout the country. The program has increased both the self-esteem and the earnings of rural women.

The Federal Ministry of Education is developing primary and secondary school curricula that will develop knowledge and values needed to build a better Nigeria. For example, the problems of drug abuse are taught in schools as well as the qualities of good citizenship.

Finally, at the adult level, public enlightenment programs are teaching people about their rights and responsibilities. Many Nigerians, particularly in rural areas, are getting more interested in politics and are learning how to ask questions about the management of public funds and property. Identifying law breakers is increasingly seen as everybody's responsibility.

Help from overseas

Individuals, groups, organisations—both national and international—have been helping to improve the lives of Nigerians. For example the United Nations International Children's Emergency Fund (UNICEF) supports rural people by sending free drugs for immunisation and child care, while the Japanese government has given vehicles to support the mass transit program.

THE FUTURE FOR NIGERIA

Nigeria is trying to bridge the gap between the rich and the poor. Rural development programs and attention to agriculture, the National Directorate of Employment, the urban mass transit program, creation of more states, and enlightening the people about their rights are all contributing to improving the lives of the poor. Despite all these attempts, and the checks that have been introduced to prevent the rich getting too rich, there are still many problems to be tackled. These include the continued devaluation of the Naira and the problem of extensive corruption. The devaluation of the Naira creates further problems when rich people save their money in foreign currencies and then buy devalued Naira later.

Rich people are not yet contributing enough to economic development. Many of them are still under-assessed for taxes and this reduces the amount of money available to the government for social services.

Despite the problems that remain, however, Nigeria is working towards a more equitable and just society.

CHAPTER 4

CHINA'S POPULATION

Lee Chun-Fen and
Yan Zheng-Yuang

Count slowly to sixty. In this time, 170 people will be born. By tomorrow, the world must feed, house and educate another 254 000 people. This high birth rate causes the world population to grow rapidly because for every 2.8 people born, only one person dies. The result is that population growth is one of the most serious problems facing the world today.

People in all countries believe that we should try to reduce death rates by improving people's health and quality of life. This means that the only way to slow population growth is to reduce the birth rate. In 1960, only two countries in the world, India and Pakistan, had official policies to reduce their birth rates. Today, 93 per cent of the world's population lives in countries with such policies. However, it seems that this is not enough to bring population under control.

POPULATION CONTROL METHODS

There are three basic ways to persuade people to have fewer children
- economic development
- family planning
- socio-economic changes.

Economic development

Demographers (scientists who study population changes) examined the birth and death rates of countries in western Europe in the nineteenth century. They found that, as industry developed, death rates declined before birth rates declined. This meant that the population growth experienced in Europe changed from fast to slow to zero, and eventually to a slow decline in population. This process is called the **demographic transition** (see Figure 4.1).

By 1989, Austria, Belgium, Bulgaria, Czechoslovakia, Denmark, Germany, Finland, Greece, Hungary, Italy, Luxembourg, Norway, Portugal, Spain, Sweden, Switzerland and the United Kingdom all had a rate of population growth of about zero. However, these seventeen countries between them account for only 6.3 per cent of the world's population.

Population pyramids show the situation clearly. In India, the birth rate is high and so is the death rate. The effect is shown in Figure 4.2a. The pyramid is triangular and the numbers of people in each age group reduces with age. When the large number of people under the age of fifteen have children of their own, the population will expand even more rapidly. In the United Kingdom, shown in Figure 4.2b, each generation is only just replacing itself and the pyramid will probably remain straight and may even become top-heavy. When a country has more people aged over fifty than under fifteen, then its population will usually fall for at least half a century. Furthermore, the people who are still working must support more retired people.

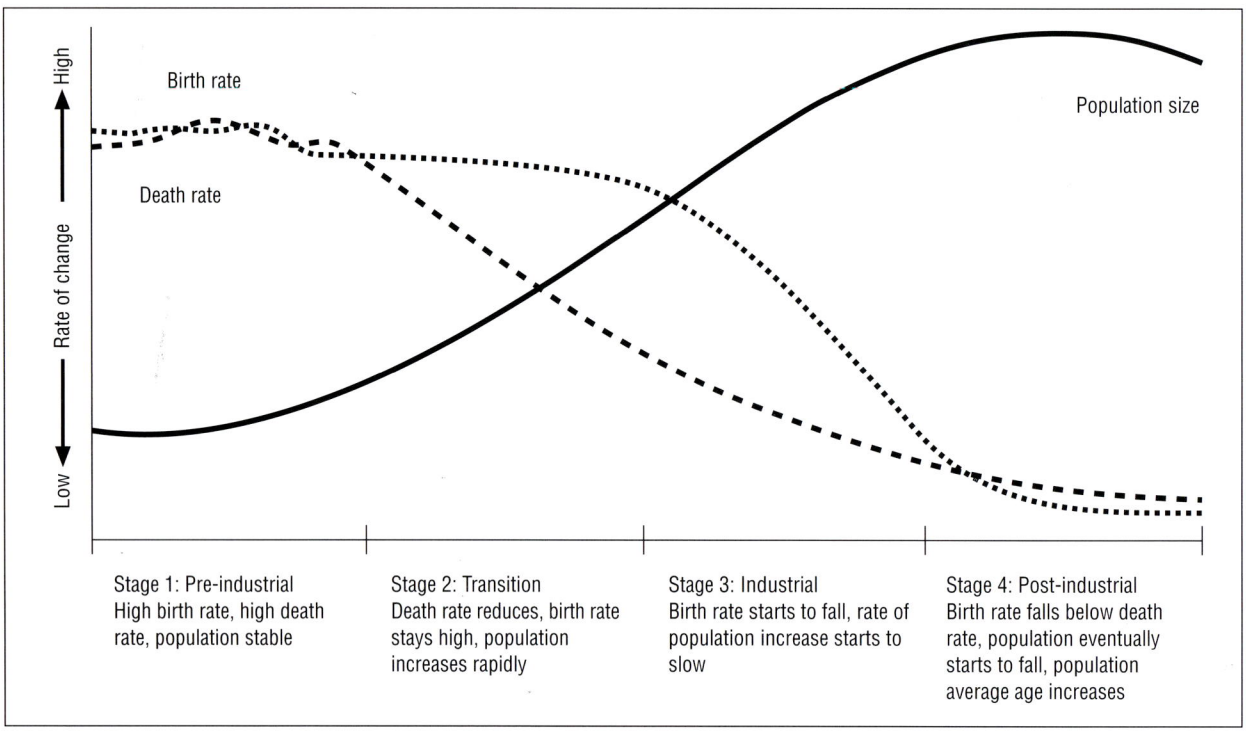

Figure 4.1 The demographic transition shown diagrammatically

Stage 1: Pre-industrial
High birth rate, high death rate, population stable

Stage 2: Transition
Death rate reduces, birth rate stays high, population increases rapidly

Stage 3: Industrial
Birth rate starts to fall, rate of population increase starts to slow

Stage 4: Post-industrial
Birth rate falls below death rate, population eventually starts to fall, population average age increases

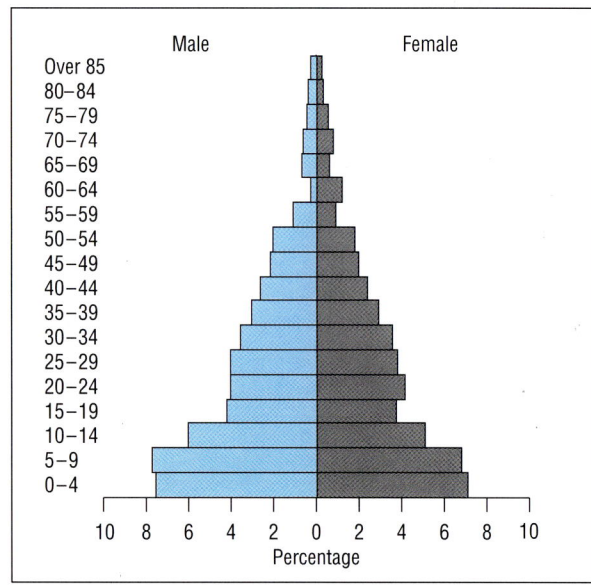

Figure 4.2a The population pyramid for India

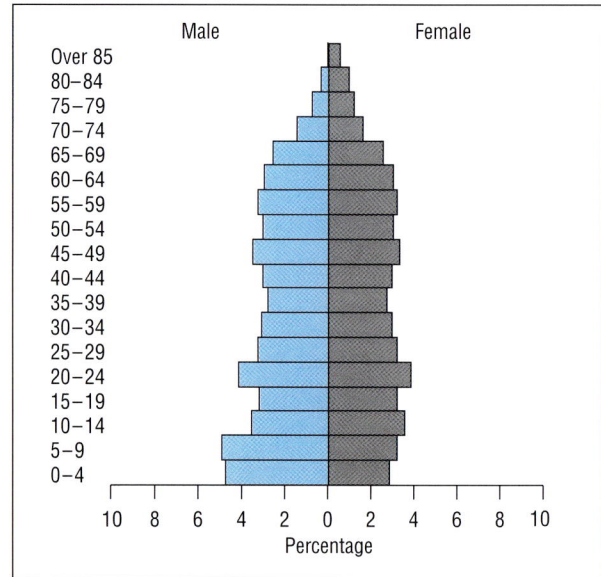

Figure 4.2b The population pyramid for the United Kingdom

1 Discuss reasons why
  a birth rates and death rates are high in pre-industrial societies
  b death rates start to decline as the economy develops
  c birth rates decline more slowly than death rates
  d birth rates eventually become lower than death rates.

2 Find the population statistics for your own country and draw a population pyramid. Discuss the future structure of the population.

Most of the developing countries of the world are in the transition stage now. Some demographers are afraid that their population growth is so great that their economies will never pull them into the next stage. If this happens, death rates will start to rise again and those countries will slip back into the pre-industrial stage.

Family planning

Family planning programs provide educational and clinical services to help couples choose how many children they have. Such programs can reduce a country's population faster than waiting for the demographic transition to take effect. About 70 per cent of women in more developed countries use contraception, but only about 39 per cent of women in less developed countries (other than China) do so. If contraception were available to all the women in less developed countries, there would be 5.8 million fewer births a year and 130 000 fewer abortions every day. This would mean that by the year 2100, 2.7 billion fewer people would need food, water, shelter and health services.

Socio-economic changes

A third way to encourage smaller families is by increasing rights, education and work opportunities for women and by using economic rewards and penalties.

One-third of the world's paid workforce is women, and most women earn less than men for doing similar work. Women also do most of the domestic work and child care without pay and produce more than half of the world's food. Women work two-thirds of all work hours in the world and receive one-tenth of the world's income. Many studies have shown that better education and prospects for women lead them to have fewer children. However, tradition makes these changes very difficult in many countries.

Some countries offer payments to people who are sterilised or who use contraceptives. In India, for example, a man receives the equivalent of about two weeks' wages if he is sterilised. Other countries penalise couples who have more than one or two children. In Singapore, Hong Kong, Ghana and Malaysia there is no tax deduction for a third child. Persuading people to have fewer children is usually best, but if population growth becomes too rapid, stronger methods, such as those used in China, may be necessary.

The situation in China

Between 1958 and 1962, there was great famine in China and many people died. Since then, China has grown enough grain to feed its population, has reduced its birth rate from 32 to 18 per 1000 people and reduced its fertility from 5.7 to 2.1 children per woman. China has done this by adopting the strictest population control program in the world. The main aspects of this program are
- couples are strongly encouraged to marry later in life
- education is available to everyone
- contraception, sterilisation and abortion are free and easily available
- couples who sign pledges to have only one child receive extra salary, extra food, larger pensions, better housing, free medical care, free schooling for their child, while single children are given preferential treatment when they seek jobs
- couples who break these pledges must pay back all the benefits
- women who are pregnant with a third child are persuaded to have abortions
- one parent of a two-child family must be sterilised
- sterilisation, family planning advice, health care and education are taken to rural areas by mobile units
- local people are trained to promote family planning
- leaders must set an example with their own family size.

3 Discuss the reasons why more education and better job prospects lead women to have fewer children. What is the position of women in your country? Do women have opportunities equal to those of men for developing their own careers?
4 Should rewards and punishments be used to control population? Do you think poor people may feel that they have to accept them to survive?
5 How acceptable would the Chinese regulations be in your country? What would have to change for them to become acceptable?

China is the most highly populated country in the world. According to the 1990 census, the total population is 1134 million (not including Taiwan, Hong Kong and Macau). This is 21 per cent of the world's total, and the population density averages 118 per square kilometre. This is far higher than the world average of 36 per square kilometre. As a developing country, China must make great efforts to control the birth rate, and strengthen family planning work. China believes that population growth should adapt to economic development, as well as to the carrying capacity of the physical environment.

China is currently in her eighth Five-Year Plan (1991–95), and is working on the Ten-Year Program (1991–2000). The aim of this last decade of the century is to improve people's living standards, to develop the economy, to double the country's GNP again and to lay a good foundation for further development in the next century. The Chinese must grasp the opportunities offered by history, meet the challenges and work hard to attain the strategic objective of socialist modernisations, while keeping watch over population growth.

ECONOMIC DEVELOPMENT AND POPULATION GROWTH

During the seventh Five-Year Plan period (1986–90), China undertook major reforms and became more open to the outside world. Major industrial and agricultural production increased and all targets were reached.

The seventh Five-Year plan created conditions for sustained economic development during the eighth Five-Year Plan period (1991–95). However, population growth was greater than planned and this added new pressure on economic growth. During the seventh Five-Year Plan, China recorded the third highest birth rate since the founding of New China in 1949.

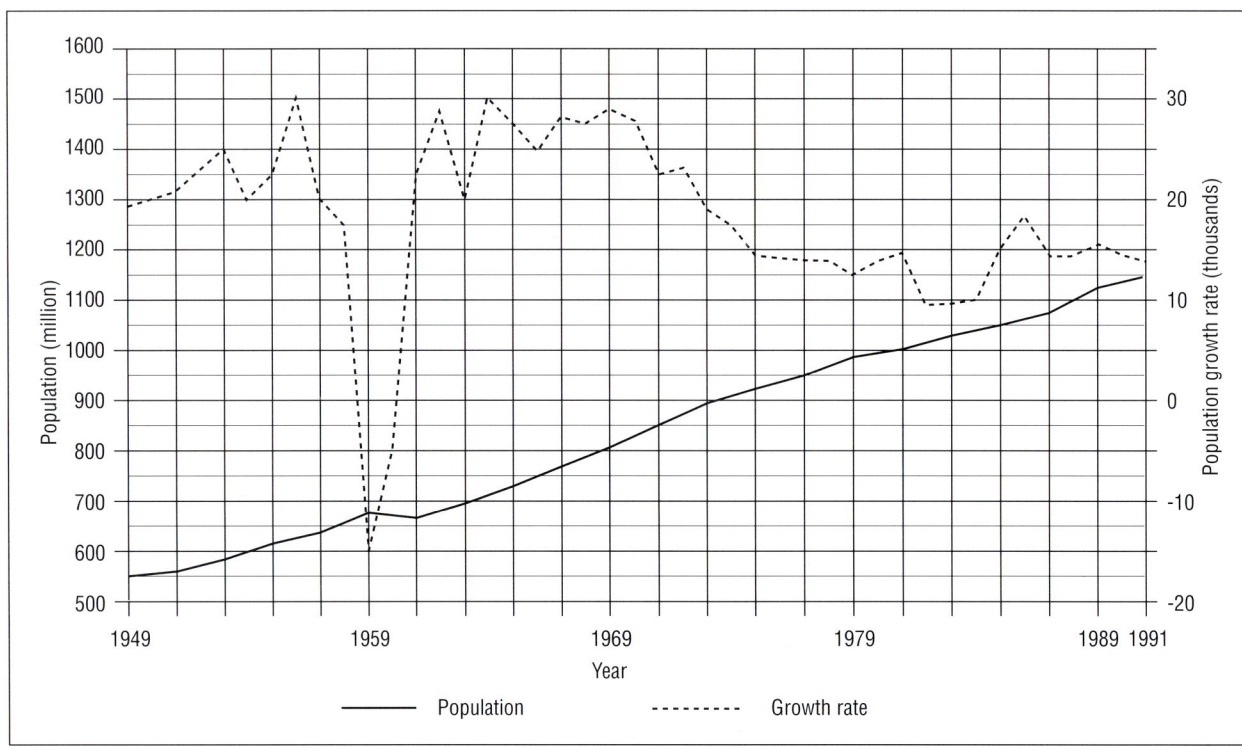

Figure 4.3   China's total population and rate of population growth, 1949–91

The large population is responsible for the low average output of the main industrial and agricultural products. The average income of farmers, who represent 72 per cent of the population, in 1990 was 600 yuan. This represents an average annual increase rate of about 10 per cent over the past five years. The average income of urban dwellers was 1360 yuan in 1990, almost twice the 1985 figure, or an average annual growth of 14.7 per cent. These figures are low compared with more developed countries.

On 14 April 1989, the population size of China reached 1.1 billion. The State Council decided to regard this day as 'the Day of China's 1.1 Billion population'. It is neither a holiday nor a celebration but a warning to every citizen that population growth must decelerate.

This 1.1 billion population was more than double the 540 million population in mainland China in 1949. The Chinese 1.1 billion population is 36 per cent of Asia's 3 billion. In just over one hundred years, from 1840 to 1949, the Chinese population had increased by only 100 million. At the present rate of more than 15 million every year, the population of China increases by 100 million every six to seven years. Although photographs can show scenes of congestion in cities such as Shanghai, they cannot give any sense of the huge size of the Chinese population nor can they indicate the rate at which that population is growing.

Figure 4.4   Scenes in Shanghai—a bus queue and a bustling street

> 6   Discuss China's movement through the demographic transition. On a copy of Figure 4.1, mark each of the stages.

In 1985, the number of women of child-bearing age (fifteen to forty-nine) in China was 276.7 million. China's population will continue to grow for at least the next ten years as more women enter this age group each year. It will be 330 million in 1995 and 340 million in 2000. Despite success in reducing the population growth rate each year, China will probably have a population of 1.3 billion by 2000 and 1.5 billion by 2030.

CHINA'S POPULATION

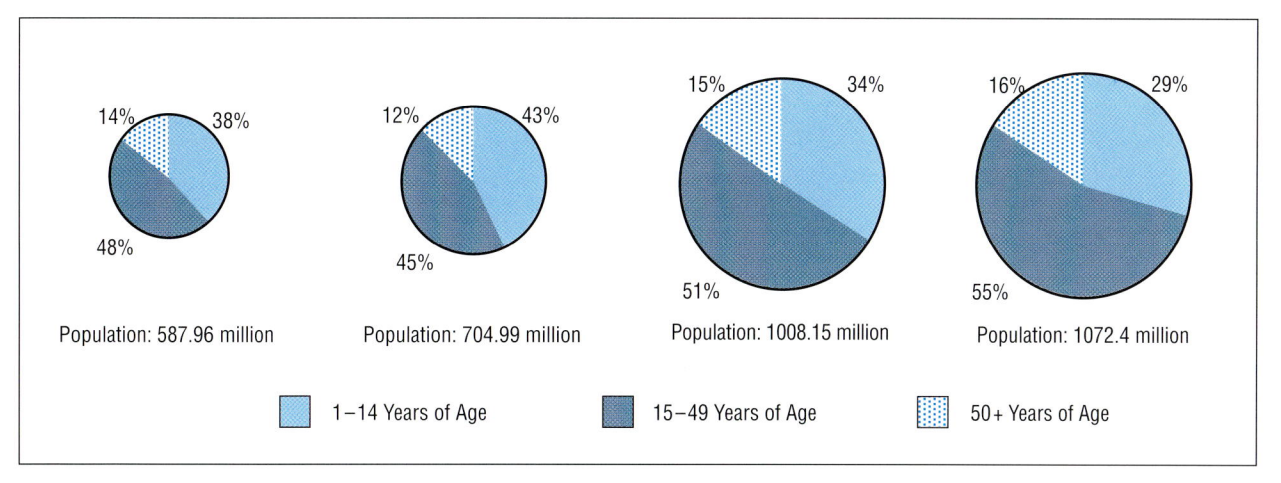

Figure 4.5 The structure of the Chinese population in 1953, 1964, 1982 and 1987

PROBLEMS ARISING FROM POPULATION PRESSURE

Although China has 21 per cent of the total world population, these people live on only 7 per cent of the world's cultivated land. Such a high population places enormous pressure on the standard of living. Furthermore, this huge population is not spread evenly across the land area of China.

> 7 From the information given in Table 4.1, describe the changes that have taken place in
> a the area of cultivated land in China
> b the amount of cultivated land available per person
> c the yield of grain gained from this land
> d the amount of grain produced per person.
> Discuss the ways in which China has increased the amount of grain available per person despite population growth.
> 8 Compare the distribution of population shown in Figure 4.7 with Figure 4.8 which shows the relief of China. Discuss the factors which may influence the population pattern.

The per capita output of grain in 1988 was 730 jin, an increase of 22 per cent since the founding of modern China. However, this 730 jin is raw grain, including beans and yams, and not all is available for human consumption. About 20 per cent is used for forage, industry and medicine and the removal of chaff and other waste reduces the rest by another 10 to 20 per cent. The result is that only half the total figure is available for people to eat and the grain ration in some areas is short, leaving 40 million people unfed, so China imports about 10 million tonnes of grain each year. This is the equivalent of 3.3 per cent of China's own grain production.

The Chinese landscape is most mountainous and arid, and there is little spare land for expanding cultivation. Moreover, the total area of arable land is declining by 5 to 7 million mu every year as the demand grows for houses, roads, factories and reservoirs from the ever increasing population. China already has one of the smallest areas of cultivated land per person in the world. Only by increasing the yield per unit area can we solve or ease the problem of grain shortage.

Table 4.1 The relationship between China's cultivated land, its output and its population

Year	Population (millions)	Cultivated land (million mu)	Area of cultivated land per person (mu)	Grain yield (jin per mu)	Output of grain per person
1741	143.41	588	4.1	280	1148
1840	412.81	842	2.1	300	600
Late 1940s	455.59	1275	2.8	220	600
1952	574.82	1860	3.2	180	560
1962	672.95	1820	2.7	180	480
1979	975.42	1810	1.8	360	680
1985	1050.44	1450	1.4	520	730

Note: 1 mu = 1/15 hectare
1 jin = 1/2 kilogram

FAMILY PLANNING AND POPULATION CONTROL

Since the late 1970s China has made great achievements in family planning. Population growth has reduced greatly compared with that of the 1950s and the 1960s. Between 1978 and 1987, 100 million fewer babies were born than

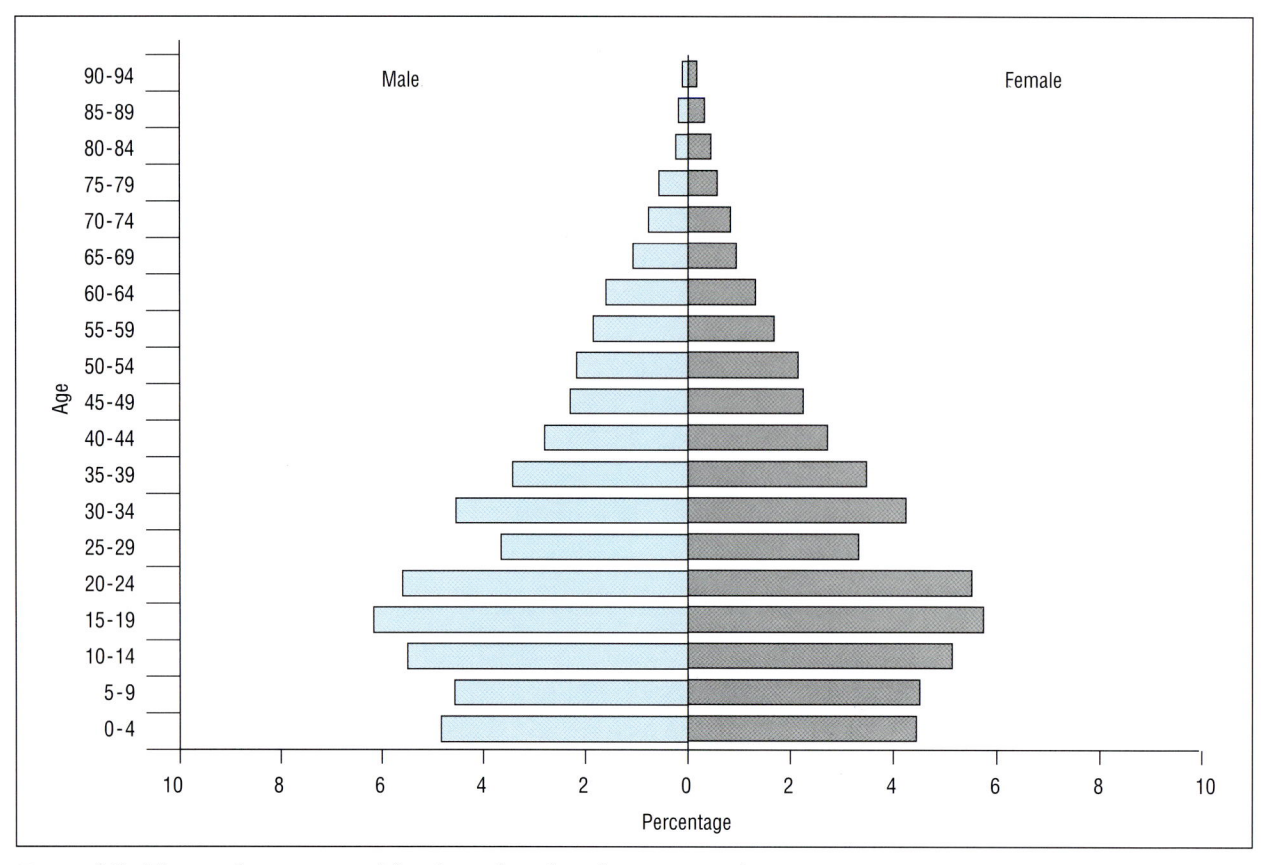

Figure 4.6 The population pyramid for China, based on the 1987 sample census

might have been expected. This has played an important role in promoting socialist modernisation and increasing people's material and cultural quality of life.

Despite the great achievements, the national family planning efforts are unbalanced throughout the country. The policies have been difficult to enforce, especially in the countryside. Chinese traditions, such as the duty of sons to care for their parents in their old age, and the need to have children to work on the land make people resistant to the family planning policies. The result is that some people have reverted to early marriage and larger families.

In 1988, the Party Central Committee reasserted China's family planning policy: late marriage and late child-bearing, fewer but healthier pregnancies and, especially in the cities, each couple to bear only one child.

In the countryside, people such as parents of one child who are faced with particular difficulties may ask to have a second child and may be permitted to do so after several years. However, a third child is strongly discouraged.

Family planning is a progressive and civilised undertaking, through which the human race may adjust its numbers. There are many difficulties, but we must uphold family planning for the sake of China, and the health of its descendants.

It is essential that the growth of China's population be controlled. However, efforts to do so have created new problems. For instance, as people live longer, the proportion of older people in the population will increase. At present, people of sixty-five years old and above form 7 per cent of the national total while 10 per cent are over the age of sixty. Although the size and structure of the present population cannot be changed, changes in the future can be anticipated. Plans must be made to deal with the problems which will face us.

9 Discuss the ways in which the Chinese population will probably change in the future. What are the implications for these changes?
10 Use the population pyramid you created in question 2 for your own country or find one in an atlas. Do you have a 'young' population or an 'ageing' population? What does the future hold for the population of your country?

FACTORS RESTRICTING 'POPULATION CONTROL'

The arrival of the day of China's 1.1 billion population is an inevitable historical outcome of population development since the founding of the New China. The socialist system has improved medical and health provisions so that the death rate has fallen from 20 per 1000 in 1949 to 10.8 per 1000 in 1957. In the early days of the New China, population growth was encouraged and increased from 16 per 1000 in 1949 to 24 per 1000 in 1954. It reached 33.33 per 1000 in 1963.

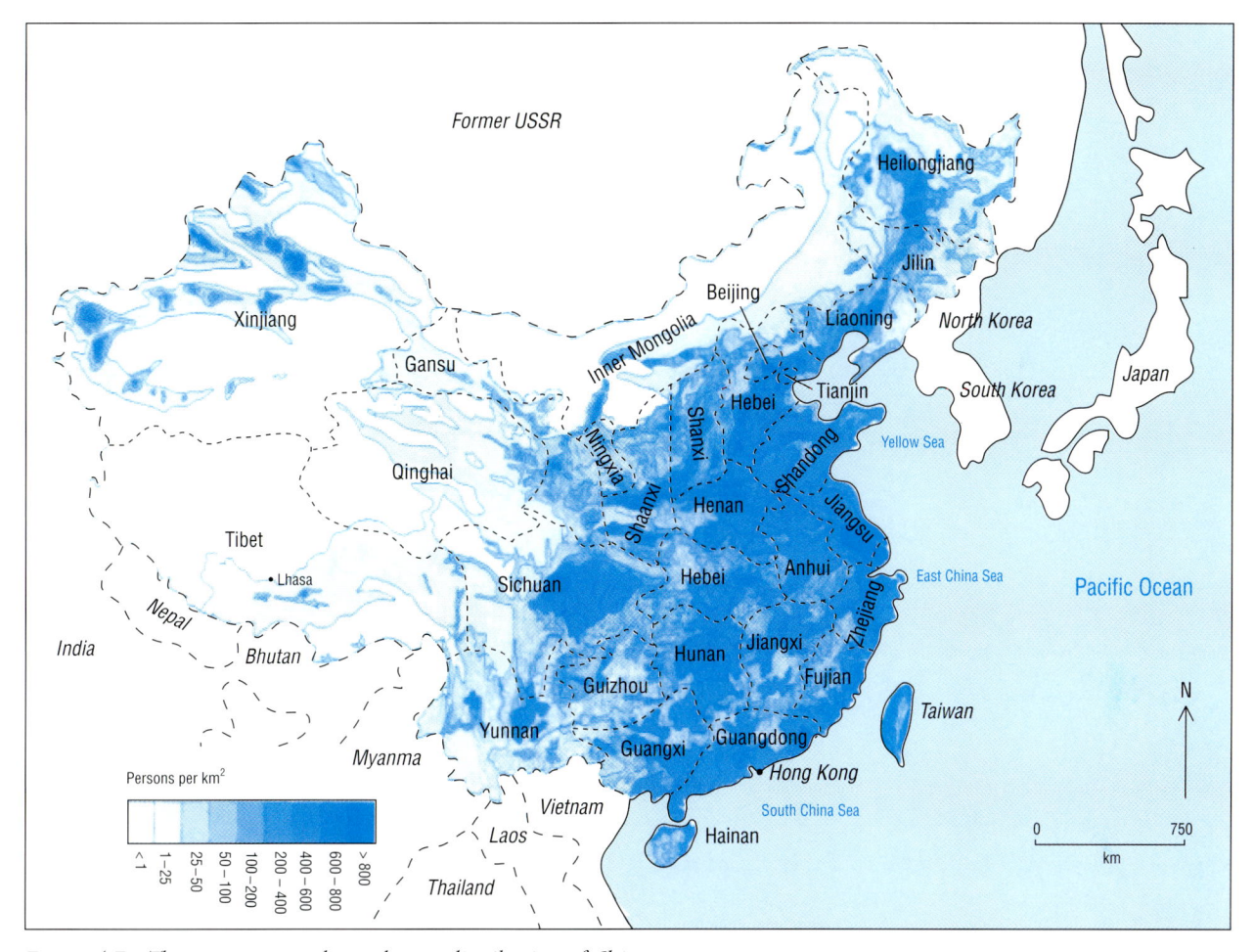

Figure 4.7 The provinces and population distribution of China

During 'The Cultural Revolution' of the 1960s, there was no regulation, the fertility rate rose and the national population increased rapidly. 'High fertility rate, high mortality rate and low growth rate' before the founding of the state had changed into 'high fertility rate, low mortality rate and high growth rate'.

The growth was rapid and unprecedented. Due to the large population base, the number of people added each year is enormous.

The link between economic development and population development has been explained by the theory of demographic transition. Many developed western countries now have birth and death rates that are about equal and China is moving towards this stage. To achieve this, China has tried to enforce family planning. However, a survey in 1988 showed that this was not totally successful. Table 4.2 shows how the various provinces of China differ in their population growth rates, use of family planning and family size.

> 11 Survey your class to discover how many students come from families with two or more children. Discuss the advantages and disadvantages of your findings for your country.

> 12 On an outline map of the provinces of China, shade in those provinces in which the percentage of households with two or more children is less than 10 per cent. In a different colour, shade those provinces where the percentage is over 20 per cent. Discuss the pattern revealed by your map.

In some provinces, people have interpreted the 'one-child' policy as a 'one-son' policy, while elsewhere, people have permitted themselves to have two children. The result of this has been that the rate of population growth rose from 10.8 per 1000 in 1984 to 16.16 per 1000 in 1988—although data announced in May 1993 suggests that since 1988, the rate has dropped greatly.

THE EFFECT OF ECONOMIC DEVELOPMENT

Although the theory of the demographic transition suggests that population growth rates fall as economic development increases, the relationship may not be as simple as that. In a country where annual income per head is under US$750, economic development often leads to rapid population growth. On the other hand, when income per head rises above US$750 it has zero or little population increase.

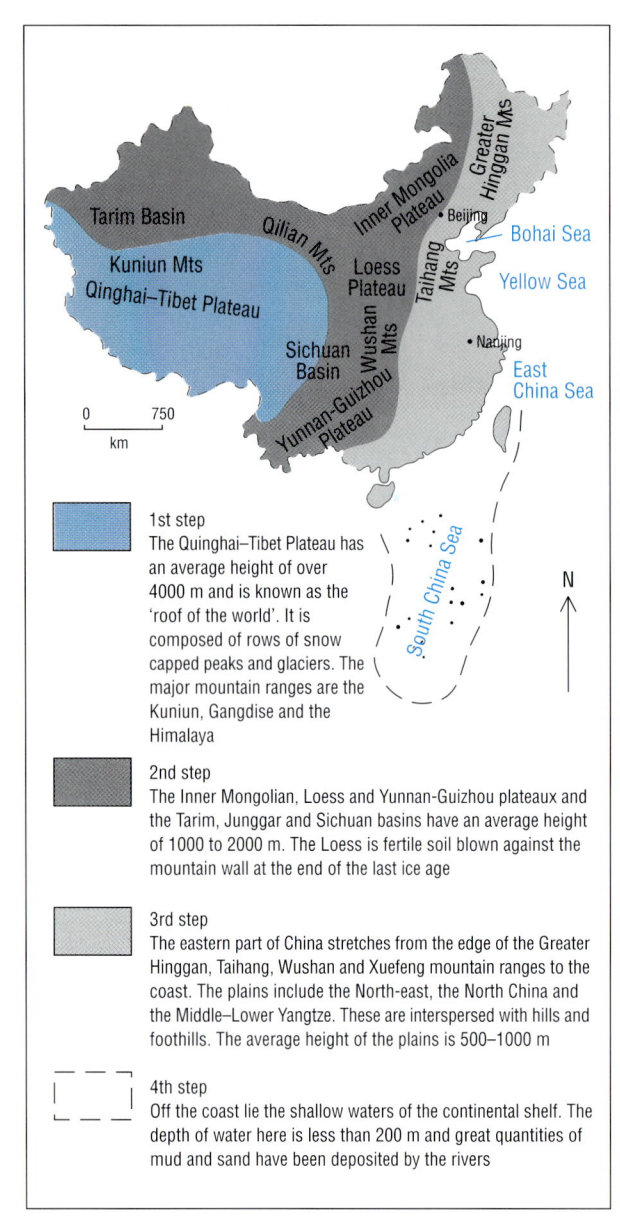

Figure 4.8 China's relief may be imagined as four steps going down from west to east

In China, an income of 1400 yuan per head is a dividing line. In areas such as Jing–Jin–Hu (Beijing–Tianjin–Shanghai) the average income is above 2000 yuan. Here, the average fertility rate increased from 13.9 per 1000 in 1985 to 16.48 per 1000 in 1987 and the total fertility rate of women of average child-bearing age is under 2.1. This means that each couple produces only enough children to replace themselves. In Qinghai, Yunnan and Henan the average income is under 700 yuan. The average fertility rate increased from 14.17 per 1000 in 1985 to 25.19 per 1000 in 1987 and the total fertility rate of women is 2.99.

In 1989, the State Statistical Bureau pointed out that another baby boom for China was inevitable and called for increased efforts to reduce population growth. They emphasised education particularly.

Table 4.2 Variations in population growth rates, family planning and size of families in the provinces of China, 1988

Region	Total population by the end of year	Rate of natural growth per 1000	% households practising family planning	% households with 2 or more children
Beijing	10 810 000	8.86	85.68	1.79
Tianjin	8 430 000	10.27	80.98	2.59
Hebei	57 950 000	14.82	50.25	9.33
Shangxi	27 550 000	13.86	50.23	17.10
Neimenggu	20 940 000	14.25	63.02	12.64
Liaoning	38 200 000	10.71	94.51	1.41
Jilin	23 730 000	12.72	87.41	2.41
Heilongjiang	34 660 000	12.71	71.78	6.83
Shanghai	12 620 000	6.40	97.77	1.12
Jiangsu	64 380 000	10.14	70.74	6.11
Zhejiang	41 700 000	9.19	79.85	2.64
Enhui	53 770 000	15.20	53.04	14.17
Fujian	28 450 000	14.71	36.93	17.84
Jiangxi	36 090 000	13.99	32.01	21.49
Shandong	86 010 000	11.50	63.98	12.37
Henan	80 940 000	15.59	53.46	17.01
Hunan	51 850 000	12.64	56.40	16.98
Hubei	58 900 000	16.50	40.32	13.44
Guangdong	59 280 000	15.83	42.21	24.08
Guangxi	40 880 000	15.82	69.29	29.97
Hainan	6 280 000	15.37	42.97	33.73
Sichuan	105 60 000	11.70	78.06	6.35
Guizhou	31 270 000	17.80	44.09	28.30
Yunnan	35 940 000	16.88	65.30	22.53
Xizang	2 120 000	17.18	—	—
Shaanxi	31 350 000	14.93	46.36	23.78
Gansu	21 360 000	15.35	46.25	21.69
Qinghai	4 340 000	14.59	57.54	25.63
Xingxia	4 450 000	19.55	79.95	28.40
Xinjiang	14 260 000	13.73	14.33	46.43

Note: Figures for the total population and natural growth rate of each region are from the 1988 sample survey. For Shanghai, Jiangsu, Zhejiang, Anhui, Guangxi, Xizang, Ningxia and Xingjiang, the figures are for households. The percentages of households practising family planning and with two or more children in each province are provided by the Family Planning Committee for the first half of 1988

CHINA'S POPULATION 35

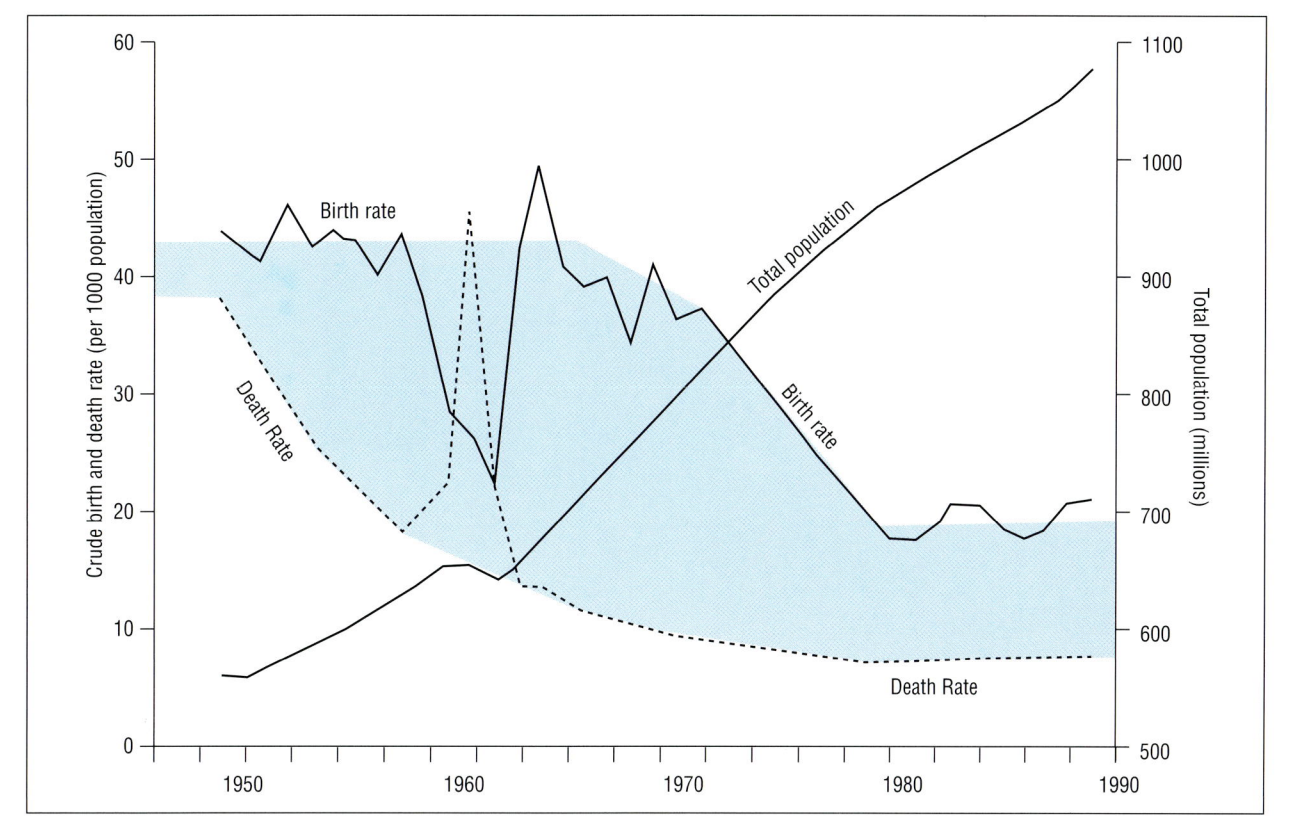

Figure 4.9 China has moved quickly through the demographic transition, although birth rates are still higher than death rates and the population is still growing

13 Summarise your conclusions about Table 4.3 which shows the relationship between education and family size. Discuss the reasons why this pattern may emerge.
14 Is there a similar relationship between education and family size in your country? In what ways are the reasons for this likely to be similar to and different from those for China?

Table 4.3 The relationship between the educational level and family size of fifty year old women in China, 1982

Highest level of formal education reached	Average number of children borne
Little or no schooling	5.86
Primary schooling	4.80
Junior secondary schooling	3.74
Upper secondary schooling	2.85
College	2.05

The broad base to the population pyramid for China (see Figure 4.6) means that the number of women of child-bearing age will increase year by year. This means that even if every Chinese couple practises family planning, the birth rate will continue to rise for some years. We can try to control and regulate fertility rates, but we cannot change the number of people of child-bearing age already in the population. Since the population base keeps on increasing, population control will become more difficult.

Despite the recent increase in fertility rates, China's leaders want to reach near zero population growth by 2000, followed by a slow decline in population over the next century. They think that 750 million people is the ideal population for China. Since over one-third of China's people are under fifteen years of age, this may be difficult to achieve, but at least some techniques used by China to reduce its population could be useful for other countries to adopt.

CHAPTER 5

FIGHTING THE WAR AGAINST HUNGER IN INDIA

Savita Sinha

Ever since human beings appeared on earth, there has been hunger and starvation. Initially, people hunted animals and gathered fruits and roots. When this failed to satisfy their basic need for food, they learned the arts of cultivating crops, breeding animals, and processing, storing and trading food. Despite these advances, hunger and starvation have continued to affect some people in every society. Even today, when science and technology enable the world community to produce enough food for everyone, many people go to sleep hungry every night. Feeding the world's people is a major global challenge. Many countries are fighting a war against hunger. India is one.

WHY DOES INDIA HAVE A PROBLEM WITH FOOD?

India is a vast country with an area of 3.28 million square kilometres. It has a wide diversity of people and landscapes. Despite these differences, the shared monsoon climate and common political and cultural heritage have given India a sense of unity.

India has many natural resources including fertile soil, abundant water, dense forest and rich mineral resources. The large areas of fertile arable land, the variety of climates and long growing season have made it possible to grow a variety of crops like cereals, pulses, oil seeds, cotton, sugar cane, jute, tea and coffee. Between 1987 and 1989, India produced over 20 per cent of the world's rice, second only to China, and ranked fourth in wheat with 9 per cent of the world's production.

> 1 For each of the landscapes shown in Figure 5.1 suggest ways in which the landscape offers a valuable resource to India.
> 2 Compare the range of landscapes and resources of India with those of your own country.

Despite these achievements, nearly one-third of India's people (29 per cent) live below the poverty line. This means that they cannot afford to buy the minimum food needed for their survival.

Why is it that a country so rich in natural resources—the land and water needed for agriculture—has not been able to feed all its people? Even today, many people in India are hungry and some still die from starvation. In the past there have been famines in which many millions of people have died. Before going on to examine the ways in which India is fighting the problem of hunger, it is important to understand the differences between hunger, starvation and famine. Figure 5.2 explains these basic differences.

THE HISTORY OF FAMINE IN INDIA

In earlier times, food shortages before the harvest season were common due to insufficient food preservation techniques and a lack of food storage facilities. As a result some people, especially the poor, went hungry. However, the

FIGHTING THE WAR AGAINST HUNGER IN INDIA

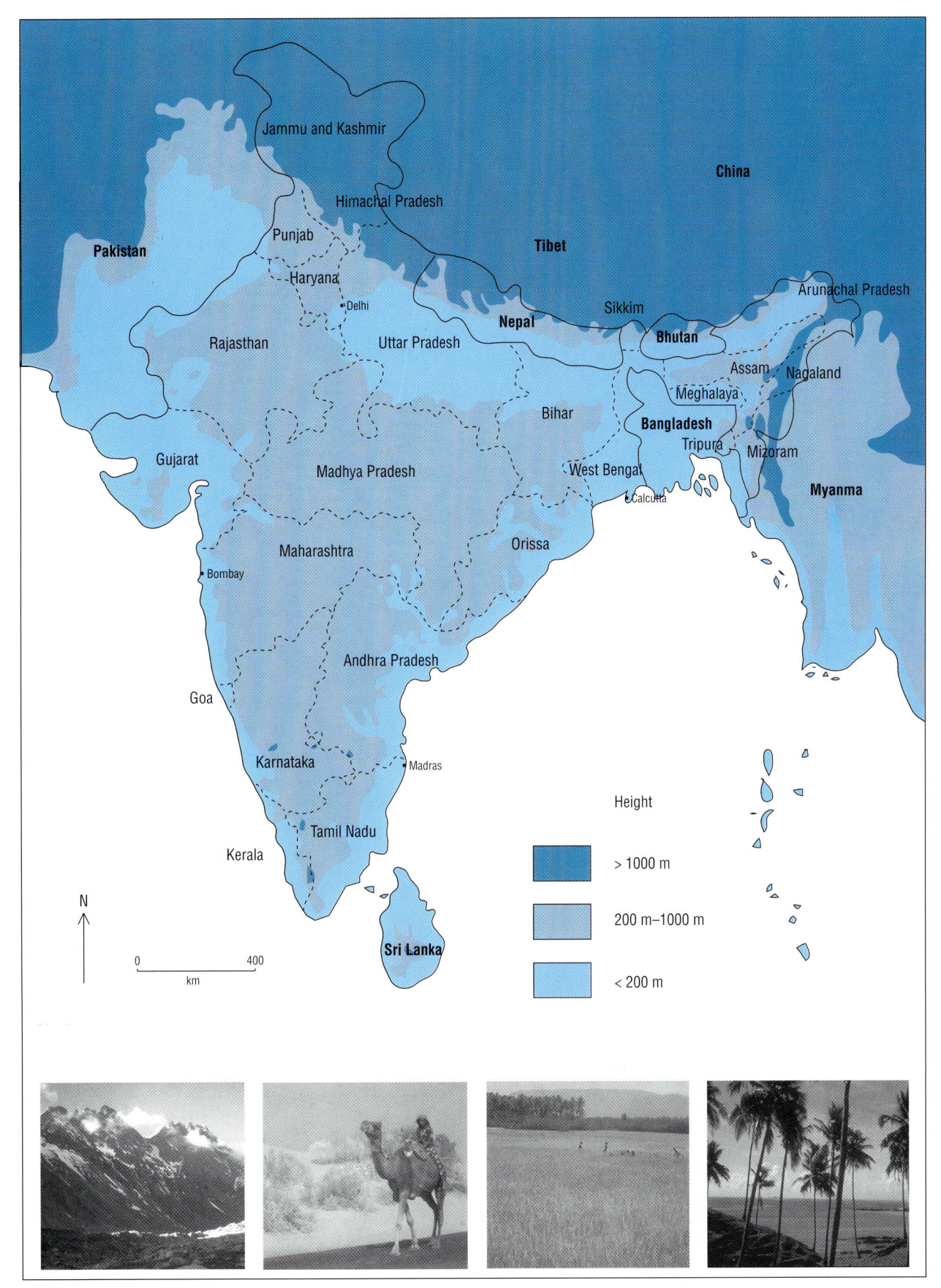

Figure 5.1 Map of India showing some of the various landscapes

problem was sometimes made worse due to crop failure caused by poor physical conditions such as drought, flood, frost, insects and diseases. Figure 5.3 shows a harvesting dance from West Bengal. Such dances, which represent thanks for a successful harvest, illustrate the importance of the harvest to the people. Crop failures often led to many people dying from hunger and starvation—a famine. However, although crop failures often caused famines, all famines were not due to crop failure. All over the world, human factors such as war, poor transportation and communication facilities, overpopulation, economic policies, political decisions and social systems have also resulted in famines.

Between AD 297 and 1943 there were seventy major famines in India. Of these, only eight can be blamed on physical factors alone. Others were caused or made worse by various social upheavals, including wars. Nearly half the famines occurred during the period of British rule, between 1707 and 1943. The famines during this period were also much worse than many of the others. Many of the famines that killed millions of people in the last few years of the nineteenth century occurred because farmers were encouraged to grow industrial crops such as cotton to export to Europe and even food was exported to pay for the costs of administering the country.

Hunger
Hunger means a painful sensation or a state of weakness caused by the need for food. We all feel the need to eat regularly. As soon as we eat, we feel satisfied. This is such a normal routine for many of us that we can hardly imagine what hunger really means, how intense it can be and what kind of suffering it brings to people.

Starvation
Food is needed for our survival and sustenance. Both the quantity and quality of food are important because they provide energy and nutrients. The desire to eat is generated by the body's need for energy rather than its need for other nutrients. Thus a person may die due to nutrient deficiency by not eating the right kinds of food without ever having the feeling of hunger. While the main cause of hunger is the inadequacy of food in terms of quantity, starvation often occurs due to inadequacy of quality. Nevertheless, acute and persistent hunger is often suffered together with starvation and leads to death in the long run.

Famine
While hunger in some form has always existed in every society and some people die of starvation, the death of many people in a society is called famine.

Figure 5.2 Differences between hunger, starvation and famine

The worst, and last, famine was the one that affected Bengal in 1943 in which over a million people died. This famine was caused when the British government in India, fearing invasion by Japanese troops, prevented rice planting and removed all stocks of food from the area. So great was the anger in India at these unnecessary deaths from starvation that independence was declared in 1947.

THE FIGHT AGAINST HUNGER

Soon after independence, India started to plan its economy to ensure a steady improvement in the standard of living of its people. Agriculture required immediate attention. Methods of cultivation were traditional. There was a shortage of such facilities as irrigation, electricity, and credit. Most of the farmers were only tenants who did not own the land they farmed but rented it from a landlord. This meant that the productivity of the land was very low.

One of the first acts of the new government was to encourage more farmers to own their own land. Laws were passed to limit the total amount of land that could be owned by a single person so that more farmers could own land. The government also redistributed land to create workable farms that were not split into many small parcels. New arrangements for supplying farmers' needs and marketing their produce were introduced.

As a result of these changes, India recorded appreciable growth in agricultural production, productivity and investment. Despite both drought and flood in various parts of the country, there have been no famines in India since independence. Thus, the country has won a major battle against the biggest human tragedy—famine.

However, there is still the other battle to win—the fight against hunger. It is difficult to count the exact number of hungry people or to measure the intensity of their hunger. We may, however, get some idea from the percentage of people who live below the poverty line. The poverty line refers to that standard of living which provides the barest minimum of food that will sustain life.

Table 5.1 The percentage of the Indian population living in poverty, 1972–88

	1972–73	1977–78	1983–84	1987–88
Rural dwellers	54.1	51.2	40.1	33.4
Urban dwellers	41.2	38.2	28.1	20.1
Total	51.5	48.3	37.4	29.9

3 Draw three line graphs to show how the percentage of rural people, urban people and the total population who live in poverty has changed between 1972 and 1988.

4 For each group, write a sentence or two to describe the changes that have taken place.

5 The percentage of the population who live in poverty has reduced greatly during this period. Does this mean that the total number of people living in poverty has reduced? Explain your answer.

India has adopted three main approaches to reducing the number of people who suffer from hunger and starvation
- increasing food production
- checking population growth
- alleviating poverty.

INCREASING FOOD PRODUCTION

After independence, the problem of feeding the huge population was so great that the emphasis of India's economic policy was placed on producing more grain for food. Food production in India has been increased first by bringing more land under cultivation and second by increasing the yield from the land through improved methods of farming.

Increasing the area of agricultural land

Figure 5.4 shows the changes in the areas devoted to the various food grains between 1949 and 1990.

6 Examine the changes that have taken place in the area devoted to each of the grains and the total area of food grains between 1949 and 1990. For each graph, identify periods of rapid growth and/or decline in area as well as periods of relative stability.
7 For each graph suggest possible reasons for these periods of growth, stability and decline.

Today, about one-third of the area under food grains is devoted to the cultivation of coarse cereals under rain-fed conditions. These crops are mainly grown by resource-poor farmers on small and marginal farms. While there has been a slow but steady growth in the yield and production of these crops, the area they cover has declined during the 1980s.

Figure 5.3 A harvesting dance from West Bengal

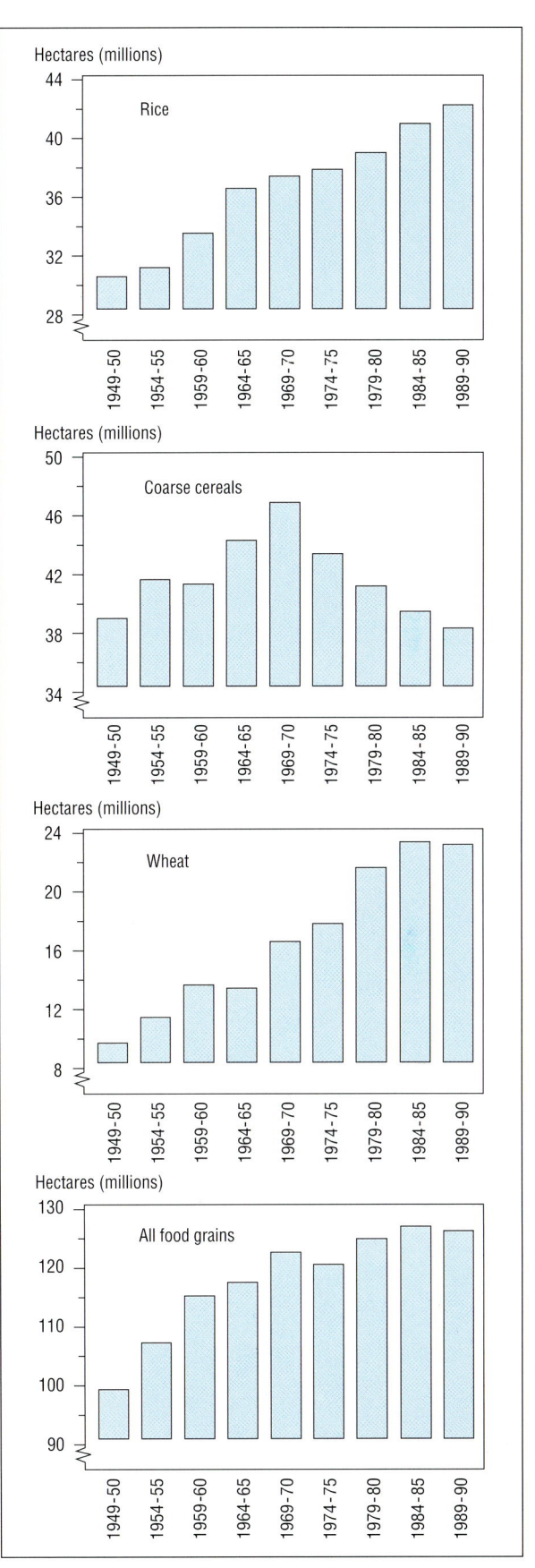

Figure 5.4 The area under food grains, 1949–90

Investment in agricultural inputs other than land area

In the mid 1960s, the 'green revolution' was encouraged and the government provided support for 'package technology'. The term 'green revolution' is used for the rapid increases in rice and wheat yields brought about by introducing high yielding varieties of seed combined with the expanded use of fertilisers and other inputs. Package technology emphasises the use of high yielding varieties of seeds, fertilisers and irrigation. These are all expensive inputs and poor farmers had difficulty in finding the money for them.

The government helped in two ways: First, by supplying seeds and fertilisers directly to farmers at heavily subsidised prices. Second, by setting up a system of lending money to farmers at low rates of interest. Sometimes farmers have been unable to repay these loans and the government has then had to waive them.

Despite problems such as these, package technology has contributed to remarkable changes in agriculture. The use of fertilisers for food grain production increased rapidly from an average of about 18 000 tonnes in 1950 and exceeded 5 million tonnes by 1984. Progress in providing irrigation is comparatively slow. Irrigation increased from an average of about 18 million hectares in 1949–50 to 1951–52 to about 38.7 million hectares in 1981–82 to 1983–84. However, it was the use of high yielding varieties of crops that really marked the start of the era of the green revolution. From zero coverage before 1964–65 it spread to over 49 million hectares during 1982–82 to 1983–84, surpassing the irrigated area.

8 Calculate the percentage change between 1950 and 1986 for
 a the total area of crops
 b area sown more than once per year
 c total irrigated area
 d area irrigated more than once per year.
 (Hint: The percentage increase in the total area sown between 1950 and 1986 is (140.92 minus 112.75) divided by (118.75 x 100%).)
9 Describe the changes that have taken place in each of the aspects of farming mentioned.
10 Comment on the possible association between the area under irrigation and the area sown more than once.
11 Which aspect of farming has changed the most over the total period—the total area sown or the amount of land being irrigated?
12 Draw graphs to show changes in each of the aspects of farming for which figures are given in Table 5.2. Label your graphs to show any changes that appear to have occurred after the green revolution in the mid 1960s.

Table 5.3 shows the changes in the grain production, yields and the use of fertiliser, irrigation and high yielding seeds in India between 1950 and 1990.

Table 5.2 Changes in the use of agricultural land from 1950–86 (millions ha)

Year	Total area of crops	Area sown more than once per year	Total area under irrigation	Area irrigated more than once per year
1950–51	131.89	13.14	22.56	1.71
1955–56	147.31	18.55	25.64	2.88
1960–61	152.77	19.57	27.98	3.32
1965–66	155.28	19.08	30.90	4.56
1970–71	165.79	25.52	38.19	7.09
1975–76	171.29	29.64	43.36	8.77
1980–81	172.64	32.63	49.78	11.06
1985–86	178.83	37.91	54.65	12.57

Source: Based on data from the Government of India, Ministry of Agriculture, Directorate of Economics and Statistics, *Agricultural Statistics at a Glance*, March 1991

Table 5.3 Changes in grain production, yields and the use of fertiliser, irrigation and high yielding seeds in India, 1950–90

	1950–51	1990–91
Production (million t)		
Rice	20.6	74.6
Wheat	6.5	54.5
Total food grains	50.8	176.2
Yield (kg/ha)		
Rice	668	1751
Wheat	663	2274
Total food grains	522	1382
Agricultural inputs		
Area under irrigation (millions ha)	18.0	82.8
Area under high yielding seeds (millions ha)	nil	67.00
Consumption of chemical fertiliser (kg/ha)	negligible	72.27

Source: Based on data from the Government of India, Ministry of Agriculture, Department of Agriculture and Cooperation, *Annual Report 1990–91* and Ministry of Finance, Economic Division, *Economic Survey 1991–92*, Part II, Sectoral Development

Figure 5.5a Solar energy is used to pump water for irrigation in a village in Uttar Pradesh

Figure 5.5b Mechanised farming in Suratgarh, Rajasthan, showing how part of the desert has been converted to good agricultural land with the aid of irrigation

Figure 5.5c Spraying a mustard crop

13 Use the information in Table 5.3 to help you describe the extent of the changes that have taken place in Indian agriculture between 1950 and 1991. Which changes do you think are the most dramatic?
14 For each of the photographs on page 41, find out if similar activities take place on farms in your own country. Discuss the advantages and disadvantages of each approach to farming.

a In what ways could methods of farming in your country benefit from the approaches used in India?
b In what ways could Indian farmers learn from the experiences of your country?

Growth in production

The growth performance of food grain production has been impressive. India was a country facing food deficit until the mid 1960s, after which it became self-sufficient—even producing a small surplus in the 1980s.

The area of food grains increased from 99.3 million hectares in 1949 to 125.5 million hectares in 1990. Of this increase, two-thirds took place in the years before the green revolution.

Table 5.4 provides details of the population, net food production and the amount of food grown per head of population for India from 1951 to 1991. In the period 1967 to 1984, production of only three crops, wheat, sorghum and ragi, exceeded population growth rates. Wheat tends to be consumed by the more wealthy people in India. Since coarse grains are consumed mainly by the poorer sections of the society, more rapid growth in the production of coarse grains would be most beneficial in reducing hunger.

15 Draw line graphs to show the changes in population, production of food grains and amount of grain grown per head of population.
16 Explain why the large growth in the production of food grains has led to only a small increase in the amount of food grown per head of population.

Table 5.4 Population and food production, 1951–91

Year	Population (millions)	Net production of food grains (million t)*	Food grown (kg/person)
1951	363.2	48.1	130
1961	442.4	72.0	160
1971	55.3	94.9	170
1981	688.5	113.4	160
1991	849.6	154.2	180

* Net production has been taken as 87.5% of gross production: 12.5% has been allowed for seeds, food requirements and wastage

Source: The Government of India, Ministry of Agriculture, Department of Agriculture and Cooperation, *Annual Report 1990–91*

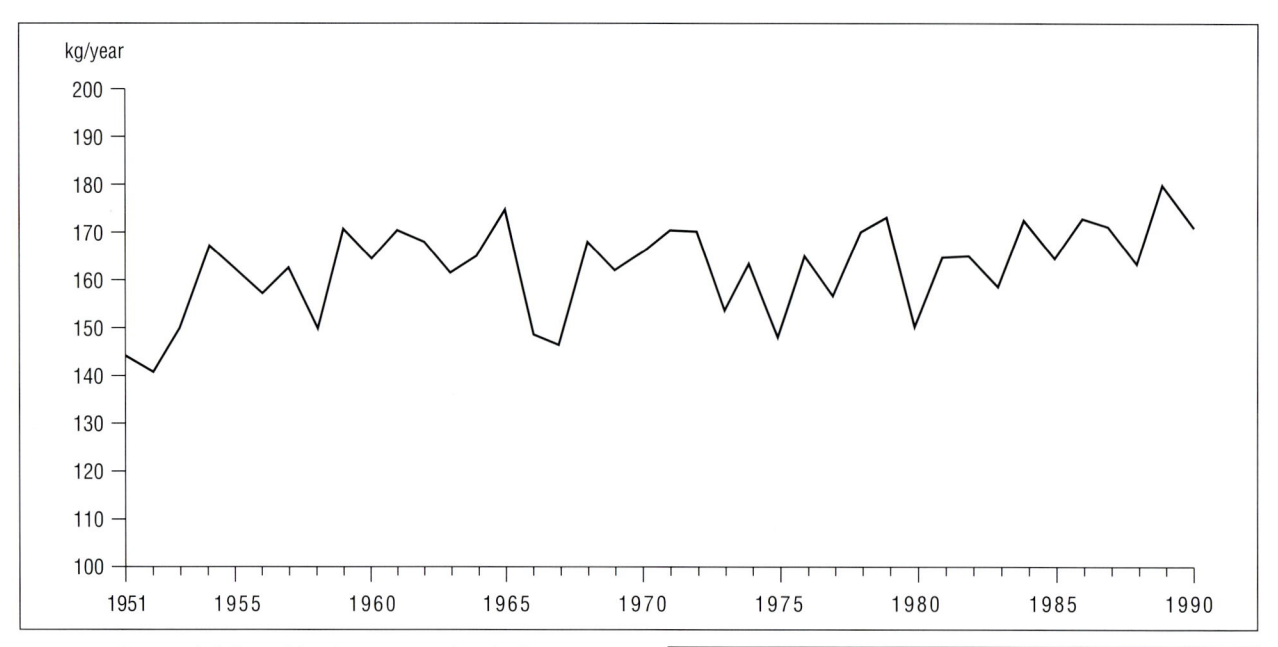

Figure 5.6 Availability of food grains per head of population, 1951–90

The availability of food grains per head of population in India during 1951–90 has fluctuated, varying in the range between 140 and 180 kilograms a year. This is shown in Figure 5.6. This graph is based on net production (after wastage, seeds and other losses are deducted from total production), net imports (the excess of imports over exports of grain) and changes in government stocks. Improvement in the production and yield of food grains has been largely absorbed by population growth, reduction in imports, and building up of stocks.

17 *a* Trace Figure 5.6. Draw a line of best fit to show the changes in food grain per head between 1951–65 and between 1967–90. Mark 1965–67 on your tracing as a period of abnormal drought, and 1965–67 as the start of the green revolution.
b Summarise the other information you have learned about food supply in India as notes on your traced graph.

The consumption pattern of food grains and the income levels of people are closely linked. Sample surveys conducted by the National Sample Survey Organisation to examine the consumption pattern of food grains in rural as well as urban areas cutting across various groups reflect some interesting features. Figure 5.7 shows the amount of the different grains eaten by rural and urban dwellers. Figure 5.8 shows how the amount of grain eaten changes as people earn more money.

18 Examine Figure 5.7 and list the conclusions that you can draw from it about the differences between the eating habits of rural and urban dwellers.

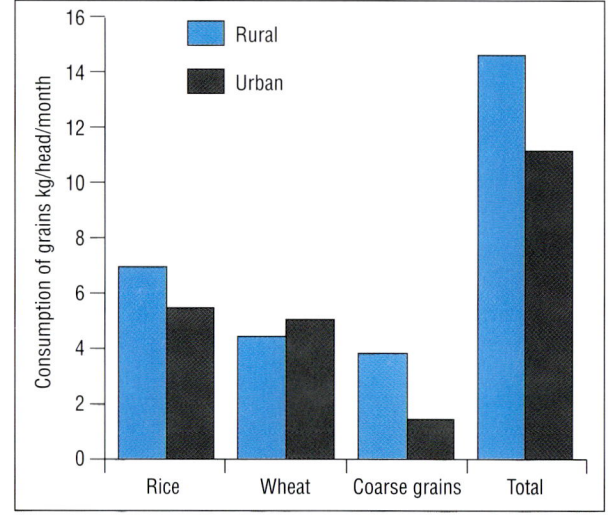

Figure 5.7 The amount of the different grains eaten by rural and urban dwellers

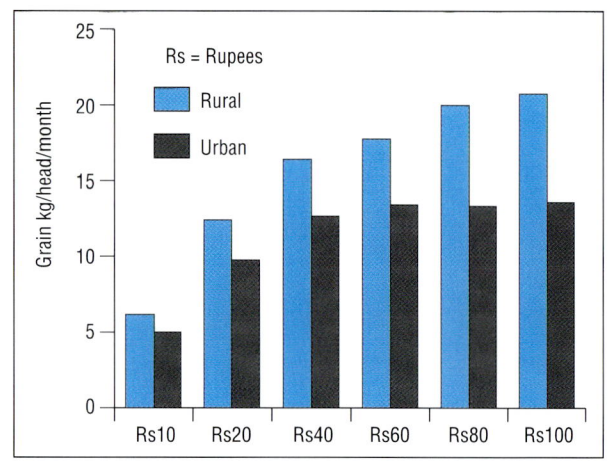

Figure 5.8 The influence of income on the amount of grain eaten by rural and urban dwellers

FIGHTING THE WAR AGAINST HUNGER IN INDIA

> 19 Trace Figure 5.7. On your tracing draw two lines to represent the changes in the amount of grain eaten by rural and urban dwellers as they earn more money. Describe the changes that take place as income increases. What conclusions can you draw about the differences in diet of poorer and more wealthy people in rural and urban areas?

Here are some more conclusions that were drawn from the surveys
- cereals constitute about 94 per cent of the total food grains consumed
- consumption of food grains is much higher in rural areas than urban areas
- the consumption of food grains rises initially with increases in wages, and then reaches a saturation point and only rises a little after that
- the consumption of wheat and rice has increased comparatively faster in rural areas than urban areas, perhaps because of the rapid expansion of Fair Price Shops
- the consumption of coarse cereals has declined in both rural and urban areas.

> 20 *a* For each of the statements above, explain the conclusions that can be drawn about food supply among different groups of people in India.
>
> *b* What suggestions can you make about the future supply of grains and other foods in India?

Some people have described the green revolution as a disaster for poor people in third world countries, because they have been forced to leave the land and go to the cities in search for work. [When asked by the editor of this book to expand on some of the reasons for the bad publicity the green revolution has received in many western countries, Dr Sinha gave the reply shown in Figure 5.9.]

CHECKING POPULATION GROWTH

India is one of the most populous countries in the world. With over 844 million people in 1991, it is second only to China. Its population is expected to exceed 1 billion by the turn of the century.

The size of a country's population has a strong impact on its economic development. A large population may be a major source of wealth and provide a market for goods and services. On the other hand, it may not only prove to be unproductive, but even neutralise all the gains of economic development. We have already seen this in the case of food production in India. Table 5.5 shows how the Indian economy has changed from 1950 to 1990. It also shows how the population has changed.

It is true that a number of reports have concluded that the green revolution has adversely affected the rural poor. However, more recent evidence clearly shows that although exceptions exist, as a general rule the green revolution has resulted in a very significant improvement in the material well being of the poor.

These studies have also tried to find out where the earlier reports went wrong, and have identified four main areas. First, the studies failed to distinguish between early and subsequent adoption of new technology. The studies undertaken soon after the release of the first high yielding varieties of rice and wheat found that only big farmers adopted them together with the need for fertiliser and irrigation. However, they failed to recognise that small farmers would follow once the uncertainty was reduced by observing success under the new conditions. Second, the benefits to the poor as consumers of rice and wheat through lower prices was largely overlooked. Third, practically no attention was paid to the multiplier effect of the green revolution and hence its impact on incomes of the rural poor. Fourth, the impact of the green revolution was frequently confused with the impact of institutional arrangements, agricultural policies and labour saving mechanisation.

In fact the green revolution has been beneficial to the rural poor through changes in their assets, incomes and the price they pay for food. High yielding varieties of rice and wheat have been adopted by producers, irrespective of farm size or land ownership. In fact, soil quality and access to irrigation water are much more important than farm size in influencing adoption. Since the yield increases, even a small farmer earns much more using package technology than before.

The green revolution has also helped in creating more employment opportunities in the agricultural and allied sectors through the extension of irrigation, improved banking and credit services, and the development of agriculturally-based and other industries. In some states, such as Punjab and Andhra Pradesh, farmers generate a huge surplus and invest the money in other activities.

Wages in the rural areas have increased as a result of the new employment opportunities and now even landless labourers can earn more than they could before the green revolution. Finally, the increases in food production have caused prices to go down and this helps poor consumers even more.

Figure 5.9 The green revolution: disaster or saviour?

Figure 5.10 Poultry farming in a village in Punjab—farmers invest their profits from grains into other economic activities like this one to generate more income

Table 5.5 Selected economic and social indicators for India, 1950 and 1990

	1950–51	1990–91
Gross domestic product (GDP)		
GDP at current prices (million Rs)	89.79	3951.43
Net national product per head at 1980 prices (Rs)	1127	2142
Production of selected goods		
Food grains (million t)	50.8	176.2
Finished steel (million t)	1.04	13.4
Cement (million t)	2.7	48.9
Electricity (billion kWh)	5.1	264.6
Selected social indicators		
Population (million)	318.91	849.51
Birth rate (per 1000)	41.7	29.9
Death rate (per 1000)	27.4	9.6

Rs = Rupees
Source: The Government of India, Ministry of Finance, Economic Division, *Economic Survey 1991–92*, Part II, Sectoral Development

> 21 *a* For each of the four products in Table 5.5, food grains, steel, cement and electricity, calculate the quantity produced per million people for 1950 and 1990. (Hint: Divide the amount produced by the population for that year.)
> *b* Has the increase in Indian production of these items kept pace with the increase in population?
> *c* What would have been the probable result if the population growth had been less?

The Indian government, aware of the problems of a rapidly growing population, introduced the National Family Planning Program in 1951. The emphasis then was only on promoting contraception. Today, that program has expanded into a community oriented service. The long term goal of the Ministry of Health and Family Welfare is for India to reach a zero population growth rate by 2050 with an estimated population around 1300 million. A multi-pronged strategy has been adopted to attain the demographic goals. Besides the family welfare programs, emphasis has been laid on creating awareness among the people regarding the need to bring down the growth rate of population.

Table 5.5 also shows the changes in the birth rate and death rate for 1950 and 1990. These figures show that the birth rate has fallen by nearly one-third as a result of the family planning program. However, during the same period, the death rate has fallen by over two-thirds. The health and family welfare programs have two goals: 'Health for all' and a national population growth rate of zero.

Improvements in health care and better and more food have resulted in the reduction in the death rate. One aspect of the improved health care has been the Integrated Child Development Service which was launched in 1974. This service provides a package of nutrition, immunisation and health checks for children from birth to six years and for expectant and nursing mothers. The net result has been that the Indian population has continued to grow. The average annual rate of population growth from 1981 to 1991 was 2.11 per cent.

If this growth rate continues, then the Indian population will double again in thirty-six years.

> 22 *a* What is the growth rate for your country? How many years will it take for your country to double its population?
> *b* Some countries have a falling population and they too are worried. How does the government of your country try to influence rates of population change?

ALLEVIATING POVERTY

Poverty is an evil in itself. People who live in poverty often find themselves unable to raise their own standard of living. They also often have larger numbers of children than other groups. It is therefore important to alleviate poverty in any society. In India, the main strategies that have been adopted to remove poverty are food distribution, asset distribution and generation of income among the poor.

Food distribution

It is not enough for India to produce more food. The food must be distributed throughout the society and be available throughout the year. Besides improving the methods of farming, the government also ensures that the farmers are paid a

Figure 5.11 A wheat mandi, or collection centre, in Haryana

high enough price for their produce for them to earn a fair living and be encouraged to grow more. This is achieved by the government fixing minimum prices for various agricultural products. The government buys the required stocks of essential commodities and releases some of them for sale at the market price and some is provided to the Fair Price Shops.

The seven essential commodities supplied to the states and union territory governments for distribution to poorer people through Fair Price Shops are rice, wheat, edible oils, sugar, coal, kerosene and cheap cloth. The Fair Price Shops are part of the Indian Public Distribution Systems (PDS)—one of the largest in the world. It has been in operation since the Second World War. It started at a time of shortage of essential goods, though it continues even when shortages do not exist. Now a general concern about the low consumption levels of the poor keeps the PDS in operation. The PDS keeps prices under control and ensures a supply of essential commodities at reasonable prices to weaker and poorer sections of the society.

Over the years, the network of Fair Price Shops has increased from 302 000 in 1984 to 354 000 in 1989. About 75 per cent of these shops are in the rural areas. The Fair Price Shops are important for the poorer people, especially in rural India. However, not all these poorer people are living in poverty.

The system does have several weaknesses which need to be removed. Though it covers the whole population in principle, the criterion is to issue ration cards to all those households that have proper registered residential addresses. As such, homeless poor or migrant workers are left out of the scheme, although slum dwellers have an address and so can obtain a ration card. People who lack enough money on a regular basis (such as daily wagers, who earn money on a daily basis) cannot afford to buy their ration from the shops. Finally, in rural areas, Fair Price Shops are dispersed over large areas and many people are unable to get to them. Efforts are being made to bring 1700 more blocks (an administrative unit smaller than a district), especially in the backward areas, under this scheme.

Asset distribution and generation of income

The first section of this chapter described the importance of land reforms in India, which have helped to redistribute land to the people who actually till the soil. However, there are also schemes to create other ways for people in the countryside to earn their living.

The world's biggest program to create assets for the rural poor is the Integrated Rural Development Program (IRDP). The main objectives of IRDP are to raise families of the identified target group above the poverty line, and to create substantial additional opportunities of self employment in the rural sector.

There are two sub-programs to IRDP. These are the Training for Rural Youth for Self Employment (TRYSEM) program and the Development of Women and Children in Rural Areas (DWCRA) program. The TRYSEM program provides training and technical skills to young people while the DWCRA program encourages rural women to undertake economic activities. Both programs help people to create work by providing them with credit to buy the materials they need and by subsidising their costs. Bee keeping is one activity that has been encouraged by the TRYSEM program (see Figure 5.12). It has been estimated that since 1985, when the IRDP was introduced, 18.2 million people have been helped. This means that about another 3 per cent of the population have been lifted above the poverty line.

Figure 5.12 Bee keeping, seen here in a village in West Bengal, is one activity that has been encouraged by the TRYSEM program

> 23 *a* What programs in your country are designed to help young people earn their living?
> *b* Make a list of the ways in which people are helped to escape from poverty in your country.

THE FUTURE

In the last fifty years, India has changed from being a country faced with famine and recurrent food shortages to being almost self sufficient in food and even growing some surpluses. Its production of almost all its requirements has increased both in terms of total amounts and in terms of amounts per head, even though its population has grown rapidly. Not only has there been an increase in the amount of food grown, but the ways in which it is distributed to the people have been improved by the system of Fair Price Shops.

Despite all these achievements, hunger still exists in India. The answer to this problem lies in faster rates of growth so that workers move to more productive occupations. In 1992, the Indian government introduced a number of reforms designed to improve the technologies of production, storage and marketing food and raw materials. The aim is to move beyond self sufficiency and for India to become a regular exporter of agricultural products. At the same time, the PDS will be extended.

However, India cannot achieve everything on its own. The more developed countries of the world can help by making their more advanced technology available to speed up economic development. They can also help by reducing the instability of world food markets and permitting countries such as India to trade with them on fairer terms.

> 24 Find out how much trade exists between your country and India. What tariffs and import duties make this trade more difficult for India?
> 25 Find out how many people in your country are often hungry or live in poverty. What is being done to help them? What can your country learn from India in fighting the problem of hunger and poverty?
> 26 In what ways does your country and its people help other countries of the world that suffer from famine, starvation and hunger?

CHAPTER 6

URBANISATION IN BANGLADESH

**Mesbah-us-Saleheen,
A.H.M. Raihan Sharif,
Md Mozurul Huq and
A.K.M. Abul Kalam**

Bangladesh, situated at the head of the Bay of Bengal, has been an independent nation only since 1971. In the ancient past, the people of Bangladesh enjoyed self-government at the local level, but the Indian subcontinent has often been subject to foreign rule. The Mughals, who came mainly from central Asia, were early invaders, while British colonial administration began in 1757. At this time, the area which is now Bangladesh formed the Indian province of East Bengal. India received independence from British colonial rule in August 1947 and Pakistan was created as a new country in two parts—1760 kilometres of Indian territory separated the new East and West Pakistan. East Pakistan was the territory that is now Bangladesh. In December 1971, after a war of liberation with Pakistan which lasted nine months, Bangladesh emerged as an independent country.

Bangladesh is now a member of the Association of Commonwealth Countries and of the United Nations Organisation.

Bangladesh is a small country in area, but in terms of population it is the eighth largest nation in the world. The population census of 1991 records its total population as 108 million living in 143 998 square kilometres. With 750 people per square kilometre, Bangladesh has one of the highest densities of population in the world. Only city–states such as Hong Kong and Singapore have densities higher than this. If the total population of the world gathered in Australia, the density would be approximately equal to that of Bangladesh!

Bangladesh is one of the poorest nations of the Third World. Agriculture is the basis of its economy and most of the population lives in approximately 68 000 rural villages. Only about 10.29 per cent of its population lives in the urban areas, giving Bangladesh one of the lowest urban–rural population ratios in the world. Despite this, the problems of urban management are still large since 60 per cent of the total population lives below extreme poverty level, and many urban dwellers are unable to satisfy their basic needs. This chapter describes the process of urbanisation that is taking place in Bangladesh, the problems that are being encountered and the ways in which these problems are being solved.

THE HISTORY OF URBANISATION IN BANGLADESH

Although Bangladesh is one of the least urbanised countries in the Third World, it has a glorious urban tradition. Historical records show that urbanisation started in this part of the world more than two thousand years ago. The ancient and medieval urban centres were the focus of administration, trade and commerce, and religious festivities. During the period when the Mughals ruled the area, urban centres were also important for defence purposes. Many of these urban centres either declined or disappeared. Under British rule, the urbanisation process and the urban centres took on a typically colonial character. At this time, urban growth in Bangladesh was slow and limited to some geographical locations which could provide easy administration and transport facilities, particularly sea and river ports. For example Dhaka, the capital city of Bangladesh, developed as a major urban centre for British administration.

With Indian and Pakistani independence in 1947, urban growth in the then East Pakistan gained impetus. Major investments took place in the capital city of Dhaka and the port cities of Chittagong and Khulna, which were old British district headquarters and major industrial centres. The West Pakistanis dominated the government of Pakistan and the colonial tradition of concentrating development in a few urban centres continued. Existing major urban centres began to experience many problems as Bangladesh experienced rapid, unplanned, urbanisation from the mid-1960s, and especially since its own independence in 1971.

Table 6.1 shows that Bangladesh has experienced a steady increase in urban population from the beginning of the twentieth century. In 1901, less than 3 per cent of its population lived in urban areas, and the proportion had only risen to 5 per cent in 1961. This represents a very low average rate of urban growth.

Immediately after the creation of Pakistan, between 1951 and 1961, there was, however, a higher rate of urban growth compared to previous census periods. This was due mainly to the unprecedented migration of Muslims from India that started with the partition of India and Pakistan. These migrants settled mostly in the major urban centres. During that period, many Hindus also moved from East Pakistan to India, especially the province of West Bengal. This period also saw an increase in rural–urban migration which accentuated the process of urban growth. Over time, this process led to the development of new small towns throughout the country. The government has encouraged this trend since the early 1980s.

Table 6.1 The growth of urban population in Bangladesh, 1901–91

Year	Total population ('000)	Urban population		Increase of urban population
		Population ('000)	% total	
1901	28 928	702	2.43	—
1911	31 555	807	2.56	14.96
1921	33 254	878	2.64	8.80
1931	35 604	1 076	3.02	22.55
1941	41 997	1 537	3.66	42.85
1951	42 063	1 826	4.34	18.80
1961	50 841	2 641	5.19	44.63
1974	71 480	6 274	8.78	137.56
1981	87 120	8 041	9.23	28.16
1991	107 992	11 112	10.29	38.19

1 Draw a line graph to show the changes in both the total population and the urban population of Bangladesh from 1901 to 1991. Label your graph with the various stages in Bangladesh's history over this period. Mark the time when urbanisation developed most quickly.

RECENT URBAN GROWTH

The urban population began to increase at a higher rate in the mid-1960s and reached about 9 per cent of the total population in 1974. From 1961 to 1974, the total increase in urban population was 137.56 per cent. This was an increase of more than 10 per cent each year.

Another striking feature in the urbanisation of Bangladesh is that from 1901 to 1991 the population in the towns has always grown faster than in the rural areas.

Rural poverty and migration

Rural–urban migration has been a major factor in urban population growth in Bangladesh, as in many other Third World countries. Migration from rural areas accounted for almost 50 per cent of the total increase in urban population between 1961 and 1974. The estimated number of rural

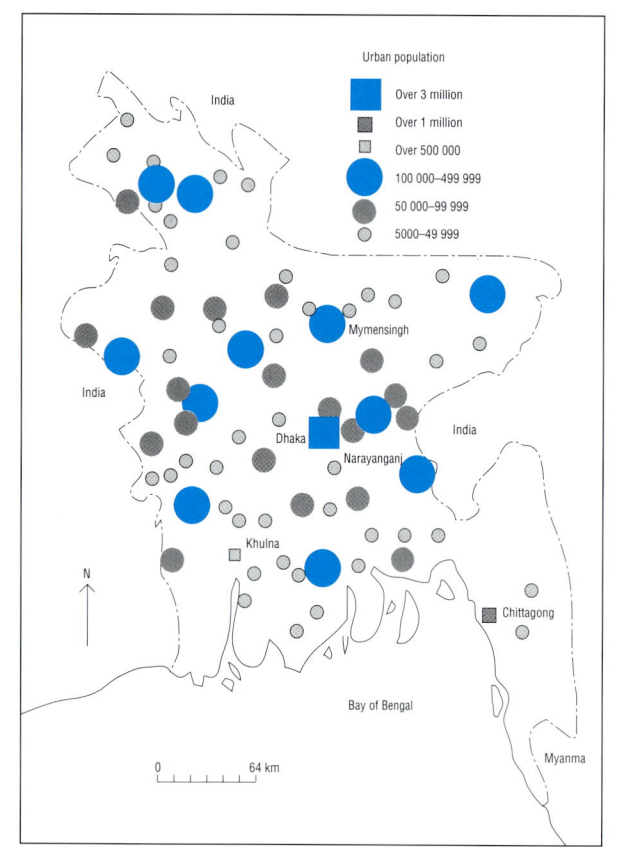

Figure 6.1 The distribution of the urban population, 1981

migrants to the urban areas was about 1.8 million during this period.

People in rural areas were both pushed and pulled towards the cities. They were pushed by natural hazards such as river bank erosion that removed farmland, leaving its owners destitute. They were pushed by the lack of roads and other facilities that enable farmers to earn a living. These push factors led to increasing unemployment and underemployment. Rural people were pulled towards the increasingly dominant large urban centres while improvements in transportation and communication opened their eyes to the possibilities available in the towns. Table 6.2 shows the reasons given by rural people for migrating to Dhaka city in 1990. Besides the rural–urban migration, there is also a general movement of people from smaller urban centres to larger urban centres.

Table 6.2   Reasons for migration to Dhaka city

Reason	%
Economic reasons (for example, landless and poverty, unemployment, getting charity)	57.30
Environmental causes (river bank erosion)	25.00
Personal or family reasons (loss of husband, dependants, family feud)	8.90
Socio-political reasons (social factors, village politics, brought by relatives)	1.00
Other reasons	7.90
Not stated	0.10
Total	100.00

2   Draw a bar chart to show the reasons for migration to Dhaka. Briefly describe the main reasons for people making such a move.
3   Imagine you have met a rural family on the road to Dhaka. Write the conversation which may follow when you ask them why they are going to Dhaka.
4   Survey students in your school to identify which families have moved into your area from elsewhere. Discover the main reasons for them making this move. Present your findings as a chart and briefly describe the main reasons. To what extent are they similar to those found in Bangladesh?

Urban spread into agricultural areas

During the 1980s, the government chose many smaller regional centres for development as future small towns. The intention is that many small towns will help to slow the migration of population from rural areas to the major urban centres by distributing the facilities of modern life to the rural villages. As part of this policy, the government upgraded thirty-three subdistrict headquarters to district headquarters and 460 thanas (police stations) to upazila (subdistrict) headquarters between November 1982 and February 1984.

In the last decade, these newly upgraded places have become the focus of national economic development and new urban facilities.

One result of this growth of many small towns has been that new housing areas, industrial sites and other economic activities have encroached on agricultural land. Private landowners, who often break existing state planning laws, are responsible for much of the urban encroachment on agricultural land. The continuous growth of population in the major urban centres and such urban sprawl in the smaller centres may increase the problems of urban management in the future.

THE PROBLEMS OF THE MAJOR URBAN CENTRES

Studies of urbanisation in Bangladesh have identified six major urban centres including the four cities of Dhaka (the capital), Chittagong, Khulna and Rajshahi. Dhaka, being the capital and a commercial and industrial centre, is the largest city of the country. Chittagong and Khulna are the two sea port cities of the country. Rajshahi is much less developed, but, like the other divisional headquarters, has both a university and colleges. Two other major urban centres are Narayanganj and Mymensingh. Narayanganj is an industrial and commercial centre with a major river port. Mymensingh is an old district headquarters with important educational establishments, such as the Agricultural University, Medical College and Women's Cadet College.

All of the major urban centres in Bangladesh are suffering from an enormous increase in population, particularly poor people, and from haphazard growth and expansion. The aspects of the urban environment that suffer most are landuse and housing, health and sanitation, water resources, garbage disposal, transportation, education, and social and aesthetic appeal.

Urban congestion

Urban congestion occurs for many reasons. Overcrowding is a major cause but an imbalance between the ratio of urban functions and the population served adds to the problem. The city plan of Dhaka has not been reviewed for a long time. Parking and providing open space have not been considered. There has been a great increase in the number of vehicles, particularly slow forms of transport like rickshaws and carts. Many city roads are used for storage and loading and unloading of goods and merchandise during the working day. Traffic jams, the fluctuating population, street beggars, vendors and hawkers, add to the existing overcrowding. When roads are blocked for municipal and other emergency functions, the chaos can last all day.

Figure 6.2 Congestion in the city streets of Dhaka, typical of many urban centres in Bangladesh

Slums and squatters

Most of the large urban centres in Bangladesh face common problems of slums and squatters but the problem is especially acute in the four major cities of the country. In many South American cities, the shanty towns have developed on the outskirts of the main towns, but in Dhaka there are many slums and squatters distributed over the whole of the city area. Slums exist even near the central business district and high class residential areas. While the average density of population living in the slums of Dhaka city is approximately 741 per hectare it is much higher in some other urban centres.

Access to urban land and housing in the big cities of Bangladesh is very unequal. In Dhaka city, for example, 70 per cent of the population lives on 20 per cent of the total residential land. The most wealthy 30 per cent of the city's population controls over 80 per cent of the residential land.

Slum dwellers, who are mostly migrants from rural areas, live in unhygienic environments. A lack of living facilities, poor sanitation and health care are common problems. In bad weather, they face even further hardships from the lack of adequate shelter and drainage. The results of a large population in a poor city affect everyone.

Figure 6.3a Slums in the heart of the central business district of Dhaka

Figure 6.3b Roadside dumping of garbage in a residential area of Dhaka city

Figure 6.4 Unhygienic and poor sanitation system of the slum dwellings in Dhaka city

Floating population

The population census of 1991 records 5 252 500 people described as the floating population of the country. This floating population is 0.49 per cent of the total population. Of the large number of migrants seeking employment in the cities, many fail to find rooms for living, even in the slums. Many of these people become beggars—their only means of livelihood. This group of migrants select pedestrian spaces or shoulders of the quieter roads for their shelters, where they stay until they are forced to move somewhere else.

Pollution

All urban people suffer from the effects of overpopulation and the increase in vehicle pollution and industrial and municipal wastes. However, the urban poor suffer more than others because their substandard living environment does not protect them from human and other wastes. Pollution in major urban centres has been a growing concern over the last two decades. In Dhaka, open dustbins are commonplace. Household wastes are often dumped by the roadside. In low-income residential areas, the problems are more acute due to lack of waste disposal facilities, poor sanitation and, above all, lack of consciousness about the effect of pollution on urban life. Throughout Bangladesh, municipal waste disposal services are inadequate. Even in the small urban centres, problems in urban services are acute.

Figure 6.5 A well-planned area in Dhaka city

Informal economic activities

Informal economic activities include all those ways in which people earn money without having officially recognised jobs. In Dhaka, and the other major cities, nearly two-thirds of people who engage in informal economic activities provide basic needs such as food, clothing, shelter and transport. Others provide various household necessities, health and personal care and recycle old or waste materials.

Of the people engaged in the informal sector, 70 per cent are migrants. Many of these people take up street vendoring, petty retailing, shoe-polishing, garment-repairing and other such jobs due to the absence of formal employment opportunities. Although those who arrive in the city find they have no other option, the possibilities of the informal sector themselves attract some migrants. These migrants exert further pressure on the available urban land. Thus, although this sector of the economy meets many needs of Dhaka's citizens, it also causes many problems. For example, Dhaka now faces increasing growth of slums, urban congestion, prostitution, begging and crime. Many of these problems result from the poor economic conditions of the low-income people in the city.

Lack of urban planning and management

A United Nations report in the 1970s lamented that many earlier development plans tended to ignore urbanisation. Most of the urban centres in Bangladesh suffer from a lack of planning and management of urban functions and services. This further aggravates the problems of urban life. Urban plans rapidly become outdated and they are rarely evaluated and monitored in the light of experience. Problems accumulate over several years before another master plan comes before the urban management authority, by which time problems are often beyond the capacity of the authorities.

> 5 *a* Make a list of all the problems facing Dhaka city that are mentioned in this chapter. Discuss the extent to which each aspect of life that you have listed exists in the cities of your country and the way in which each is treated by the authorities of your country.
> *b* In what ways should each of these aspects be regarded as problems and in what ways may they be regarded as advantages?

THE FUTURE

Dhaka has another face. Some people live in conditions that may be compared favourably with those in any city in the world. However, just as in most other cities, only a relatively few people can live in such splendour. Dhaka has many more people living at the other extreme of the line between rich and poor than most other countries.

However, despite the problems faced by the slum dwellers and the floating population and the problems that the large number of such people cause for the major cities, most urban people in Bangladesh enjoy both a higher standard of living and better economic opportunities than the rural dwellers. Consequently, the government is undertaking development programs for both the urban poor and for rural areas.

If nothing is done to help the people of the rural areas, the surplus population will continue to migrate to the major urban areas in search of employment. Urban growth in the largest cities may soon become unmanageable if the rural–urban migration rate is not considered. The solution to the problem of rural–urban migration depends greatly on the redistribution of economic improvements.

A great start has been made by encouraging the growth and development of the small towns to redistribute the large number of rural labourers who tend to migrate to the major urban areas. During the last few decades, the road transport network linking rural and urban areas has improved greatly. More recently, air links between the various parts of the country have been established. Over the last decade many more people in rural areas and small urban areas have had better access to cars, colour televisions and radios. Such developments reduce the pressure on the major cities and indirectly help to reduce undesirable urban problems.

The Bangladesh government is now preparing plans for the new urban centres to ensure that urban sprawl and larger populations do not create new problems. With this end in mind, a successful urbanisation policy will ensure that economic development and the distribution of resources are more equitably provided across the landscape of Bangladesh.

> 6 Discuss the ways in which Dhaka shares the same urban problems that afflict many other cities in the world. What can other countries learn from the situation in Bangladesh?

CHAPTER 7

URBANISATION IN BRAZIL

Sônia Maria Marchiorato Carneiro, Antônio Lineu Carneiro and Zeno Soares Crocetti

In most of the countries of the world today, more people live in urban areas than in rural areas. In many countries, a large proportion of the population lives in the major cities. While cities in all countries have many aspects in common, they also have features peculiar to their own country and its history. This chapter explores the evolution of cities in Brazil. Some Portuguese words are difficult to translate. These are explained in Table 7.1.

Table 7.1 Explanations and pronunciation of some Portuguese words used in this chapter

Portuguese	Pronunciation	Meaning
Alagados	Alagadooz	Marshy land
Barracos	Barracooz	Dwelling units of the favelas
Cortiços	Cortesooz	Slums or decaying over-peopled buildings
Favela	Favela	A slum-like town of low dwellings made out of any useful waste material
Favelados	Faveladooz	Inhabitants of the favelas
Tropeiros	Troparooz	Herdsmen of beasts of burden

A BRIEF HISTORY OF BRAZILIAN CITIES

Most of the major Brazilian cities of today originally developed to serve the export of primary products such as sugar in the sixteenth and seventeenth centuries, gold in the eighteenth century and coffee, cacao, tobacco, cotton and timber from the mid-nineteenth century to the mid-twentieth century.

The first sugar plantations established in Brazil were along the north-east coast. A flourishing triangular trade soon developed: importing slave labour from West Africa to work on the plantations which produced sugar to be exported to the markets of Europe. From the sixteenth century to the beginning of the nineteenth century Portuguese colonial cities involved in the sugar and gold trade developed along the Atlantic coast.

The whole purpose of these cities was to further Portugal's trading interests with other European countries. Even major trading and administrative centres, such as Salvador, Recife and Rio de Janeiro, were merely trading posts for importing and exporting products between Portugal and its South American colony.

As more immigrants settled along the coastline, the King of Portugal divided the Brazilian coastline and its hinterland as far west as the Tordesillas line between fourteen hereditary 'captains'. The Tordesillas line, which lies between 48° and 49° west, was agreed between the Spanish and Portuguese at Tordesillas in 1494 as dividing the New World between them. However, when King Philip of Spain took the throne of Portugal in 1580, the line was forgotten and the new Brazilians pushed their way westwards. When Portugal once again became independent, they refused to abandon the new lands and established Brazil's boundaries as enclosing about half the area of the South American continent.

Despite this expansion, the 'captains' wanted the sugar cane plantations to be self-sufficient and tied directly back to Portugal. This discouraged the growth of independent cities and internal trading in Brazil since the rural estates were more dependent on the cities of Europe than on those of their own country.

From the middle of the seventeenth century the Portuguese sugar market in Europe faced competition from the West Indies or Antilles (Central America), colonised by the Spanish, English, French and Dutch. Portugal reacted by establishing government-owned companies to control the production and export of agricultural goods. These companies created a demand for financial and other urban services and so the coastal Brazilian towns at last began to grow.

By the end of the seventeenth century, the search for gold and diamonds led to further immigration from Portugal and internal migration both inland and further south towards Minas Gerais. These movements of people in turn led to the building of roads, especially linking the gold mining area in what is now Minas Gerais state to Rio de Janeiro.

From this time on, there was more exploration and occupation of inland Brazil and its natural wealth. The development of cattle raising encouraged internal trading of consumer goods. The tropeiros opened trails and routes linking the south-east of Brazil (the main mining region of the colony) to the southern and north-eastern regions, where large farms were established to breed cattle, horses, donkeys and mules. By the eighteenth century, Minas Gerais state and some other inland areas had a number of cities.

By the end of the eighteenth century the Brazilian gold rush was declining. The great ore strata were almost exhausted by available methods of extraction.

Coffee, which had first reached Brazil in the eighteenth century, then developed rapidly as an export crop and remained the most important national product until the 1930s. Coffee plantations, which were founded along the Paraiba river valley to take advantage of the slaves before 1850, spread across neighbouring states in south-east Brazil. Throughout the nineteenth century, and into the twentieth century, other cities continued to develop, until the present pattern of cities emerged.

Rio de Janeiro and São Paulo already had a higher population density and greater financial resources than other states or regions and so gained most from the growth of the coffee industry. They established a transport network and this led to the development of industries such as textiles, soaps, beer, chemicals and metal foundries.

The balance between coffee exports and the import of industrialised goods was disrupted by the two world wars (1914–18 and 1939–45) and Brazil had to rely on its own production. This economic change led to the decline in the political power of the rural aristocracy and the rise of an industrial middle class.

Industrialisation was almost confined to the areas of Rio de Janeiro and São Paulo until the 1950s. However, by the 1970s, existing industries had spread to other regions, new industries had emerged and Brazil was trading in international markets. The need to distribute raw materials and consumer products led to an expanding transport system and closer links between Brazilian cities.

1   Identify the phases of urbanisation in your country. Research the main factors that contributed to the urban development in each phase.

BRAZILIAN URBAN DEVELOPMENT: PROBLEMS AND ISSUES

The growth of industry since the 1950s and the steadily growing demand for services and consumer goods have led to great growth in Brazil's cities. However, this growth has been accompanied by a decrease in rural population so that by the 1970s, the majority of Brazil's people lived in the cities.

2   *a* From Figure 7.2 identify the year in which the Brazilian population was half urban and half rural.
    b From the slope of the two lines on the graph, what conclusions can you draw about the reasons for the change from a rural to an urban society?

Figure 7.1 Major Brazilian cities and states

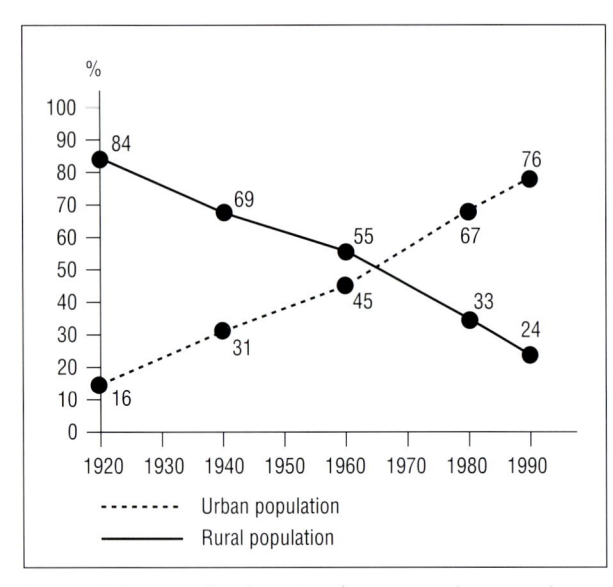

Figure 7.2 Brazil—changing from a rural to an urban society

Table 7.2 The changing population of Brazil, 1950–90

Year	Rural population ('000)	% rural population	Urban population ('000)	% Urban population	Total population ('000)
1950	33 162	64	18 782	36	51 994
1960	38 767	55	31 303	45	70 070
1970	41 054	44	52 085	56	93 139
1980	38 566	32	80 436	68	119 002
1990	35 669	24	114 699	76	150 368
1991	38 000	26	108 100	74	146 100

Source: Brazilian Institute of Geography and Statistics

> 3 Use the statistics in Table 7.2 to draw divided bar charts to show the total population of Brazil divided into urban and rural dwellers for each year from 1950 to 1991. Write sentences to explain what has happened to the total population of Brazil, the total number of rural dwellers and the total number of urban dwellers during this period.

Brazil's urban population rose from 36 to 74 per cent between 1950 and 1991. There were 4491 municipalities in Brazil in 1991 but almost a quarter of the whole population lived in only fourteen of those municipalities—just fourteen cities.

Table 7.3 The main urban centres in Brazil, 1991

City	State	Population
São Paulo	São Paulo	9 480 427
Rio de Janeiro	Rio de Janeiro	5 336 179
Belo Horizonte	Minas Gerais	2 048 861
Salvador	Bahia	2 056 013
Fortaleza	Cearó	1 758 334
Brasilia	Distrito Federal	1 596 274
Nova Iguaçu	Rio de Janeiro	1 286 337
Recife	Pernambuco	1 290 149
Curitiba	Paranà	1 290 142
Porto Alegre	Rio Grande do Sul	1 262 631
Belém	Pará	1 246 435
Goiãnia	Goiás	920 838
Campinas	São Paulo	846 084
Manaus	Amazonas	1 010 558

Source: Brazilian Institute of Geography and Statistics

> 4 Locate each of these cities on Figure 7.1. Discuss the distribution of the fourteen major cities of Brazil.
> 5 Discover the populations of each of the largest cities in your own country. What proportion of the population lives in these cities?

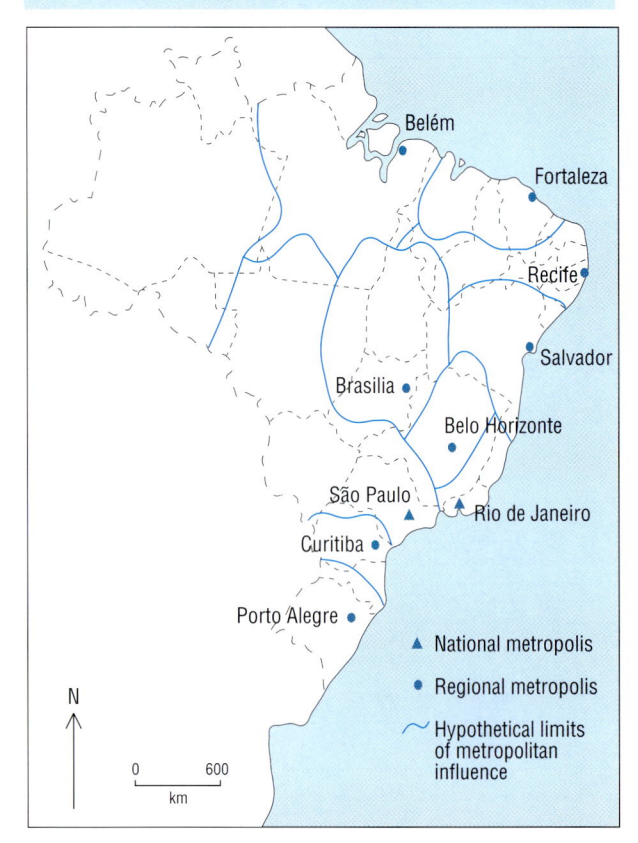

Figure 7.3 The areas of influence of the major cities of Brazil

With the exception of Brasilia, the national capital, the nine largest cities of Brazil have been designated as national metropolises by the Brazilian Institute of Geography and Statistics. The hypothetical areas of influence of these cities are shown in Figure 7.3. However, the areas of influence are constantly changing as the cities grow. The two largest Brazilian cities, São Paulo and Rio de Janeiro, are also international metropolises because they are worldwide centres of economic and cultural production and exchange.

6 What do you understand by the term 'hierarchy of settlements'? Discuss the ways in which the hierarchy of settlements in Brazil may be different from that in your own country. (Hint: Usually the capital city of a country is also the largest city.)

The continuing urbanisation process in Brazil is either through the development of new cities or through the growth of already established cities.

Table 7.4 Rural and urban populations in the five major regions of Brazil

Regions	1970		1990	
	Rural	Urban	Rural	Urban
North	54.9	45.1	45.2	54.8
North-east	58.0	42.0	42.7	54.8
South-east	27.2	72.8	10.0	90.0
South	55.4	44.6	21.2	78.8
Centre west	51.7	48.3	21.0	79.0
Brazil total	44.0	56.0	24.0	76.0

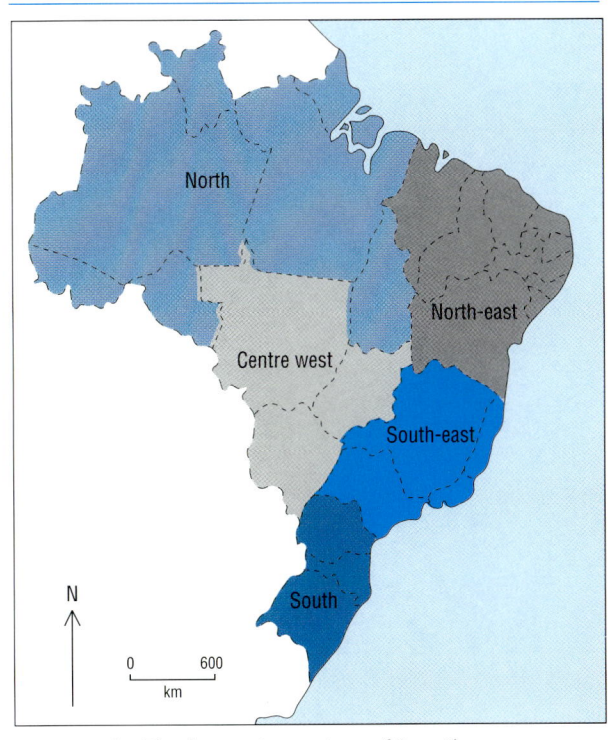

Figure 7.4 The five major regions of Brazil

7 Discuss the figures in Table 7.4 and explain in which regions further urban growth will take place through expansion of existing cities and in which regions new cities will probably emerge.
8 In your class, make a list of your perceptions of each of the major cities in Brazil. What image do you have of these cities and for what are they most famous?

PROBLEMS IN BRAZILIAN CITIES

The rapid growth of cities and industries in Brazil has been caused by many people leaving rural areas. This rapid growth has also caused many people to leave rural areas. Rio de Janeiro and São Paulo have received many people, both from the rural areas which surround them and from the north-east region.

Rural people have been pushed from the land and pulled towards the city. Factors which **push** people from rural areas include

- mechanical agriculture which has forced many labourers from farms
- many bosses are unwilling to obey laws designed to help rural workers and consequently won't pay minimum wages, holiday pay, and social taxes
- joining small and medium sized rural estates together, estates being taken over by other estates or by agricultural production companies
- small farms taken over to grow export crops
- deforestation and desertification in the north-east
- poor living conditions.

Factors which **pull** people towards the cities include
- displaced labourers seeking work
- people seeking better living conditions, including higher salaries, better medical assistance, better educational opportunities, facilities of modern life.

Brazilian cities such as Rio de Janeiro, Salvador, Fortaleza and Brasilia were not prepared for the population

Figure 7.5 Rubbish disposal is one of the basic services that the cities of Brazil can not provide

explosion. In the early 1970s, about 150 migrants per hour arrived in São Paulo and were directed towards the city's outskirts, where they did not find even the most basic public services.

In the early 1980s, only 10 per cent of Salvador's total population of 1.5 million people had access to sewerage. São Paulo, which then had 12.5 million inhabitants, could provide only 40 per cent of homes with sewerage and 55 per cent with tapped water. Even by the late 1980s, Ceilandia, one of the satellite-towns of Brasilia, the nation's capital, had no sewerage system at all.

Table 7.5 The provision of basic services and household goods for Brazil from 1940 to 1980

Services or goods	% households supplied				
	1940	1950	1960	1970	1980
Basic services					
Sewerage	—	—	27	22	39
Water supply	38	39	43	54	76
Electrical energy	47	60	72	75	88
Durable goods					
Television sets	—	—	9	40	79
Radio sets	16	n/a	61	72	73
Refrigerators	—	—	23	42	65
Cars	2	—	—	13	28

9 Discuss the information shown in Table 7.5 and prepare a brief report on the changes that have occurred in the provision of basic goods and services in Brazil in the period shown. What are likely to be the results of the pattern of service provision shown?

Sanitation is the most important service provided in any city. Non-treated wastes and open sewers, so common in poor areas of Brazilian cities and towns, are the main cause of several infectious and epidemic diseases. Contaminated water, largely consumed by poor families, causes dehydration—particularly in children—with a high death rate the result. This occurs mainly during summer.

10 *a* Look at Figure 7.6 and describe how the pattern of infant mortality has changed in Brazil over time.
    b Discuss possible reasons why the mortality rates in the cities have been less than those for Brazil as a whole, despite the sanitation problems of the cities.
11 Find out the rates for infant mortality for your country over the same period. In what ways have they changed? What reasons can you discover for these changes?

Despite a significant lessening in a twenty year span (1960–80), the child mortality rate in Brazilian capital cities is still very high. This is largely due to the poor quality of life.

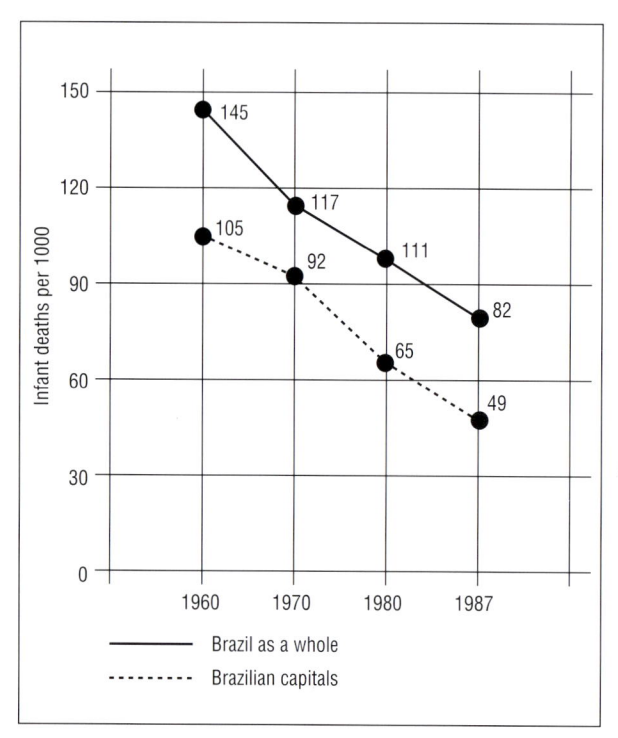

Figure 7.6 The child mortality rate in Brazil (deaths per 1000 live births)

Figure 7.7 The most recent arrivals in a Brazilian city are forced to seek space on the very outskirts

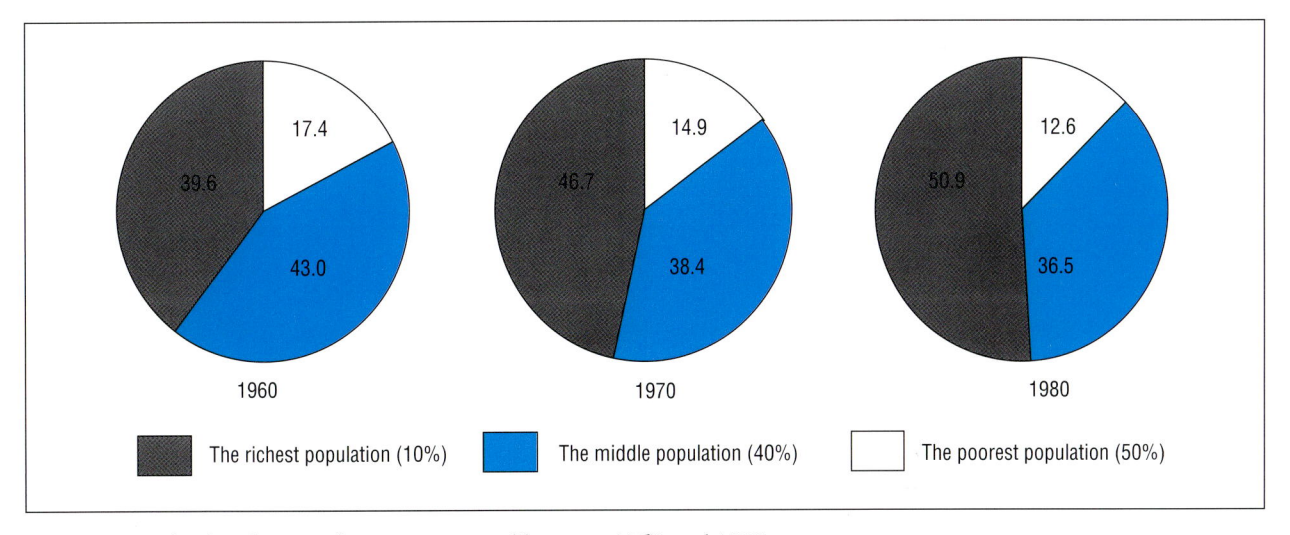

Figure 7.8 The distribution of income in Brazil between 1960 and 1980

POVERTY IN BRAZILIAN CITIES

Underdeveloped urban areas in Brazilian cities are generally located far away from the city centre, or other residential, administrative and industrial districts or areas. These underdeveloped areas are the only ones available to poor working people (see Figure 7.7), whereas better situated areas remain under the control of those with money and power.

In the city of São Paulo, about 45 per cent of urban land is empty space. Rio de Janeiro, Salvador, Porto Alegre, Belo Horizonte and Recife also have about 40 to 50 per cent of their central areas as vacant space. The result is a city plan which is an irregular pattern of empty and occupied areas.

People with low incomes who are forced to live on the very edge of the city are at a disadvantage in two ways. First, the municipality must pay more to provide services a long way from the centre, and second, the people have to pay more both in time and money to travel to work. By the 1980s, transport expenses in Rio de Janeiro and São Paulo had reached 10 to 15 per cent of a working family's monthly budget.

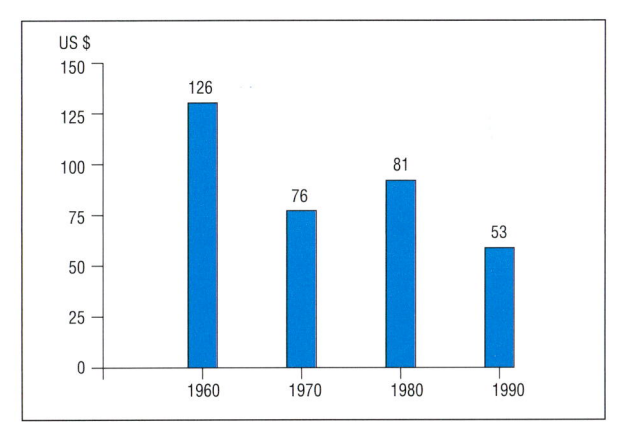

Figure 7.9 The value of the mean monthly wage in Brazil, 1960–90

Figure 7.8 shows how the incomes of Brazilians were redistributed during the 1960s and 1970s. Figure 7.9 shows how the value of this income fell between 1960 and 1990. The large numbers of rural people coming to the cities also compete for available work and this competition keeps wages low.

Table 7.6 The increase in the favelas and barracos of Rio de Janeiro and São Paulo

Rio de Janeiro	1950	1960	1967	1970	1982
Number of favelas	105	147	230	300	309
Total population of favelas	169 305	335 696	575 696	1 000 000	1 800 000
Number of barracos	44 000	69 680	162 741	185 000	n/a
São Paulo	**1971**	**1972–73**	**1974–75**	**1980**	**1983**
Number of favelas	163	542	916	763	1986
Total population of favelas	39 000	56 000	108 000	359 000	414 572
Number of barracos	8 552	14 504	23 948	79 286	91 419

12 Describe the change that occurred in the proportion of income owned by the richest 10 per cent of the population during this period. Where did this extra share of the wealth come from? Which group in society would have been most affected by the changes shown in Figures 7.8 and 7.9?

Such poverty reflects on the kind of houses those people can afford for themselves. Many people live either in the favelas—precarious dwellings made from any available materials, clustered on slopes, along roads or over marshy stretches—or in cortiços—overcrowded and decaying buildings in the city itself. It is practically impossible for these people, and even most of the middle-income urban families, to buy the simplest house or apartment even with the help of government-run savings and loan plans.

Table 7.7 The population of the city of São Paulo in 1990

	Population
Total population 1990	11 573 553
Population of cortiços	6 040 851
Population of favelas	1 030 400

For the reasons outlined above, the population of the favelas has increased greatly in recent years. Table 7.6 shows how the favelas and barracos—the shacks in which people live in favelas—of Rio de Janeiro and São Paulo increased in size. Figures are difficult to come by, so the dates for the two cities are not the same.

Figure 7.10 Conditions typical of the favelas of many Brazilian cities

13 *a* Draw graphs with the same horizontal scale to show the growth of the favelas, their total populations and number of dwelling units. Where was the growth of favelas most rapid—Rio de Janeiro or São Paulo?
 b Calculate the average number of people who lived in each of the barracos at the beginning and end of each group of figures.
14 Table 7.7 shows the situation in São Paulo in 1990. Calculate the percentage of the total population who are living in cortiços or favelas.

The living conditions of the poor in other cities are similar. By the 1970s, 50 per cent of the habitations of Recife were barracos. In Salvador about 100 000 poor people were pushed into 15 000 cheap houses built by the state government in the alagados, a muddy and pollution drenched area on the edge of the city. In 1990, 75 per cent of the 2.2 million inhabitants of the Federal District, municipality of Brasilia—the nation's capital—lived in the so called satellite-towns. These are eight suburbs within 12 to 45 kilometres from the central city, almost entirely lacking in basic urban installations and services.

The social and economic inequalities between the rich and the poor in Brazil have led to great discontent, particularly in the major industrial urban centres. Since the late 1970s there has been action of various kinds, including

- a series of protests and strikes for better salaries and living conditions
- invasion and occupancy of idle urban areas by the so called landless militants
- spontaneous riots with destruction of buses and railroad cars, because of poor public transport and ever increasing fares.

The worst aspect of large cities in Brazil today, however, is urban violence, which includes traffic misbehaviour, power abuse by the police, robbery, assaults and rapes, street gangs of youngsters, and recently, organised crime in connection with the drug trade. This violence reduces the quality of life in Brazilian cities but is caused by the low quality of life for many people.

15 To what extent do the social problems mentioned occur in the cities of your country? Discuss the reasons why they may occur.
16 What areas near you are known for their social problems? Why do you think that these problems exist in particular areas?

THE WAY FORWARD

Brazil's cities have grown very rapidly. Both São Paulo and Rio de Janeiro are among the ten largest cities in the world and by 2000 São Paulo is forecast to be second only to Mexico City in size.

Brazil now realises the mistakes it made in the 1960s and 1970s when the National Bank of Habitation financed a housing policy to move favela residents from central Rio de Janeiro and Brasilia into peripheral housing blocks far from places of work, schools and shops.

The Brazilian Constitution of 1988 acknowledges the need for environmental protection and urban development policies that are based on understanding the interactions between the social functions of a city. Plans for the future will reorganise the municipalities' boundaries to recognise the links between housing, transport, energy, sanitation and ecological concerns and basic public services.

This kind of planning needs to be done at local and regional, rather than at national level. The 1988 Brazilian Constitution gives more power and money than before to local areas. In 1960, local municipalities controlled the spending of only 8.6 per cent of all taxes. By 1987, this had risen to 18.3 per cent and by 1993, to 23.6 per cent. The constitution also gives more power to local municipalities to set up social organisations to plan their own areas and to decide how to spend this money.

The municipality of Curitiba, with 2.5 million people living in and around the city, is being particularly successful in improving its urban lifestyle. There is a mass transport system which takes 1.2 million passengers each day. Even though Curitiba has the highest density of cars of all state capitals, many car owners choose to rely entirely on public transport. In areas where garbage collection is difficult, people can take rubbish to central depots where they can exchange it for bus tickets, food or classroom items for students.

While there is still an urgent need to extend sewerage to the whole population, depollute the rivers and improve the conditions in its slums, Curitiba is planning to clean up 11 kilometres of rivers, lay 20 kilometres of sewerage mains and plant more than 100 000 trees in 1993 to celebrate the three hundredth anniversary of its foundation. Other schemes to improve the quality of life of its citizens include 'family stores' where basic foods are sold at 30 per cent discount and 'stork vouchers' which are given to expectant mothers to use at the city's dispensaries.

17 Discuss the advantages and disadvantages of planning decisions made by central governments rather than local councils.

18 What opportunities are there in your country for citizens to take part in urban planning?

19 Discuss how best the large cities of Brazil can improve the quality of life of their citizens. What could Brazil learn from the experiences of your country? What can your country learn from the experiences of Brazil?

Figure 7.11 Inner city Curitiba

CHAPTER 8

DEVELOPMENT IN BHUTAN: GOOD OR BAD?

● ● ● ● ● ● ● ● ●

Jagar Dorji

Until recently, the small Kingdom of Bhutan, in the foot hills of the Himalaya mountains, has remained isolated from the rest of the world. While other countries were undergoing development, Bhutan stood still and its people continued to live their traditional lifestyle. During the reign of the late King Jigme Dorji Wangchuk, the father of the present King, Bhutan began to develop its economy through a process of planned modernisation. This chapter suggests that because Bhutan started later, it has had the chance to learn from the mistakes of others.

The problems facing any country trying to develop its economy without damaging its environment are very great, but Bhutan is working towards solving them, even if it means slowing down the process of modernisation.

Bhutan is roughly rectangular in shape and has an area of 46 500 square kilometres with a population of about 1 400 000. Bhutan lies at the eastern end of the Himalayas. The land surface is mountainous with very little flat land other than that which occurs in the inner Himalayan valleys and in the foothills adjoining the vast plain countries of Assam and Bengal in India to the south. Bhutan is one of the most rugged countries in the world and altitudes can vary from 150 to 7500 metres in a distance of less than 100 kilometres.

Most of the people live in the settlements that occur in the broader river valleys and in the foothills, although other parts of the country are also occupied by subsistence farmers and herders scattered over the mountainsides. However, over 40 per cent of the total area of Bhutan is mountainous and of little use for agriculture. The difficult terrain has made transport and communication difficult both within the country and with the outside world.

> 1 *a* Use an atlas to calculate the distance from Thimphu, the capital of Bhutan, to the nearest coast.
> *b* Calculate the size of Bhutan in terms of the distance from north to south and east to west. Compare the size of this whole country with the size of your own country and the size of the local region in which you live.
> 2 Discuss the reasons why Bhutan may have imposed a life of isolation from the rest of the world on itself and its people. What may have been the advantages and disadvantages of such a policy?
> 3 Make lists of the ways in which the Bhutanese landscape both helps and hinders the people of Bhutan.

DEVELOPMENTS SINCE 1961

In 1961, a cautiously planned series of development programs were launched in Bhutan, to be reviewed and implemented on a five year cycle. The main objective of these development programs was to raise the incomes and improve the welfare of the people of Bhutan.

During the past thirty years there has been a steady change in the social and economic situation. Until 1961, the

DEVELOPMENT IN BHUTAN: GOOD OR BAD?

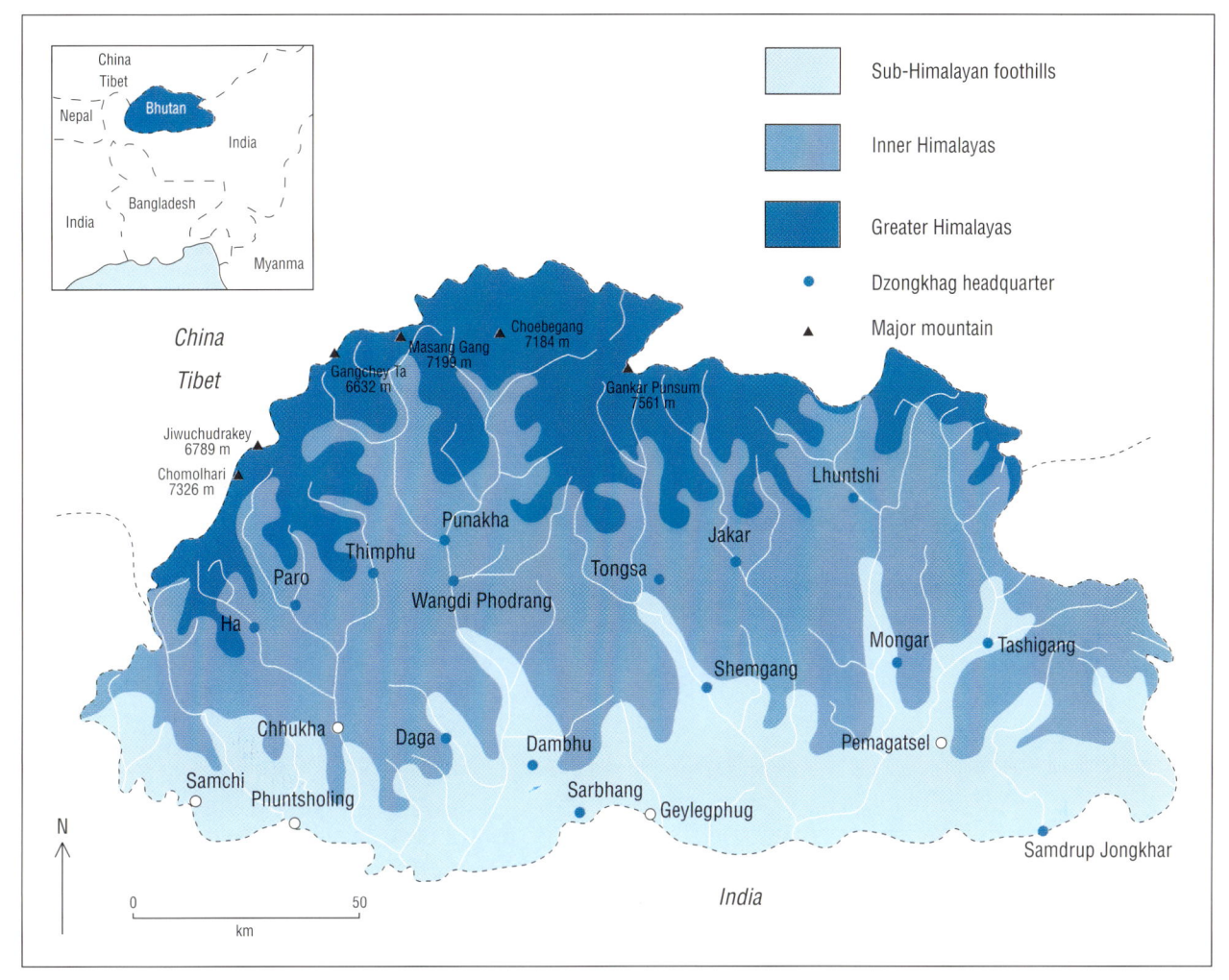

Figure 8.1 The relief of Bhutan

Figure 8.2 The scenery of northern Bhutan

Bhutanese people were mainly subsistence farmers who exchanged goods and services with one another using a system of barter. This system has now been transformed into a modern monetary system. The purchasing power of the common people has increased dramatically and, as a result, standards of living and the health of the people have improved greatly. Some of the achievements are described below.

Table 8.1 Comparison of basic services and infrastructure between 1961 and 1990

Type of activity	1960	1990
Motor roads	just started	2280 km
Motor cars	nil	7000
Local telephone connections	n/a	1990
Post office and wireless stations	5	145
Schools	59	240
Health care centres	16	143

Source: Central Statistical Office (CSO), 1990

The achievements

Changes in a country can be observed in different ways. The writer of this chapter asked an elder from a remote village how life had changed and was told that, in his youth, it used to be difficult to get enough to eat to have the energy to build a house. Now, most people have a good diet, proper houses, land to cultivate and access to health services so that they are healthier than ever before. Some idea of the changes that have taken place in Bhutan may be gained by examining the figures for the availability of electricity, the gross domestic product (the total value of all goods and services produced in a country) and the demographic trends (changes in births, deaths and population).

The availability of electricity in Bhutan in 1989 is shown in Table 8.2. In 1960, Bhutan did not have an electricity grid at all. Table 8.3 shows how the gross domestic product of Bhutan is expected to change in the years between 1980 and 1991. In the 1970s, the average income per head in Bhutan was about US$80 per year. Recent information suggests that the average Bhutanese now earns up to US$400.

Table 8.4 shows the changes that have occurred in the demographic characteristics of Bhutan in the twenty years from 1970 to 1990. The improvements shown in these figures may be due to many changes. Improved housing and food are obviously important, but there have been other improvements in people's lives. Bhutan has a very successful immunisation program which reaches the highest proportion of children in the whole of the South Asia region. In the next year or so, it is expected that the child immunisation program will be universal. Two-thirds of the population now has access to regular medical facilities. Clean drinking water supply and smoke free stoves are also widespread in the country. The latter was initiated by the National Women's Association of Bhutan (NWAB).

Table 8.2 Electricity consumption, 1989

	Number
Towns having access to electricity	20
Villages having access to electricity	171
Individual consumers in both	14 092
Per capita consumption (in units)	90

Source: CSO, 1990

Table 8.3 Gross domestic product (GDP), Bhutan†

Activity	1980	1986	1991*
Agriculture	25	56	79
Mining and manufacturing	5	11	43
Trade and transport	2	5	19
Finance	6	14	10
Services	5	14	19

†Figures in millions US$ at 1991 exchange rate
*Figures are projections only

Source: CSO, 1990

Table 8.4 Changes in demographic trends

	1970	1990
Average life expectancy at birth	45	49
Infant mortality per 1000	144	102
Maternal mortality per 1000	n/a	7
Crude birth rate per 1000	44	39
Crude death rate per 1000	23	1

Source: CSO, 1990

4 What proportion of the families in your country have access to electricity? Discuss the effects on the lifestyle of your family if you either had your electricity supply taken away, or suddenly had an electricity supply provided.

5 Table 8.1 lists a number of services that have been provided in recent years. Discuss the importance of these services in providing a good quality of life. What other service facilities could have been more important in improving the living conditions of the people of Bhutan?

6 If you have electricity in your house, calculate the average number of units you use. (Take the annual total and divide by the number of people who live in the house.) If it is more than the 90 units average per year for Bhutan, discuss the changes that you would have to make to reduce your consumption to that level.

7 Draw divided bar charts to show the contributions of the various economic activities to Bhutan's gross domestic product. Describe the changes that have occurred in the total GDP between 1980 and 1991, and the changes in the make up of those totals.

8 Suggest possible reasons for the increase in the importance of mining and manufacturing in the Bhutanese economy.

9 Discuss the changes that have occurred in the demographic characteristics of Bhutan between 1970 and 1990.

10 Discuss the reasons that may have made it possible for Bhutan to introduce such a successful immunisation program.

11 Compare the demographic statistics for Bhutan with those of your own country. How does your country compare with Bhutan? How have the statistics for your country changed in the last twenty years?

> 12 Use the information provided in the first part of this chapter to write a statement on how Bhutan has changed since economic development was initiated in 1961.

The effects of economic development have certainly changed the lives of the majority of the Bhutanese people. However, such changes in the socio-economic structure of a country are also bound to affect the original landscape.

VISUALISING THE IMPACT OF DEVELOPMENT

In almost all developing countries three factors—population growth, poverty and environmental degradation—interact as a vicious circle which impedes forward planning.

Many of these countries, particularly in the sub-Saharan region of Africa, are witnessing a decline in their economies as well as ecological degradation. Having started late, Bhutan has the advantage of observing closely the problems of modernisation that are confronting these countries at present and has noted with alarm some of the effects. Changes that can have major effects on the natural environment include those in the areas of

- population
- forest cover
- livestock
- mining
- water resources
- roads
- urbanisation and pollution
- tourism and migration
- economic development
- industry.

Population

With an estimated population of some 1 400 000 people, Bhutan has a very small average population density of about 28 per square kilometre. However, since only about 16 per cent of the total land area can be cultivated, the density can be recalculated at about 175 per square kilometre of cultivable land. This may seem, to a non-Bhutanese, a very favourable situation, but the population is at present growing at an annual rate of more than 2 per cent. If this rate of increase continues, the population of Bhutan will double in less than thirty-six years.

All the arable land is already under cultivation and there is no sign of a dramatic increase in yield in agricultural production, which is already very low. The figures for Bhutan's GDP (Table 8.3) show how important agriculture is for the economy as a whole. However, they do not show that nearly 90 per cent of the Bhutanese people rely on farming for their livelihood. Most of the farmland is owned by the women, who have very high status in Bhutanese society.

A typical family in the valleys of western and central Bhutan will earn its living from about 1 hectare of private land, common grazing land, forest products (for timber, fuelwood and leaves), the labour of the family, animals and their products, grain, straw, vegetables and fruit. Almost all the food is used for the family and the straw, bran and manure is returned to the soil to make the ecosystem sustainable. Some of the grain, such as rice or wheat, may be sold or exchanged for tea, salt, blankets and kerosene.

With such an economy, the current rate of population growth can obviously not be sustained. New off-farm jobs in trade, industry and service sectors are emerging, but very slowly, and not at a rate which will keep pace with population growth.

At present Bhutan has very few landless farmers and unemployed people. The government provides free education and medical services and drinking water facilities. However, if the present rate of growth is allowed, it will very soon be difficult to maintain a healthy environment and a balance between arable land and the population which depends on it.

Forest cover

The forests provide the basic natural resources for Bhutan. Farmers depend on a relatively free access to the forests and their products. Fertility of the terraced farmland is maintained through a constant input of biomass from the forest. Most of the fodder for domestic animals comes from forests. More than 90 per cent of the Bhutanese depend on forest for their fuelwood. The non-wood products, such as bamboo, medicinal plants and edible plants, are also collected from the forests.

Table 8.5 Landuse distribution, 1991

Landuse type	%
Forests	57
Water, snow, pastures	26
Agriculture and settlements	16
Uninterpreted	1

Source: Department of Forestry, 1991

A report by the Bhutan Department of Forestry in 1974 showed that 64 per cent of the land in Bhutan was covered in forest. A later study showed that between 1978 and 1988, the annual loss of forest cover was around 0.33 per cent. This is insignificant when compared with the amount of forest cover lost in other parts of the Himalayan region, but it is still cause for concern. The growing number of sawmills, the rapid growth of human population and an equally rapid increase in livestock population, indicate that forest cover in Bhutan will be reduced greatly in the future.

Livestock

According to an old Bhutanese saying, 'a farmer without cattle is a poor farmer'. As in many countries in Africa and India, one of the ways by which a family's wealth is measured in Bhutan is by the number of cattle it owns. Almost all rural households own some cattle. They are used as draught animals, for dairy products such as cheese and butter, and their manure is mixed with leaves to fertilise the soil.

Due to the limited amount of pasture land, most of these animals graze in the forests. This is perhaps the greatest threat to this precious resource base. Cattle and sheep not only prevent natural regeneration of plants by trampling and eating the new shoots, but also cause erosion on the slopes by the impact of their hooves. Due to the geologically unsettled topsoils in the Himalayas, the large number of cattle adds considerably to the problems of soil erosion and landslip and this increases the destruction of the forests.

The government of Bhutan is faced with two problems which contradict one another. The cattle are destructive to the forests and soils but they are also an economic and social investment for the people. Most Bhutanese are Buddhists and the Buddhist religion forbids direct butchering of livestock. There seems little chance of reducing the number of livestock in the near future.

> 13 In what ways is 'wealth' recognised in your country? What are the effects on the environment of your country of seeking greater wealth?

Mining

Bhutan has large deposits of limestone, dolomite, graphite, gypsum and marble. These can be exploited and mined on a large scale for processing into manufactured goods, such as cement at home, or can be exported as run-of-the-mine products to neighbouring countries to be processed there.

While the development of mining industries can provide off-farm employment opportunities, it is also bound to upset the fragile ecosystem of the Himalayas by damaging the forest cover and displacing the other living beings from their natural home. A few small scale limestone and dolomite mines in the foothills, such as the one in Figure 8.4, have given enough evidence that mines must be properly and carefully planned. Overlooking these important steps would involve heavy environmental costs later.

Figure 8.3a   A herd of yak, typical upland cattle

Figure 8.3b   Typical lowland cattle in Bhutan

Table 8.6   Livestock population, Bhutan in 1989 and projection to 2000

Livestock type	1989	2000
Cattle	350 315	511 500
Yak	37 639	53 725
Sheep	48 044	80 000

Source: Planning Commission, 1991

Figure 8.4   Labourers working in a gypsum mine

DEVELOPMENT IN BHUTAN: GOOD OR BAD?

14 Discuss the advantages and disadvantages to Bhutan and its people of developing manufacturing industry based on the mineral deposits compared with exporting the minerals in their raw state.
15 From an examination of Figure 8.4, suggest ways in which these mines may cause environmental problems.

Water resources

Bhutan has rich water resources in the form of ground water, springs, lakes and the monsoon rains. The large forest cover has helped maintain the ground water in the mountains and this water reappears at lower altitudes as sources of rivers and streams. A recent survey by the Department of Power showed that Bhutan could generate up to 20 000 mega watts of electricity from its water resources.

However, even this resource is at risk from development. The freshness of the water for drinking is threatened by pollution from towns and larger settlements while hydro-electricity generation is possible only if the flow of water in the rivers is constant and their silt loads minimum. Deforestation and bad agricultural practices will disturb the constant flow of water, increase silt loads and upset the plans for harnessing sufficient commercial energy from water.

Figure 8.5 Fast flowing streams provide a potential source of power

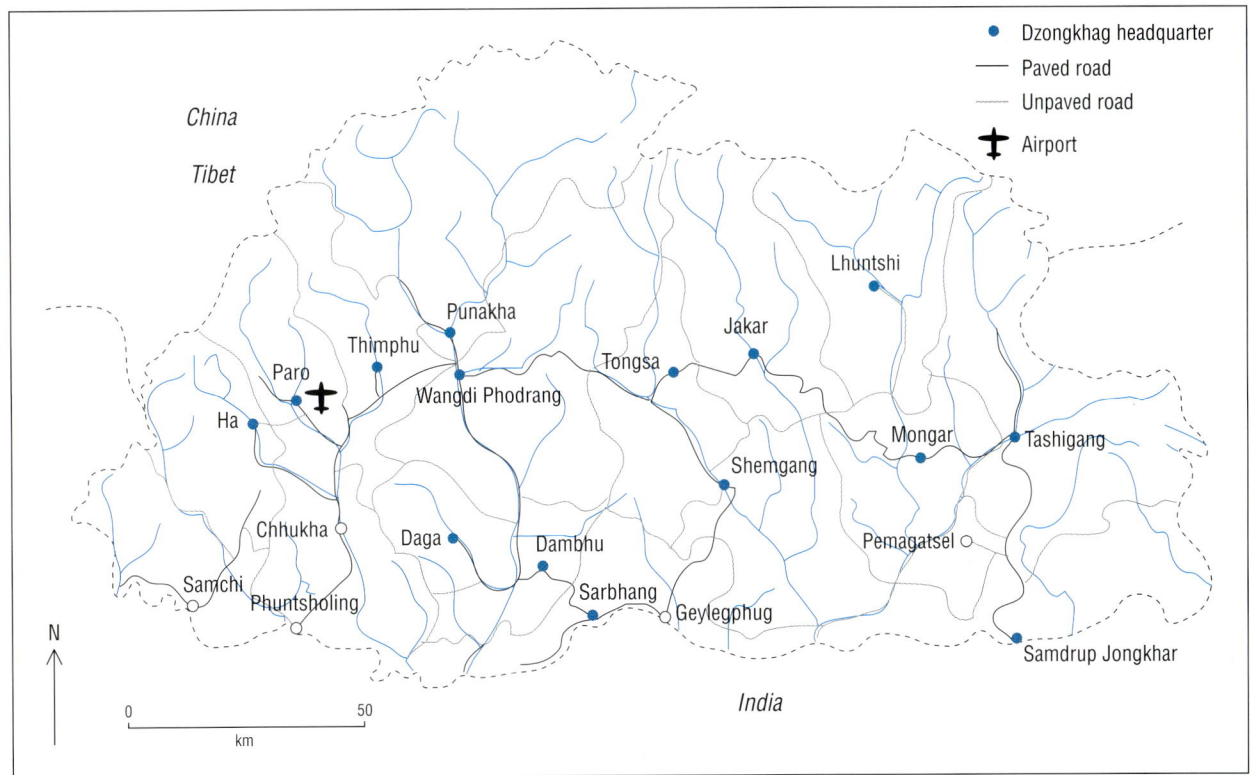

Figure 8.6 The network of rivers and roads in Bhutan

Roads

The rapid development of a system of roads has helped open up rural areas of Bhutan for modernisation. However, these same roads have also brought problems. The process of building them across the steep mountain slopes has resulted in many large landslides, particularly during the monsoon season, while the vibrations of vehicles and the occasional earthquakes may also cause landslides that block or destroy the roads, especially in summer.

Figure 8.7a   A typical road in the central valley area of Bhutan

Figure 8.7b   Landslides can easily block roads like these

Urbanisation and pollution

Urbanisation is a new concept in Bhutan. The problems of pollution in Bhutan at present are relatively minor as the population is small, industries are few and urbanisation is at an early stage. But there are signs of future problems already appearing on the landscape. Non-biodegradable wastes such as plastics, cans and glass are to be found along tracks near urban areas.

For the majority of the Bhutanese population, these wastes are new, and people tend to dispose of them in just the same way as they disposed of biodegradable wastes in the past.

Tourism and migration

By ending its centuries-old isolation, Bhutan has opened its doors to the people of other lands and their cultures. Tourists were first allowed into the country in the early 1970s. Later, more people came as expatriate residents, teachers, advisers and labourers. They brought with them habits, styles of dress, religion and ways of thinking, some of which are universal and some unique to their own country of origin, not necessarily fitting in the host society. In addition, the media, such as cinemas, videos, television, magazines and journals, have played a major role in bringing new ideas to Bhutan.

Bhutanese culture has been affected by all these features in the past thirty years. One particular effect may be seen in the ways in which people dress. For many Bhutanese, alien dress is more glamorous than the local style. In former years, some of the elder Bhutanese thought that some kind of cultural erosion had started, but now the effects do not seem so alarming.

The job opportunities that have been created by development, the healthy and unspoiled environment, the variety of climatic conditions and the chance to carve new agricultural land from the forests have attracted people from neighbouring countries, especially Nepal. The high growth rate of Bhutan's population is partly due to illegal immigrants.

> 16 Discuss the influences of other cultures on your own traditional culture. Do you feel that these changes are a form of cultural erosion? Are older people in your culture happy with the changes that are accepted by people of your generation? Do you think that the changes are for the better or the worse?
> 17 Have you migrated or ever considered migrating to another country? Discuss the factors that would influence you in your decisions
>   *a* to leave your own country
>   *b* to choose another country in which to live.

Figure 8.8   Traditional weaving in Bhutan

Table 8.7 Bhutan's balance of payments, 1981–89†

	1981	1982	1983	1984	1985	1986	1987	1988	1989
Current account balance	−16	−23	−28	−35	−35	−43	−43	−25	−39
Aid grants and loans	17	23	29	32	32	49	51	42	43
Other loans	0.4	2	0.8	6	6	0.3	0.3	3	11
Overall balance	1.4	2.0	1.8	3.0	3.0	6.3	8.3	20	15

†Figures in millions US$ at 1991 exchange rate

Source: CSO, 1985

Economy

Bhutan is a poor country and like most developing countries its economy is based on agriculture. More than 80 per cent of its people are engaged in traditional forms of farming and livestock raising. Yet it has successfully avoided what is called the 'foreign debt trap' into which many countries have fallen.

However, Bhutan does face a similar problem: dependence on donors and aid from other countries for foreign exchange. As Bhutan has developed its economy and imported more and more goods, it has not been able to export enough of its traditional products to earn hard currency to pay for the imports. Although Bhutan has been able to avoid foreign debts and achieve 7.5 per cent growth during 1980–90, in 1988–89, Bhutan had a 10 per cent deficit in its GDP. This means that its growth is mainly being paid for by other countries, especially India.

Industry

The Bhutan government has worked hard to establish industries that can improve Bhutan's ability to earn money. By 1989, seven new types of industry had been established in Bhutan and most are now privately owned. Figure 8.8 shows the traditional weaving that is generally carried out by women. Clothes manufactured in a factory may be cheaper but undermine small industries such as these.

While these industries may earn Bhutan money from exports, they also cause problems. The cement and wood processing plants are already damaging their surroundings through dust pollution, overuse of forest resources and landslides, and some of this damage may be irreversible.

> 18 For each of the types of industry that have been introduced into Bhutan, discuss the ways in which it may cause damage to the environment. For each problem, suggest ways in which Bhutan may be able to use its resources wisely and avoid such problems.
>
> 19 In your opinion, which is more important for a country, to have many people employed in simple industries or to achieve low costs by employing fewer people in highly mechanised factories? What are the factors that influence your opinion in this matter?

WHAT DOES DEVELOPMENT MEAN FOR BHUTAN?

The purpose of development for Bhutan is to give the greatest possible happiness for its people. While the changes have brought increased income and welfare to the Bhutanese, many people in the government have become very concerned about future generations. The very process of development that gave Bhutan access to information about other nations revealed the problems that were being faced by other developing nations.

The changes in income, consumption patterns, economic situation and lifestyle that have come with development have created an immense appetite for material goods in the Bhutanese people. This has led to

- more intensive forest use than ever before
- an increase in the number of livestock and in the area used for farming
- the replacement of green fields with towns and cities.

Many developing countries have encouraged tourism as a way of earning foreign currency. Bhutan made the decision to restrict tourists. So far, the number of tourists allowed into Bhutan has never exceeded 3000 in any year.

Dependence has become Bhutan's biggest problem. In its attempts to improve the Bhutanese economy, the government has been faced with many difficulties. The mountainous terrain and the long distances from the sea make transport of goods difficult. The relatively small amount of land suitable for agriculture limits the potential for increases.

Table 8.8 Types of manufacturing industry, 1989

Types of industry	Number of factories
Mining	13
General manufacturing	62
Food processing	10
Textiles and clothing	110
Wood and paper based	28
Chemical production	29
Mineral based	40

Source: Department of Education, 1992

Figure 8.9a   Thimphu in 1966

Figure 8.9b   Thimphu 1986

The scattered rural settlements, often with long distances between them, make it difficult to provide health, education and other services to the people. The main aim of the government is self reliance for Bhutan, but it is a difficult aim to achieve without increasing environmental degradation.

> 20 The Bhutanese have developed an increased appetite for goods. Can you imagine a time when you have enough of the material goods of the world? Do you think that human beings are insatiable?
> 21 In what ways does your country earn its foreign currency to pay for its imports? What are the main problems facing your country in increasing these earnings?
> 22 Do you agree that the aim of governments should be to encourage the greatest possible happiness for its people?

WHAT IS BEING DONE?

In the last couple of years the government has adopted a policy by which attempts are being made to ensure that development is sustainable and will remain so in the future. This means putting a limitation on the exploitation of natural resources and delaying the pace of development. It is now working on a process whereby developmental programs will continue but future sustainability is ensured. This policy was formulated in 1990 following a workshop funded jointly by the governments of Bhutan and Denmark and the United Nations Development Program.

> 23 Discuss the extent to which Bhutan has maintained a balance between development and environmental destruction so far. Do you agree that development should be slowed down in order to limit the risks of environmental damage?

The following are some of the important steps taken so far.

Population planning

The government has proposed a bill on population policy to the National Assembly which, if passed, will help reduce the fertility rate from the present 140 per thousand and growth rate from 2.3 per cent. There are incentives for couples who will limit their family size. These incentives are

- free schooling for two children per mother—fees will be charged for the third child and will be raised for every successive child
- education and employment opportunities will be increased for women—adult literacy campaigns will be targeted towards women especially
- couples who have limited their children to two will be given priority when being considered for low interest or interest free loans
- couples who limit their family size will be assured of old age pensions if the children die before them.

(*Source:* Planning Commission, 1991)

> 24 Discuss the proposed incentives to encourage couples to have smaller families. Do you agree that such incentives will encourage people to have fewer children? What other factors might influence a couple's decision about how many children to have?

Sustainable use of renewable natural resources

Over the years, farmers in Bhutan have adopted different methods of survival by practising sustainable resource use such as shifting cultivation and migratory cattle herding. This approach works well when there are relatively few people and livestock. However, recent increases in both population and livestock numbers now threaten this balance. The government, in its seventh cycle of planned programs, has decided to integrate a development approach which is to be known as Renewable Natural Resources Development (RNRD). This means the development of crops, livestock and forestry is included within watershed management activities. The aim is to ensure that farmlands, forests and other elements of the natural environment mutually support one another to ensure the sustainability of all. Table 8.9 shows how these principles may be used to solve some of the problems currently being faced.

Already, many of the programs are underway. Within the last eight years or so, for example, some 11 936 hectares of degraded forest have been replanted through the social forestry activities annually.

Maintaining bio-diversity

Bhutan has some of the greatest bio-diversity in the world for a country of its size. Wildlife varies from almost tropical to extreme cold creatures. Strict restrictions on hunting, together with the general Buddhist principle of compassion for all living creatures, have helped preserve the wildlife which existed in the country. Some 20 per cent of the total surface area is protected as wildlife parks. An Environmental Trust Fund of US$20 million has been established recently with the help of the World Bank and the World Wide Fund for Nature.

Master plans

A long term plan on forestry is being prepared. It is to be effective from 1992, with conservation of the forest environment as its guiding principle. A similar plan for hydro-power is underway to ensure its use in a most ecologically suitable way.

National Environmental Committee

A government committee on the environment has been established, under the leadership of the Planning Commission. This committee is supported by the National Environmental Secretariat (NES). One of the most important function of the NES is to assess the environmental impact of

Figure 8.10 Students work to plant trees to replace those that have been cut down

Table 8.9 Some current problems and possible solutions

Problems	Alternative plans
Agriculture	
Low productivity of crops	Set up agro-ecological zone of farmers
Inadequate technological support	Improve distribution of high yielding seeds
Poor water management	Ensure access to credits
	Reform community organisations in management of irrigation and other inputs
Animal husbandry	
Imbalance between feed resources and livestock	Encourage cross breeding
Poor breed and low production	Feed and fodder development program
Traditional values encouraging keeping of large herds	Urea paddy straw treatment
Inadequate coverage of animal health facilities	Feed conservation
	Improve traditional methods of ploughing to reduce requirements of bullocks
	Disease control programs
	Restriction of forest grazing
	Progressive tax on all grazing livestock to discourage maintaining large herds
Forestry	
Pressure to transform forest land to other uses	Encourage farmers to grow trees for fodder, fuel and timber for local needs within the farm or its vicinity
Increased demand for fodder, timber, fuelwood	Provide information and education services through which people are helped to understand the value of forest resource management
Lack of community participation in management of forest cover	Maintain 60 per cent of the total area as forest cover
Lack of sufficient trained workers to manage extensive forest cover	Social forestry as an annual feature

any project proposed and the future of the project will depend on the results of the assessment.

> 25 Find out how the environmental impact of new projects is assessed in your country. Is sustainability an important factor in reaching these decisions?

Formal education

At present only between 20 and 40 per cent of the Bhutanese people can read and write. Bhutan hopes that by teaching children in schools, the children will help their parents to understand the importance of the sustainable use of natural resources. To help this process, the whole school curriculum has been changed in the past two years.

The focus of school subjects like science, social studies and language has been changed from the traditional style of fact learning to a concentration on such issues and values as population growth, environmental conservation, resource management, small family norms and the important role of the forests. Primary school children learn to be aware and to love their environment and how to take care of it. Tree planting is part of a social forestry program and takes place each year.

> 26 To what extent does the school curriculum of your country focus on the future health and happiness of people?

Non-government organisations

There are at present only two non-government organisations based entirely in Bhutan. These are the Royal Society for the Protection of Nature (RSPN), and the National Women's Association of Bhutan (NWAB). There are also international organisations such as the World Wide Fund for Nature who assist in special projects.

Voluntary organisations such as RSPN and NWAB can do a great deal to look after people and to change people's attitudes about matters of importance. For example, the RSPN is involved with the protection of rare animals and birds such as the rare black neck crane. It organises nature clubs, summer camps and awareness courses for school children. The NWAB is a very powerful agency, since women have an important role in the family. The NWAB has introduced new kinds of cooking stoves for family use and is at present involved in developing literacy skills for adults and children who drop out of school.

> 27 What non-government organisations are there in your country which are working towards development and environmental sustainability? Do you contribute to them in any way? Find out how you can become involved in the work of one that interests you.

THE FUTURE

The Bhutanese philosophy believes that: 'We always have to give something in order to gain something. But we are willing to give anything if the gain makes us happy. Progress in development activities will be more meaningful and its results will be enjoyed by everyone in the society if the natural resource base is renewed and sustained. Every parent has responsibilities towards their children and one of these responsibilities is to leave enough bread for them and for their descendants. Without a sustainable resource base, future development will be hampered.'

Saving the environment and the natural resource base has to be a joint effort—with all countries participating. In terms of geographical area, Bhutan is just a very tiny part of the world and its efforts, however successful, can mean very little if the richer and bigger countries do not make some efforts, too.

> 28 Discuss the problems that face Bhutan and decide how many of them face your own country. How many of the solutions that Bhutan is attempting might work in your country?
> 29 Of all the actions that the Bhutanese government has taken to achieve sustainable development, which do you think are the most important? Explain your reasons for your decision.
> 30 Review the chapter and make a list of all the good news for Bhutan's future.

CHAPTER 9

SAVING AUSTRALIA'S SOILS

Marilyn Wiber

We all depend on the land for our survival, but for hundreds of years people throughout the world have abused the land on which they depend. Many people think of the land as a resource that belongs to them, to be used in any way they wish. However, this attitude often leads to the abuse that eventually destroys the land. If people change their attitude to think of the land as a resource to which they belong, they may begin to use it with the respect it deserves.

Across the whole world, farmers are trying to feed 86 million more people each year. In recent years, world grain production per capita has markedly declined as droughts have cut harvests. Croplands have shrunk by 7 per cent in China since 1978 due to industrial development and by 13 per cent in the former Soviet Union through land mismanagement. Twenty-four billion tonnes of topsoil is being lost each year, chiefly from over tilling. In parts of Australia, 7 tonnes of soil is lost for every tonne of wheat that is harvested.

Managers of land in Australia must understand the concept of the total ecosystem. They must appreciate the problems affecting the world today—unchecked pollution, land mismanagement and population growth. They must be aware that without better land management there could be a global food shortage and millions may starve.

> 1 What is the state of the soil in your country? Does it vary from place to place? Make a list of the reasons why the soil may not be as productive as it used to be. (Hint: It may be because of soil erosion, the expansion of towns and roads, or the poisoning of the soil.)
>
> 2 Find out what is being done at present to overcome these problems.

SOIL PROBLEMS IN AUSTRALIA

Some environmentalists consider that Australia is a 'ravaged land where much pastoral land is in a state close to abandonment'.

These are harsh words. There are areas of degraded pasture with gaunt, skeleton trees, expanses of salt affected land, areas with deep gully erosion and regions affected by devastating floods and loss of topsoil. In fact, half of Australia's useable land is now degraded, some parts losing up to 100 tonnes of soil per hectare a year because of cropping. It has been shown by seabed sediment tests that soil blown from Australia stretches far out into the Pacific and Indian Oceans, up to a metre thick. Salinity is a major problem, especially in Victoria, and this soil problem costs A$55 million a year in lost agriculture. Land degradation problems affecting Australia are so severe that in 1990, the federal government began a A$32 million-a-year land care program.

The Aborigines, the original inhabitants of the continent, had lived in harmony with the environment for at least 40 000 years before the British settled Sydney in 1788. They hunted and gathered food and fire was used to hunt animals and stimulate plant growth. Devastating fires that got out of control could not be extinguished and early European settlers reported that when the fires were followed by heavy rainfall, the land was often badly eroded.

The first British settlers were forced to exploit the land in order to survive and to create a self-sustaining colony. The first settlers experienced an environment with an erratic climate, low rainfall, droughts, low fertility and fragile soils. Soil erosion has resulted from droughts, heavy rainfall and bushfires throughout Australia's development, but it became increasingly severe as the demand for land increased and the use of the land became more intense. Through the need to become a self sufficient agricultural nation Australia's land became damaged and degraded.

ACTIVITIES THAT DAMAGED THE LAND

Clearing and hoofed animals

For two centuries, Australian farmers have seen trees as competition for the water, nutrients and space they needed for pasture and crops. As a result, large areas of trees have been cleared for cultivation. No consideration was given to the fragility of the land being cleared as farming and grazing were considered vital to the needs of the people. The land was then subjected to grazing pressures of sheep and cattle. These animals ate the vegetation and damaged the soil with their hooves by compressing it so that water could not soak in, and breaking up the surface so that the wind could erode it. The removal of the trees and introduction of hard hoofed animals from Europe exposed the soil to both wind and water erosion.

Gold mining

Large numbers of people mining and fossicking for gold placed much stress on the land. Mining methods, such as sluicing the crushed ore to extract the gold, caused soil erosion, while the chemicals used, such as cyanide, also poisoned the land for future generations. After the mining had ended, many miners turned to farming, about which they had little knowledge, and poor land management often resulted in soil erosion.

Early settlement schemes

After 1861 land settlement schemes were established. These caused very bad management practices and landowners often demanded more from the land than it was capable of yielding. In the Murray Valley, for example, the land was irrigated without making any provision for drainage. This resulted in increased salinity. The settlement schemes also encouraged more people to move on to the land.

Rabbits

The introduction of rabbits led to some of the worst devastation of the land in Australia. In 1859, an Englishman in Geelong introduced twenty-four wild rabbits for hunting. These rabbits spread quickly and devastated the vegetation and the land. So much soil erosion occurred that, in 1871, the first Rabbit Act, to outlaw rabbits, was passed in Tasmania.

Export pressures

As the population of Europe grew, food and fibre from the 'New World', including Australia, became more important. In the twenty years from 1830 to 1850, Australia's wool exports grew from 894 200 kilograms to 18 830 000 kilograms. The increase in sheep led to increased damage to the fragile lands. From 1890 to 1920 there was great agricultural expansion—the area under wheat expanded from 2.23 million hectares to 6.07 million hectares. A severe drought from 1895 to 1903 was broken by flood rains which caused massive erosion. Overgrazing in the drought years and a plague of rabbits devastated much land in the arid and semi-arid areas.

Irrigation

Irrigation schemes had occurred because drought dominated the 1860s and 1870s. Early scientists knew about the salinity of the groundwater of much of Australia but no one thought that this had anything to do with the surface vegetation. Salting was not recognised as a serious problem in Australia until the 1970s—the increase in irrigation has continued to make this a problem in Victoria. Tree planting programs designed to lower the watertable and allow the salt to be washed out of the soil only began after 1983.

Other mining

In 1841, lead ore (galena) was discovered and later, copper, zinc, tin, silver, iron, uranium and bauxite were all mined. These other types of mining did not cause population pressures on the land as gold had. However, the act of mining did lead to land degradation. In 1853 copper was discovered in Queenstown. For twenty years the area was cleared for building material and for fuel. Smelter fumes denuded large areas. The destruction of vegetation, together with a heavy annual rainfall, caused massive soil erosion.

Urbanisation

Australia is the most urbanised country in the world. Today the capital cities of the eight states and territories contain 80 per cent of Australia's population. There were many problems associated with building roads and railways, areas needed for the supply of water, gas and electricity, and laying telephone cables. These developments, together with building water storage dams, electricity generation plants and industrial sites, placed great demands on the land.

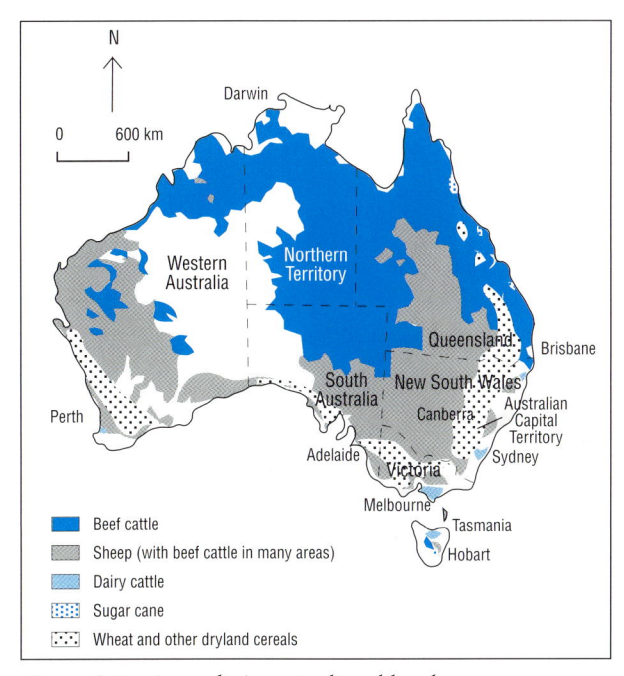

Figure 9.1 Australia's agricultural landuse

LAND DEGRADATION PROBLEMS IN AUSTRALIA TODAY

Land degradation is the decline in the quality of the land resource commonly caused through improper use. To prevent erosion, vegetation must be maintained on the land surface in the form of plants and organic matter. Removal of this vegetation cover leaves the soil vulnerable to erosion by water and wind.

The intensity of the landuse has a particular effect on the type of degradation. Farming, forestry, mining, recreation, urban and industrial developments all contribute to land degradation.

Australia's land can be easily degraded. In many parts of the world the topsoil is several metres thick. In Australia the average depth of the topsoil is only 50 millimetres, with 90 per cent of the soil too poor or too dry to support any agriculture other than grazing, and much of the land too salty to farm.

Figure 9.2 Contour ploughing on the Darling Downs of Queensland

3 Make a list of the ways in which wind and water have affected the land in Australia. Describe the processes which have led to major land management problems.
4 To what extent do you think that farmers have been to blame for land degradation in Australia? Justify your answer.
5 What changes to the types of vegetation cover have taken place in your region over the past two hundred years? Discover the reasons for any changes that have taken place.

THE BATTLE AGAINST SOIL DEGRADATION

In some parts of Australia, where farms have been established on sloping land and natural vegetation has been cleared, especially in Queensland with its high intensity summer storms, there is a major soil erosion problem. The early settlers with their European farming methods did not realise that clearing the natural vegetation and ploughing the soil into a fine seedbed, or letting stock overgraze the land, allowed the soil to be washed away when rain fell.

Falling raindrops reach the ground at high speed. Vegetation usually absorbs this raindrop energy but when the land is bare, the energy of the raindrops shatters soil particles into tiny fragments and splashes them in all directions. On sloping land up to three-quarters of these fragments fall back to the surface on the downhill side and the soil is slowly moved down the slope. These fragments also block the natural air spaces between the soil particles and seal the soil surface. The amount of water that soaks into the soil is reduced and water builds up on the surface and starts to run off.

This effect can be countered by ensuring that the land is always under some kind of vegetation cover. It is important to control the number of animals on the land so that they do not eat all the grass and break up the soil with their hooves. Much agricultural land is now farmed by methods that avoid over tilling. A number of crops may be planted together so that harvesting one does not leave the ground bare.

Once trees and other vegetation are removed, the wind can carry away the light fertile topsoil while the heavier particles are blown along the ground where they break up the larger soil particles and expose them to further erosion. When this soil erosion continues, it leads to widespread deserts—areas that are difficult to restore.

Water also attacks cleared land and leads to major soil loss, silting of rivers and flooding. Normally, during heavy rain, tree canopies, undergrowth and litter reduce the effects of raindrops and help the absorption of water into the soil. Surface litter slows the runoff and helps to prevent erosion. Water runoff produces sheet and rill, gully and tunnel erosion.

Another problem that occurs when trees are removed

from the upper slopes of hillsides is excess soil salinity. Trees remove soil moisture, but when they are felled, sub-surface water runoff may increase, leading to a rise in the level of the watertable lower down the slope. If the watertable rises to the surface in areas where the groundwater is saline, it evaporates, the salt accumulates on the surface. A similar problem arises when farmers irrigate the land with highly saline water. Eventually, the soil salinity may rise sufficiently to kill off vegetation, and this leads to increased soil erosion.

Sheet and rill erosion

On sloping land the excess water on the soil surface runs down the slope and can carry away a thin layer of soil from the entire soil surface. This is called sheet erosion. Sometimes the water flows in a series of small channels, called rills, as it flows downhill. This water moves faster and has the energy to break away large soil particles and carve larger grooves. Rill erosion can remove even more soil than sheet erosion.

The soil from both these types of erosion is deposited along fence lines, over roads and railway lines, and can silt up dams and watercourses. The smaller particles also block the air spaces on the surface and discourage water penetration. Contour ploughing creates small terraces that encourage water to penetrate the soil rather than run off downhill.

Gully erosion

When rills become so large that they cannot be crossed by farm machinery, they are called gullies. Gullies present major problems for farmers in both cropping and grazing areas. Gullies, or steep sided channels, are created in a variety of ways, but the basic reason is that water is concentrated into an area of unstable land. If gullies are not attended to, they may become many metres deep and several hundred metres long.

The Wimmera region, which stretches north-westward from the town of Stawell (see Figure 9.9), has the most severe erosion in Victoria. For every 1 square kilometre of land, there is 1 kilometre of gully erosion.

> 6 Calculate the size of the region in which you live. Use the information above to estimate how much gully erosion there might be in your area. Use your findings to estimate how much of your village or town would be waste land if these figures were applied.
> 7 What problems might there be in your area if so much land were made completely useless?

Gullies may begin as stream channels where the surrounding land has been cleared of trees and where there is little vegetation to stabilise the soil. Left unchecked, such gullies can become very large. The rate of erosion and the width of the channels increase over time with further land clearance, especially if this occurs upstream.

Figure 9.3 Dean's Gully in the Wimmera region, Victoria—the rate of erosion and the width of the channel have increased over the last twenty years resulting in millions of tonnes of soil flowing down the gully

Figure 9.4 This gully has formed along the line of an old wagon track

Rescuing the land from the effects of gullying is a major task. One technique is to construct a cement wall, called a drop structure, across the channel. The idea of a drop structure is to act as a spillway for the water so that soil can build up behind the structure and eventually a level surface will form. The technique can be very effective, but sometimes the rate of erosion may be too great.

> 8 Describe the process by which a gully is formed and grows.

Stream bank erosion

Stream banks are naturally protected by tree roots and grasses. When these are removed, the scouring effects of stream flow may undercut the banks and cause them to slump. Clearing the land and cultivating it right up to the edge of a stream both removes the natural vegetation and causes water to flow over the land during periods of heavy rainfall. This erodes the banks. Slowly the banks of rivers are being protected and restored in some parts of Australia by using cement blocks and by growing willow trees.

SAVING AUSTRALIA'S SOILS

Figure 9.5a The process of tunnel erosion—water penetrates through the topsoil

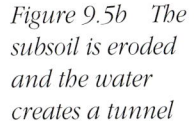

Figure 9.5b The subsoil is eroded and the water creates a tunnel

Figure 9.5c The tunnel collapses to form a gully—which will be enlarged if it is neglected

Figure 9.6 Undercutting the banks of the Latrobe River in east Gippsland, Victoria

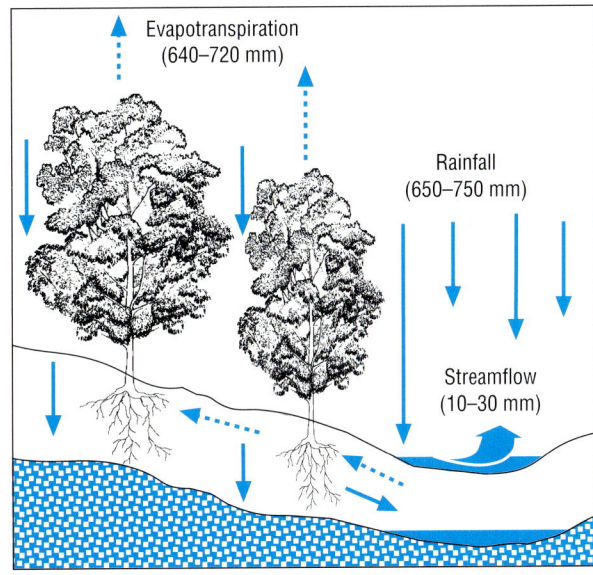

Figure 9.7a Water balance before clearing—the water was used where it fell

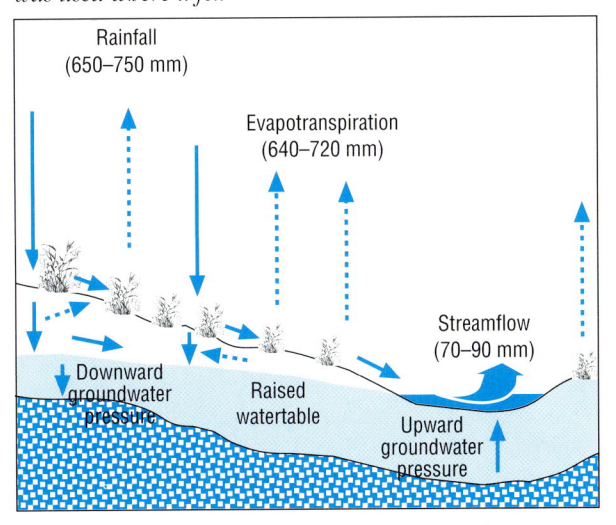

Figure 9.7b Water balance after clearing—saline groundwater rises and affects shallow-rooted pastures, salt is concentrated on the surface by evaporation and vegetation is affected

Soil salting

When you dig a hole deep enough so that you find water, you have found the watertable. In Australia, bores and wells are sunk to obtain water from the watertable to be used for cattle and sheep and sometimes for irrigation. However, billions of tonnes of salt lie under much of Australia's landscape. It comes from the beds of ancient inland seas, from the breakdown of rocks to soil, and is carried in from the sea on the wind. This salt leads to high levels of groundwater salinity.

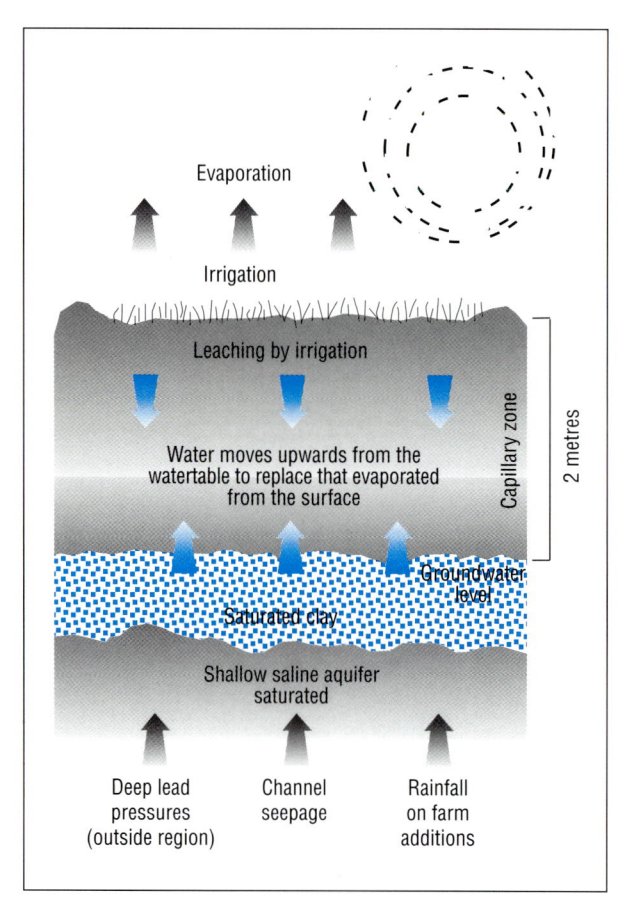

Figure 9.8 The process of wetland or irrigation salting—if the watertable rises to within 1 metre of the surface, waterlogging and salinisation occur

Figure 9.7 shows the process of dryland salting with the clearing of trees. Trees and plants remove water from the soil through their roots and out through their leaves. As trees are removed the watertable rises, and as the groundwater rises through the soil it collects salts. If the amount of salt dissolved is high enough it can kill the plants. Deep rooted trees will show signs of salting first.

While this process leads to dryland salting, a similar process can lead to what is known as wetland or irrigation salting. This is caused when irrigation is used to such an extent that it contributes to rising watertable levels. With this process, when more water is put into the soil than the plants can absorb, excess water is added to the groundwater. As the watertable rises, plant roots come in contact with the salty water and the plants die. The results in the long term are similar to those of dryland salting.

In the northern part of Victoria, a shallow watertable threatens about 385 000 hectares of productive land. The effects of salinity are far reaching and include a reduction in the productive capacity of affected land, degradation of the environment and wildlife habitats, loss of water quality for household supplies and damage to household equipment. In some areas, production losses have caused significant social and psychological hardship as farmers' earnings have

Table 9.1 Simulating the salinity in different environments

Container number	Amount of salt added (mg)	Environment simulated by container
1	0	Control: distilled water only
2	0.15	Upper limit of fresh water (150 mg/L)
3	1	Upper limit of marginal water (1000 mg/L)
4	3	Upper limit of brackish water 93 000 mg/L)
5	35	Salinity of sea water (3500 mg/L)
6	130	Recorded once in a creek feeding the Murray River in northern Victoria (9 130 000 mg/L)

Note: 1 level tsp holds about 5 g salt

Table 9.2 The salinity limits for some common plants and animals and for use in industry

Uses of water	Upper limits of salinity (mg/L)	Upper limits of salinity (EC)
Irrigation		
Tobacco	50	83
Citrus, legumes, garden plants	1 000	1 667
Vines, grass, cabbages	1 500	2 500
Cotton, lucerne	2 500	4 167
Domestic animals	1 000	1 667
Agricultural livestock		
Poultry	3 500	5 833
Pigs	4 500	7 500
Horses	6 500	10 833
Milking cows and ewes	7 000	11 667
Beef cattle	11 000	18 333
Sheep	15 000	25 000
Secondary industry		
Rayon	100	167
Paper	150	250
Petroleum	350	583
Carbonated beverages	850	1 417

Note: The approximate relationship between electrical conductivities (EC) and total dissolved salts (mg/L) is: EC x 0.6 = mg/L

Source: Groundwater Victoria, Department of Industry, Technology and Resources, Melbourne, 1987

SAVING AUSTRALIA'S SOILS

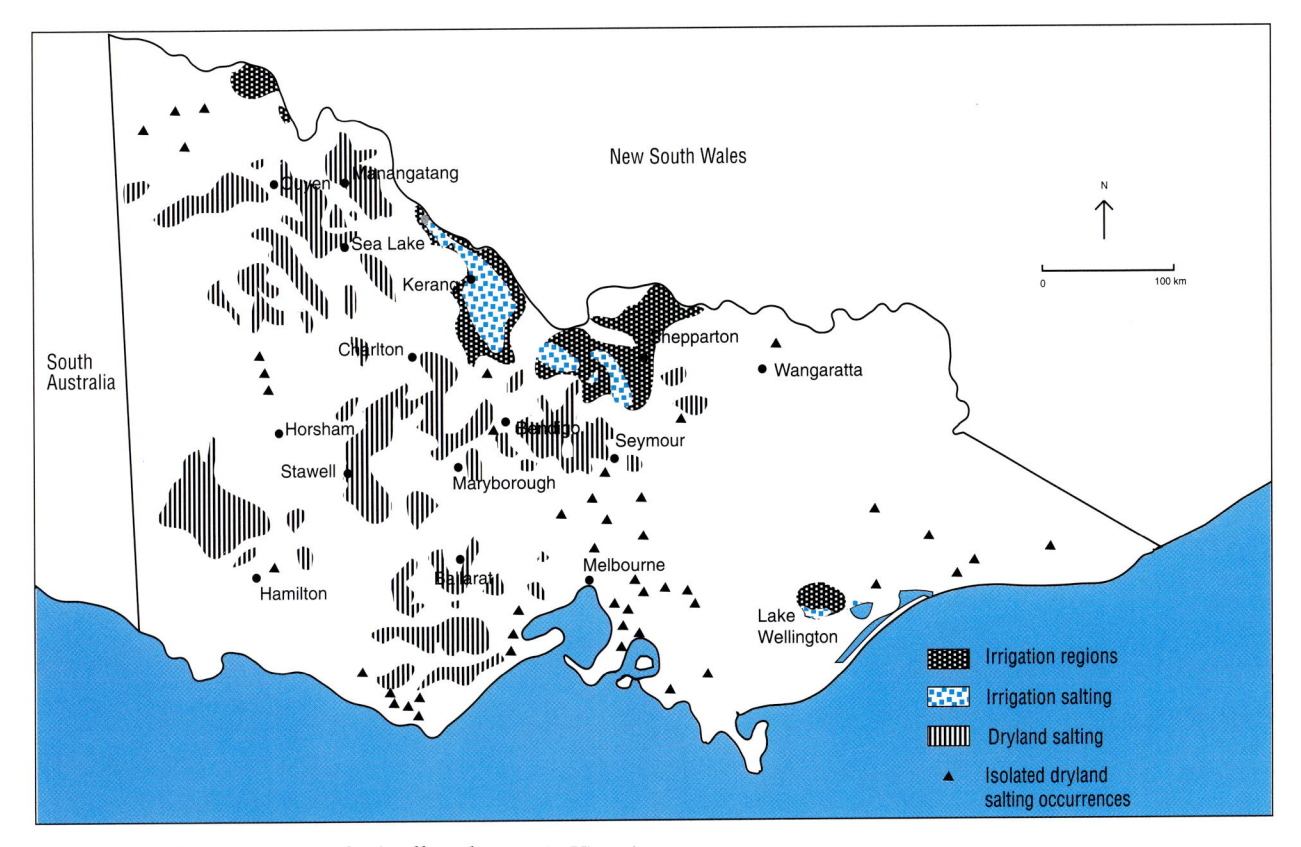

Figure 9.9 The distribution of salt affected areas in Victoria

fallen to such an extent that they cannot afford to take any actions to improve their land.

9. What is salinity like? This activity can enable you to taste water of known salinity and to compare this with water from your own area. You should prepare six full 1 litre containers of distilled water. Add the amounts of salt shown in Table 9.1 to each container.
   a Taste each of the six solutions in turn. Cups should be carefully rinsed out after each tasting.
   b Compare these solutions with water in your own area. (Find the electrical conductivity (EC) of your local water. Multiply this figure by 0.6 to determine the salinity in mg/L (total dissolved salts). This will enable you to compare the salinity of water in your area with the samples you have made.)
   c Table 9.2 shows the salinity limits for some common plants and animals and for use in industry. Compare the solutions you tasted with the tolerance of these uses. What conclusions can you draw?
10. With a partner, compose a list of the possible problems which can follow extensive land clearing. For each point made explain why you have included it.
11. In your own words, explain how the removal of trees can upset the balance of water in the soil and so increase the risk of soil salting.

12. a The salinity problem is like 'being flooded from below'. What does this mean?
    b How would the removal of trees contribute to this 'flood'?

At the turn of the century, the saline watertable lay 25 metres below the surface. Today, in parts of northern Victoria, it is less than 2 metres and in many places less than 1 metre below the surface. As the salt rises into the root zones of trees, pastures and native vegetation, large areas will die, placing at risk the future of more than 7000 farms and twenty-six towns.

If nothing is done, the northern part of Victoria would lose almost a third of its production over the next fifty years, along with thousands of jobs, much of the wildlife and most of the tourism industry. The solution to this problem could take between fifty and a hundred years. If something is not done quickly, what might cost millions of dollars now may cost billions in the future.

CONSEQUENCES OF SOIL DEGRADATION

Even though most Australians live in urban areas, the whole of society will lose as a result of the various forms of soil degradation, not just farmers.

The general community loses due to
- the costs of removing silt from watercourses, dams and estuaries—at the taxpayers' expense

- the increased risk of flooding because of the increase in water running off areas not protected by vegetation
- the pollution by silt and agricultural chemicals of rivers and dams used as town water supplies—this pollution may also affect aquatic life and cause algal blooms
- the increase in food prices when crops fail and farming costs rise
- the loss of natural areas that could have been maintained as wildlife reserves and national parks.

Farmers lose due to
- the loss of valuable and irreplaceable topsoil
- reduced productivity—in parts of south-east Queensland, where wheat is grown, 7 kilograms of soil are eroded for every 680 gram loaf of bread produced
- costly and time consuming repair work
- loss of seed and fertiliser—work is often wasted when these inputs are washed away when erosion occurs
- reduced stock carrying capacity in salty areas.

This means that the soil is kept where it belongs on the farm, instead of being blown or washed away. Controlling soil erosion is called soil conservation. Erosion can be reduced if soil conservation methods are used.

A farmer can conserve soil in a number of ways. For example, areas of sloping land can be ploughed around the contours. Water collects in the ploughed channels and soaks into the ground instead of washing away the soil. To stop heavy rainfall from eroding soil, this idea can be taken further and large earth banks, called contour banks, may be built.

On flat land, strip cropping is the best soil conservation method. Strip cropping means growing crops in strips across the slope to spread out and slow down runoff water. Alternate strips of different crops are grown side by side. Water spreads out when it hits a strip with a growing crop. The idea is to keep the water spread out as much as possible so it cannot build up and start to cause erosion when it flows

WHAT IS BEING DONE?

Australians have become very aware of the responsibility they have for their land. In a country with such fragile soils and such a harsh climate, the care and maintenance of good, productive land is essential. Productive land is still under pressure from development, salinity, topsoil erosion, erosion caused by poor forestry management and soil pollution due to the excessive use of agricultural chemicals. There is a need for action to care for the land and all over the country there is increasing interest in achieving this goal. Across Australia
- landholders are planning their properties to ensure that land is used to its best potential without being damaged
- farmers are using conservation farming techniques to minimise soil erosion and improve soil fertility
- landholders are planting trees, conserving native plants and retaining areas for wildlife habitats
- groups of concerned citizens are forming land care committees to promote the adoption of conservation practices and to foster cooperation between the community, all land users and government agencies.

Even in the cities people are caring for their land. They are doing this by educating school children, planting trees, restoring river banks and protecting natural areas.

Soil erosion can generally be controlled.

Figure 9.10a   Strip cropping is particularly appropriate on flat land

Figure 9.10b   Low tillage farming avoids breaking up the soil surface

on to the next strip without a crop. Strip cropping also limits wind erosion.

Low tillage farming also contributes to limiting the amount of erosion. This type of farming involves crops being grown and harvested without the surface of the soil being disturbed by ploughing or harrowing.

The battle against salt is also being fought, particularly in Victoria. In 1991 farmers, government and local authorities in Victoria launched an A$840 million campaign against salinity. This campaign included

- farm planning, tree planting, improved irrigation technology and drainage
- environmental plans to revegetate, protect rivers from groundwater inflows
- pumping and better drainage of sub-surface salt water
- improvements to surface drainage and disposal of salt water in huge evaporation basins.

Victoria has been divided up into nine salinity control regions. In each, the community has elected a committee of landholders and residents. These people will help decide how their region will cope with the salt.

There are three options.

- The amount of water getting through to the watertable can be minimised by revegetation, using more efficient irrigation practices and land forming so that the soil drains better. Many farmers are using laser grading which allows paddocks to be formed with an even slope, eliminating places where water forms ponds.
- The watertable can be lowered by pumping the water out and putting it somewhere else, such as into big evaporating basins.
- Growing salt tolerant crops and high water using species such as phalaris. However, productivity is likely to drop and some land may be taken out of production altogether.

Using methods such as these, salinity can be controlled but many of the solutions are long term and are not the responsibility of landholders alone. To improve Australia's land conditions, farmers are working with scientists, farm advisory services and government officials. In the 1990s, farmers will recover the A$4 million production losses caused directly by salinity in the 1980s.

Restoring the land

Although preventing a gully forming is better than trying to rectify an eroded landscape, gullies can be repaired. Sometimes small gullies can be filled in with soil, the gully fenced and planted with grass.

To help farmers in western Victoria, school students spent a weekend weeding, planting seedlings and small trees, and mulching. Another scheme, the Salt Action Project, has also undertaken a huge community education program. Four hundred schools in Victoria are involved in a program where schoolchildren measure the salinity of their regions and observe the effects of salt on their environment.

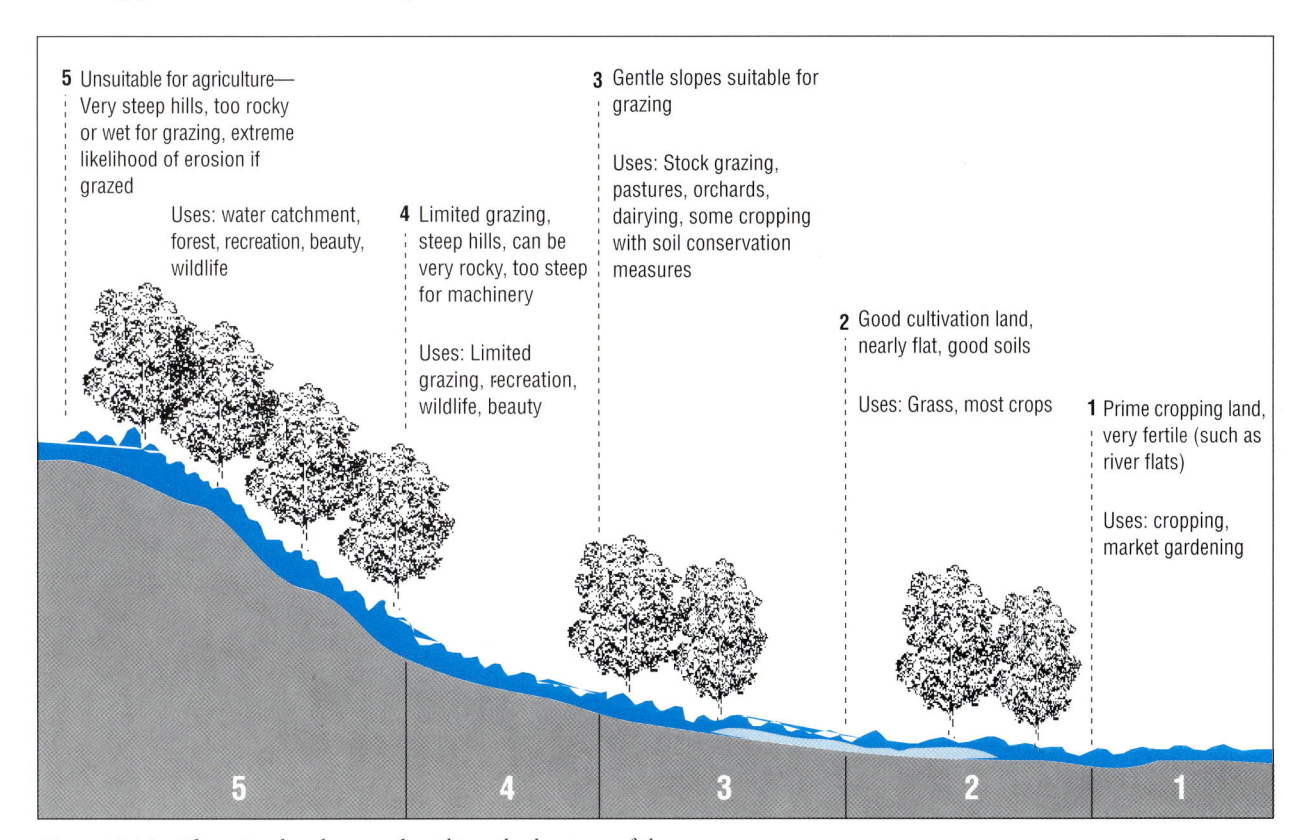

Figure 9.11 Planning landuse and making the best use of the resource

Farm planning

These approaches to reducing soil erosion and salinity are important, but the most important factor in maintaining the health of the land is its wise use. Land on farms should be used for the purpose to which it is best suited and managed according to its needs. A farmer must consider three things when planning landuse
- type and fertility of soil
- slope of the land
- climate and exposure to wind.

The fertility of the soil and soil type often vary across a region. On the top of a steep hill there may be shallow, rocky soil which is probably not fertile. Down the slope there might be deep, clay soils which are fertile and would hold water. These soils, however, can erode easily. On flat land near rivers there might be alluvial soil which is made up of sand and silt which has been deposited by rivers in flood. This soil is fertile and is ideal for growing crops.

> 13 With a partner, discuss Figure 9.11 which shows the ideal use of a landscape.
> *a* Decide on which section(s) of land you would grow a wheat crop and on which section(s) of land you would graze cattle.
> *b* Why should you leave forest on section 5? Explain your reasons for your decisions.

> 14 What kind of land care is being carried out in your region? If nothing is being done, see if you can find out why.

We must look after our land, no matter where we live. Saving our soil is one way we can provide enough land for future generations. What are you going to do to try and 'save the soil' in your country?

> 15 Have you any signs of soil erosion in your school grounds? What could you do in your school? Try these suggestions.
> *a* Form a small group with three or four other students.
> *b* Draw a sketch map of your school, marking on it the buildings, play areas etc.
> *c* Check the school grounds for signs of soil erosion. Mark these on your map.
> *d* Find out what has caused the erosion. Develop plans to prevent any more erosion from occurring. These plans may include fencing off the area, planting grass, trees and other vegetation or persuading your fellow students to use different routes around the school grounds.
> With the help of your teachers, try to carry out your plan.

CHAPTER 10

DAMS: THE ENVIRONMENTAL HAZARD

Patricia Green-Milberg

Water is the most abundant resource on the earth's surface. Oceans, ice caps, glaciers, rivers and lakes cover well over 70 per cent of the planet. Although Canada has only 1 per cent of the world's population, it has 9 per cent of the fresh surface water. Much of this water is stored in lakes and wetlands in the less settled areas of the north, while large areas of southern Canada suffer from water shortages.

Since Canada has both vast water resources and areas of great water shortage, it is not surprising that the country has tried to manage the water it possesses in order to maximise the benefits for its people.

People have been moving water around for thousands of years and some of the great civilisations of the world have been based on large scale irrigation systems that brought river water to farmlands. Of all the measures taken to manage water resources, dam building is the measure taken most often.

However, there has been much controversy about many of these schemes. Environmentalists claim that such water transfer upsets the natural balance of streams, lakes, estuaries and terrestrial ecosystems. Among the environmental costs of many water projects are the loss of free flowing rivers that are either drowned by reservoirs or turned into long sterile irrigation canals which result in

- altered stream flows
- altered groundwater levels
- increased salination
- silt deprivation
- increased erosion downstream
- raised watertable below dams
- flooding of natural habitats and changes to water nutrient levels.

Dams have also been criticised for using public funds to increase the value of privately held farmland and for encouraging agricultural development and urban growth in arid lands where other uses might be more appropriate.

On the other hand, benefits of dams and storage reservoirs include flood control, energy production, making water available for farming, industrial and municipal use, and providing recreational facilities.

The Rafferty–Alameda Dams of Saskatchewan and the dams of La Grande River in Québec have both been the subject of great controversy. While dams in the prairie provinces are generally built to store water for irrigation and prevent flooding, those in northern Québec are usually built for hydro-electric generation. Despite the benefits to be gained in both cases, the costs in terms of money and environmental and social disruptions are often very high.

THE RAFFERTY–ALAMEDA DAMS OF SASKATCHEWAN

Rivers in the prairie lands of Canada vary from season to season and between one year and the next. In spring the melting of accumulated snow and ice causes flooding and

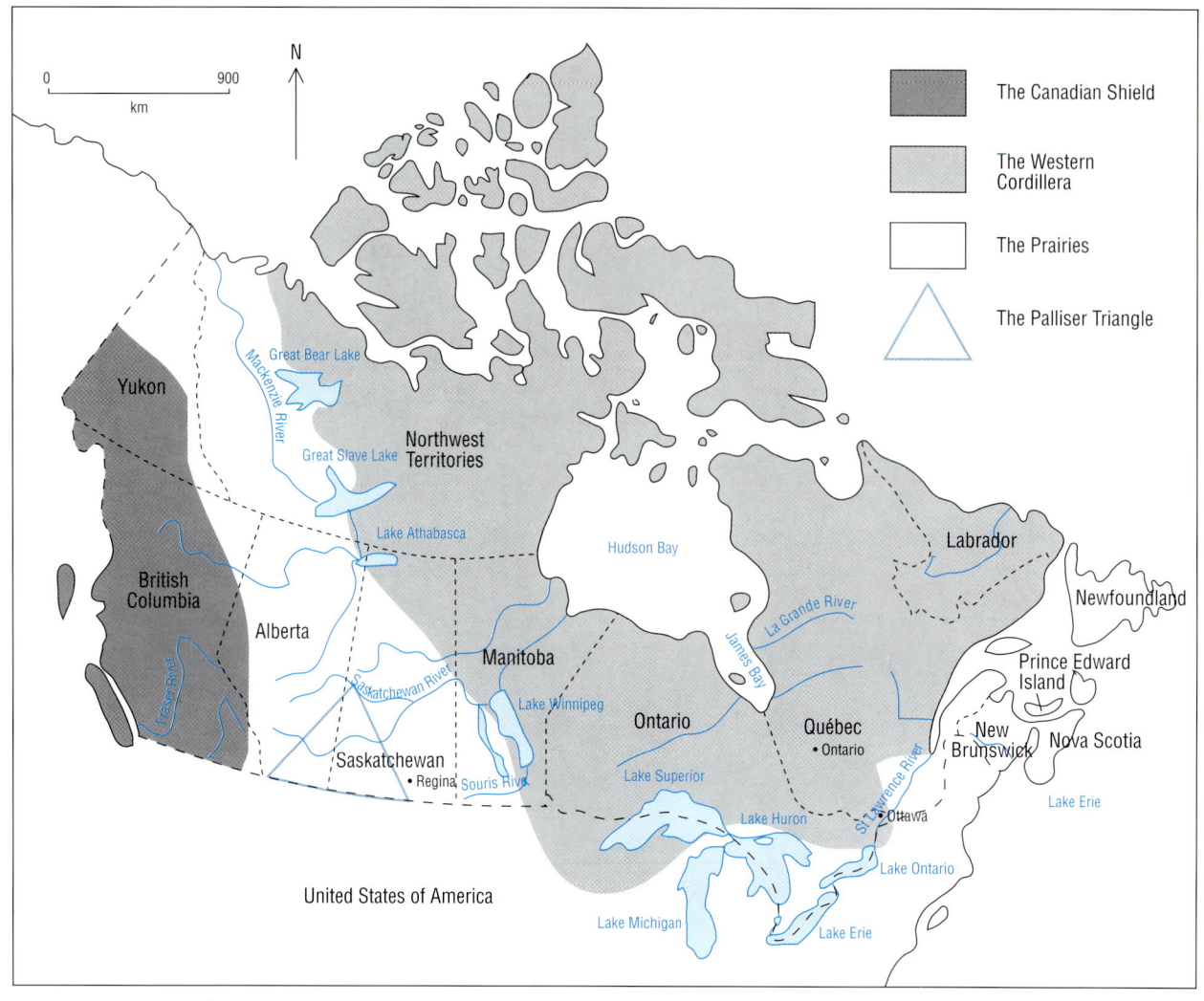

Figure 10.1 Canada

damage to personal property and farmland. In summer, when the demand for irrigation water is greatest, the rivers are at their lowest levels. Under natural conditions, forests soak up the rainfall and slow down the melting of snow in spring, while wetlands store the spring runoff water and release it slowly in the dry summer season. The problems in the prairies today are partly caused by clearing forests, draining wetlands and building cities. On the other hand, rainfall often varies greatly between years.

1. Examine the maps of water shortage and areas of flooding and major reservoirs in Figure 10.2. Describe the distribution of each feature in Canada. Discuss the reasons for

   a the location of many major reservoirs in areas which have no water shortage

   b major flooding in areas of water shortage.

2. Discover the policy in your country towards building dams. Discuss the extent to which the potential harmful effects of large dams have occurred in your country. To what extent have such dams become major political issues?

3. Compare the yearly pattern of precipitation and river flow at Estevan. Explain why the two patterns are different (Figure 10.3).

4. a Calculate the highest and lowest flows of the river for the two periods, 1933–39 and 1943–49.

   b Calculate the range from highest to lowest river flow as a percentage of the average river flow over the thirty year period 1951–80. Comment on your result.

   c Discuss the problems that would have arisen if river management planners had based their decisions on the average annual discharge for 1933–39.

5. Discuss the effects of such wide annual variations on the lives of those who live in the prairies.

6. Calculate the percentage variation in the river flow or annual precipitation in your area. What effects does this variation have on your life and that of your country?

Shortages of water have been a problem from the very first days of European settlement in the prairie provinces. Settlers ploughed the grasslands and converted them to grain fields. In the centre of the prairie lies the Palliser Triangle (named after Captain John Palliser who explored the lands between the Red River of Manitoba and the Rocky Mountains in 1857). Captain Palliser described the triangle as unfit for agriculture and even today the heart of the triangle is difficult to farm. The centre of this triangle, which includes south-western Saskatchewan and south-eastern Alberta, extends 608 kilometres along the 49th parallel and 400 kilometres northwards. The soils are brown and support short grass, pasture sage, prickly pear cactus, broom weed and sagebrush. Around this zone are darker brown soils which support mixed grasses, willows and aspens. Topsoils in these grassland areas may be 60 to 120 centimetres thick because of the humus added each year when the grass dies.

During the 1930s, and again during the 1980s, very little rain fell for a number of years and farmers suffered from both drought and depression. In 1935 parts of the Palliser region were declared a 'dust-bowl'. Programs to deal with the 'dust-bowl' conditions included the construction of farm dugouts (water holes) stock-watering dams and irrigation reservoirs. The Souris River is a slow flowing, sediment laden stream which flows sluggishly southwards into the state of North Dakota in the United States of America and then doubles back northwards into the Canadian province of Manitoba. The statistics shown in Figure 10.3 reveal that periodically the precipitation in the Souris area is unexpectedly heavy and the river experiences a surge of water. Under natural conditions, such surges lead to the river overflowing its banks on to its floodplain. This is a perfectly natural occurrence, but such floods may be unwelcome to people who have chosen to live on the floodplain and who are not expecting such an event.

In the early 1980s, the town of Minot in North Dakota was damaged in one of these rare floods and this led to great political wrangling about what should be done.

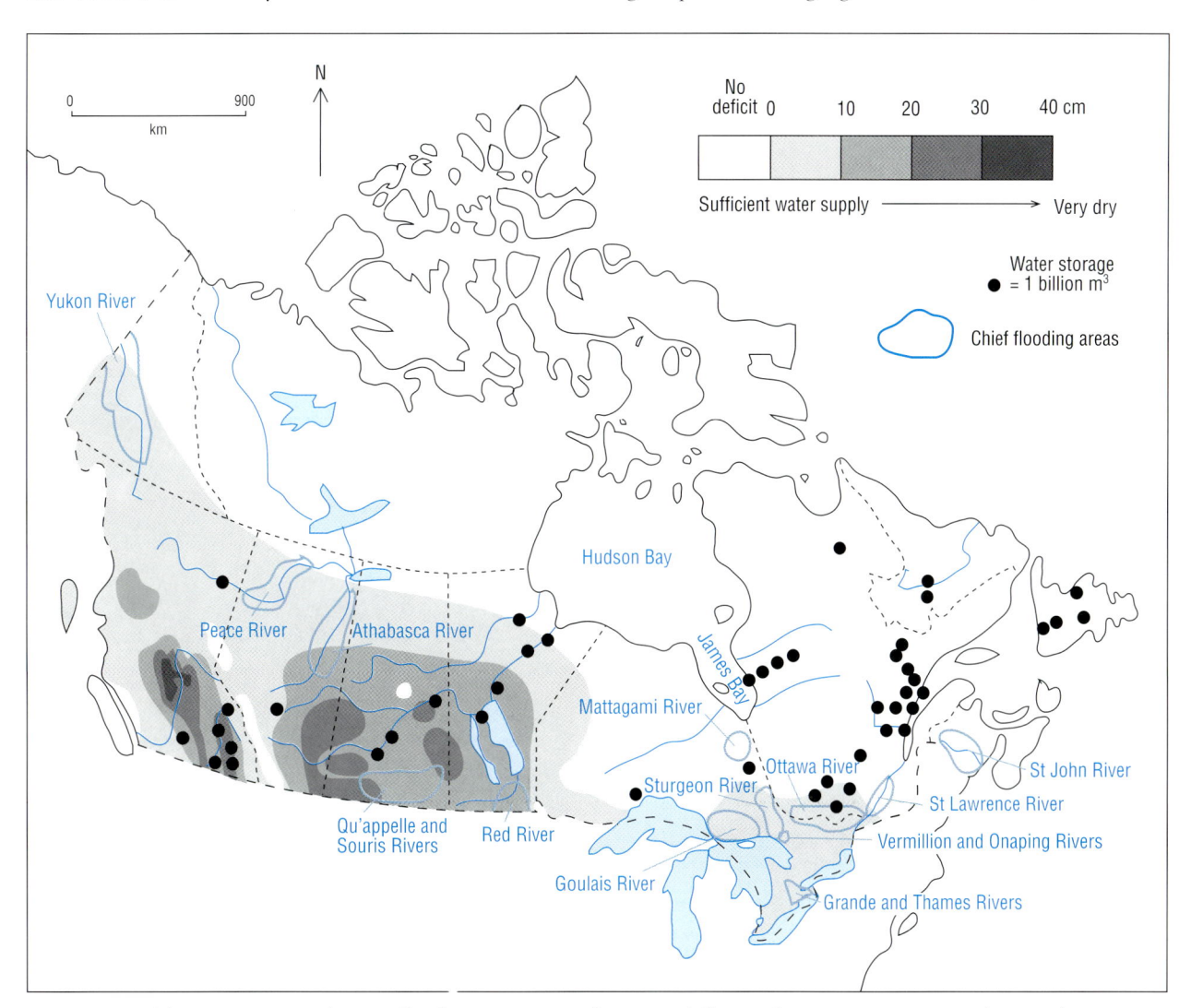

Figure 10.2 The main areas subject to flooding, reservoirs of over one billion cubic metres capacity and water shortage areas in Canada

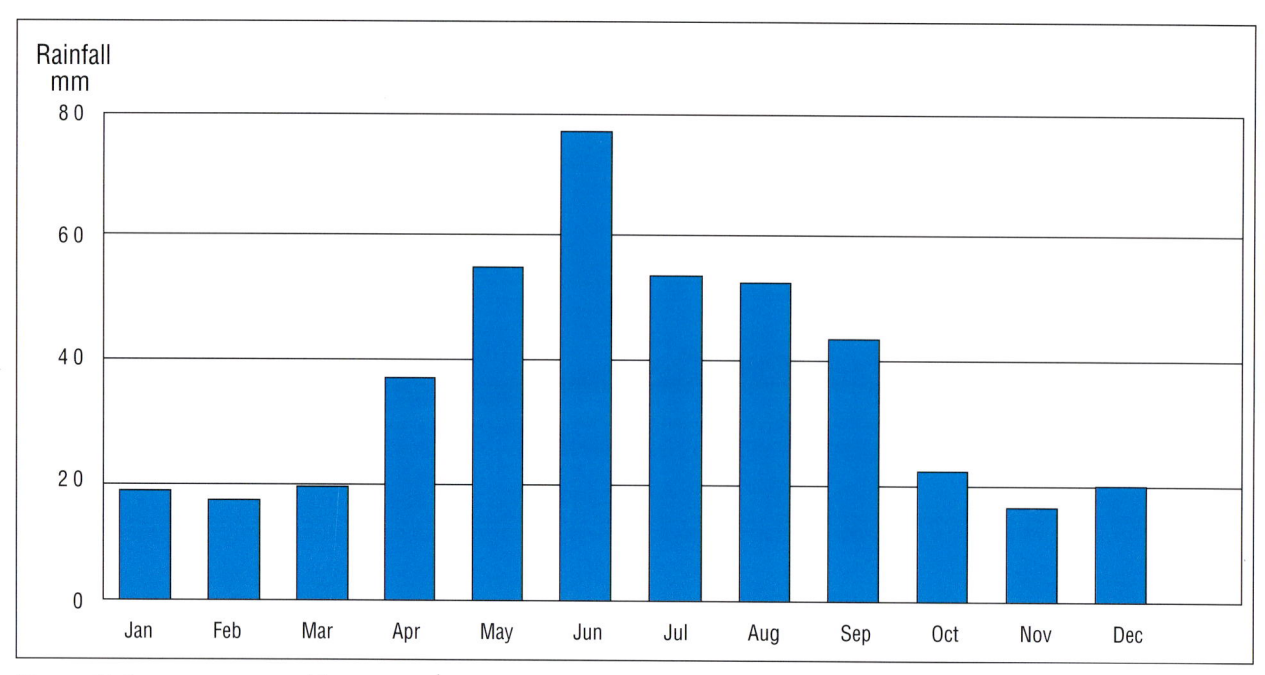

Figure 10.3a   Average monthly precipitation, Estevan, Saskatchewan, 1951–80

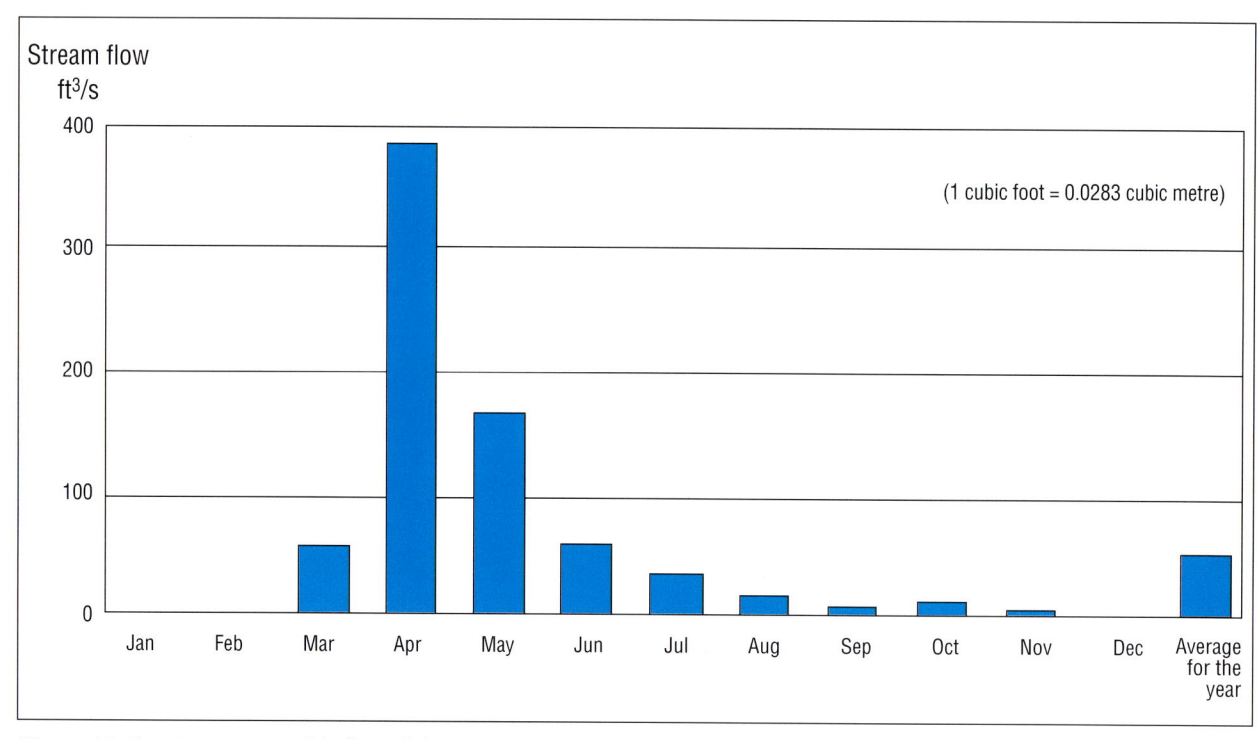

Figure 10.3b   Average monthly flow of the Souris River, Estevan, Saskatchewan, 1951–80

At that time, there was strong opposition to building flood control dams and all dam building in the state of North Dakota was forbidden by the US Congress. Later, in 1986, however, Congress passed a water bill which allocated US$41.1 million to the Canadian province of Saskatchewan to build a dam higher up the Souris River to protect the people of Minot. Such a dam would also provide irrigation water. A Canadian newspaper report in 1990 claimed that 'Political manoeuvring turned one dam into two dams—one in the Premier of Saskatchewan's riding of Estevan and the other in the riding of his then-deputy premier'.

The political process from then on is summarised in the timeline which follows.

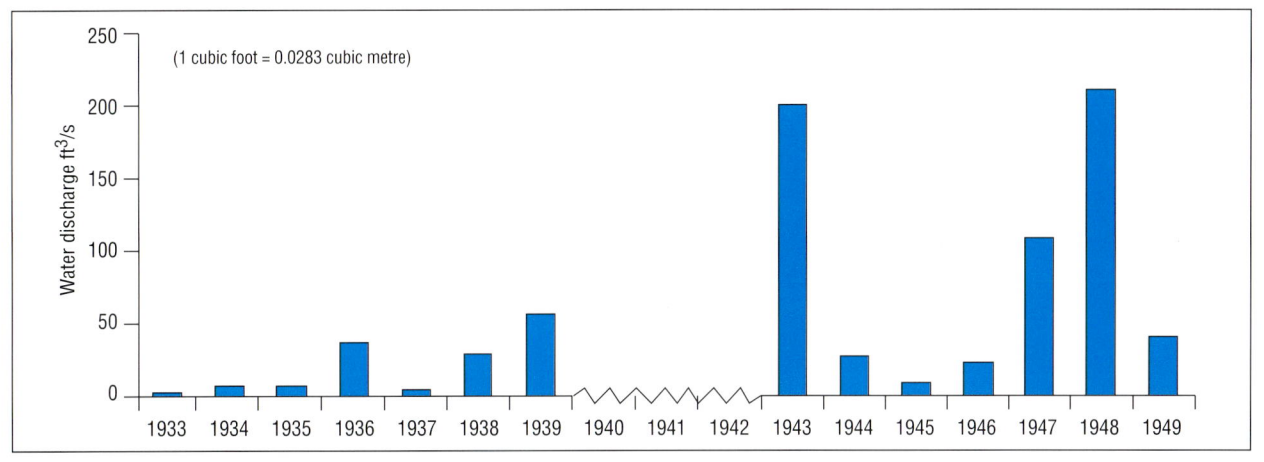

Figure 10.4 Annual average flow of the Souris River at Estevan, Saskatchewan between 1933 and 1939 and between 1943 and 1949

Table 10.1 Timeline of the political process

September 1987	Environmental review of the dam proposal conducted by Saskatchewan provincial government in six centres Critics claimed that both the monetary and environmental cost outweighed the benefits of the project Environmentalists also claimed that if the Rafferty Dam had been started in 1912 it would have taken until 1958 just to fill with water and the accumulating sediments that would clog the reservoir would represent a loss of valuable nutrients
15 February 1988	The provincial environment minister granted final approval for the project
19 March 1988	On site preparation work began on the Rafferty Dam
April/May 1988	Furious environmentalists in Saskatchewan appealed to the federal environment minister for a federal environment assessment The Minister told members of the House of Commons that the federal environment process would be followed
June 1988	A federal permit to proceed with construction was issued without further review in return for Saskatchewan's commitment to translate its provincial laws into French and establish the Grasslands National Park
19 January 1989	The Canadian Wildlife Federation challenged the federal permit and claimed that the minister had failed to follow the review process and had broken the law
12 April 1989	The new federal environment minister pushed through an environmental assessment in the record time of four months
19 April 1989	Mr Justice Bud Cullen agreed with the Canadian Wildlife Federation, quashed Saskatchewan's licence and ordered the federal government to comply with the environmental guidelines Construction on the Rafferty Dam was suspended
31 August 1989	A new federal permit was issued for the construction to begin
September 1989	The Canadian Wildlife Federation went to court again, stating that the minister had again broken the law by not holding a full public enquiry
28 December 1989	The court agreed and stated that Saskatchewan's licence would remain quashed unless a federal environmental review panel was appointed by 30 January 1990
January 1990	The federal minister agreed that the federal government would pay Saskatchewan Can$1 million a month in compensation up to a maximum of Can$10 million while an environmental review panel studied the full impact of the building of the dams
January 1990	The premier of Saskatchewan claimed that he would not be bound by an oral agreement and that the project must be finished to make it safe Environmental groups complained to federal government that work was continued on the dam, but government failed to respond

5 September 1990	Premier of Saskatchewan and the new federal environment minister met in Ottawa Officials said that they agreed orally to allowing Saskatchewan to finish both dams and review the situation afterwards
4 October 1990	The environmental review panel appointed by the federal government announced that it was suspending its review because Saskatchewan was continuing excavations at Rafferty
October 1990	The angry federal environment minister told the premier of Saskatchewan that he must respect the court order of 28 December 1989
The Saskatchewan government stated that the federal minister did not have the right to intervene in a provincial affair
US Fisheries and Wildlife Service expressed concern to Canadian federal government that a Canadian province could proceed with a project that had international implications
(Remember who had asked for and funded the project in the first place)
25 October 1990	Court agreed that construction of the Rafferty Dam could continue for another week until a hearing in Regina on 1 November 1990
29 October 1990	Federal environment minister sought another court order against work proceeding at Rafferty–Alameda
February 1991	Law suits still awaiting hearing by the courts
Work on the project had come to a stop because of the winter freeze up
1991–92	Nature took a hand
Heavy rains and a freak water surge caused the reservoir behind the unfinished dam to start to fill up, and Saskatchewan was ordered to resume work on the dam in order to make it secure
11 March 1993	The minister for natural resources announced a deal with the two farmers whose lands have been flooded by the dam
The government will pay them Can$250 000, return part of the 16 hectares taken for the dam and will keep the reservoir only one-third full
The government hopes that this will save them years of legislation

For some of the people of southern Saskatchewan, a 26 kilometre reservoir created by what has been described as 'a long, low-slung pile of earth and stone that stretches across the Souris River valley for more than a kilometre—a little pimple of dirt' brings the prospect of water to a region that is rich in potash, coal and oil deposits, but which lacks water. For others, both in Saskatchewan and nationally, such dams represent further destruction of the natural environment and may encourage more people to move into an arid area.

This has led to a battle between the federal government in Ottawa and the government of Saskatchewan. Many Saskatchewan residents see it as a battle to run their own affairs and control their own resources without input from Ottawa. If Saskatchewan wins, the implications for other projects like Québec's Great Whale project may mean that federal influence on environmentally sensitive schemes is limited and environmentalists would find it more difficult to oppose such projects.

7 Discuss the factors that may influence the people of Saskatchewan to support the Rafferty–Alameda dams while the federal government opposes them. How would you vote if
   a you lived in Saskatchewan
   b you lived elsewhere in Canada?
   How should such issues be resolved?

THE GRAND RIVER PROJECT OF QUÉBEC

The Canadian Shield covers most of the provinces of Québec and Ontario, the peninsula of Labrador, and parts of northern Manitoba and Saskatchewan provinces. This area of over 4.6 million square kilometres represents over 40 per cent of Canada's territory but has only 8 per cent of its population.

The rocks of the Canadian shield are some of the oldest on earth. When the earth first cooled from its molten state more than three billion years ago, the first solid land masses that formed became the central cores of the continents.

Once the Canadian shield was higher than the present-day Rocky Mountains in western Canada. However these mountains were gradually worn away by the processes of weathering and erosion until today the shield averages about 65 metres above sea level.

The great ice sheets of the last Pleistocene glaciation melted from the southern regions of the shield about 10 000 years ago, and the remainder of the shield about 13 000 years ago. They left behind a landscape of bare rock, thin soils, enormous areas of poorly drained, swampy land—known as muskeg—and thousands of small and large lakes. These lakes formed when the streams of melt water were blocked by huge rock barriers dumped by the melting ice. There are many other features of glacial deposition, such as the eskers in James Bay shown in Figure 10.5.

Figure 10.5 An esker in James Bay—eskers like these are long ridges of material eroded by glaciers and deposited in tunnels under the ice, which remained when the glaciers melted

Since the retreat of the ice, rivers have eroded new beds in the deposits creating terraces. During the ice age, the shield was compressed under the weight of ice over 1000 metres thick. After the ice sheets retreated, the land gradually rose. This isostatic uplift is still occurring at a rate of 1.5 metres every 100 years.

The area drained by James Bay extends from 49° to 55° north in latitude, and 70° to 80° west in longitude. This is more than six times the area of the British Isles and three times larger than France.

8 On a piece of tracing paper, draw an oblong which covers an area spanning 10° of longitude and 6° of latitude using a world map in your atlas. Using the same atlas world map, what proportion of your country does this area represent? Make a list of the countries in the world that would fit into such an area.

The physical environment of the shield is not favourable for agriculture. The average annual temperature of the region is –4°C (11°C lower than Montreal). Summers are short

Figure 10.6 Terraces and meanders on La Grande River

and July temperatures average only 12°C. The average temperature in January is –23°C, but temperatures can drop as low as –50°C.

Precipitation increases from west to east across the shield as the prevailing winds move masses of humid air from James Bay towards the higher land. Annual precipitation is approximately 760 millimetres and more than one-third falls as snow.

The area around James Bay is partly boreal forest and partly sub-arctic forest. The boreal forest is found in the south of the James Bay region, and consists mostly of slow growing coniferous trees, white spruce, black spruce, balsam fir, grey pine and larch. There are lichens and moss, as well as hundreds of shrub and wild flower species. Further north is the sub-arctic forest of stunted coniferous trees, mainly spruce and larch. The winters are long and harsh with little precipitation. The subsoil is frozen all year round—**permafrost**—and plant growth is slow.

The area around the James Bay has a great diversity of natural wildlife. Lakes and rivers are well stocked with fish, including lake trout, char, pike, walleye and white fish. Black bear, moose, caribou, beaver, muskrat and lynx inhabit the region. James Bay and its shoreline is a habitat for whales, seals and water fowl and is a breeding ground for millions of migratory birds.

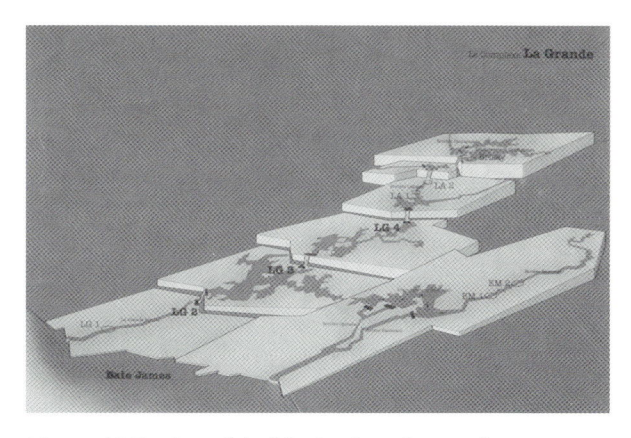

Figure 10.7 A model of the La Grande complex

Figure 10.8 The spillway of one of the hydro-electric generating stations of La Grande 2—it has a potential power capacity of 10 282 megawatts

Using the rivers of the shield

In 1964, Hydro Québec began seeking new energy sources and was attracted by the immense hydro potential of La Grande River. In 1971 the James Bay project was launched. The La Grande complex, a model of which is shown in Figure 10.7, is one of the world's major hydro-electric developments. The first phase of the project, called La Grande 2 (La Grande 1 has yet to be started) was completed in 1985.

Many rivers discharge into the James Bay including La Grande River and La Grand Rivière de la Baleine, the two main rivers and their tributaries that have been developed or designated for hydro development.

These rivers experience two floods a year. The major flood occurs during the spring thaw (May and June) and accounts for more than 40 per cent of the annual runoff. The autumn flood caused by heavy rainfall is generally smaller. Runoff almost ceases in winter.

In its natural state, the 800 kilometres of La Grand River had a catchment of 176 000 square kilometres (an area equal to that of England). In 1983 it had an average discharge of about 1700 cubic metres per second, making it the third largest river in the province of Québec.

Although the flow of La Grande is considerable, the river only drops about 376 metres along its 800 kilometre length. This represents an average drop of only half a metre per kilometre. Furthermore, there are no natural waterfalls and only a few rapids.

In order to increase the potential of the river to generate electricity, engineers decided to increase the flow of La Grande River by diverting water from two other rivers—the Eastmain River and the Caniapiscau River.

Figure 10.9 The Eastmain River, Québec, after water has been diverted to La Grande River

Figure 10.10 The present site of Chisasibi, at the mouth of La Grande Rivière

Figure 10.11 An ice bridge on La Grande Rivière

The 720 kilometre Eastmain river, with its tributaries the Opinaca and the Petite Opinaca, runs parallel to La Grand River approximately 150 kilometres to the south. By blocking these rivers with a dam and diverting their flow, the discharge of La Grande was increased by 807 cubic metres per second. However, since water has been diverted to La Grande the Eastmain River has been left as kilometres of dry river bed along which the fishing and wildlife habitats have been destroyed.

The Caniapiscau is a powerful river which flows eastward to Ungarva Bay. By damming the upper reaches of the river and creating a huge reservoir, Lake Caniapiscau, the higher levels of the lake enable the Caniapiscau River to flow into La Grande via the Laforge River.

In 1983 a preliminary study of the second major river of the area, La Grande Rivière de la Baleine, proposed construction of three power stations with a potential of 3000 megawatts.

As a result of such schemes, over 80 per cent of the total provincial electricity generating capacity of Québec comes from hydro stations located on the shield at the cost of flooding 11 500 square kilometres of land with reservoirs.

The effects of the hydro schemes on the people

Much of the area of Canada is claimed by native Americans who assert that their land was taken from them unjustly by European settlers. The region around James Bay is a vast, thinly populated area to which access is very difficult. About 9000 native Cree Indians and Inuit live there. Most of the settlements are small, with fewer than 1000 people. Chisasibi is one of the larger Cree settlements with about 2500 people. Until the early 1980s most of the residents lived on Fort George Island, an old Hudson's Bay fur trading post, situated at the mouth of La Grande Rivière.

Engineers warned that building dams on La Grande Rivière might change the river currents so that the sandy island would be slowly eroded. The settlement was therefore moved to the banks of the river. In fact the island has not been eroded and some of the Cree have returned to live there. However, the currents have changed enough so that an ice bridge (see Figure 10.11) no longer forms across the river mouth in winter. This means that the Cree hunters are no longer able to cross to their northern traplines.

ADVANTAGES AND DISADVANTAGES OF THE HYDRO SCHEMES

Since its inception there has been a great deal of debate over the real value of the La Grande scheme. At present three dams (La Grande, 2, 3 and 4) have been built and 11 500 square kilometres of land have been flooded. The land has also been changed by the building of numerous

Table 10.2 The perceived advantages and disadvantages of the James Bay hydro-electricity schemes

Advantages	Disadvantages
The scheme will supply much needed hydro-electricity for Québec	Artificial lakes will flood traditional Cree hunting grounds
Surplus power can be sold to the United States	With increasing energy conservation, mega projects are unnecessary
Thousands of jobs will be provided	Few jobs are permanent after the construction is complete
An infrastructure of roads and airports will provide communication links into a sparsely occupied area of Canada	More than 6000 native people will have their lives disrupted
New resources will be opened up	The climate and balance of nature will be upset
There is little to show that the environment will be upset in any way	
Tourists will bring money to the area	
The native peoples can have a choice of hunting elsewhere or finding employment at the project	

dams, spillways (artificial waterways), powerhouses, artificial lakes and power corridors. Although no formal environmental impact assessment study was ever undertaken, a number of assertions were made by those on each side at the start of the project. These are summarised in Table 10.2.

The results so far

It is now more than a decade since the first dams at James Bay were constructed and some of the impacts of the project can be seen clearly, as listed below.

- Recent studies have shown increasing levels of mercury in fish life, caused by the decomposition of foliage. This means that the Cree no longer eat fish from the reservoirs.
- Diverted rivers, like the Eastmain, no longer have sufficient water to supply the communities along their shores, and the Cree must travel long distances to find fish or get water.
- A particularly tragic event took place in 1984 when 10 000 caribou were swept over the Limestone Falls on the Caniapiscau River by a surge of water released from the Caniapiscau Reservoir upstream. They were all drowned.
- The promised jobs have not materialised and traditional hunting grounds have been destroyed.
- By 1992, only twelve of the workers employed on the James Bay project were Cree.
- Closer links to the outside world have brought increasing social and family problems to the indigenous people, with rising rates of alcoholism and violence.

On the other hand, the James Bay developments have brought some benefits to the traditional owners of the land. The Cree and Inuit nations were awarded Can$90 million and the federal government agreed to fund an income security program that allows many Cree to continue trapping for a living. Chisasibi has a Coop Store and Northern Store, an office for Creebec, the Cree airline, a modern office for the band council, a branch of one of Canada's main banks, a modern hospital and CreeCo Construction is building an office complex. The new Cree School Board is training Cree teachers with the support and encouragement of Québec universities. The Cree have also achieved much greater levels of self-government than other aboriginal peoples in North America.

Environmentalists see dams as hazards that can be avoided by more efficient use of the water we have. Other points of view suggest that hydro-electricity is one of the least damaging sources of energy production upon which we depend. On the other hand, a human being requires only 2 litres of water a day to survive. Canadians currently use 7100 litres a day.

9 Hydro Québec now proposes to include the Great Whale River, to the north of La Grande River, in the scheme.
   a What factors may influence the Cree and Inuit nations in reacting to further hydro-electric proposals in their traditional lands?
   b How should these views be weighed against the growing needs of Québec, the rest of Canada and the USA for more energy?
   c How do you regard the environmental effects of hydro-electricity when compared with other methods of obtaining energy (see also Chapter 19)?
10 Discuss the two dam schemes described in this chapter. In what ways are they similar and in what ways are they different? Compare the advantages and disadvantages that they cause for human beings and the natural environment. Should such schemes be encouraged or discouraged?

Acknowledgment: Patricia Green-Milberg acknowledges Mr Ted Milberg, Ms Janet Wood, Ms Suzanne Taylor and the John Abbott College, James Bay Nursing Project for assistance with photographs, Mr Patrick Busque for preparing the original computer graphics, and the Société de Baie James Hydro Québec for permission to visit the 'La Grande' complex.

CHAPTER 11

A NEW AIRPORT FOR HONG KONG

● ● ● ● ● ● ● ●

Tammy Yim Lin Kwan

Hong Kong is one of the few remaining colonies of Great Britain, situated on the southern tip of mainland China, overlooking the South China Sea. Hong Kong island was originally occupied by a number of fishing villages, but as part of the opium wars between European countries and China, Great Britain gained control of the area in 1842 and established a trading centre. In 1860, the Kowloon peninsula was added to the growing colony, and in 1898, Britain reached an agreement with China to lease the other islands around Hong Kong and the area which is now called the New Territories. This lease was for ninety-nine years and will expire in 1997.

It has been agreed between the Chinese government in Beijing and the British government that in that year, the whole of Hong Kong, which now comprises Hong Kong Island, Kowloon Peninsula, the New Territories and the group of outlying islands—of which Lantau Island on the west is the biggest—will be returned to Chinese sovereignty.

Although we often think of Hong Kong as being very urbanised, over 80 per cent of the total area of just over 1000 square kilometres is hilly and not suitable for development. On the other 20 per cent, however, Hong Kong houses 5.82 million people—an average population density of over 5390 per square kilometre. Most of these people live along the narrow coastal strip of lowland and this gives rise to an even higher population density in the actual urban areas. Figure 11.1 shows Tsuen Wan, viewed from Tai Mo Shan (the highest point in the whole of Hong Kong)—only 20 per cent of Hong Kong is built up with high density housing such as this, most of the area is covered in lush subtropical vegetation.

Figure 11.1 The Tsuen Wan new town in the New Territories

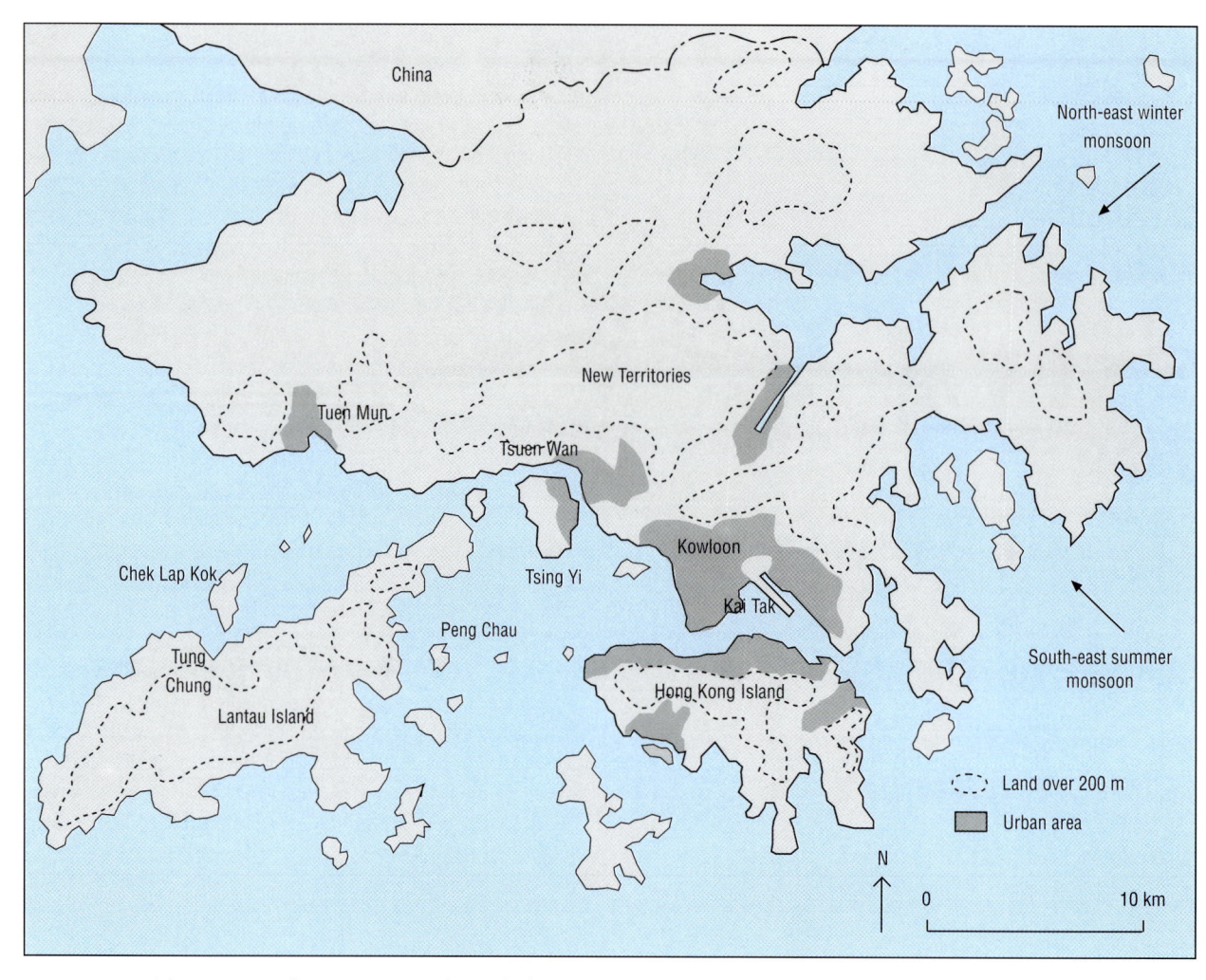

Figure 11.2 The position of Hong Kong and its relief, prevailing winds and population distribution

Figure 11.3 The runway of Kai Tak airport is built on reclaimed land in Victoria Harbour

A NEW AIRPORT FOR HONG KONG

In order to create more flat land for living, land has been reclaimed from the sea. In recent decades, the total land area available for building has been increased by 75 square kilometres. One major scheme for reclaiming land from the sea was the building of the Kai Tak Airport, Hong Kong's international airport. Figure 11.3 shows the Kai Tak Airport runway projecting out into Victoria Harbour in a north-west to south-east direction, towards Lei Yu Mun (Carp Channel).

1 Discuss in class your images of Hong Kong. How many people have thought of Hong Kong as being mainly open countryside with subtropical vegetation?
2 Find the average density of population and the percentage of land that has been built up in your own country. Compare these with those of Hong Kong. What are the advantages and disadvantages of high density living?

LOCATION OF KAI TAK AIRPORT: PROBLEMS

Being located at the focal point of major routes between east and west, Hong Kong has grown into an international city. In 1989, Kai Tak Airport was served by thirty-seven scheduled international airlines which operated 80 512 passenger flights and 5643 cargo flights. These flights linked Hong Kong directly to 121 major world cities. Due to the great increase in demand by passengers, cargo handling and aircraft movements, great problems have been created for the management of both ground and air space. Furthermore, a major airport sited in the centre of the urban area creates many problems for nearby residents.

3 Compare the photograph, Figure 11.4, with the map in Figure 11.2. Identify the airport runway projecting into the sea. Describe the location of Kai Tak Airport.
4 *a* Discuss the advantages and disadvantages of having Kai Tak Airport in the urban centre of Hong Kong.
b In what ways may the opinions of the residents who live close to the airport be different to those of travellers and business people?
5 *a* What problems can you see for travellers and business people if the demands on Kai Tak Airport continue to grow?
b In what ways could the problems facing Hong Kong with its airport be solved?

The issue of what to do about the ever growing Kai Tak Airport has been the subject of hot debate in Hong Kong since the mid-1970s. The activity which follows will illustrate the nature of the debate which was conducted in the 1980s.

6 Read the boxed information on page 94 and Table 11.1. Consider each of the options described and decide on the advantages and disadvantages of each.
Option 1: To limit the number of aircraft Kai Tak can take and be prepared to accept the economic penalty.
Option 2: To develop and expand Kai Tak to its maximum potential through large scale investment in order to add a few more years to its life.
Option 3: To construct a new airport in Hong Kong which will allow room for future expansion.

Figure 11.4 The site and location of Kai Tak Airport

Table 11.1 Statistics for Kai Tak Airport

Year	Passengers ('000)	Cargo ('000 t)	Aircraft movements ('000)
1969	1 541	40.6	34.5
1979	5 797	237.0	53.5
1985	9 707	419.4	56.6
1986	9 923	447.7	60.7
1987	11 067	558.7	66.5
1988	13 230	624.4	77.0
1989	15 863	704.6	89.6
Maximum capacity	30 000	n/a	n/a

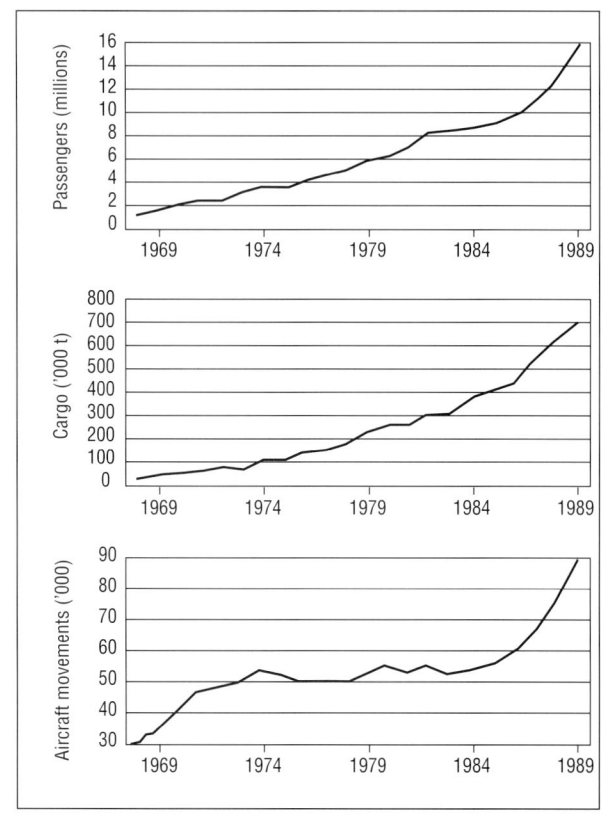

Figure 11.5 Passenger numbers, aircraft movements and cargo handled for Kai Tak Airport, 1968–89

One option has been to expand the capacity of Kai Tak Airport itself. Another has been to build another new airport elsewhere in Hong Kong. While this debate was going on, Kai Tak continued to grow, and has already undergone several phases of expansion and redevelopment. Despite these changes, Kai Tak Airport is still approaching saturation and it is forecast that further expansion on the present airport will be impossible after 1996.

After much debate, the continued growth of Kai Tak led to the conclusion that a new international airport elsewhere in Hong Kong had become inevitable. It was considered that a new airport built to accommodate the expanding air traffic would permit Hong Kong to maintain her international prosperity and continue to develop her import and export trade. Furthermore, the removal of Kai Tak Airport from the existing site would reduce the stress on nearby

---

Information about Kai Tak Airport

- Kai Tak occupies an area of 2.5 square kilometres and is worth HK$100 billion.
- Airport revenue from poll tax and other service charges is expected to rise from HK$900 million in 1984–85 to HK$1900 million in 1994–95.
- The airport is sheltered against typhoons by the surrounding hills.
- The airport is surrounded by commercial, industrial and residential activities. Heavy traffic congestion is found in areas like Kowloon City, To Kwa Wan and Kwun Tong.
- Buildings in the north-eastern part of Kowloon and the north-eastern coastal region of Hong Kong Island, on the main flight paths, are subject to height restrictions. The flight paths also prevent the construction of a bridge over Lei Yue Mun.
- The north-west to south-east trend of the runway allows the best use of the prevailing easterly wind coming through Lei Yue Mun, reducing the amount of fuel and the length of runway needed for takeoff and landing. This single runway is approaching saturation with between thirty and thirty-four aircraft movements (arrivals and departures) during peak hours from 12 noon to 4 pm.
- Aircraft movements are only permitted between 6.30 am and 12.30 am due to the noise abatement regulation.
- Kai Tak Airport's cargo operations are the sixth largest in the world. Statistics for air transport breakdown are shown in Table 11.1.
- It is estimated that Kai Tak Airport's runway and parking apron will reach its maximum capacity by 1992. This could cost Hong Kong as much as HK$10 100 million in trade and other commercial benefits.
- Some expansion of the airport could be achieved by clearing the nearby temporary housing area and reclaiming land from Kowloon Bay in order to construct more aircraft parking aprons. Road widening and the construction of a second airport tunnel are also suggested to smooth the traffic both inside and outside the present Kai Tak Airport.
- However, due to the narrow gap between northern Kowloon and Lei Yue Mun on Hong Kong Island, there is no hope of building one more runway, which is regarded as a longer term solution to the airport.
- The removal of Kai Tak Airport would release an area of 250 hectares for redevelopment as housing.

A NEW AIRPORT FOR HONG KONG

residents caused by traffic congestion and noise pollution. It would also release much already reclaimed land for future housing.

> 8 What are the main problems to be faced in your country in terms of landuse and land management? Make a collection of newspaper headlines to illustrate the debates that are going on.

THE ISSUES TO STUDY

Although the conclusion was that Hong Kong needed to consider the building of a new airport to solve the environmental and economic problems faced by Kai Tak, this decision led people to consider other issues, including the following questions.

- What are the conditions for an ideal site of a new airport?
- How can Hong Kong decide on the best site for the new airport?
- What would be the impact of a new international airport development on the site selected?
- Would a new airport solve the problems of the present Kai Tak Airport completely?
- Would Hong Kong be creating new problems without solving the old problems?

The next activity will help you to join in these debates too.

> 9 Where to build the new airport? The list below discusses conditions that may need to be considered in choosing a suitable site for a new airport.
> a Do you think that the list of conditions is complete? Add to the list any new conditions that you think are necessary.
> b Using your revised list and the map (Figure 11.2), suggest where the new airport to replace Kai Tak should be built.

An ideal site for an airport

- The airport requires a large area of flat land which
  — is large enough to meet the predicted demand for air transport
  — is well linked with other parts of the local region
  — allows room for further expansion
  — has access to sufficient air space not over urban areas and outside established flight paths in case of emergency.
- The airport should be built so that its runways are parallel to the direction of the prevailing winds, but sheltered from typhoons.
- The airport should always have a high degree of air visibility. This may be affected by
  — heavy rainfall or fog
  — industrial pollution.
- The airport should be near the existing urban area so that labour and supporting services can be obtained easily.
- The airport should require minimal costs of construction, supporting infrastructure and land resumption, but offer the opportunity to maximise revenue creation.
- The location of the airport should minimise the air flights over urban areas.
- The airport should support the master plan of development of the larger region.
- The airport should not be a cause of environmental damage in its vicinity.

If you have found it difficult to help Hong Kong to find a suitable site to build a new airport, you are in the same situation as that in which the Hong Kong government found itself in the early 1980s. At that time, the government decided to concentrate on the expansion and development of the existing Kai Tak Airport. It seemed at that time that the problem was solved. However, in reality, the problem was just delayed.

Figure 11.6 The island of Chek Lap Kok with Lantau Island in the background

Figure 11.7 Peng Chau and its nearby islands—Lantau Island is on the right

In 1989, new forecasts showed that if nothing was done about reaching a decision on building a new airport, both Kai Tak and the whole of Hong Kong would face great economic problems by 1996. So, finally, the government took up two suggestions from the consultants who were invited to consider possible sites for a new airport for Hong Kong. The consultants suggested two sites for further consideration. These two sites are shown on Figure 11.2 as Chek Lap Kok and Peng Chau.

Deciding between the two sites

Information about the proposed airport site at Peng Chau Western Harbour

- Peng Chau has an area of 8500 square metres but is occupied by more local residents (about 10 000) than Chek Lap Kok. The cost to resettle these families will be very high. In the past, most of the people earned their living by making handicrafts, such as pottery, or running small-scale industries, such as making light bulbs. With rapid population growth in recent decades, more and more people are now working in the urban areas in Hong Kong.
- The small island has limited space for aircraft movement. Hence, an area of 27 square kilometres will have to be reclaimed for site construction. At the site, the water is over 7.3 metres deep and it is near to the fastest water flowing near Tsing Yi Island.
- After reclamation, the new airport will provide adequate scope for dual runways with 2000 metre separation. This satisfies the standard set by the International Civil Aviation Organisation of 1300 metres apart.
- The site is exposed to the prevailing easterly winds and this gives advantage to aircraft landing and taking off.
- The reclamation work will narrow the waterway between Lantau Island and Tsuen Wan. Thus, water currents will flow faster, which in turn will increase erosive power. As a result, more sediments will be brought into Victoria Harbour and aggravate the silting problem in the harbour.
- On the other hand, with more rapid water current, the purification of the water will be increased as the amount of dissolved oxygen in the water will be increased.
- The 1979 estimate of costs to construct the airport was HK$34 billion. The project will take nine years to complete.
- Its location is nearer than Chek Lap Kok to the existing city centre, about 10 kilometres.
- Some 55 kilometres of new roads will be needed. They can produce HK$1000 million a year as revenue.
- There will be approximately 5 square kilometres of land available for private property development. It will bring about HK$50 000 million in revenue.
- At night, the flight routes from this site will provide a good view over the beautiful scenery of Hong Kong.

Information about the proposed airport site at Chek Lap Kok

- Chek Lap Kok has an area of 2.5 square kilometres. The official population is around 400, but the actual number of inhabitants is less than 100. The small number of local residents means that the cost of land resumption will be lower. Most of the inhabitants are older residents or children whose parents work all week in other parts of Hong Kong. Market gardening and poultry keeping are the main economic activities on the island.
- It is sheltered against the prevailing easterly winds of Hong Kong by Lantau Peak but is exposed to attack from typhoons which come from the north-west or south-west.
- A runway on the island would have to be built north-east to south-west so that aircraft taking off and landing could avoid Lantau Peak. However, this does not make very good use of the prevailing easterly winds and so a longer runway will be needed.
- The first runway will be 3700 m in length and the parallel runway 3400 m, separated from each other by 900 m. (This is less than the international standard which requires that runways be 1300 m apart.) Nevertheless, the new airport will handle twice as many passengers and twice as much cargo as Kai Tak.
- An area of 17.7 square kilometres will have to be reclaimed. At the site, the water depth is less than 3.6 metres.
- Since reclamation is needed for site construction, the work will narrow the waterway between Lantau Island and Tuen Mun. Thus, water currents will flow faster, which in turn will increase the erosive power of the sea. As a result, more sediment will be brought into Victoria Harbour and aggravate the silting problem there.
- On the other hand, with more rapid water currents, the purification of the water can be increased as the amount of dissolved oxygen in the water increases.
- The 1979 estimate of costs to build the airport was HK$29 billion. The project will take nine years to complete.
- This airport site is 24 kilometres away from central Hong Kong. It will take thirty minutes to reach it by jet foil and about two hours by outlying island ferry link.
- It will be necessary to build 58 kilometres of new roads to link up the airport with the urban centres. These roads can produce HK$1060 million a year as revenue.
- Some 2.5 square kilometres of land will be made available for private property development and will be worth HK$7600 million.
- This project can help to develop one of the most remote areas of Hong Kong—Lantau Island.

A NEW AIRPORT FOR HONG KONG

> 10 Use the evidence provided above to help you decide which site should be adopted for the construction of the new airport. You should examine the evidence from the point of view of
> a local residents who may be affected
> b the Hong Kong Civil Aviation Authority
> c the civil engineer responsible for the construction
> d an economist employed by the Hong Kong government.

THE GOVERNMENT'S DECISION

In October 1989, the Hong Kong government finally decided to build the new airport at Chek Lap Kok. Depending on your point of view, your decision may have been different from the official one. The government's decision to choose Chek Lap Kok was probably not influenced by a desire to achieve least conflict, but to optimise the economic benefits. In fact, the 1989 government decision was not confined to finding a location for the new airport, but developed into a larger 'bold plan' for a Port and Airport Development Strategy (PADS). PADS has established a framework for the long term expansion of port and airport facilities, together with associated land uses and transport infrastructure. The plan includes a number of important elements

- to set up a Provisional Airport Authority early in 1990 to oversee matters related to the building of the new airport at Chek Lap Kok
- to outlay HK$127 billion to build the new airport at Chek Lap Kok with the first of two runways open in early 1997

Figure 11.8b   Fishing junks at Tung Chung pier

- to build a high-speed rail system and six-lane highway joining North Lantau and Tsing Yi Island with West Kowloon and onward to Hong Kong Island through a new Western Harbour Tunnel
- to build a new town for 150 000 people in the Tung Chung valley near the new airport site
- to build two new container terminals—terminal 8 on Stonecutters Island and terminal 9 on reclaimed land south-east of Tsing Yi Island
- to build a large breakwater between Lantau and Lamma Island, and dredge a new shipping channel west of Lamma.

The announcement of the bold plan raised even more questions. Can we work fast enough to complete the airport before Hong Kong returns to Chinese sovereignty in 1997, especially as it will involve so much major engineering work? Is it financially sound to launch such a bold plan? To what extent will the building of the new airport disturb the beautiful green islands of Chek Lap Kok and Lantau? What the government calls the 'bold plan' is nicknamed 'the rosy garden' by local people. Can the environmental and economic problems of Kai Tak be solved by moving to Chek Lap Kok?

Figure 11.8a   Inlets such as this on the east and west of the island will soon be reclaimed to give land for the twin runways

Figure 11.8c   A quiet spot away from the urban hassle

Present and future

11 Figure 11.8 shows three aspects of Chek Lap Kok and Tung Chung village shortly before reclamation work began in February 1991. For each photograph, write one or two sentences to describe your feelings about these places.
12 Figure 11.9 shows graffiti on Chek Lap Kok. One Tung Chung villager commented: 'If there is an airport, the area will be turned into a second Kowloon'. Discuss how life on Chek Lap Kok and in Tung Chung will be changed by the construction of the new airport. To what extent do you consider these changes to be good or bad, desirable or undesirable?

THE FUTURE

Hong Kong is a tiny dot on the world map. Unlike many of the other developed and developing countries, Hong Kong's survival does not rely on natural resources, but rather on the attitude of the Hong Kong people towards solving their problems.

The most obvious advantage for Hong Kong to prosper is the very favourable international location which attracts the people, cargo, capital and technology needed to sustain economic prosperity. Hence, Hong Kong relies heavily on the viable operation of the airport. However, Kai Tak Airport has effectively reached saturation point even with the considerable development and expansion over the past two decades. Despite awareness of the many implications of either building or not building a new airport, and of the further implications of deciding where one could be built, Hong Kong had ultimately to reach a decision. While not everyone agrees with the decision, the government has decided that a new airport can no longer be shelved and delayed. However, this means that many other questions must be answered, such as where to build the new airport and what to consider in order to avoid new problems.

A decision has been made and the construction work on preparing the island of Chek Lap Kok has begun. However, the situation is still not finalised as the Chinese government in Beijing, who will take over responsibility for Hong Kong in 1997, has expressed concern over the great cost of the project and whether Hong Kong will be left heavily in debt. This new factor must now be included in renewed discussions if the new airport is to open in 1997 as proposed. It may be that further changes to the plan will still be necessary. The lesson to be learned from the long history of Hong Kong's airport debate is that there is unlikely to be any perfect solution to such a large problem, but that if we continue to explore many possibilities with open minds, we may eventually reach a peaceful agreement.

Figure 11.9a This sign on the back of a pig sty says: 'The blood and sweat of the islanders is destroyed in one day'

Figure 11.9b The sign on the gate of the only school on Chek Lap Kok, now deserted, reads: 'My home is destroyed by the building of "the Rosy Garden"'

13 Make a list of major planning decisions in your own country for which there appears to be no general agreement. Study the processes that are being adopted to reach a satisfactory conclusion. Can you think of ways to improve the decision making process so that more people are involved and better decisions may be reached?

CHAPTER 12

INDUSTRIAL POLLUTION IN TAIWAN

Linda Chung-Ling Ouyang

Although economic growth is important in the modern world, the most important elements in our lives are water, air and earth. If the human race allows these to become polluted, it will pay a high price—it may even dig its own grave. Taiwan has changed from being a poor, mainly farming society to being a modern industrial state in a little over thirty years. However, this rapid progress has been at a cost to the natural environment. This chapter describes and explains some of the problems that have been experienced in Taiwan and the lessons that have been learned.

The industrial revolution that began in Europe in the nineteenth century led to major changes in the patterns of human economic activity. The standard of living in countries that embraced industrialisation increased dramatically. These countries became known as 'developed', whereas countries without high levels of industrialisation were described as 'developing'. It is not surprising that many countries have seen industrialisation as the best means for progress and there is no doubt that it has proved to be a panacea for many.

Table 12.1 shows how the contribution of agriculture, industry and services to the economies of seven countries has changed since 1960. It also shows the gross domestic product (GDP) per head for each country. GDP per head

Figure 12.1   The island of Taiwan and its location

Table 12.1 The contribution of agriculture, industry and services, selected economies, 1960–88

Country	Agriculture				Industry				Services				GDP US$/head
	1960	1970	1981	1988	1960	1970	1981	1988	1960	1970	1981	1988	
United States	4	3	2	2	38	35	32	29	58	62	66	69	19 780
Japan	13	6	3	3	45	47	41	42	43	47	56	55	21 040
Korea	37	27	14	11	20	30	41	44	43	44	45	45	2 099
Taiwan	29	16	6	4	29	41	50	43	43	45	44	53	6 335
Philippines	26	28	27	—	28	30	33	—	46	43	40	—	630
Thailand	40	28	17	—	19	25	30	—	42	46	53	—	1 000
India	47	43	35	27	19	20	27	27	28	28	38	46	330

represents the total value of all the goods and services produced in a country divided by the number of people.

> 1 For each country shown in Table 12.1, select a way of illustrating how the contributions of agriculture, industry and services to the economy have changed since 1960. Comment on the relationship between the GDP per head and the contribution of agriculture to the economy.
> 2 Discuss the reasons why service industries are the major contributors to the economies of each of these countries.

Manufacturing industries may be divided into **light industry**, which makes goods light in weight or small in size—such as television sets or refrigerators—and **heavy industry**, which makes products large in size or heavy in weight—such as steel bars and railway locomotives. Both are very important to industrial development.

Although there are many benefits to be derived from industrial growth, there are also problems. Not all things produced in factories are useful. Some of them are waste products and are harmful. Some of these even cause environmental problems. We call this pollution.

> 3 List the light and heavy industries that are to be found in your area. For each industry, discuss the types of pollution caused and the effects on the natural environment.

INDUSTRIAL DEVELOPMENT IN TAIWAN

Taiwan is a mountainous island about 200 kilometres from the coast of mainland China. The island occupies a total area of 35 960 square kilometres and has a population of about 22 million people.

From 1895 to 1945, Taiwan was a dependency of Japan. During this period, Taiwan developed as a colony and although there was some investment in housing and transport, there was little industrial development. The island was primarily an agricultural community.

As a result of the conflict which led to the creation of the People's Republic of China as a communist state, the Chinese nationalists under Chiang Kai-Shek took over Taiwan in 1949 and, with the help of the United States, established a separate economy. China still regards the issue of Taiwan's independence as an unresolved domestic dispute.

With the benefit of the money, technology and skills brought from mainland China, and aid from the United States, Taiwan began to recover from the effects of the war very rapidly. Textile and food manufacturing became particularly important.

Between 1953 and 1963, industry in Taiwan focused on providing the food and building materials needed for its rapidly growing population. Electricity generation was also developed and this provided the basis for the industrial growth which followed.

In 1964, aid from the United States ended and Taiwan began to look for international trade to maintain its economic growth. Many light industries were established to provide goods for export—particularly electronic products, textiles and plastics. These industries were based on the ready supply of electricity and had access to a relatively cheap labour supply in the many rural villages. Heavy industries, such as steel making, car and machine manufacturing, also began to grow.

After 1974, an international energy crisis, global economic recession, increasing wage costs in Taiwan and increasing competition with other developing countries led to a slow-down in Taiwan's economic growth. The Taiwan government, therefore, began to promote more heavy industry and high technology light industries in which skill added great value to the finished product. The success of this policy is shown by the list of products that are exported by Taiwan. The list includes: cars, aeroplanes, ships, petrochemicals, iron and steel, machinery, electrical appliances, computers, consumer electronics, textiles, garments, sporting goods, footwear, toys, processed food and handicrafts.

In 1991, Taiwan's exports grew by 12.6 per cent over 1990. This made Taiwan the twelfth largest exporter in the world. Table 12.2 gives more details of Taiwan's economic performance in 1990 while Table 12.3 shows the pattern of international trade of Taiwan.

INDUSTRIAL POLLUTION IN TAIWAN

Table 12.2 Taiwan's economic output, 1991

Economic performance	1991
Gross national product (GNP) (US$ billion)	178.4
GNP per head	8 718
GNP growth rate (%)	7.0
Inflation rate (%)	4.0

Major output	1991
Cement (million t)	18.46
Colour television sets	2 098 900
Computer monitors	7 277 406
Cotton yarn (t)	203 937
Ethylene (t)	775 662
Integrated circuits (billion)	2.5
Artificial fibres (million t)	2.57
Motorcycles	1 055 297
Passenger cars	353 888
PVC (t)	920 954
Sewing machines	2 514 727
Steel bars (million t)	5.2
Telephone sets	13 992 431

Table 12.3 The international trade of Taiwan, 1991

Major exports	%	Major markets	%
Electric/electronics	23.6	United States	32.4
Textiles	15.3	European community	16.0
Machinery	8.6	Hong Kong	12.7
Metals/metal products	7.8	Japan	12.4
Rubber/plastic products	6.6	Singapore	3.3
Footwear	5.2		

Total exports, 1991: US$77.0 billion

Major imports	%	Main suppliers	%
Electric/electronics	18.2	Japan	29.2
Consumer goods	12.1	United States	23.0
Chemicals	10.7	European Union	13.3
Metals/metal products	10.1	Australia	3.0
Machinery	9.8	Hong Kong	2.6
Transport equipment	7.1	Singapore	2.6

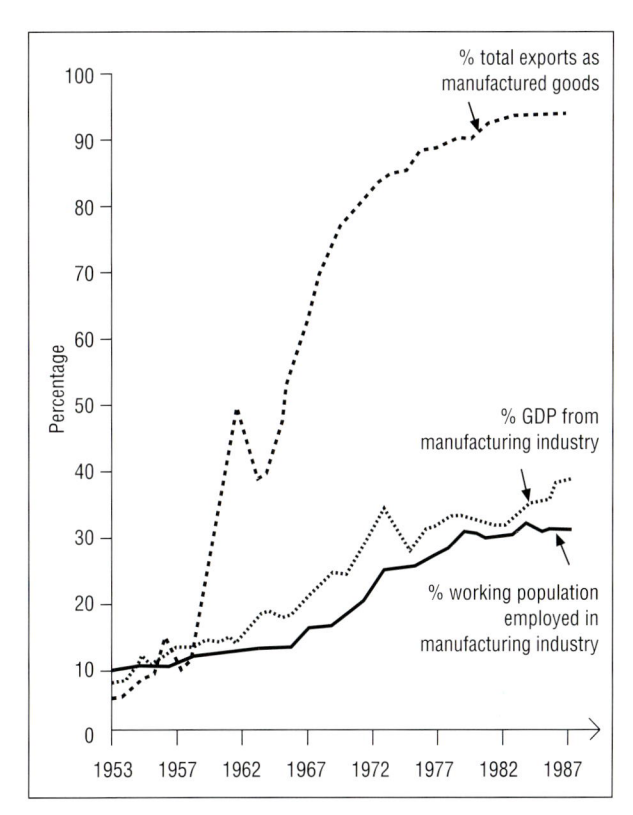

Figure 12.2 Industrialisation in Taiwan, 1953–87

4 Figure 12.2 shows how the proportion of Taiwan workers employed in manufacturing industry, the contribution of manufacturing industry to GDP and the contribution of manufacturing industry to Taiwan exports increased from 1953 to 1987.
   a On a copy of this graph, label the stages in industrialisation as described above.
   b Comment on the changes in the rate of industrialisation at each stage in the process. What changes do you think may occur in the future?

THE PROBLEMS OF DEVELOPMENT

Although the GDP and the standard of living in Taiwan have risen quickly, environmental problems have sometimes been neglected. Investors have not always calculated the cost of maintaining high environmental quality and many serious environmental pollution problems have arisen.

Figure 12.3 Effects on the environment of small workshops and factories

5 Discuss the extent to which industries in your country have polluted the natural environment. What arrangements are there to prevent such pollution occurring?

The atmospheric and water pollution is visible and is therefore relatively easy to prevent. Not all pollution, however, is so easily identified.

Cadmium pollution in Taoyuan prefecture

Taoyuan prefecture lies to the south-west of Taipei City in the north of Taiwan. This area is on the edge of the growing urban and industrial area of Taipei and in the early 1980s already had significant industrial development. Figure 12.4 shows how the town has changed in recent years, but much of the rest of the prefecture area is still occupied by farmland and villages consisting of houses like the one shown in Figure 12.5. Many of the farmers grew rice in their fields around the factories. As Figure 12.6 shows, much of Taoyuan already has over 75 per cent of its people living in the urban area.

Figure 12.4a An old street in Taipei

Figure 12.4b Taipei today

Figure 12.5 An old house like those in villages in Taoyuan

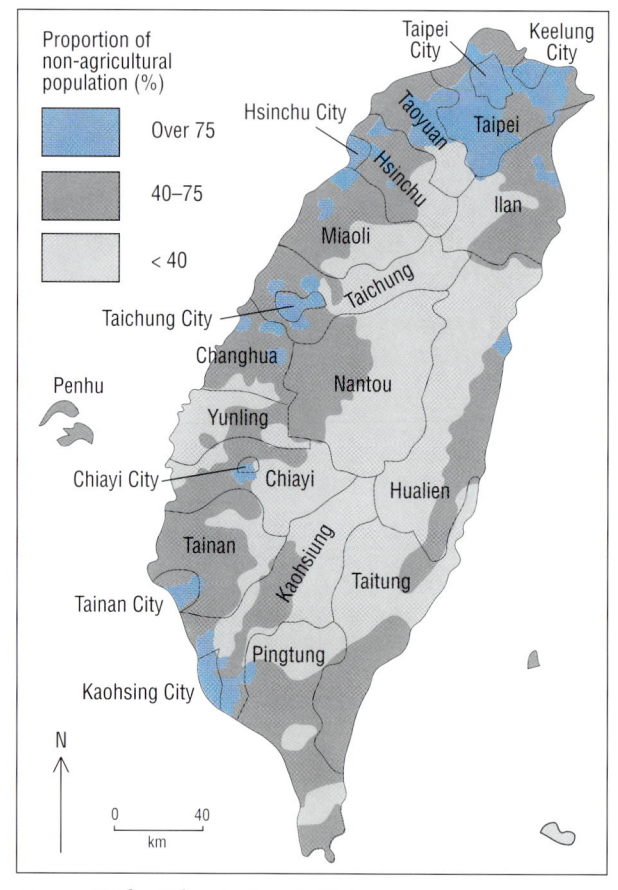

Figure 12.6 Urbanisation in Taiwan

By 1983, new factories had been located on the edges of many villages. The processes used in these factories involved the production of cadmium, lead, zinc and stearic acid. Plastic stabilisers were used to remove waste water.

In Tatan village, Kuanyin county, and Chunfu village in Luchu county, the waste water from the factories was allowed to run away into the irrigation ditches used by local farmers.

The cadmium-polluted water soaked into the soil and was taken up by the rice plants. Although the rice grew well and looked and tasted just like any other, it was poi-

Figure 12.7 A chemical factory on the edge of a village in Taoyuan

Figure 12.8 Former rice fields must be left idle for years until the cadmium poison breaks down

sonous to human beings. The effects are not felt immediately, but people who eat cadmium rice for some time develop a disease called osteomalacia which causes aching all over the body.

By the time that the Environmental Protection Administration of the Taiwan government discovered the cause of the pollution, the soil was too polluted to be used. Today it is left idle. The cadmium pollution will break down in the soil eventually, at which time the fields may be used once more. In the meantime, however, the farmers in the village have lost their livelihoods and many have had to move to other villages. This fate has befallen the twenty-seven families who gained their livelihoods from the 17 hectares polluted in Tatan and all the families who lived on the 200 hectares that were polluted in Chunfu.

THE FUTURE

Taiwan has gone through a number of stages in its industrialisation in a very short time. Thirty years ago, people in Taiwan wanted and needed the basics of modern life such as food, clothes, houses and transport. Later they wanted higher incomes and this was achieved for many people by increasing exports of the goods needed elsewhere in the world. Now, Taiwan sees its future in developing the next generation of high technology products. This new type of industry, and the people who will work in it, demands high environmental standards in air, water and food.

In the early growth stages of Taiwan's economy, many small factories producing components for larger firms were established in agricultural areas. The local planning authorities in these rural areas did not understand the processes that were used in these factories and did not appreciate the need for careful planning and disposal of wastes. In recent years, the Taiwan government has expanded the Environmental Protection Administration and has created strict laws to protect the environment, together with inspectors to ensure that the laws are obeyed. In some cases, pollution or the abuse of natural resources in the past has done irreversible damage but planning for the future can solve many problems and prevent the mistakes of the past being repeated.

Developed and developing countries face different problems. Countries generally try to solve their most pressing problems first. The main problems facing many developing countries are poverty, inadequate housing and an insufficient food supply. The aim of the governments of such countries is usually economic development. Once these problems are solved, the developed countries may concentrate on raising the standard of living of their people as well as on the protection of the environment. Effective policies require political and social planning as well as economic planning. Taiwan has achieved a high rate of economic growth in the past thirty years. Taiwan is now determined to achieve high standards of environmental consciousness and care.

However, such care costs money. In the face of rising production and labour costs in Taiwan, its businessmen have looked overseas to set up new factories, especially in Southeast Asia and southern mainland China. More than 1000 Taiwan-owned factories have been set up in South-east Asian countries such as Thailand, Malaysia, the Philippines and Indonesia since 1987. More recently, many Taiwan companies have moved their less skilled and more labour intensive industries to mainland China where wages are lower, many people need jobs and the language is the same.

6 Do you regard Taiwan's investment in other developing countries as representing a sharing of progress or causing increased pollution elsewhere?
7 Do you agree that countries concentrate on solving their economic problems before their environmental ones? To what extent did the countries of Europe and North America go through the same process in the nineteenth century? Discuss ways in which the developing countries of today may be helped to avoid the 'pollution stage' of economic development.

CHAPTER 13

BULGARIA: AT A GEOGRAPHICAL CROSSROADS

Dimitar Kanchev

Human beings are generally very sociable animals and we often describe ourselves in terms of the groups to which we belong. These groups may be based on the area of land in which we live, our religion, our race or some other grouping which is important to us. One of the most important ways in which we are grouped is by the country in which we live. Atlases include maps which show the various countries. Some countries have been very stable over long periods of history, while differences within other countries have led to great instability.

Problems of instability in our political organisations form one of the major issues facing the world. Studies of how the spatial aspects, or the 'geography', of a country change as a result of the ways in which people define their loyalties and political decisions both within a country's own borders and in the wider world show the importance of both history and geography in helping us to understand this major issue.

This chapter discusses how Bulgaria has changed through its long history while still maintaining its identity.

THE GEOGRAPHICAL LOCATION OF BULGARIA

The changes in Bulgaria's development are closely associated with its geographical location. Bulgaria is situated in south-eastern Europe and occupies one-fifth of the area of

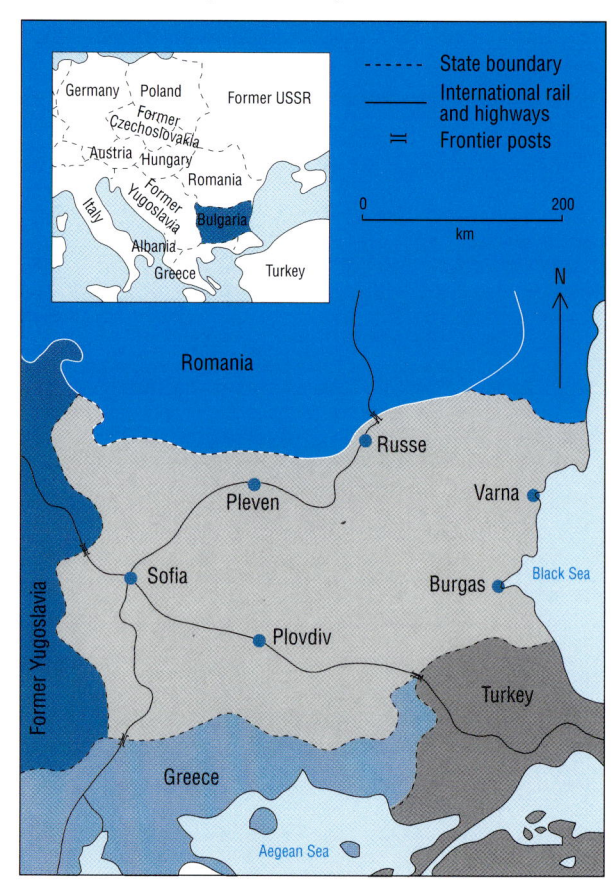

Figure 13.1 The location of Bulgaria—at an international crossroads

the Balkan Peninsula. Bulgaria is one of six Balkan countries and is located near the Mediterranean basin, without having an outlet to it.

The northern border between Bulgaria and Romania is the River Danube and to the east lies the Black Sea. The Danube is a strategic waterway and permits Bulgaria to trade with Germany, Austria, Slovakia, Hungary, the former Yugoslavia, Romania and the former Soviet Union. A railway and highway bridge in the town of Russe facilitated close ties with the countries of eastern Europe for much of this century. There are many islands in the Danube and since the border follows its midstream, some of them remain in Bulgaria and others in Romania. Many of these islands are still under dense forests of willow and poplar, while others provide excellent conditions for growing vegetables.

The eastern Black Sea boundary is 378 kilometres long. The Black Sea is a semi-closed intra-continental basin, separated from the Mediterranean by the narrow strait of Bosphorus. The Black Sea connects Bulgaria with the former Soviet Union and Turkey while the straits of Bosphorus and Dardanelles give the country access to the Mediterranean region. The Black Sea is warm and its many sunny days in summer, sandy beaches, scenery and resorts, attract large numbers of tourists, especially from eastern Europe. However, as it is an intra-continental basin, the Black Sea is faced with serious ecological problems, partially caused by the heavily polluted Danube and Dnieper rivers which flow through some of the most industrialised areas in the world.

In contrast to the northern and eastern boundaries, which are natural, the western and southern boundaries of Bulgaria are entirely land frontiers that were forcibly imposed after the First World War when Bulgaria was among the defeated countries. The western boundary was defined to the benefit of the former Yugoslavia while the southern boundary lies 40 to 50 kilometres from the Aegean Sea. This fact can be explained by historical and political reasons.

Despite these problems of its frontiers, Bulgaria's geographical location means that it lies on a major international crossroads. Figure 13.1 shows how Bulgaria forms a bridge between Europe and Asia. Furthermore, the direct railway and motorway connections from northern and eastern Europe to the Mediterranean region pass through the capital city of Sofia. Despite its location in the western part of Bulgaria, Sofia may be regarded as a major nodal point both for Bulgaria and for Europe.

Before continuing with the study of Bulgaria, a number of broader issues about political geography must be considered.

COUNTRIES AND NATIONS

When we speak of a country, we are often thinking of both the area of land as shown on the map as well as the people who live on that area of land. This means that the words 'country' and 'nation' are often used as if they mean the same thing. While this assumption is true for many of the countries of the world, it is not true for all. Some countries, such as France, Egypt, Japan and Uruguay, have boundaries which come very close to enclosing true nations of people. Other countries, such as the United Kingdom, Switzerland, Kenya, Uganda and China, enclose areas which do not coincide with the distribution of members of single true nations. Furthermore, while countries may change their boundaries and may even disappear as a result of some political upheaval, nations of people continue to live within the changed boundaries and country names. Some nations, such as the Kurdish people, have never occupied a country of their own, but live as minority groups in Turkey, Iraq, Iran, Syria and Armenia.

In order to understand how people feel about countries, we must therefore distinguish between our nationality as people and the state, or political organisation, in which we live. As explained above, these will be the same thing for many people. For many others, however, the two words mean different things. In these circumstances, the problem of divided loyalties may emerge for both the individuals concerned and for the states in which they live.

What is a nation?

A nation is a group of people who share cultural characteristics such as language and racial origins, and values such as a common religion. As the political geography of Europe developed, a series of nation–states were created, both by negotiation and by force. A number of these, such as France, were states in which a single nation formed a single state. Other states, such as Switzerland, Belgium and Great Britain, contained people whose traditional languages, religion, history and cultural backgrounds were very different.

What is a state?

Most of us are members of one or other of the states that are marked on the world map. There are also many people in the world who are not accepted as members of any particu-

Figure 13.2 The Black Sea coast at the Albena resort

lar country or state or who have left a country in which they have lived for some reason. These people may be described as 'stateless'. Refugees who have left their country of origin and who are unable to return there are stateless people.

The countries that are shown on the world map are independent states. Our maps tell us that states are areas of land and water with clearly defined, internationally recognised boundaries within which a group of people lives with its own political system. It also usually means that at least some other countries recognise the independence of a particular state.

However, states are not just areas of the world's surface in which groups of people live. They are regions of cities, towns and hinterlands, linked by communications networks of railways, roads, telephone lines and air routes. They have administrative subdivisions, school and hospital systems. They are a maze of circulation and movement as people, raw materials, manufactured products and information flow to and fro.

States exist to serve their people, but they also demand their taxes, their obedience to the laws and even their loyal service in times of war. To succeed in all these things, a state must create a sense of unity and pride.

This definition of a state goes beyond the notion of an area with clear boundaries. The political geographer, J. Gottman, suggested that the real difference between one country and another can be described as its **iconography**. An icon is a symbol of some religious, historical, social or political memory that is shared by the majority of people, often with pride. Figure 13.3 shows some of the national symbols of Bulgaria. The map is striped with the national colours (white, green, red), the lion is the national symbol and the number 1300 indicates that Bulgaria dates its foundation from 1300 years ago. The girl in the picture is wearing traditional national dress and is picking roses. Bulgaria is known as the 'country of roses'.

These symbols are formally or officially recognised, but countries may also have informal or unofficial symbols by which they are known elsewhere in the world and which their people regard as representing important features of their lives. In Australia, the tune of 'Waltzing Matilda' is an unofficial anthem and is better known than the 'official' national anthem. For many years, blue jeans and Coca Cola were regarded as a symbol of young people in the United States and today these products have been adopted by young people across the world as symbolising a 'youth culture'.

Many countries have symbols such as these and support for them may be more important in creating unity than a shared language, history or racial background. Despite the importance of symbols, however, race, language and ethnicity have had a great influence on history and some of the most stable states on earth have been identified as nation–states. A nation–state is one which mainly comprises people of a single nation.

> 1 With a friend, make a list of the official symbols that represent your country and then a list of the informal symbols that you regard as representing what makes your country special. Discuss how you feel about each symbol and which are most important for you.

The origin of nation–states

Few of the current state boundaries marked on maps of the world have existed for anywhere near as long as the patterns of culture, ethnicity and languages. Over time, boundaries, countries' names, and even those who have been allowed to live in particular areas, have changed. Figure 13.4 shows the national boundaries in Europe that existed over 400 years ago, those that came into existence between 200 and 400 years ago and those that have only come into existence within the past 200 years. The boundaries between France and Spain along the western Pyrenees, between Spain and Portugal, and of Switzerland and the Low

Figure 13.3 The national symbols of Bulgaria

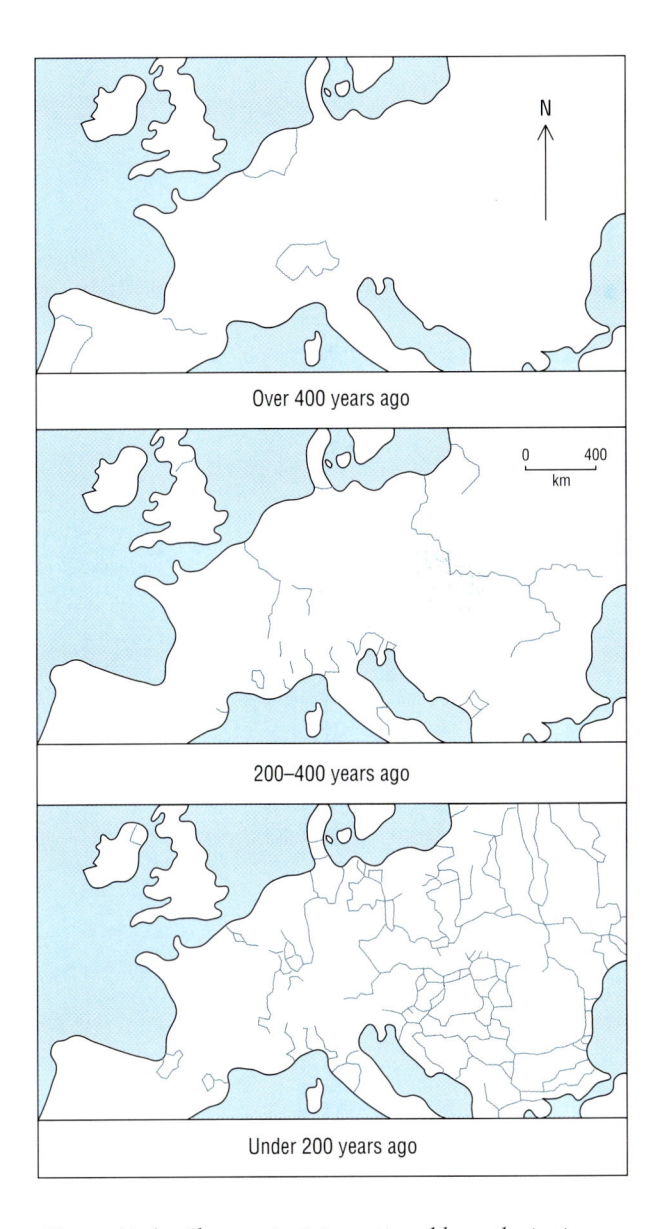

Figure 13.4 Changes in international boundaries in Europe since the fifteenth century (after Haggett, 1975)

2 Investigate the boundaries of your own country and the ways in which they have changed throughout history. What kinds of boundaries does your country have? (For example, physical boundaries such as sea, river, or mountain ranges or boundaries that have been decided arbitrarily on land.) Which of these boundaries have endured the longest?

Despite the creation of the modern pattern of states across Europe, the complex pattern of language groups remains. The most common language group in Europe is the Indo-European family and about half of the world's people speak languages within this group. Figure 13.5 shows the main languages in this family and the links between them. However, some parts of Europe speak languages that come from the Ural-Altaic family. These include Finnish, Basque and Turkish. As people move between countries to live and work, and the amount of communication between people increases, language becomes less important as a means of discriminating between them. Many students reading this book in English will speak other languages with their friends and in their homes.

3 Carry out a survey to discover how many languages are spoken by the people in your class or your school. Why is there this range of languages among your colleagues? Are different languages used for different purposes?

During the nineteenth century, the idea of the nation–state came to be regarded as an ideal form of government across the world. Japan, already a single nation state, wanted to emulate European achievements, undertook major reorganisation and even moved its capital city from the ancient city of Kyoto to the coastal town of Edo, and renamed it Tokyo. Similarly, when the old colonial empires disintegrated, many of the peoples of Africa wanted to achieve nation–states based on the European model and thus tried to create unified countries from still-divided peoples, secure their national territories and boundaries, develop economic and other systems of organisation, and assert their national strength—often by creating expensive military machines. In Africa particularly, the old colonial boundaries that marked the lines between the opposing European armies were kept as the borders of the newly emerged states, even though they bore no relationship to the ethnic boundaries of the people who lived there.

COUNTRIES, NATIONS AND STATES IN THE BALKAN PENINSULA

Until 1990, the state boundaries of Europe that were set after the end of the Second World War appeared to be firmly established. In the last few years, however, Germany, which had been divided into the German Federal Republic in the

Countries have changed little since the fifteenth century, while others, such as those between France and Germany and those of eastern Europe, have changed a great deal.

In the seventeenth century, Europe was divided into a very complicated patchwork of small states, most of which had ill-defined boundaries. Powerful royal families struggled for supremacy and most of the states were very politically unstable. As a result, there were frequent wars and many of the governments repressed their peoples. As trade, agriculture and industry developed, merchants and business people demanded political recognition. Money and influence became more and more concentrated in the cities and many European countries increased both their power and wealth by taking over large areas elsewhere in the world as colonies.

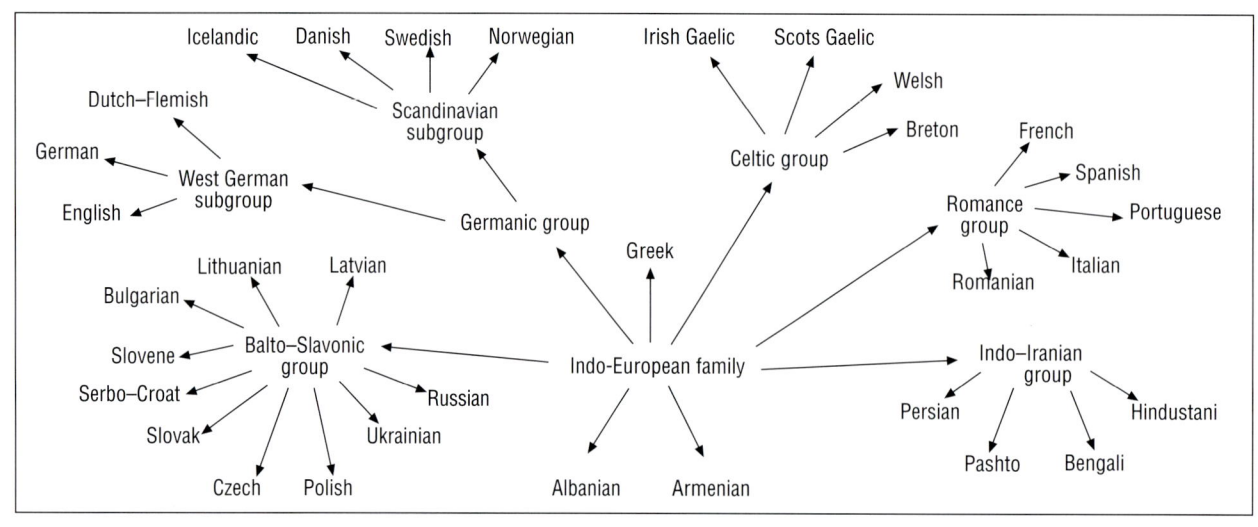

Figure 13.5 The Indo-European family of languages (after Haggett, 1975)

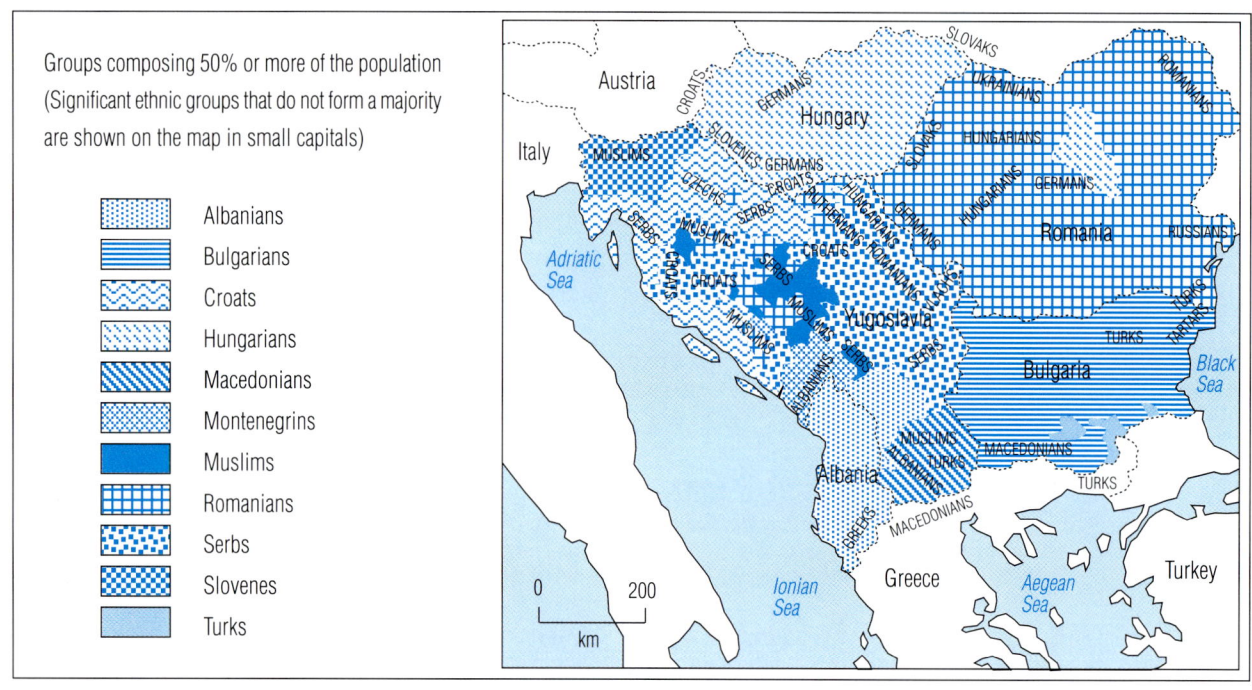

Figure 13.6 South-eastern European ethnic groupings

west and the German Democratic Republic in the east, has been reunited, while the countries of the former Yugoslavia, which was a single state for over half a century, have become split into a series of smaller independent states according to ethnic and language divisions.

While the reunification of Germany has been achieved relatively peacefully, the division of the former Yugoslavia has been accompanied by much bloodshed and misery. The complicated pattern of different ethnic groups in the former Yugoslavia offers some explanation of the problems that have occurred in that area while the relative homogeneity of Bulgaria may give some clue to the stability of that country.

In 1993, Bulgaria acknowledged the national boundaries established in 1945 and did not make any territorial claims on her neighbours. However, the people of Bulgaria are well aware that during the twentieth century the countries of Europe have fared very differently. Some have been favoured by being able to annex territories, others, like Bulgaria, have been deprived of land which they had previously governed. Furthermore, while the frontiers between the Scandinavian countries, for example, are symbolic, frontiers between countries on the Balkan Peninsula have traditionally been barriers.

Historical background to national boundaries

Bulgaria is one of the ancient states in Europe, founded 1300 years ago, but for five centuries it was under Ottoman (Turkish) rule. The Russo–Turkish war of liberation in 1878 put an end to the domination of the Ottoman Empire, freed Bulgaria and restored its autonomy. Immediately after the liberation neither the Great Powers nor the neighbouring countries opposed the necessity of stretching Bulgaria's southern boundary to the Aegean Sea. Later, several wars broke out to unite the territories settled by Bulgarians, but all transformations concerning the southern frontier were to the detriment of Bulgaria.

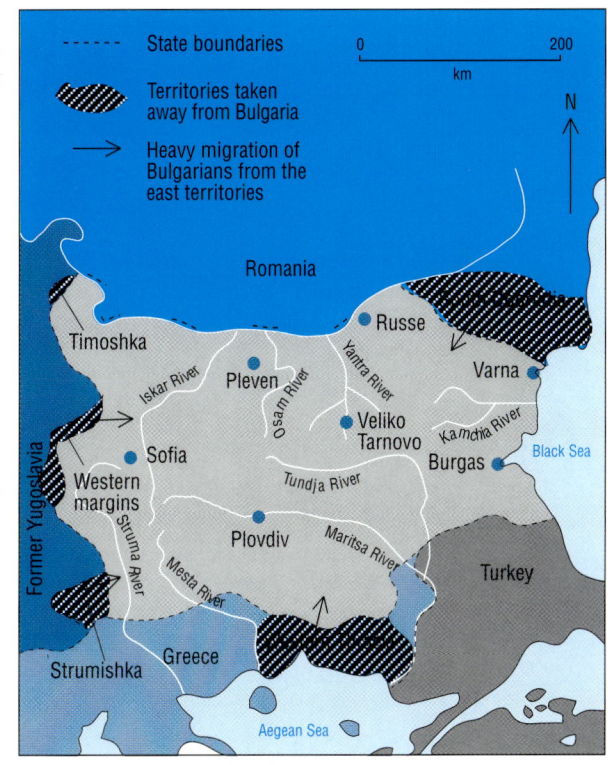

Figure 13.7 Bulgaria's boundaries

In 1913, after a war against Serbia, Greece and Romania, Bulgaria lost South Dobrudja to the north and most of Macedonia to the west. The end of the First World War brought a real national catastrophe to Bulgaria because Western Thracia was taken away and, hence, Bulgaria was cut off from the Aegean Sea. At this time, many Bulgarians migrated from the areas that changed hands back within Bulgaria's new boundaries. The loss of the lands bordering the Aegean Sea had an adverse effect on both Bulgaria's foreign trade and agriculture.

In 1940 Bulgaria concluded a peace treaty with Romania according to which it gained the return of South Dobrudja. The agreement required that 70 000 Bulgarians, living in North Dobrudja, should resettle into Bulgaria and that the Romanian people in South Dobrudja should move back to Romania. Those Bulgarians, who migrated from North Dobrudja, got plots of land in South Dobrudja and some of them went to live in the big towns (in Varna there is a housing estate still called 'Dobrudjanski'). The main crops that grow in South Dobrudja are maize and wheat and therefore this region is known as Bulgaria's granary. This exchange of people and territory is a good example of how a complex international political conflict can be solved peacefully.

4 The exchange of territory and people solved the political problem of the boundaries, but what about the people who had to move their homes? Discuss the feelings of the people who were involved in this exchange.
5 Many people in the world move countries because they are no longer comfortable with the political situation. Some migrate voluntarily and some become refugees. Where do the migrants and refugees in your country come from? Discover the main reasons for them wanting to move into your country.

The development of the Balkan countries after their liberation from Turkish rule was dictated by the Great Powers of England, France, Germany, Russia and Austro–Hungary. German and Russian influence was felt most strongly in Bulgaria, French influence was felt in Serbia, while English influence was greatest in Greece. The effects of these influences were felt also in the years following 1945, after the Second World War, when the southern boundary of Bulgaria with Greece and Turkey turned into a border-line dividing the communist Warsaw–Pact countries and the western NATO countries. The constant opposition of the two large military and political blocs in Europe was the main reason why Bulgaria's southern and western boundaries were fortified. These fortifications prevented communication across the frontier other than at specially prepared frontier posts.

6 Imagine that you and your family have lived in Bulgaria for many generations. How would you feel about the changes that have occurred to the boundaries of your country in the past century?
7 Discuss ways in which problems of national boundaries may be solved without resulting in war.
8 Discuss the reasons for creating boundaries between people of different ethnic groups.
9 Make a list of the various ethnic groups that live in your country. What is the relationship between these ethnic groups? How can the differences between the various ethnic groups in a country be minimised for the good of people of all ethnic backgrounds?

Changes since 1989

On 10 November 1989, the totalitarian communist system in Bulgaria was overthrown. Numerous meetings were organised and joined by hundreds of thousands of people. Bulgaria, like the other eastern European countries, took the road to democracy. A new parliament was established by free elections, a pluralistic society came into existence, great progress was made in guaranteeing human rights, and a painful transition began from central planning to market economy.

The Bulgarian government adopted a foreign policy of non-commitment and priority was given to integrating Bulgaria within European political and economic structures. The so-called 'Europeanisation of the Balkan Peninsula' was under way. At first it was believed that the borders between the Balkan nations would cease to perform isolating functions and would promote economic and cultural links. However, the heritage of the past has proved to have a strong influence on interstate relations in this part of Europe and old animosities between different ethnic groups have flared up again in some areas. Bulgaria itself, with its long history as a nation–state, shared history and relatively homogeneous ethnic mix has remained stable.

THE PRESENT AND THE FUTURE

Under the new circumstances, how is the geographical location of Bulgaria likely to influence Bulgaria's future development? In recent decades, there has been a strong move in north-western Europe towards creating the European Union (formerly the European Community) in which the participating countries agree to maintain their own national identities while reducing the importance of their national boundaries as barriers to the movement of people, goods and ideas.

Bulgaria would like to move closer to these countries and its position as a bridge between Asia and Europe and as a nodal point for land transport will encourage this change. Plans are already in hand for the European Union to encourage the further development of pipelines, highways and railways (allowing 250 kilometre per hour speeds), stretching from east to west and from north to south. These will cross Bulgaria.

The big navigable river Danube will play an increasingly important role in the trade of both the European Union and Bulgaria. Completion of the canals which link the rivers Rhine, Main and Danube to form a huge trans-European waterway system will connect Bulgaria and the Black Sea not only with the mid-European countries but also with western European countries. It is likely that the Bulgarian ports of Russe, Lom and Vidin will attain greater significance.

Until 1989 Bulgaria maintained economic links primarily with the Soviet Union and the countries of the eastern bloc. Now it is working to reorient its exports to the western European market. The trade relations with its old partners will be given further impetus as well but they will be based on the principle of mutual economic benefit and will not be subject to political and ideological aspirations.

There are also interesting possibilities relating to the southern boundary. Bulgaria badly needs an outlet to the Aegean Sea and so to the Mediterranean. As Bulgarian–Greek relations become more friendly, Bulgaria could be allowed to use some ports like Thessalonika and Kavala. The practice of countries exporting through the ports of their neighbours has been common in western Europe for many years and Bulgarians hope the Balkan countries will be able to enjoy similar opportunities.

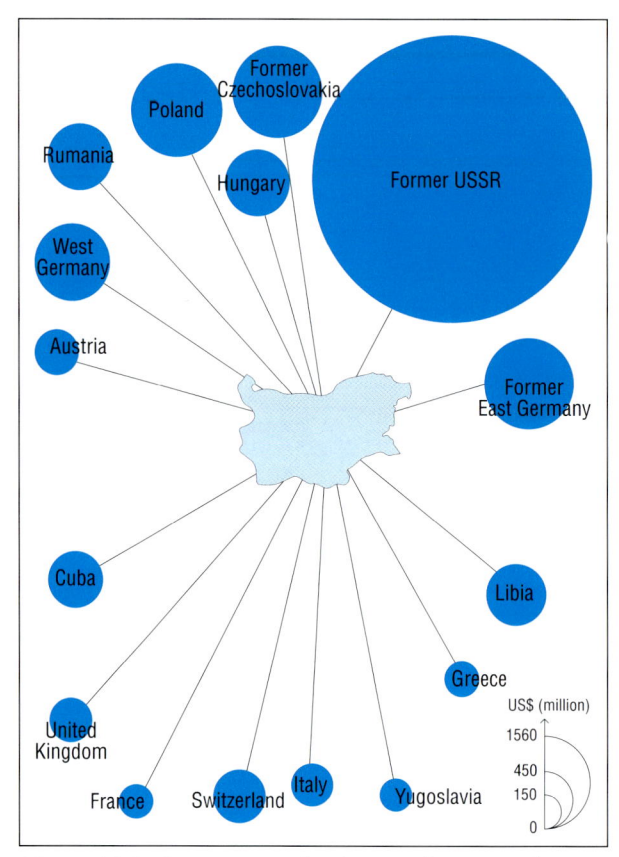

Figure 13.8 Destination of Bulgaria's foreign trade before 1989

Economic and cultural exchanges between the Bulgarian, Greek and Macedonian towns along the frontiers will go on at accelerated rates. For instance, the towns of Kardjali and Giumurdjina, Smolyan and Ksanti, Petrich and Seres-Strumitsa can form 'pairs' on the basis of intensive economic and cultural ties. This is likely to happen because, on the one hand, they are too far from the major centres in their own countries, and on the other, they belong to geographical unities, artificially divided by political boundaries.

Despite the history of conflict in the Balkans that has come about largely through the artificial creation of state boundaries that conflict with people's ethnic, cultural and language loyalties, Bulgaria is now in a position to lead the other countries of the Balkans and the former Warsaw Pact countries into a new relationship with the other countries of Europe. This unity will be mutually beneficial and will contribute to strengthening the peace of the Balkan Peninsula and to the creation of a new Europe, while maintaining the pride and traditions of ethnic origins and nationhood.

CHAPTER 14

THE DIAMOND TRADE: RICH WORLD– POOR WORLD

● ● ● ● ● ● ● ● ●

Ann Verhetsel

In 1992, more than one in every ten women in the United States and Japan acquired a piece of diamond jewellery. However, although diamonds have been valued for their beauty and strength from ancient times, it has only been relatively recently that many ordinary people have aspired to owning them.

From early times to the seventeenth century, India was the sole supplier of diamonds to the world. Diamonds were first mentioned in the Book of Exodus (28:18) and in Greek literature from the eighth century BC. A Sanskrit book called 'Artha-Câtra' (The teaching of profit), written in the fourth century BC, describes a sophisticated diamond trade in those days, with details of cutting, quality and trade. During early Christian times in the west, diamonds were regarded as being associated with superstition and interest did not re-emerge until the fifteenth century. Elsewhere in the world, kings and princes wore diamonds as a symbol of strength and invincibility.

In 1477, Archduke Maximilian of Austria gave a diamond ring to his beloved Mary of Burgundy. He placed it on the third finger of her left hand because of the ancient Egyptian belief that the vena amoris (the vein of love) ran from the heart to the top of that finger.

In 1948, the giant De Beers diamond corporation asked an American advertising agency to come up with a slogan

Figure 14.1   The map shows the location of Antwerp and Belgium in relation to the rest of Europe

that associated diamonds with eternal love. The agency suggested that 'Diamonds are forever' might work. Trade in diamond jewellery grew rapidly until the early 1990s and diamonds became the main gift of love for many women in the developed world. Although the trade has slowed down with the world recession, many people would still like to own a diamond.

Diamonds are not only used in jewellery. Their hardness makes them invaluable in many industries. Their earliest use in industry was as an abrasive powder for sawing and polishing and for grinding metal-cutting tools. Many kinds of drills, particularly geological drills, use diamonds as cutters. Fine wires, like those needed for electric lamp filaments, are made by drawing the metal through a hole in a diamond. Diamond cutters are also used for cutting and engraving glass and porcelain, for dental surgery and for bearings in mechanical watches. Diamond powder is used for polishing optical lenses.

This chapter describes the influence of the diamond trade on relationships between the richer countries of the north and the poorer countries of the south.

Belgium, a small country in the centre of western Europe, is one of the biggest commercial and industrial centres for diamond in the world. Although no rough diamonds are mined in Europe, about one-third of the international trade of rough diamond and cut diamond passes through Belgium. This does not mean that there are little diamond shops on every street corner. The whole diamond business is located in a small area of one city—Antwerp.

Figure 14.2a Uncut natural diamonds

Figure 14.2b A row of cut natural diamonds and a gem quality cut diamond

THE NATURE OF DIAMOND

Even though diamond is the hardest of all known gemstones, it is the simplest in composition. Chemically, it is common carbon, like coal and the graphite in a pencil. However, it has a melting point which is two and a half times higher than the melting point of steel. The diamonds that are mined today began their life billions of years ago as carbon gas in the boiling magma deep below the surface of the earth. As this carbon seeped upwards towards the earth's surface, it cooled under pressure to become crystals of diamond.

Scientists have calculated that carbon can only crystallise into diamond under pressures of more than 70 000 tonnes per square centimetre and temperatures of over 2000°C. These conditions exist only at depths of 200 kilometres. The

Figure 14.2c The grading laboratory of the Diamond High Council, Antwerp

volcanic mass, in which this crystallisation took place, was later thrust upwards and broke through the earth's surface as small volcanoes. After the eruptions, the magma cooled in the volcanic vent and formed what are known as kimberlite pipes. Kimberlite was named after Kimberley, a city in South Africa where such rocks were first identified. These kimberlite pipes, most of which were formed in the Cretaceous period, some 70 to 140 million years ago, contain most of the diamonds that are mined today. This means that diamonds originated at the time of the major movements of the earth's surface when the earth's tectonic plates—on which Africa and South America lie—moved apart to form the Atlantic Ocean.

In the time since the volcanic activity, the earth's surface has been attacked by the forces of weathering and erosion. When the kimberlite is eroded, diamonds are released and are carried by water towards the sea. Often they are deposited in river and ocean sediments.

Anything that is in high demand and is also extremely rare will fetch a high price. Diamonds, formed billions of years ago, are rare in that only a few survived the hazardous journey from the depths of the earth to the surface. On average, 250 tonnes of ore have to be extracted, washed and filtered for each carat of diamond. Of diamonds mined today, only about 20 per cent are judged to be of gem quality. Even fewer are large enough to be cut into diamonds that are much bigger than the head of a match. The remainder are used for industrial purposes.

However, the price of diamonds has also been maintained by the actions of a group of major diamond traders who form the Central Selling Organisation. This organisation, which is run by the Diamond Trading Company, De Beers, buys up diamonds when either supply increases or demand falls. The company stockpiles them until prices rise. In this way, the prices of gem diamonds have been kept high for over fifty years. Until recently, only the former Soviet Union was not controlled in this way.

Scientists have been able to make synthetic diamonds for industrial uses for many years and since 1970 have been able to create synthetic diamonds of 'gem quality'. However, the process is so expensive that synthetic diamonds are not profitable on the gemstone market.

For the gem market, the expertise of many skilled and experienced craftsmen is necessary for the complicated process of extracting and finishing a diamond. A rough diamond before it is cleaned looks just like a pebble so that most people would pass it by without a glance. Once cleaned, it looks like a pearl. However, it is the skill of the diamond cutter that unlocks the real beauty that lies within. The knowledge required for this incredibly demanding art has been passed down over the centuries from generation to generation. If the diamond cutter makes a mistake, he risks not just the diamond itself, but also several months of work and his reputation.

THE DIAMOND TRADE: AN INTERNATIONAL INDUSTRY

At first glance the diamond industry appears to be a truly international affair (see Table 14.1). If you were to shade all the countries named in this table on a map of the world you would have shaded in a good proportion of the world's surface. However, the distribution of the various stages in the process of transforming a rough diamond into a piece of jewellery to be worn suggests a different pattern.

> Uncut diamonds are graded in laboratories such as that of the Diamond High Council in Antwerp. The quality and the value of a diamond are judged by carat, clarity, colour and cut (the four Cs). Of these, the cut is the one most directly influenced by human work. The other three are dictated by nature.
> - *Carat*—As with all precious stones, the weight of a diamond is expressed in carats. One carat is 0.2 grams. One carat is divided into 100 points so that a diamond of 25 points is described as a quarter of a carat or 0.25 carats. The natural cut diamonds in Figure 14.2 are 75 points.
> - *Clarity*—Almost all diamonds contain minute traces of non-crystallised carbon. Most are not discernible to the naked eye. These inclusions are nature's fingerprint and make every diamond unique. However, the fewer there are, the more valuable the stone will be.
> - *Colour*—Diamonds can cover the entire spectrum of colours from the black diamonds of the Argyle mine in Western Australia to completely colourless. The majority range from a yellow to a brownish tint. The most valuable are colourless.
> - *Cut*—It is the cut that enables a diamond to make the best use of light. When a diamond is cut to good proportions, light is reflected from one facet to another and then dispersed through the top of the stone. If the cut is too deep or too shallow, the light escapes before it can be reflected. After cutting, the diamond is polished.

> 1. Comment on the numbers of countries that produce, cut and trade in diamonds. Where do you think the greatest profits are to be made?
> 2. Design appropriate symbols for diamond producers, diamond cutters and diamond traders. Draw a map of the world and label the countries involved in the diamond trade. Use your symbols to show the different stages in the diamond trade.
> 3. Describe the patterns of diamond production, cutting and trade that are revealed by your map. Which stages in the trade are mainly undertaken in less developed countries and which in more developed countries?

Table 14.1 The main production, cutting and trading centres for diamonds in the world

Production centres	Cutting centres	Trading centres
Angola	Belgium	Belgium
Australia	Brazil	Hong Kong
Botswana	China	Israel
Brazil	France	Japan
Central African Republic	India	South Africa
China	Israel	Switzerland
Guinea	Korea	United Kingdom
Indonesia	Malaysia	United States
Lesotho	The Netherlands	
Liberia	Tunisia	
Namibia	USA	
Sierra Leone	Former USSR	
South Africa		
Tanzania		
Former USSR		
Venezuela		
Zaire		

For most of the past fifty years, the price of diamonds has been kept high and stable by careful buying and selling by the Central Selling Organisation of the Diamond Trading Company. More recently, two sources of diamonds that are not controlled in this way have opened up and reduced the price of diamonds on the world markets

First, the former Soviet Union released large quantities of cut diamonds onto the Japanese market at prices 10 per cent below those being charged by the De Beers company. Second, in mid-1992, low rainfall followed by the start of the dry season led to a fall in the level of the River Cuango in Angola. This exposed river sediments in a band running 100 kilometres from Lurendo in the north to Zambia in the south that contained huge quantities of rough diamonds. More than 50 000 Angolans, increasing at the rate of 500 a day, swarmed into the area to search for them.

Before 1991, De Beers had an agreement with the Angolan government that a royalty would be paid to the government for all diamonds mined and that only a controlled amount of diamond would be released onto world markets. Until 1991, it was illegal for individual Angolans to be in possession of rough diamonds at all, but a change in the law and the low river levels meant that diamonds were smuggled out of the country. These began to flood world markets at the rate of US$6 million a week. In order to continue to control prices, the Central Selling Organisation was forced to buy up as much of this extra rough diamond as it could in order to stockpile it.

In newspaper reports, a De Beers company spokesperson has termed these diamonds 'illicit' diamonds and suggested that it is not in the interests of Angola to allow people to seek for diamonds and sell them direct to diamond merchants. In fact, it is almost impossible for the area in which diamonds are found to be fenced and controlled by the police.

4 Discuss the advantages and disadvantages of a cartel such as that run by the De Beers company to keep diamond prices high and stable for
 a individual Angolans
 b the Angolan economy
 c the world diamond traders.

Figure 14.3 The scramble for diamonds in Angola—these people are searching the dry bed of the River Cuango for rough diamonds

Table 14.2 The output of diamonds by the main producers, 1989 (million carats of diamonds)

Producing country	Gem quality	Industrial quality
Australia	17 540	17 540
Botswana	10 676	4 576
USSR	4 500	6 500
South Africa	4 010	5 106
Zaire	2 850	16 150
World	43 016	51 821

The flood of diamonds only slowed up when the start of the rainy season led to the river rising and heavy fighting in the Angolan civil war began again.

> 5 Using Table 14.2, calculate the proportion of total world diamond production that comes from the top five producing countries. How does this distribution of production capacity compare with the comments you made about the total pattern of production in the world?

Cutting centres

The most significant diamond cutting centres are Antwerp (Belgium), Bombay (India), Tel Aviv (Israel), New York (USA) and the former Soviet Union. Unlike the situation for most industries, the location factors for diamond cutting have little to do either with diamond production or with the market for finished diamonds. Except for the former Soviet Union, no cutting centre exists in a country which produces rough diamond. In all cases, the raw diamonds are supplied by the Diamond Trading Company. Transporting raw diamonds to the cutting centres is very cheap as they weigh very little. Similarly, transporting the finished product is not influenced by transport costs. The most important location factors originally related to the colonial relationships between Belgium and countries of Africa, and Antwerp's importance as a port.

This does not mean that it would be easy at present for any country to set up as a diamond cutting centre. Diamond cutting is likely to remain in the existing centres for a long time to come for three main reasons.

- The industry needs very specialised craftsmen. Their knowledge and skill is based on tradition, experience and intensive training. At present this is only available in a few places.
- The industry needs specialised infrastructure such as diamond bourses, diamond banks and safety-infrastructure. The existence of diamond banks gives Antwerp and New York financial advantages. Before anyone can cut diamonds enormous sums of money must be borrowed to pay for the rough diamond in cash. During the cutting period interest has to be paid on the loans, and profits only come when the finished diamond is sold. The diamond banks make cheap loans to cutting houses to buy their raw diamond.
- There is a long tradition of diamond commerce and good relations between the communities that are concerned with the diamond business in Antwerp, Bombay, London, New York and Tel Aviv. It takes time for such trusting relations to develop.

Does this mean that the most lucrative aspects of the diamond trade must remain in the traditional colonial centres?

Antwerp is famous for its 7000 very skilled diamond cutters. Although there has been some progress in developing cutting machines, these are generally used only on the smaller and less valuable diamonds. The most expensive stones are still cut by hand.

New York also specialises in expensive and high quality stones and employs 200 cutters. As in Antwerp, the high labour costs are unimportant when compared with the finished value of the very expensive big stones.

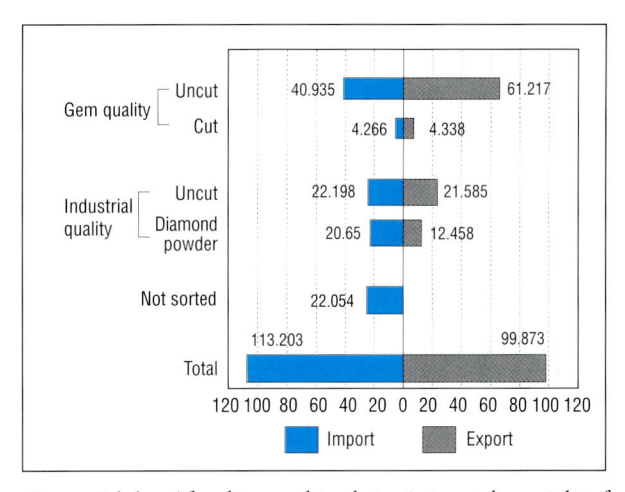

Figure 14.4a The diamond trade in Antwerp by weight of diamonds (million carat)

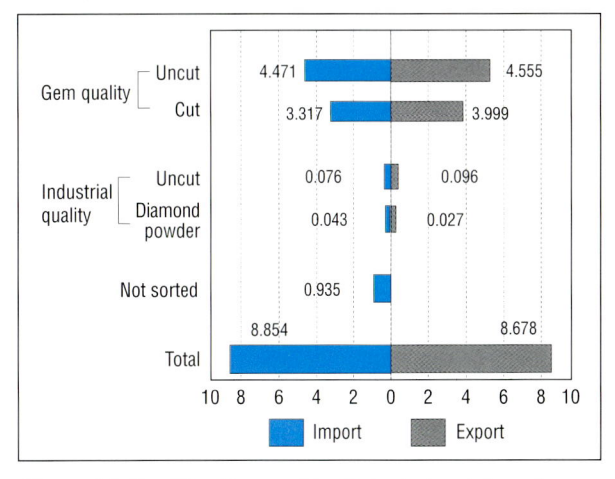

		Import	Export
Gem quality	Uncut	40.935	61.217
	Cut	4.266	4.338
Industrial quality	Uncut	22.198	21.585
	Diamond powder	20.65	12.458
Not sorted		22.054	
Total		113.203	99.873

Figure 14.4b The diamond trade in Antwerp by value (US$)

		Import	Export
Gem quality	Uncut	4.471	4.555
	Cut	3.317	3.999
Industrial quality	Uncut	0.076	0.096
	Diamond powder	0.043	0.027
Not sorted		0.935	
Total		8.854	8.678

India, on the other hand, concentrates on the least valuable little stones that are prepared by about 400 000 cutters. These are often seasonal workers with very low wages. The diamond industry is dispersed over the countryside in the neighbourhood of Bombay and organised as a home industry. The quality of the final product has been rather low, but is improving.

Tel Aviv specialises in small and medium-sized diamonds. The 80 000 employees are concentrated in a few big firms and automatic diamond cutting machines are being introduced.

Finally, the former Soviet Union developed a sophisticated diamond industry employing 4000 to 6000 very skilled employees in modern factories with very strict quality control.

Despite the advantages held by the traditional centres of diamond cutting, the industry is spreading. The activities of the Central Selling Organisation result in the prices for rough diamond being about equal for everyone.

As the market for less expensive diamonds grows, and the quality of Indian cut diamonds improves, the effects of Indian competition on Antwerp and Tel Aviv is felt more severely. The costs of cutting smaller diamonds are a large part of the finished price, and labour costs in India are generally lower than elsewhere. Outside India the diamond industry focuses on high quality diamonds, and wages form a small part of the total costs of these expensive diamonds. Furthermore, the former Soviet Union, with its own supply of rough diamond and rapidly developing cutting industry, is becoming a major rival for the other cutting centres

THE DIAMOND TRADE OF ANTWERP

Marco Polo, the thirteenth century Venetian explorer, wrote about the diamond trade from India, then the source of all rough diamonds, to Europe. The last stage of the journey was from Constantinople (now Istanbul) in the Moslem world to Venice, which held the monopoly on the diamond trade in Christian Europe. Later in the fourteenth century, Bruges developed close links with Venice and became a northern European cutting centre. Once Vasco da Gama had shown a new sea route to India and a new road was built from Lisbon, Antwerp established a diamond cutting industry also, and its good communications led the city to become the foremost diamond centre in Europe. The tools used have hardly changed today, although machines now are driven by electricity.

Today, as well as being a major centre for diamond cutting, Antwerp is also a major centre for the diamond trade.

6 Study Figure 14.4.
 a Are gems or industrial diamonds more important to Antwerp?
 b How can Antwerp apparently export more uncut diamonds than it imports?
 c What evidence do the charts provide that cut gems are worth more than uncut or industrial quality diamonds?
 d What evidence do the charts provide that Antwerp's trading role is greater than importing rough diamonds and exporting them as cut diamonds?
 e What proportion of the unsorted diamonds become cut gem quality diamonds?
 f Calculate the percentage contribution of cut diamonds to total imports and exports by weight and by value. What conclusions can you draw?
 g Calculate the percentage contribution of industrial quality diamonds and diamond powder to total imports and exports by weight and by value. What conclusions can you draw?
7 Construct pie diagrams to show the statistics for Belgium's import and export of gem quality diamonds.
 a What conclusions can you draw from the countries of origin? (Note: Rough diamonds are not mined anywhere in the United Kingdom. Where may these diamonds come from?)
 b What have the countries to which Belgium exports diamonds in common? Why should the United States, which has a diamond cutting industry of its own, import cut diamonds?

Table 14.3 Countries from which Belgium imports rough gem diamonds

Imports of uncut gem diamonds from	Weight of diamonds (carats)
United Kingdom	20 315 652
Liberia	5 283 348
Congo	2 719 749
Nigeria	1 761 806
Israel	1 285 302
Others	9 569 584
Total imports	40 935 441

Table 14.4 Countries to which Belgium exports cut gem diamonds

Exports of cut diamonds to	Value of diamonds (US$)
USA	1 124 916 100
Japan	824 030 330
Hong Kong	393 075 360
Switzerland	337 401 900
Germany	253 386 130
Others	1 066 155 480
Total exports	3 998 965 300

> *c* What conclusions can you draw about the relationship between the countries which supply rough diamonds and those which buy cut diamonds? Where are the greatest profits from the 'international' diamond trade made?

RICH COUNTRIES AND POOR COUNTRIES

After the Second World War, the contrast between the countries of the north and those of the south became much greater than previously. The industrial centres of Europe, the United States and Japan had made great strides and their control over world commerce was such that other countries found it almost impossible to compete. Only the newly industrialising countries, such as South Korea, Taiwan, Hong Kong, Singapore, India, Brazil, Mexico and Argentina, and some Organisation of Petroleum Exporting Countries (OPEC) have been able to make the jump to modern high-tech industry.

During the period of decolonisation the United Nations Organisation encouraged countries of the north to assist in the development of the former colonies. However, even though they gave up their political influence over their former colonies, their economic influence remained intact. Today, countries in the developing world are still mainly suppliers of raw materials, while the companies that operate from the north make huge profits. The traditional economic activities of the south bring little surplus wealth compared to the technology-intensive firms of the north.

Labour intensive activities remain located mainly in the south because those countries have insufficient money, technological knowledge and access to markets to move into new areas of production. The conditions under which people work are defined by the multinational corporations with their headquarters in the north.

Diamonds are an outstanding example of raw materials that are taken from the 'tropical treasuries'. After the colonial period, nearly the whole of the diamond trade has remained under the control of the companies that supply the Diamond Trading Company. They continue to control the production, buying and selling of rough diamond. They buy rough diamond in the south and sell it in the north. The major profits are made by selling cut diamonds as jewels or investment diamonds to rich countries such as the United States, Japan and the Middle East. Only in India, with her low wages, has a diamond cutting industry, although of lesser quality stones, been established. It may be that India, which was for so many years the world's only source of rough diamond, may regain some of the wealth that is involved in the diamond trade—which for so long has stayed in the richer countries of the north.

CHAPTER 15

DEFENDING FINLAND FROM ACID RAIN

● ● ● ● ● ● ● ●

Lea Houtsonen

Warnings have been issued for a long time concerning the problems likely to be caused by air pollution. The question first arose with the spread of industrialisation in the nineteenth century. Rain water in the industrial city of Manchester, England, was discovered to be more acid than in the surrounding areas as early as the mid-nineteenth century.

No special attention was paid to this acid rain until the London smog disaster of 1952, when acid rain and soot, originating mainly from the burning of coal, resulted in the deaths of over 4000 people. The London smogs showed the harmful effects of emissions on people's health, but the damage caused to the environment only became public knowledge twenty-five years later.

It is no longer a question of minor local factors affecting people's health, but changes in the environment which cover vast areas and involve serious consequences both for the natural environment and for humanity.

> 1 *a* In what areas of the world do the effects of acidification seem to be the most problematic at the present time? Examine these areas on atlas maps that show population density and industrial activity. What conclusions can you draw?
> *b* Figure 15.1 also shows areas in which emissions are expected to grow rapidly due to increasing industrialisation and population growth. Where are these potential problematic areas situated?

HOW DOES ACID RAIN DEVELOP?

Acid rain is an invisible form of pollution, caused mainly by human activity releasing sulphur dioxide, the oxides of nitrogen and ammonia into the atmosphere. It has no discernible taste or smell and its effects appear only slowly.

Sulphur emissions come mainly from coals and oils burned in power stations and factories. Unless the combustion gases are purified, this sulphur is released as emissions. Apart from power generation and industry, the most significant sources of nitrogen emissions are traffic and agriculture.

Acidity is measured on the pH scale. The lower the pH value, the higher the acidity. The pH scale ranges from 0 to 14, where 7 indicates a neutral value, that is the pH value of distilled water. The scale is logarithmic, a change of one unit indicating a ten-fold change in acidity.

The normal pH value of pure rain water is 5.6, slightly acid due to the dissolved carbon dioxide. In practice, however, the pH value of rain water varies to a great extent from one area to another due to the natural environment. In arid areas, where the bedrock or soil is alkaline, particles emitted into the air may raise the pH value of rain water almost to a neutral level. On the other hand, acidifying substances such as sulphur are released into the atmosphere from natural sources such as the soil, the sea and volcanic

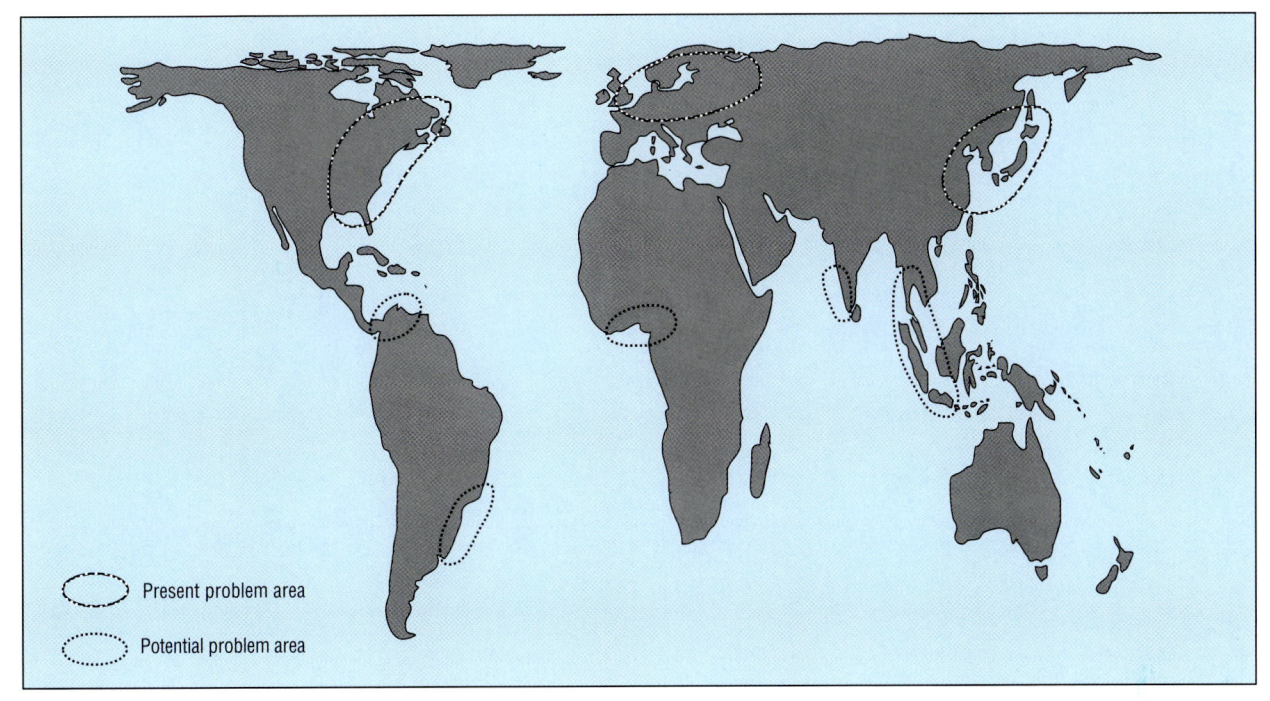

Figure 15.1 The areas of the world affected by acidification

eruptions. Natural sources of nitrogen oxides in the atmosphere include lightning and forest or grass fires.

These natural processes cause regional variation in acidity but increases caused by human inventions such as traffic, major cities, large industrial areas and power stations are the crucial effect. If the pH value of rain water in a certain area is constantly under 5, the cause is almost certainly human activity. Some of the most severe acid attacks have been measured in connection with individual storms and heavy rains. In the United States, a pH value of 2.7 has been measured in rain in Pennsylvania and even 1.5 in West Virginia, while in Europe, a figure as low as pH 2.4 has been recorded in Scotland.

THE SPREAD OF POLLUTION

Cities and industrial plants do not just pollute the air around them. The emissions are often carried by the wind over seas and national frontiers, so that they become undesirable export commodities.

Conscious efforts have been made to promote this long-distance dispersion by releasing smoke into the air at as high a level as possible. The chimneys seen in Figure 15.2 are pouring emissions into the air so that the wind will carry them further away, thus protecting the immediate surroundings. As a result of this 'tall chimney policy' pollution from central and western Europe is carried as far as the Scandinavian countries, and emissions from the eastern parts of the United States acidify the rain falling in Canada. Areas suffering from acid rain are thus often concentrated downwind of dense accumulations of power stations, smelters and large cities.

The dispersal of sulphur and nitrogen compounds in the air can last many days and extend thousands of kilometres from the source. During this process, sulphur dioxide turns into sulphuric acid by oxidation and the oxides of nitrogen turn into nitric acid. These acids dissolve in raindrops in the air and fall to the earth in the form of acid rain or snow.

The acidity of a river or lake depends on the quantity of acids deposited in its catchment area and the ability of the system to counteract these substances. Areas that are not

Table 15.1 The origin of sulphur compounds deposited over some European countries

Country	Domestic deposition %	Deposition from other countries %
Austria	10	90
Belgium	53	47
Czech Republic/Slovakia	56	44
Denmark	42	58
Finland	36	64
France	54	46
Former East Germany	80	20
Former West Germany	49	51
Italy	75	25
Netherlands	32	68
Norway	9	91
Poland	57	43
Sweden	17	83
Switzerland	14	86
Former USSR	74	26
United Kingdom	94	6

Figure 15.2 A forest of chimneys pours sulphur-yellow, lead-grey and rust-brown smoke into the air in the former East Germany

downwind of any source of emissions or which have alkaline soils or limestone bedrock which buffers the acids, are protected against the effects of acid rain.

> 2 a From the statistics in Table 15.1, draw divided bar graphs to show the origins of sulphur depositions in various European countries.
> b Name three countries in which deposition of foreign origin is small.
> c Name six countries in which deposition of foreign origin is high.
> 3 Use Figure 15.3.
> a Name the four European countries with the highest sulphur dioxide emissions.
> b Which is the dominant wind direction in northern Europe?
> 4 a On tracing overlays of Figure 15.3, shade in those areas in which the rain water is most acid (where the pH levels are lowest).
> b Use the other evidence given here to explain the pattern of acidity in western Europe.
> 5 a Comment on the relationship between the countries which receive sulphur compounds from the major source areas and the contribution of those countries to the total amounts emitted.
> b How could the amounts of deposition over the Scandinavian countries be reduced?

ACIDIFICATION: A THREAT TO PEOPLE AND THE ENVIRONMENT

The poor condition of the central European forests, which was discovered in the early 1980s, awakened scientists to the dangers lurking in the acidification of rain water. It was discovered that lakes and rivers, the groundwater and the soils were becoming more acid. Plant and animal communities were dying. Inhabitants of the most problematic sulphur deposition areas were suffering more diseases of the lungs and respiratory passages and buildings and statues were being eroded by acid rain.

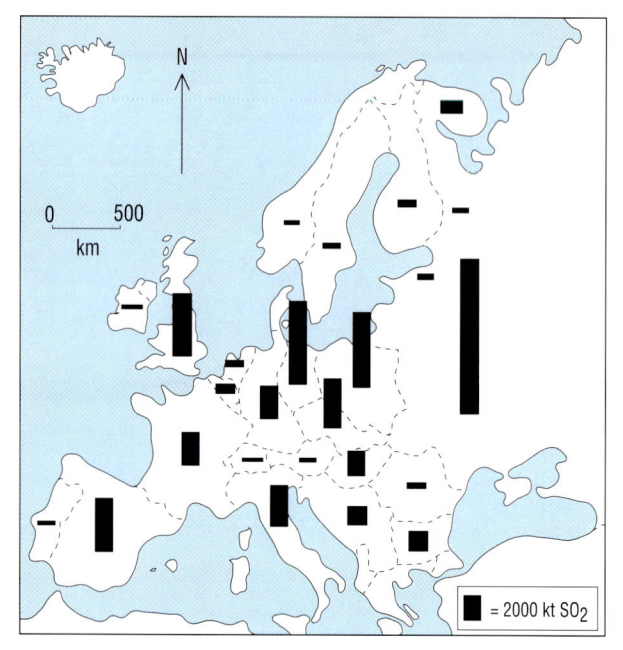

Figure 15.3a Annual emissions of sulphur dioxide in western Europe

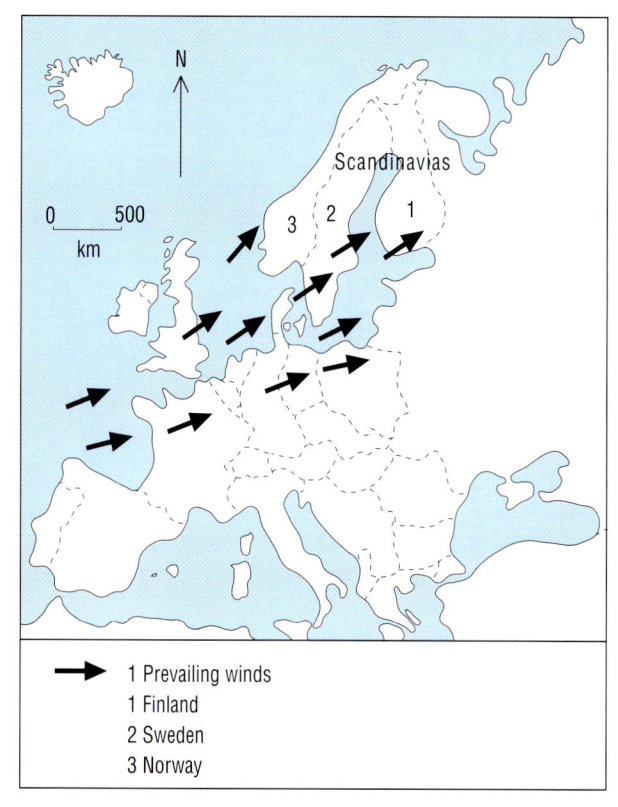

■ = 2000 kt SO_2

Figure 15.3b Prevailing winds in western Europe

→ 1 Prevailing winds
1 Finland
2 Sweden
3 Norway

> 6 Comment on the changes that take place to life in lakes and rivers as acidity increases.

DEFENDING FINLAND FROM ACID RAIN

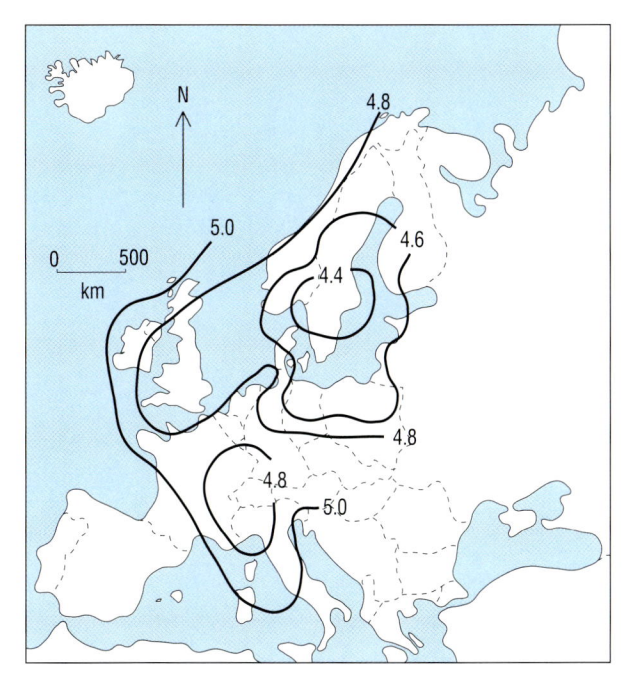

Figure 15.3c The acidity of rain water over Europe, 1986

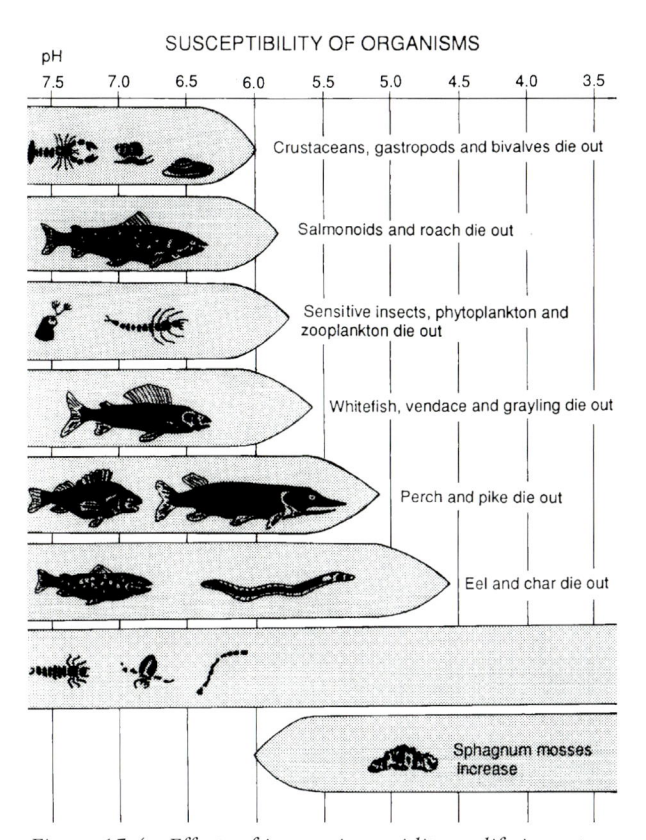

Figure 15.4 Effects of increasing acidity on life in water

Table 15.2 The proportion of West German forests damaged by acidity, 1982–88

Year	Forest damage %
1982	8
1983	34
1984	50
1985	52
1986	52
1987	53
1988	53

Scandinavia: A region particularly susceptible to acidification

The first signs of the dangers of acid deposition for natural organisms were to be seen in the water systems of the barren mountain areas of Sweden and southern Norway. In the early 1960s, it was found that salmon stocks in mountain streams were gradually declining, and a lively debate arose among scientists over the possible causes.

By the late 1960s scientists realised that the acidification which had started in the small mountain lakes and brooks was affecting many thousands of square kilometres of southern Sweden. The exhaustion of fish stocks in the salmon rivers of southern Norway made the seriousness of the problem obvious, but there are now tens of thousands of Scandinavian lakes and rivers where fish are either dying or declining in numbers (see Figure 15.5).

ACID POLLUTION IN FINLAND

Finland is the most easterly of the Scandinavian countries (see Figure 15.5). The climate of Finland is milder than other places at the same latitude, due to the warming effects of the North Atlantic Drift or Gulf Stream.

Finland's own sulphur emissions grew most rapidly in the 1960s, reached their peak in the early 1970s, and have constantly decreased since then, whereas emissions of the oxides of nitrogen have shown a slight increase, due mainly to motor traffic. Motor vehicles produce over half of these emissions.

Depositions of local origin and damage to forests are considerable in the vicinity of large factories. The chemical load in the air is also alarming in the centres of the largest towns, where lichens, which react very quickly to pollution, have disappeared entirely from the trunks of the birch trees.

However, not all Finland's pollution comes from domestic sources (see Figure 15.6). While much of the pollution can be shown to have come from particular countries, about one-third is 'background' pollution for which no particular country can be held responsible.

---

7 *a* Draw graphs to show the changes in the proportion of forests that have been damaged in the former West Germany from 1982 to 1988.
   b Comment on the spread of damaged forests.

Long distance transport starts with an accumulation of pollution in the lower layers of the atmosphere over central and eastern Europe at times when winds and vertical atmospheric currents are weak and there is no rain. This usually means a ridge of high pressure. When the high pressure system recedes, the incoming low pressure system pushes the air mass in which the pollution has accumulated towards the north-east, towards Finland. Low pressure in Finland often brings rain, which washes the impurities down onto the land. If rain occurs in central and eastern Europe, the pollution will fall there, while Finland will receive cleaner air than usual. Table 15.3 shows the monthly precipitation and sulphur deposition totals for the Jokioinen meteorological station about 100 kilometres north-west of Helsinki.

> 9 *a* Draw graphs to show the variations in rainfall and sulphur deposition from January to December.
> *b* Comment on the relationship between rainfall and sulphur deposition.

Lapland, the northern-most part of Finland, is often thought of as retaining its natural state. The eastern parts of Lapland, however, receive acid deposition from the former Soviet Union six times that caused by Finland's own emissions. The largest polluters are the nickel plants at Nickel and Monchegorsk (only 140 kilometres from the Finnish border) on the Kola Peninsula. Figure 15.7 shows how the forest and ground layer vegetation has been virtually destroyed within a radius of 5 to 7 kilometres around Monchegorsk. Damage has also been observed many kilometres away. This area represents one of the largest continuous forest damage zones in Europe.

Although the sulphur content of the air in southern Finland has decreased considerably as a result of the measures that have been taken, sulphur deposition in Lapland has constantly increased.

Another source of Finnish pollution is Estonia, situated on the southern shore of the Gulf of Finland. The electricity

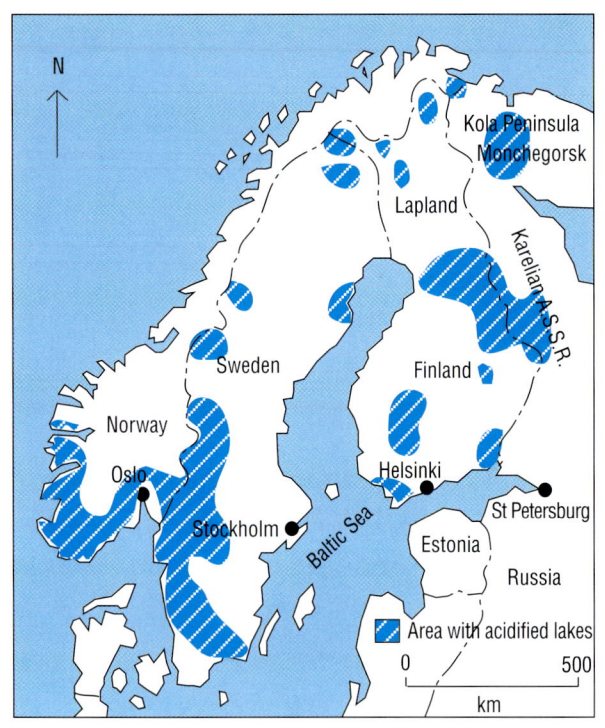

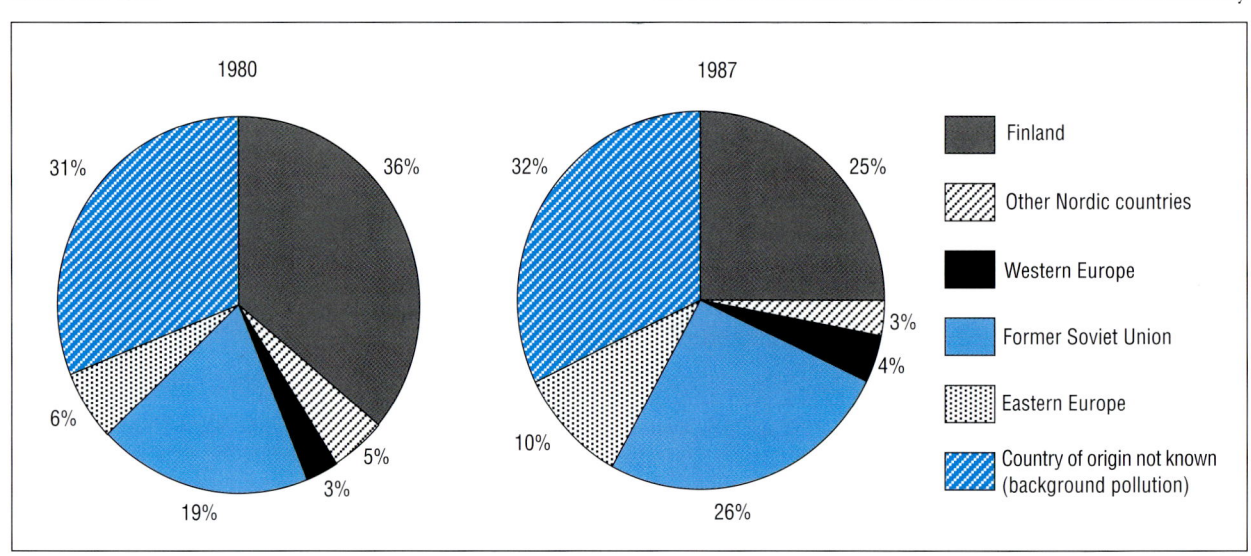

Figure 15.5 The location of Finland showing areas in Scandinavia in which acidified lakes are now common

> 8 Study Figure 15.6.
> *a* Which country increased its proportion most as a source of the sulphur deposited in Finland in the 1980s?
> *b* Which foreign area is the second largest source of sulphur deposition in Finland?
> *c* How did the proportion of the sulphur deposition caused by the Finnish emissions change between 1980 and 1987?

Figure 15.6 The origins of sulphur deposition in Finland, 1980 and 1987

Table 15.3 Monthly precipitation and sulphur deposition totals, Jokioinen

Month	J	F	M	A	M	J	J	A	S	O	N	D
Sulphur deposition (mg/m^2)	39	14	74	12	91	19	69	121	49	55	88	21
Precipitation (mm)	45	7	28	38	52	11	65	110	102	74	93	47

Figure 15.7 Forest and other vegetation destroyed around Monchegorsk on the Kola Peninsula

generating stations on the north-eastern coast of that country, which use large amounts of slate coal as fuel, are also a source of dangerous sulphur emissions.

Effects of acidification on Finland

Acidification affects many aspects of Finland, including the soils, the forests, the lakes, the groundwater and the enjoyment of the natural environment that is so important to the Finnish people.

As elsewhere in Scandinavia, Finnish soils are naturally acid and contain only a little lime, so that they are highly susceptible to acidification. Acidification of the surface soil is regarded as a serious threat to the health of natural organisms in the northern coniferous forest zone. The soils are most commonly of the acid, podsol type, which are common in the climatic zone to which Finland belongs.

Pronounced seasonal changes are typical of the Finnish climate. It is warmest in July, when afternoon temperatures in southern Finland may rise to 22°C. Precipitation is usually moderate at all seasons, being lowest in spring and early summer.

Acidifying substances fall to the ground with the rain and snow and cause nutrients in the soil to be dissolved, so that they are finally leached away. As acidification proceeds, elements such as aluminium start to dissolve, poisoning the soil and the water. Once damaged, the soil takes a long time to recover.

The influence of acid deposition can usually be prevented on farmlands, since fields are prepared, fertilised and limed regularly, although deposition naturally increases the need for liming. It has been found that berry bushes in particular are liable to be damaged by sulphur compounds, which also slow down the growth of barley, oats and peas.

The spread of forest damage

Acid rain and toxic gases affect trees both directly, by damaging the needles or leaves by destroying the cuticular wax on their surfaces and around their stomata, and indirectly, by affecting the fine root systems. Once the root system is damaged, the tree will suffer from a lack of nutrients and its needles will turn yellow.

Climate is an important factor which determines the way in which trees react to pollution. Trees growing near the northern timber line suffer more from damage to their needles and leaves and fine roots than trees growing under more favourable conditions. As a result of their poor health, trees may also become sensitive to insect damage or fungal diseases.

Figure 15.8a A typical scene in winter when the ground is permanently covered in snow up to 100 centimetres deep

Figure 15.8b Finland is a country with thousands of lakes and a landscape dominated by coniferous forests—this picture shows the lakes amidst the beautiful chain of eskers that was formed during the ice age

The forests are often referred to as the 'green gold' of Finland, which has proportionately more forests than any other European country. They not only cover some 70 per cent of the total area, dominating the landscape, but they are also vital to the Finnish economy.

> 10 Draw a pie chart to show the distribution of Finnish exports in 1988 and comment on the importance of forest products to the Finnish economy.

Table 15.4 Finnish exports, 1988

Exports	%
Textiles and clothing	0 5
Sawn timber	8.0
Paper	33.0
Chemicals	9.0
Iron steel and other metals	8.0
Metal products and engineering	31
Other industries	6.0

Several research projects were started in the 1980s to define the effects of air pollution on Finnish forests. They discovered that sulphur and nitrogen loads are a deceptive factor when assessing the condition of forests, since at first they stimulate the growth of the trees. The harmful effects are seen only later. Then yellow tips on the needles and bare patches in the treetops appear and they begin to shed their needles or leaves. The growth rate of pine forests in southern Finland is already slowing down. Alterations in the lichens growing on the trees also point to air pollution. Those of the beard lichen type, which are extremely sensitive to pollution, are disappearing from southern Finland.

Although air pollution has undoubtedly contributed to forest damage, the number of dead forests so far in Finland is fairly small. The most obvious damage has occurred in the immediate surroundings of industrial towns and near the Soviet border in eastern Lapland. The forest soils have not deteriorated so much that tree stands have become essentially poorer, although heath forests have suffered.

The situation in Finland's forests today is similar to that in central Europe some years ago. When they see what has happened elsewhere in Europe, it is easy to understand that the Finns are especially concerned about their forests, their most important natural resource.

Effects on the Finnish lakes

Finland has one of the largest proportions of lakes of any country in the world. There are large lakes, like the ones shown in Figure 15.8, that form parts of extensive waterway systems, and there are also tiny forest lakes.

The acidity of a water system depends on the concentrations of acidifying compounds in rain water and the buffer capacity of the drainage area.

The Finnish winter, or rather the melting of the snow in spring, is a significant factor for acidification. As melting commences, pollutants contained in the snow start to spread. The first meltwater flows rapidly and does not have time to be neutralised, so that the water systems receive a 'concentrated' dose of acidifying compounds.

The acidification of lakes has been studied a great deal in Finland by taking samples.

Acidification is a particular problem in small forest lakes where the surface soil is naturally acid and much of the bedrock is exposed. However, some large lakes have also been found to have reduced buffer capacity. Acid deposition is the primary cause for the acidity of lakes in southern Finland in particular, and the most acid lakes of all are to be found in the rocky areas of southern Finland and some river systems of northern Lapland, where there is most acid deposition. During the spring flooding season, acidity is so pronounced that it is believed to be dangerous for salmon fry.

The majority of the acid lakes have been acid for a long time. This water acidification is serious because of the biological changes it causes, and the biology of the water is important for both recreation and fisheries.

The appreciation of original, natural aquatic environments is growing in all industrialised countries. Water was once regarded as an inexhaustible natural resource but landuse, forestry and airborne pollution have changed the natural state of these systems, so that not even nature conservation areas have been safe from acidifying deposition.

One of the main problems for Finnish water systems is the large organic load from the wood processing industry and nutrient loading from domestic sewage and agriculture. The large rivers running into the Baltic Sea in particular are loaded with waste water to such an extent that it is difficult to distinguish the contribution of the airborne load. Even so, there are still many water areas classified as excellent in quality to be found in Finland.

Figure 15.9 Sampling the water in a Finnish lake for acidification

Clarification of the water is one of the first signs of the acidification of a waterway system. The unnatural clearness is due to the low amount of nutrients, sedimentation of organic matter on the bottom, and low biomass production, which means that the community of organisms in the lake has declined and aquatic plants are suffering.

It has been found that an increase in the acidity of a lake causes the activity of the organisms in it to deteriorate. The roach and crayfish, for instance, are especially sensitive species. Fish damage is the most crucial effect on lakes from a human point of view, and fish stocks have been found to be affected in almost a thousand lakes in Finland, with a few in the south of the country acidified to such an extent that the fish have virtually died out.

Groundwater acidification

Acid deposition from the air also affects the quality of the groundwater, and this is compounded at places such as gravel pits where removal of the surface layer allows acidifying substances easy access to the groundwater and reduces its pH. The Salpausselkä ice margin formations and numerous eskers formed at the melting stage of the ice age in Finland serve as significant groundwater catchment areas, and therefore gravel pits in these areas are a considerable risk factor for groundwater acidification.

Approximately one-fifth of the Finnish population live beyond the reach of piped water supplies, and some 350 000 families obtain their water from wells. The acidity of well water has increased in areas with sandy soils in particular. Overall, the groundwater provides over half the country's domestic water supplies. Acid drinking water is not a health hazard as such, but it can corrode metal pipes and dissolve harmful substances. Groundwater is one of the most valuable renewable natural resources, and an essential target for environmental protection.

FINNISH ATTITUDES TO THE NATURAL ENVIRONMENT

Apart from the economic significance of forests and lakes, they are also important for recreation. Most Finns feel at home in a wild, natural environment and are happy to spend their leisure time close to nature. It is this relationship with nature that is said to have maintained the creative power of Finnish culture. Many Finns are 'lake people'. Most urban dwellers have a summer cottage on the shore of a lake. Here they can spend their weekends and holidays in the bosom of nature. Every summer cottage will have a sauna, the place for freshening up and washing oneself, which is heated until it is burning hot. Fishing is also a hobby for hundreds of thousands of Finns and in winter the forests provide a perfect playground for those who enjoy skiing.

Figure 15.10   A summer cottage on the shores of a lake is almost indispensable for most Finns

11 Use all the photographs in this chapter which show lakes to help you to write a description of a Finnish lake landscape. You should consider
   a the typical features of a Finnish lake landscape
   b the atmosphere conveyed by the Finnish lake landscape
   c the possibilities offered to Finns by the natural environment for leisure and recreation
   d potential harmful effects of a major increase in the number of summer cottages
   e possible ways to protect the Finnish lake environment and landscape from the harmful effects of human activities.
12 Discuss which parts of your own country are as important to you as the lake landscapes are to the Finns.
13 Figure 15.11 shows the results of surveys of how Finnish people regarded environmental protection in 1983 and 1989. Make a list of the main ways in which attitudes changed in this period.

Reducing the effects of acidification

Attempts have been made to reduce the acidity of the soil and raise its pH value by liming the forests. This method has been used extensively in Germany, but so far only experimentally in Finland as restrictions on emissions are regarded as the major means of eliminating the problem. However, if these measures prove insufficient, liming will have to be introduced in Finland as well in order to avoid the imminent threat of forest deaths.

Approximately a hundred lakes have been limed in Finland. The method involves some risks and side effects, but fish stocks have usually recovered. The major problem with liming is re-acidification due to the turnover of water.

Controlling acidification

The most important factor involved in the prevention of acidification is the reduction of emissions. Finland's own sulphur dioxide emissions have clearly been on the decline in the 1980s, whereas emissions of nitrogen oxides have slightly increased.

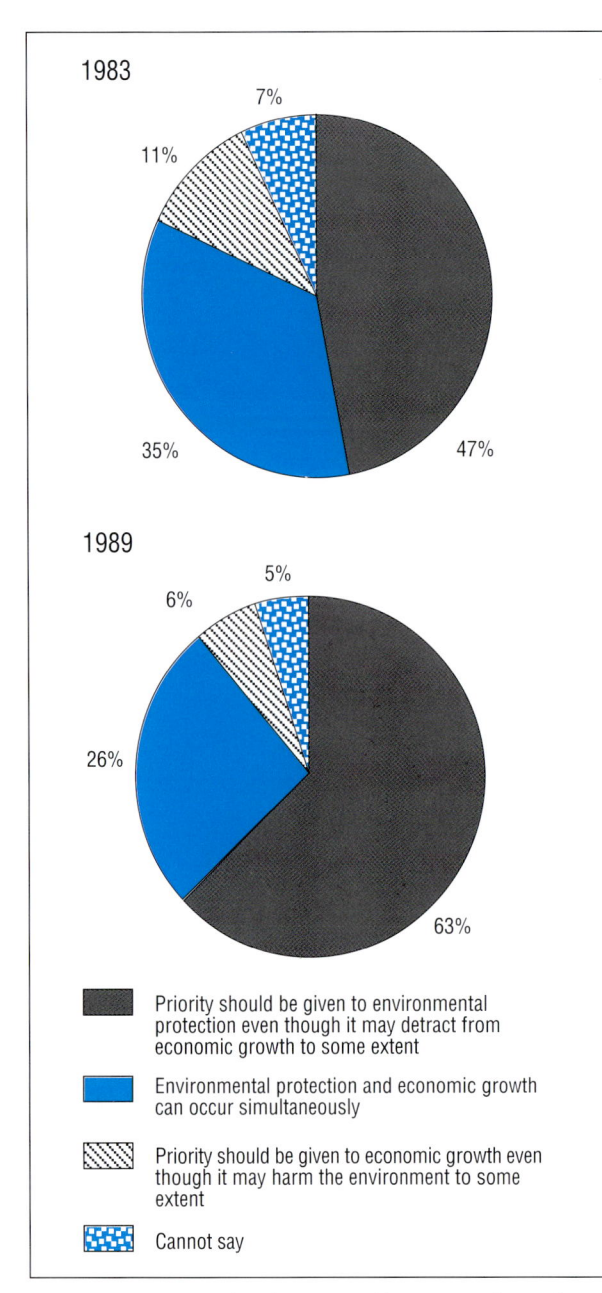

Figure 15.11 Results of surveys of how Finnish people regarded environmental protection, 1983 and 1989

Pie chart legend:
- Priority should be given to environmental protection even though it may detract from economic growth to some extent
- Environmental protection and economic growth can occur simultaneously
- Priority should be given to economic growth even though it may harm the environment to some extent
- Cannot say

1983: 47%, 35%, 11%, 7%
1989: 63%, 26%, 6%, 5%

Finland has reduced its own sulphur emissions by restricting the use of heavy fuel oil, which has a high sulphur content, and transferring to low-sulphur coal and peat. Changes in pulp manufacturing processes have led to a decrease in sulphur emissions from the forest industries. De-sulphuration plants for combustion gases are expected to reduce emissions from power stations in the 1990s, and there are plans to increase the use of natural gas, which does not release sulphur on combustion.

Reductions in emissions of nitrogen oxides in Finland can be achieved by reducing traffic exhaust. New private cars must be equipped with catalysers which purify the exhaust gases, and campaigns have been arranged to promote public transport. Speed limits, pollution taxes imposed on fuels and traffic-free zones in town centres will also contribute to a reduction in emissions.

Since acidifying emissions are transported over national borders, Finland's own restrictions on emissions will not be enough. Similar steps will have to be taken all over Europe.

Figure 15.13 shows that Finland would have a substantial area of acidified forest in ten to twenty years time without any restriction on emissions. Continuation of the present measures slow down the rate of expansion of the acidified area, and tight restrictions applied all over Europe would mean a considerable reduction of the problem.

Progress in reducing the problem

Great progress has been made in reducing the problem of sulphur, although nitrogen oxides are more difficult to control.

The first clean air agreement was signed in Geneva in 1979. In Helsinki in 1985 a number of countries agreed to

Figure 15.12 Reducing the harmful effects of acidity by adding lime to lakes

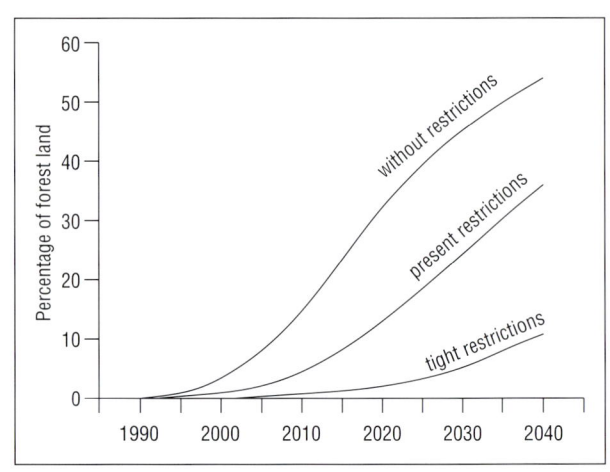

Figure 15.13 The harmful effect on Finnish forests with various levels of control

reduce their sulphur emissions by 30 per cent from the level which existed in the 1980s by the year 1993. Unfortunately, the United States, Poland and Britain, who are responsible for considerable deposition in Finland, remained outside the agreement.

The fight against sulphur emissions has been successful in Europe. Many countries have announced that they have reduced the emissions considerably more than the 30 per cent required. This was achieved because most of the emissions came from so-called spot sources, such as major power stations and nickel smelters that can be identified and controlled.

The Finnish and Swedish sulphur reduction programs may be the most ambitious in the world. The Finnish government decided in 1991 that sulphur dioxide emissions should be reduced by 80 per cent from the volume in 1980 by the beginning of 2000. By 1990, the sulphur emissions of Finland had been reduced to half the 1980 levels. Over the whole of Europe, sulphur emissions were reduced from 26 million tonnes in 1980 to 20 million tonnes in 1989. Sulphur depositions on Finnish soil have also started to diminish.

The problem of sulphur emissions drifting to Finland from the area of the former Soviet Union continues. One suggestion is for the plants to work normally when the winds are blowing away from Finland, but when the winds change towards Finland, the power plants would switch to purer fuels or cut their power output. Electricity for these areas would then be drawn from power stations in central Russia.

The Russian authorities had agreed that sulphur emissions in the Murmansk district on the Kola Peninsula would be reduced by half. In 1980 they were 724 000 tonnes, in 1989, 570 000 tonnes and by 1995, they should be only 350 000 tonnes. This can only be achieved by rebuilding many obsolete plants. Before the 1991 upheavals in the former Soviet Union, Finland had agreed to lend money at the same rate that it offers to domestic environmental investments for a new nickel smelter which would produce 90 per cent less sulphur emission. However, the political changes mean that the project has come to a temporary halt. On the other hand, the political changes may lead to some unintentional improvements. The Monchegorsk smelter uses ore with a high sulphur content that comes from northern Siberia. The fall of the central government of the Soviet Union, and the end of subsidised transport of this ore to the Kola Peninsula may bring the use of this ore to an end—thus leading to a reduction in the sulphur emissions.

The newly independent Estonia is still as short of capital as the former Soviet Republic of Estonia, but Finland finds it easier to cooperate directly with Estonia than through Moscow. In April 1992, new de-sulphuration equipment, provided with Finnish money and technology, opened at the Narva power plant.

While sulphur emissions come mainly from spot sources, nitrogen emissions come mainly from decentralised sources such as farming and traffic. Although a reduction in nitrogen emissions was agreed in Sofia, Bulgaria, in 1988, it has been difficult to achieve. The annual emission of nitrogen oxides in Europe increased from 21 million tonnes in 1985 to 22 million tonnes in 1989. This increase is mainly due to increases in road traffic.

Europe has not been able to control increases in its traffic. A particular problem is the heavy goods traffic that goes right across Europe. Italy, Austria and Switzerland in particular are concerned about the amount of traffic that passes through their countries.

Attempts to curb the increase in highway traffic include both 'carrot' and 'stick' methods. Attempts are being made to make public transport more attractive by increasing services and efficiency (carrot). On the other hand, private car transport is being made more expensive and difficult by taxation, parking restrictions, raising the price of fuel and forbidding cars from using public transport lanes (stick).

> 14 Draw a sketch or design a poster to depict the 'carrot' and 'stick' methods of controlling the use of road transport. What methods are being adopted in your country? What Finnish methods of control are not used in your country? Discuss the costs and benefits of the approaches you have identified to determine their effects on individuals, the economy of the country and the natural environment.

THE GOOD NEWS

Environmental questions are exceptionally important to Finland, since renewable natural resources mean a lot to the country's economy. At present, signs of damage in Finland can usually be seen only in extremely sensitive and seriously polluted forest and water ecosystems, although the 'techno-desert' of the Kola Peninsula is not very far away. Thus the chance has not yet been lost, and there is much that can be done to save the natural environment.

Stricter environmental rules and investment in protection mean additional costs, but they are worth it, since improvements in the condition of our environment will also increase the quality of life and provide future generations with a chance to work and live in a clean environment. Prevention of acidification is both possible and economically profitable, since the losses caused by acid rain can be huge. The Finnish experience, both at home and with international cooperation, shows that acid rain can be reduced. The Nordic countries cooperate closely together and their aim is that the high Nordic standards of health, safety and environmental protection should become the development objective for the whole of Europe. Achieving such an aim would go a long way towards truly sustainable development.

CHAPTER 16

CONTROLLING ROAD TRAFFIC IN SINGAPORE

Yee Sze Onn

Rapidly increasing populations are a problem in all large cities throughout the world. With increasing populations comes an increase in car ownership.

There are now over 400 million cars in the world. The global car fleet grows by 19 million each year. This rate of increase is lower than it was in the 1970s as most of the industrial countries, which account for 80 per cent of the total, have reached near saturation point. Nevertheless, coping with the car has become a top priority for many urban planners, and the car has taken control of the whole character of cities. Large percentages of the areas of cities are occupied by roads and parking areas. In Bangkok, roads take up 8 per cent of the total surface area of the city, compared with 20 to 25 per cent of cities such as London, Paris and New York, and over 60 per cent in Los Angeles. Yet, 140 000 cars are added to Bangkok's roads each year. Once all the ground space has been used, engineers turn to space above ground and underground. In Yokohama, Japan, there is even a floating parking area in the local bay.

The large numbers of cars have caused other problems. Traffic congestion is a reality in many cities. Rush 'hours' last for over twelve hours in Seoul and fourteen hours in Rio de Janeiro. London, where peak hour traffic speed averages 15.7 kilometres per hour, set a record in 1989 with a 53 kilometre-long traffic jam of near-stationary cars. Such average traffic speeds are similar to those achieved by horse drawn carriages a hundred years ago, but are still better than those of some Italian cities where the average speed of motor traffic at peak hour has fallen below 3 to 4 kilometres per hour. In such conditions, the noise of engines (and often horns) causes high levels of stress in the population. In Cairo, for example, the noise of road traffic is often ten times the limit recommended by health and safety standards.

Motor vehicles are the single largest source of air pollution and create a haze of smog over world cities. Smog is created when the nitrogen oxides and hydrocarbons emitted by cars react with sunlight to form ozone. Ozone, carbon monoxide and other emissions aggravate bronchial and lung disorders and are often deadly to the very old, the very young and people who suffer from asthma. Exhaust gases also contain carbon dioxide, which is a greenhouse gas. Passenger cars are responsible for over 13 per cent of the total carbon dioxide released from fossil fuels across the world—700 million tonnes of carbon each year.

> 1 Collect statistics similar to those mentioned above for your own nearest city. You can calculate the average speed of traffic in the city centre by finding out how long it takes to drive between two points in the rush hour and measuring the distance either from a map or from the car's instruments. How close to crisis do you believe your city is?

Table 16.1 Pollution emitted during a typical journey to work in the United States, 1989

Transport mode	(g per 100 passenger km)		
	Hydro-carbons	Carbon monoxide	Nitrogen oxides
Rapid rail	0.2	1	30
Light rail	0.2	2	43
Transit bus	12	189	95
Van pool	22	150	24
Car pool	43	311	43
Car (one person/vehicle)	130	934	128

Source: *State of the World*, Lester R. Brown (ed.), Allen & Unwin, 1991

Each year, over a quarter of a million people are killed in road accidents, and several million more are disabled. In developing countries, road deaths are twenty times those in more developed countries and one study of fifteen developing countries showed that road accidents are the second most common cause of death. This chapter describes the methods being adopted in Singapore to control traffic problems and improve the urban environment for the sake of its citizens.

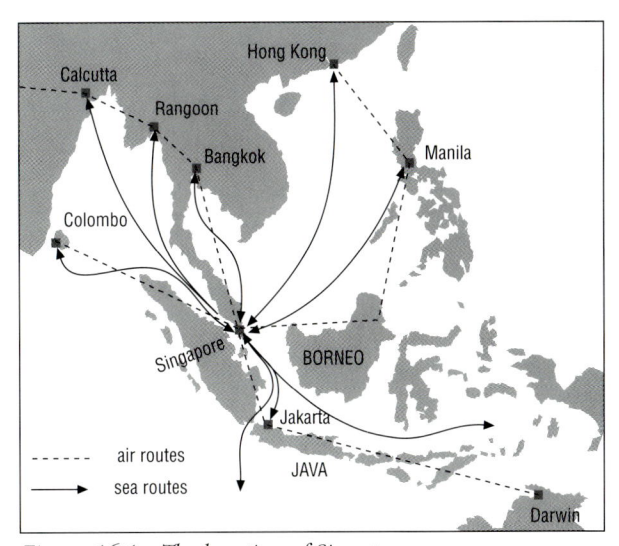

Figure 16.1 The location of Singapore

SINGAPORE

The independent state of Singapore, located at the tip of the Malaysian Peninsula, consists of the island of Singapore and about fifty-eight small islands within its territorial waters. The main island is about 42 kilometres in length and 23 kilometres in breadth. Just across the Strait of Johor to the north of the island lies Malaysia, the states of Sabah and Sarawak to the east, with Indonesia to the south and west.

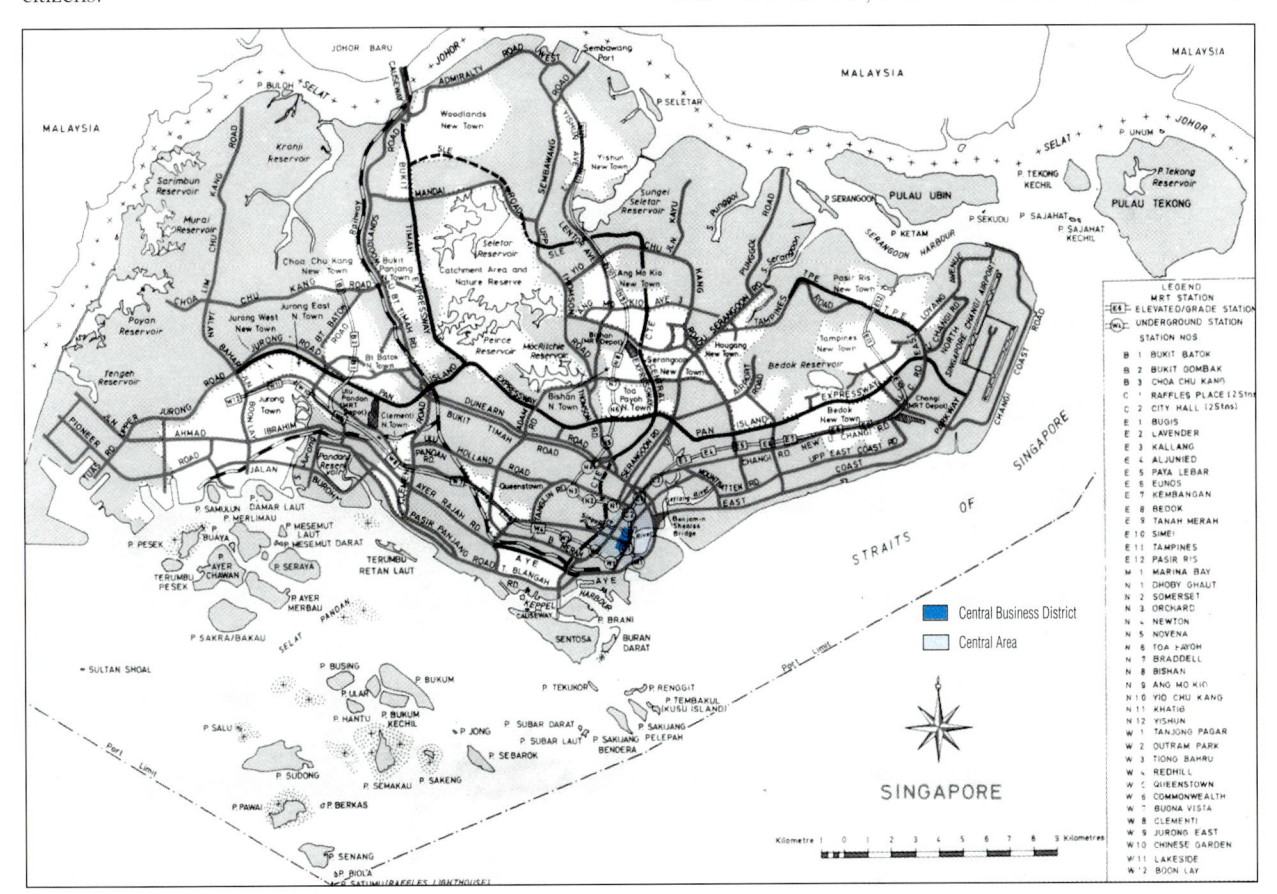

Figure 16.2 Singapore—this map shows the main routes, towns and central business district

Singapura (Lion City in Sanskrit) was well known in the fourteenth century when it was caught in the struggles between Thailand and Java for the control of the Malay Peninsula. In 1819, Sir Stamford Raffles landed at the mouth of the Singapore River in search of a location for a trading post to service British ships trading with Asia. He signed a treaty with Sultan Hussein of Johore, who then ruled the island, that allowed the founding of the new colony. Singapore became a successful trading port almost immediately.

In 1828, Raffles produced a town plan for Singapore that separated ethnic groups into kampongs, or gardens. The Chinese were given the area south of the Singapore River while the Bugis and Arabs made their homes to the north. The Europeans were housed in the middle, near to the commercial zone and government offices at the mouth of the river. The office area eventually grew to become the civic district or central business district (CBD) of today.

Singapore attained self-government in 1959, and although it joined the Federation of Malaysia in 1963, it became an independent republic in 1965.

Because it is such a small country, Singapore can only support its people through trading and manufacturing. Since the 1970s, Singapore has achieved rapid economic growth. However, the increased population has been housed in many new towns across the island and these have in turn led to problems of traffic congestion.

Traffic congestion in Singapore

Singapore, like other cities, is characterised by urban traffic congestion. Despite the various disincentives to car ownership and reductions of space, the number of vehicles has increased greatly over the last decade. This has been caused by a mix of growing economic affluence, inadequate public transport services, traffic indiscipline and a lack of road space for motorised and non-motorised vehicles. The scene in Figure 16.3 shows peak hour traffic at one junction in Singapore.

Figure 16.3 Peak hour traffic in Singapore

The total number of vehicles registered in Singapore at the end of 1991 had risen to 559 304, an increase of nearly 7.5 per cent over the 1989 figure of 520 537 (see Table 16.2). If the present rate of growth is allowed to continue it is feared that the roads will be clogged with vehicular traffic. This will have adverse effects on the economy, environment and public health.

2 Discuss the situation shown in Figure 16.3. What factors have contributed to this situation? Make a list of the effects of similar situations across Singapore on
  a commuters
  b the economy of Singapore
  c the environment of Singapore.
3 Examine the bar chart in Figure 16.4 and Table 16.2. Make lists to show which classes of vehicle have increased in number and which have decreased. Rank the lists to show which classes of vehicle have increased the most and which have decreased the most. Discuss your findings and suggest why these changes may have taken place and what their effects may be on the urban environment of Singapore.
4 Figure 16.5 shows the changes in the growth rates of vehicles in Singapore, 1981–89. Compare the figures for percentage changes in growth rate with those for vehicle numbers in Table 16.2.
  a Does a negative growth rate in a single year mean that the number of vehicles on the road has decreased?
  b Suggest reasons for the marked decline in growth rate of motor vehicles from 1984 to 1987.
  c By the end of the 1980s, the growth of all forms of motor vehicles began to increase. Do you expect this pattern of growth to occur again in the 1990s? Explain the factors which may influence the rate of growth.
  d Using the figures for 1989, calculate by which years the numbers of each form of motor vehicle listed in Figure 16.5 will have doubled. (Hint: If you divide the number 72 by the percentage growth rate, the answer is the number of years ahead when the number of vehicles will have doubled.) Which vehicle should be targeted for reduction if the road conditions in Singapore are to be preserved?
5 Find similar figures for your country and carry out a similar analysis to that suggested in question 4.

TRAFFIC PROBLEMS: CURRENT AND FUTURE MEASURES

In the past, efforts to solve the traffic problem were mostly piecemeal in nature. Methods that have been used include
* widening roads
* converting 2-way to 1-way streets to ease traffic flow
* creating more car parks to meet the demand.

However, such improvements have been overtaken by the disproportionate increase in vehicular traffic.

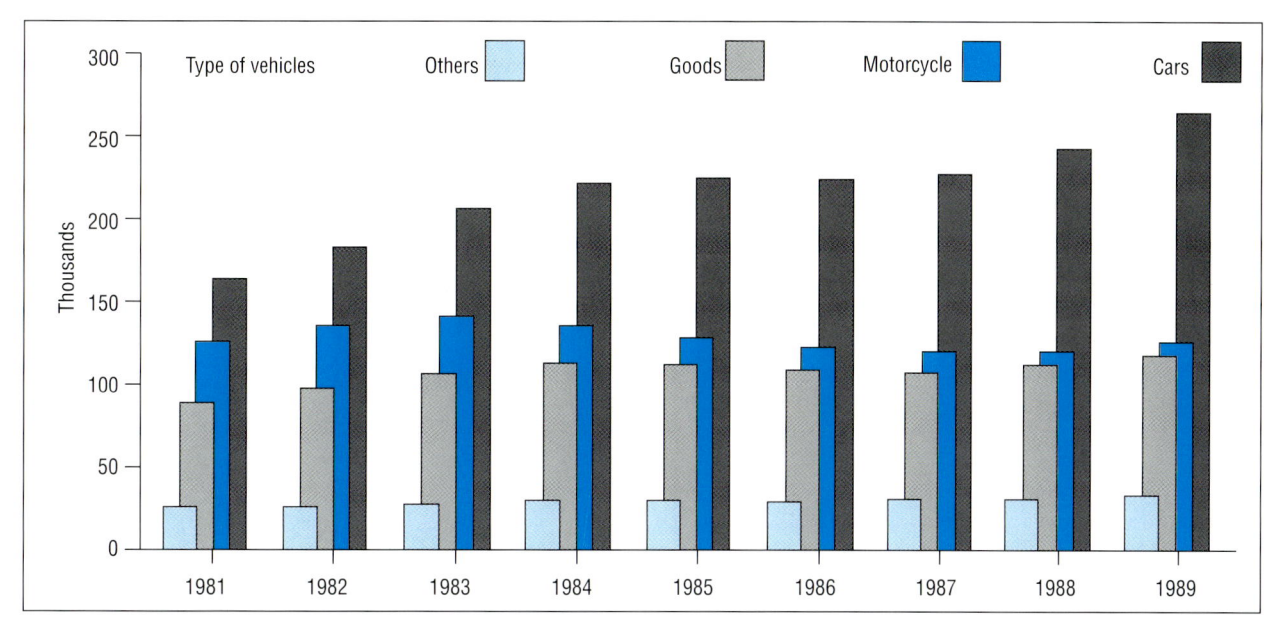

Figure 16.4   Details of the motor vehicle population of Singapore, 1981–89

Table 16.2   Motor vehicles in Singapore, 1981–89

Type	1981	1982	1983	1984	1985	1986	1987	1988	1989
Cars									
Private cars/s'wagons	143 446	160 757	182 120	195 873	200 032	200 163	201 651	215 928	234 438
Company cars/s'wagons	15 515	16 044	16 992	18 248	18 105	17 558	17 868	18 959	20 010
Tuition cars/s'wagons	888	920	1 090	1 085	1 104	910	856	957	954
Private hire cars/s'wagons	3 506	4 515	4 168	4 159	4 030	3 314	3 081	3 140	3 135
Sub-total	**163 355**	**182 236**	**204 370**	**219 365**	**223 271**	**221 945**	**223 456**	**238 984**	**258 537**
Motorcycles/scooters	**126 343**	**135 359**	**140 267**	**133 492**	**126 337**	**119 241**	**115 476**	**116 476**	**119 897**
Buses									
Omnibuses	3 206	3 219	3 287	3 354	3 597	3 530	3 482	3 410	3 304
School buses	2 530	2 736	2 733	2 645	2 573	2 427	2 345	2 207	2 047
Private buses	419	648	866	1 062	1 232	1 271	1 354	1 475	1 615
Private hire buses	408	507	616	687	779	862	944	1 039	1 174
Excursion buses	243	327	338	356	356	383	458	657	855
Sub-total	**6 806**	**7 437**	**7 840**	**8 104**	**8 537**	**8 473**	**8 583**	**8 788**	**8 995**
Taxis	**9 869**	**10 283**	**10 673**	**11 062**	**10 941**	**10 677**	**10 552**	**10 473**	**10 652**
Goods									
Goods-cum-passenger	593	555	8 757	8 959	8 781	8 634	8 562	8 525	8 468
Light goods	58 645	63 531	59 208	59 940	57 915	55 442	54 211	53 933	53 825
Heavy goods	25 418	29 173	33 198	38 436	39 298	38 241	38 756	43 183	48 491
Other	3 213	3 744	4 061	4 042	3 711	3 445	3 519	2 940	2 989
Sub-total	**87 869**	**97 003**	**105 224**	**111 377**	**109 705**	**105 762**	**105 048**	**108 581**	**113 773**
Exempted*	**7 563**	**7 958**	**7 914**	**7 922**	**7 969**	**7 561**	**8 009**	**8 506**	**8 683**
Total all vehicles	**401 805**	**440 276**	**476 288**	**491 322**	**486 760**	**473 659**	**471 124**	**491 808**	**520 537**

* Exempted category includes rollers, tractors, lorries and tippers, buses, motorcycles and scooters, and cars and station wagons

Source: Registry of Vehicles, *Annual Report 1989*

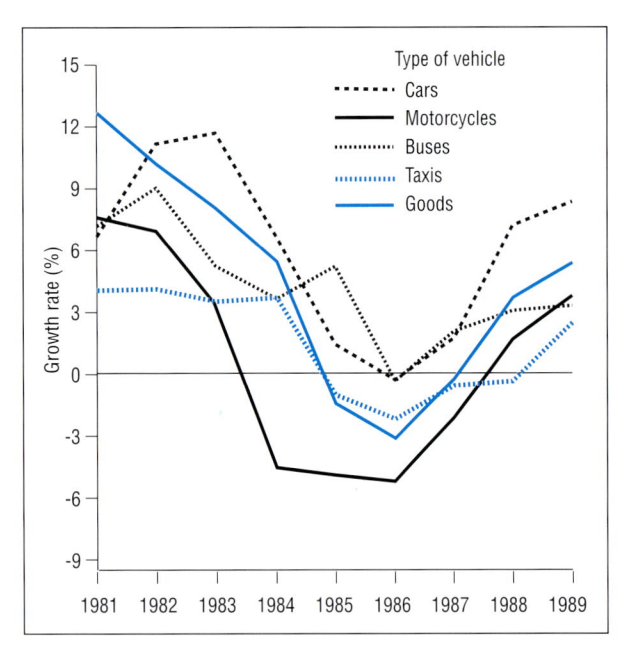

Figure 16.5 Changes in the growth rates of vehicles in Singapore, 1981–89

The next attempt to alleviate transport and traffic problems used fiscal restraint measures such as increasing import duties, taxes and registration fees. Singapore now has the highest such taxes in any country in Asia. However it was soon recognised that these measures were not appropriate for regulating car travel at congested times and in congested areas.

In the specific context of congestion four measures were selected for closer examination. They were
- vehicle metering
- toll roads
- higher parking fees
- area licensing.

Of these four measures, increased parking fees and area licensing were chosen as particularly appropriate for Singapore.

Higher parking fees

Low parking fees used to create an excess demand for parking places and increased the volume of vehicular flow and congestion. Parking fees in the CBD were increased in May 1975 to S$0.50 for the first hour and S$1.00 for the second hour and S$2.00 for each subsequent hour. The aim was to discourage long term parking and season parking so that more parking spaces would be available for short term parking. Further from the city centre, parking costs have also been increased.

> 6 What kinds of travellers are likely to be discouraged from using their cars by the introduction of car parking fees that increase as time goes by? What may this mean for Singapore?
> 7 What is the effect of imposing higher car parking charges at a fixed rate per hour outside the city centre?

Area licensing

The Area Licensing Scheme (ALS) in Singapore came into effect on 2 June 1975. It marked a major turning point in the attempt to discourage the use of cars at specific times and in designated areas where congestion was heaviest. In 1975, the CBD was cordoned off as the restricted zone between the morning peak hours of 7.30 to 9.30. A special monthly or daily licence must be purchased and displayed on the windshield of any car entering a designated restricted zone during the morning commuting hours. Figure 16.7 shows the overhead zone markings in place and Figure 16.8 shows an area licence for a single day: 28 February 1991. Commercial vehicles and buses were exempted to maintain commercial activity and encourage public transport. Car pools (defined as cars or taxis carrying at least four persons) were also exempted. The aim of this was to encourage higher vehicle occupancy and more efficient use of roads. The hours were extended from 7.30 to 10.15 am on 1 August 1975 as congestion developed after 9.30 am.

Figure 16.6 A car park outside the city centre

Figure 16.7 An overhead gantry sign at one entry to the CBD

CONTROLLING ROAD TRAFFIC IN SINGAPORE

Figure 16.8 An area licence for a single day to permit entry to the restricted zone

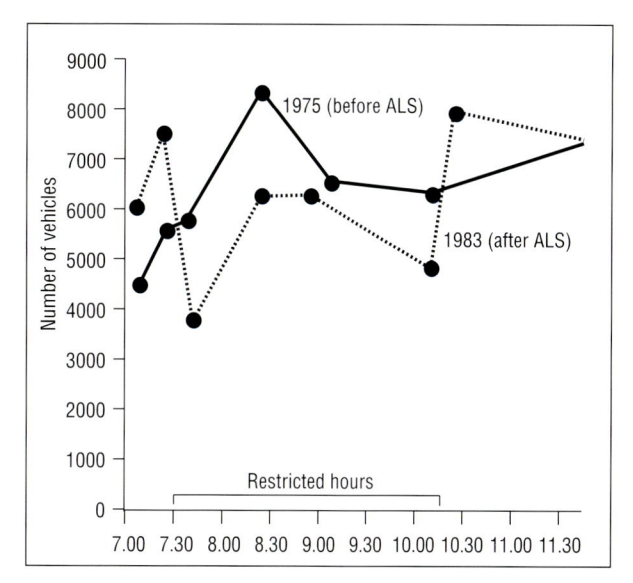

Figure 16.9b Number of vehicles entering the restricted zone, 1975 and 1983

The primary objective of the ALS was to alleviate peak hour congestion by reducing the traffic allowed into the CBD during peak hours. Another important objective was to change public attitudes to private car ownership and use.

> 8 How do you think the area licensing scheme affected different groups of travellers in the centre of Singapore? How would it affect the travelling habits of various groups of people? In what ways may this scheme change people's attitudes?

The ALS was modified with effect from 1 June 1989. In addition to the morning scheme, an evening ALS was introduced. This was subsequently brought forward to end at 6.30 pm with effect from 31 January 1991. By 1993, the ALS will be automated. This makes Singapore the first country in the world to control road use in congested areas by charging users directly for the use of the roads.

The ALS had the effect of reducing traffic flow into the restricted zone. Streams of motorists were diverted to by-pass routes or escape corridors instead of cutting through the city. It caused a major shift in travel patterns and commuter habits by encouraging people to form car pools and use public transport. Figure 16.9 shows the changes in the number of vehicles entering the restricted zone during peak hour before the introduction of the ALS and after the scheme had been operating for eight years.

> 9 Examine the graphs in Figure 16.9. Describe the pattern of car and all vehicular movements in the centre of Singapore before and after the introduction of the ALS. Explain why the patterns of car movements and all vehicle movements are different.

The weekend car scheme

In May 1991, the weekend car scheme was introduced to enable more people to own private cars without adding to traffic congestion. Cars licensed in this way can only be used between 7.00 pm and 7.00 am Mondays to Fridays, after 3 pm on Saturdays, and all day on Sundays. If the car is used outside these times, a day licence must be displayed on the windscreen. Each weekend car scheme owner is given five free day licences a year but others must be bought at $20 each. A weekend car scheme vehicle can be recognised by its red number plate. A normal car may be converted into a weekend car scheme vehicle and when this is done, the owner receives a 95 per cent reduction in road tax.

ALTERNATIVE MEASURES OF TRAFFIC RESTRAINT

The park-and-ride scheme

A park-and-ride scheme was designed to complement the ALS to provide an alternative mode of transport for motor-

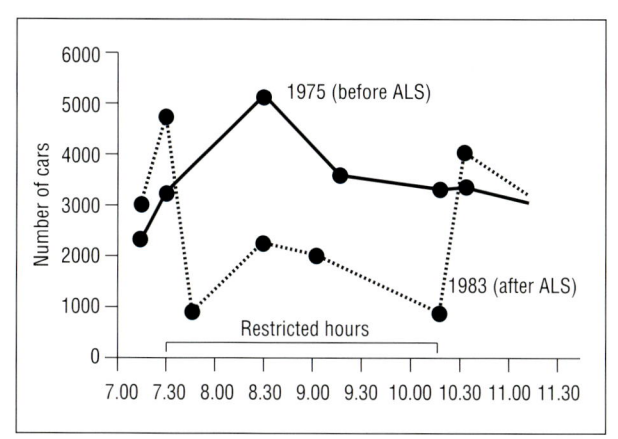

Figure 16.9a Number of cars entering the restricted zone, morning peak traffic hours, 1975 and 1983

ists who were accustomed to driving into the central area. Fifteen fringe car parks with a capacity of 10 000 cars were constructed around the periphery of the restricted zone. Motorists entering the city may use the car parks and continue their journey into the CBD by shuttle bus. The shuttle bus routes have limited stops and only seated passengers were carried in an attempt to provide a fast, comfortable alternative to the car. This scheme did not draw the projected response. Motorists preferred to leave their cars at home and travel by regular bus. Changing transport modes along a journey was apparently an unpopular idea with Singaporeans.

> 10 Discuss possible reasons why Singaporeans appear to prefer to travel the whole way to work by bus rather than use their cars and the shuttle bus. Which way would you prefer to travel?

Staggered work hours

A six month national campaign was launched on 15 July 1974 to reduce peak hour traffic congestion. The objective was to encourage two voluntary measures which could effectively reduce peak hour congestion
- staggering work hours
- formation of car pools.

The government hoped that the schemes would improve the traffic situation by reducing both the number of vehicles and congestion on the buses. However, staggered time had its limitations. In the public sector, 40 000 out of the 60 000 workers responded to the scheme. However, the nature of their work meant that only 17 500 could be given the option to choose their own starting time. Second, the staggered time worked against the car pooling scheme as it became more difficult to match participants with the same starting time.

> 11 List the advantages and disadvantages of having staggered working hours. You should consider the points of view of the workers themselves, their employers, members of the public with whom they come in contact, and the city traffic planners.

Improved public bus service

To encourage the use of public transport and to meet the needs of the commuters, efforts were made to improve the public bus service. Besides the existing Singapore Bus Service (SBS) the Supplementary Public Transport System (SPTS) was introduced in 1974.

The SPTS uses the existing pool of privately owned school buses during peak hours to provide additional services on specified routes. Private and school buses were also licensed to carry commuters.

On 21 June 1975, a new air-conditioned service was introduced to ply between several large private housing estates and the city area. A one-man-operated semi-express service running between selected residential areas and the city with limited stops on the way was also added.

Reserved bus lanes along major roads were introduced to give priority of movement for public buses during peak hours. This system affects sixteen kilometres along twenty-three roads in the CBD.

> 12 What factors contribute to making a public transport system acceptable to the travelling public? Create a questionnaire for your own area based on your conclusions.
> 13 Conduct a survey using your questionnaire to discover the satisfaction of people in your area with the public bus service.

Expressways

Seven new expressways, 141 kilometres long, were added to the existing road network to speed up traffic flow all over the island and to cater for Singapore's long term travel. The expressway network currently constructed is largely aimed at improving vehicular circulation by allowing through-city traffic to avoid the city centre. A good example is the Pan Island Expressway. This road links the eastern and western portions of the island without traversing the city areas. The grade-separated interchanges enable vehicles to maintain a high average speed.

Vehicle quota system

A further attempt was made to restrict car ownership in Singapore when the vehicle quota system was set up on 1 May 1990. Under this scheme, anyone who decides to buy a new car must first bid for an allotted licence. These licences are open to tender once each quarter and the bidding fee depends on the size of the car to be bought. A licence or Certificate of Entitlement is awarded to those people who are successful in the bid and this allows them to purchase a new car.

The mass rapid transit

The decision to study the technical, economic and financial feasibility of a mass rapid transit (MRT) system for Singapore was a major step in improving public transportation. The system is a heavy-rail system similar to the subways in London, Paris, San Francisco, New York and Hong Kong. It consists essentially of an east–west line and a north–south line with interchange facilities at two stations in the central area. Figure 16.10 shows the routes of the MRT system of Singapore. The decision to proceed with construction of the MRT was made in May 1982 and part of its route opened in November 1987, ahead of schedule.

CONTROLLING ROAD TRAFFIC IN SINGAPORE

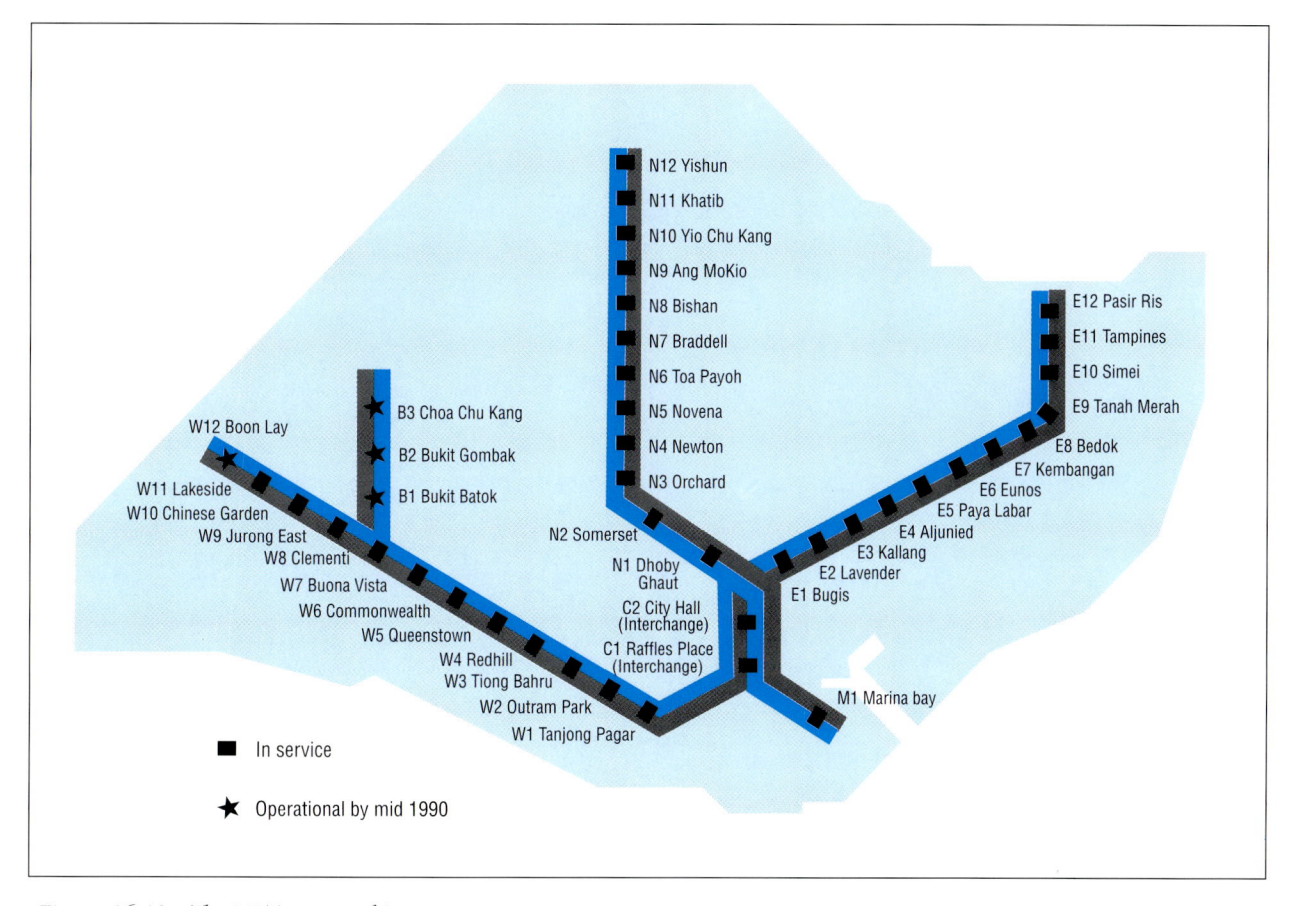

Figure 16.10 The MRT system of Singapore

14 How will the MRT system affect the following in both the short term and the long term?
   a Commuter travelling patterns
   b Patterns of landuse in the city
   c Economic activities in Singapore
15 Discuss the advantages and disadvantages of mass transit systems such as the one in Singapore for both commuters and transport planners.

16 a How many of the methods of limiting traffic congestion have been adopted in your country?
   b List the methods used in your country that have not been tried in Singapore.
   c Are there any measures that have been adopted in Singapore that you think should or should not be introduced in your country? Explain why the situation in your country may be different.
17 Which do you think is likely to be more effective in reducing traffic congestion
   a restraints on car ownership, or
   b restraints on car usage?
   Give reasons for your views.

Table 16.3 shows some examples of other schemes, used around the world, designed to reduce urban transport problems.

18 Prepare a list of all the methods of controlling traffic mentioned in Table 16.3 and the rest of this chapter. Add any others of which you are aware. Mark those that have been adopted in your country and rank them according to your opinion of their effectiveness. Discuss which of those left might be useful for adoption in your country.

Figure 16.11 Part of the MRT system—a train passing the Chinese garden, a major tourist attraction in Singapore

Table 16.3 Examples of schemes from around the world, designed to reduce urban transport problems

City	Traffic congestion control measure
Accra	Credit schemes to help people to buy bicycles, rickshaws and other non-motorised vehicles
Amsterdam	Local people may request that their street be converted into a woonerf or living yard
	In such streets, cars are free to enter as 'guests' but must navigate around trees and other landscaping
	This makes the street more open to people walking, cycling and children playing
Geneva	Provision of car parking at workplaces in the city centre is prohibited
Göteborg	The city centre is divided into five pie-shaped zones, all accessible from a large ring road on the periphery
	Automobiles are not allowed to cross the zone boundaries but public transport, emergency vehicles, bicycles and motor scooters may
Harare	City employees receive low cost loans to buy bicycles
	Merchants are required to provide bike parking in the CBD
Karachi	The Metrovile program enables people to build their own homes within walking distance of jobs and creates home-based workshops for producing textiles, furniture and other goods
Lima	Pedestrian-only streets introduced
London	Increased taxation for company cars each year since 1988
Manila	In 1975 fuel prices were increased by nearly 100%, car sales and registration fees increased and a light railway was built
	Between 1975 and 1985, petrol consumption fell by 43% and travel time on roads decreased by one-third
Munich	85 000 sq m pedestrian zone in the city centre
Paris	100 000 street parking places removed
Phnom Penh	Guarded bicycle parks at railway stations
Stockholm	Strict boundaries around cities to prevent 'sprawl'
	The city is ringed with satellite communities of 25 000 to 50 000 people each, linked with a rail network and expressway
	Shops, apartments and offices are clustered around railway stations that give people access to jobs on the periphery and in the centre
Tokyo	Ride-and-park schemes: Bicycle and car parks at stations on the periphery of cities
Toronto	Half all apartments built since 1954 are within walking distance of rapid-rail transport and 90% of all new offices are next to stations in the CBD Federal employees charged 70% of the commercial rate for car parking

Source: After *State of the World*, Lester R. Brown (ed.) Allen & Unwin, 1991

THE FUTURE

People in all the cities in the world need to work towards solving the problems caused by the increasing numbers of cars. It is ironic that the most economically advanced countries of the world have the greatest problems with traffic. Many people in these countries regard using a private car as a symbol of success and of good living. However, this habit results in their spending more hours travelling to work, is more expensive and reduces their health through increased pollution. Few drivers in the United States, for example, realise the full costs of motoring. They pay about US$21 per 100 kilometres for fuel, maintenance, insurance, depreciation and finance charges. In comparison, travelling by public transport costs about US$9 per 100 kilometres.

Although more public transport may seem the solution, this is not so. About one-quarter of all households in developing countries cannot afford to use public transport. In the developed world, a study of world cities has found that low urban densities of houses and jobs are associated with high dependency on cars. Sprawling cities in the United States and Australia are highly car-oriented. Medium density cities in Western Europe and Canada have greater use of public transport. And highly concentrated metropolises in Asia have more commuters who walk and cycle.

The message of these findings is that careful urban planning must go hand-in-hand with provision of public transport if cities are to keep their arteries open. While Singapore has undertaken several creative schemes to control its traffic, it has also introduced a major low-cost housing program to place jobs and homes close to each other to relieve CBD congestion without expanding the transport system at all. Time that is not spent travelling to work is available for more enjoyable pursuits. This raises the quality of life, reduces pollution and increases the health of the people and helps the economy.

Singapore has shown that it is possible to restrain the ownership and use of private cars through taxes and other measures. The ALS has reduced peak hour traffic and congestion in the CBD without hurting either the commuters or the economy. If such aims are to succeed in the long term, the secret is to reduce car usage by providing acceptable alternatives. Singapore may provide an example to inspire planners in other cities.

CHAPTER 17

PAST FLOODS: UNDERSTANDING THE GREENHOUSE EFFECT

David Wright

The greenhouse effect—is it true? Scientists are still uncertain about what will happen and many people who are not scientists are confused about what to believe. Table 17.1 lists some of the arguments that have been put forward by people on both sides of the discussion.

Table 17.1 The greenhouse effect

Yes: Warnings about the enhanced greenhouse effect are true	No: Warnings about the enhanced greenhouse effect are false
Most scientists now say that the world is getting warmer	Twenty years ago, many scientists were saying the opposite! In twenty years, will it be 'all change' again?
Temperature statistics from many weather stations show that the world is warming up	Towns and cities have grown greatly and so the 'heat islands' around cities are bigger and more noticeable. Many weather stations are in or near big cities: are they just measuring bigger 'heat islands'?
More air pollution and greenhouse gases will trap more heat	Will more air pollution make the sun shine less brightly, which could block heat reaching the earth?
A warmer day means another warmer day tomorrow, and so on ...	Extra heat can lead to more evaporation, which will lead to more cloud which will result in less heat from the sun reaching the earth
A warmer world means that the ice sheets melt faster so sea level will rise	It could mean that much more snow falls on the ice sheets ($-3°$ is warmer than $-5°$, but it is still below freezing). If more snow falls than melts, sea level could still go down
Lots of icebergs will melt	This definitely has no effect on sea level. If a block of ice melts in your cold drink, the level of drink in the glass stays the same
Extra carbon dioxide in the air will cause a warmer world	The extra carbon could be absorbed in the sea and sea creatures eventually turn it into calcium carbonate (coral, limestone etc). This has been happening for millions of years—it could just happen a bit more quickly

Pollution of the oceans could slow the making of coral	In some places that are exceptionally polluted this could be true, but there are still millions of healthy corals busy making excellent coral limestone

> 1 Discuss each of the arguments put forward in Table 17.1. Continue the argument on each line by thinking of other factors that need to be considered.

After all the arguments, the conclusion today is—we're not certain about the greenhouse effect. But we are certain that air pollution causes lots of harm and we are certain that coastlands have been lost to the sea. So it is worthwhile studying the effects on coasts—even though there is no proved link yet to the greenhouse effect.

WILL THE SEA INVADE THE LAND?

Many people do not realise that 'mean sea level' is below sea level for half of every day. Countries such as Great Britain have quite a big tidal range—the difference between high tide and low tide—even on normal days. Twice a month,

---

£7m sea defence cash is letdown

An extra £7 million earmarked for the crumbling flood defences of Norfolk and Suffolk was described by the chairman of Norfolk County Council last night as 'a drop in the ocean'.

The two counties will get the lion's share of the £24.7 million national sum from the government.

But news of the extra cash—part of which must be met by community charge payers (local taxes)—comes only weeks after a water expert said £200 million was needed to maintain the region's sea defences over the next 10 years.

Junior agriculture minister David Curry told Waveney MP David Porter in a written reply to a parliamentary question that the extra money was in recognition of 'the particular problems of the area'.

Norfolk County Council chairman Harold Rockcliffe said last night more cash was needed to safeguard the county's fragile coastline.

'It will help, but it's a drop in the ocean. It's a long, long coastline for Norfolk to make safe', he said.

---

at full moon and at new moon, there are spring tides when the high tides are much higher than usual for a few days. If there is a strong onshore wind, the problem is worse. Anywhere less than 5 metres above mean sea level will be below the level of the waves.

Figure 17.1 shows the areas of Great Britain that would be at risk if sea levels rise because of the enhanced greenhouse effect. You can undertake a similar study for any country with a coastline. Countries made of coral islands which lie close to mean sea level, such as the Maldives (a group of 1800 islands), may disappear completely.

One answer that has been suggested is to spend more money trying to protect the coast. Some people believe that human beings are stronger than nature, but others say that defending the land from the sea is money down the drain—the sea will always win in the end.

> 2 Read the boxed text above. What do you think?

While Norfolk and Suffolk have emphasised their particular problems, there are many other areas along the coastline of Great Britain that are also at risk from rising sea levels.

> 3 Figure 17.1 shows the fourteen areas most at risk from coastal flooding in Great Britain.
> *a* South-east England is sinking because of the ice retreating from northern England and Scotland. Which two areas are therefore at risk of flooding even without a rise in sea level because of the enhanced greenhouse effect?

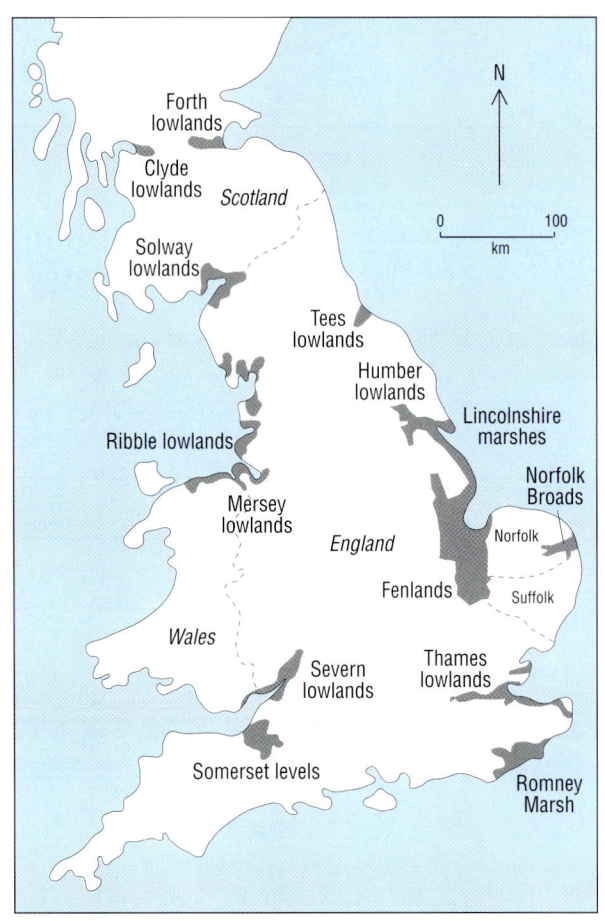

Figure 17.1   Great Britain: areas at risk from coastal flooding

PAST FLOODS: UNDERSTANDING THE GREENHOUSE EFFECT

b Estimate the relative areas at risk of flooding on the east and west of Great Britain. Study an atlas map of Great Britain which shows the areas of high and low land. Suggest reasons why one side of the country has a greater area at risk.
c Using your atlas, list the major cities or towns that are at risk.
d In your library, discover the location of Britain's nuclear power stations. List those that are at risk from flooding.

THE NORTH SEA FLOODS OF 1953

If the enhanced greenhouse effect is reality and if sea level rises and the climate changes, then looking back into history at previous extreme events is a good way of understanding what the future may bring. The greatest storm to hit the North Sea this century occurred in 1953 when tides were unusually high and winds along the east coast of Great Britain were onshore. Just as in the Netherlands, the dunes and sea defences in many areas were breached and large areas were flooded.

What has happened since 1953?

One expert in coastal geography, Professor J. A. Steers, shortly after the 1953 floods, said

> Conditions like the 1953 floods are fortunately rare—but they can and doubtless will recur. The storm of 1897, and those of earlier times, were just as severe as the 1953 storm, but the number of houses which existed on marshes then was negligible ... the great loss of life and property in 1953 resulted almost entirely from recent bungalow [single storey house] development.

In the future there will still be high and low tides, calm seas and storms. Even in the future, floods are only likely when there are both rough seas and high tides. However, rising sea levels and more severe storms will make floods more likely.

When very high tides occur off the south-eastern coast of England, especially with easterly winds, water is channelled up the Thames estuary. Much of the City of London (near Tower Bridge) upriver to Westminster and the Houses of Parliament is on low lying land and was liable to flooding. After the 1953 floods, and when they realised that south-eastern England was sinking, the Greater London Council laid plans to build a barrage to prevent the Thames from rising and flooding the centre of London.

To avoid the possibility of this happening, a barrier was built across the River Thames downstream from London at a cost of about £450 million. The barrier, shown in Figure 17.3, consists of ten 20 metre high gates that lie on the river bed. If a storm surge is threatened, the gates are raised to keep the water down river.

Press statement: From the Greater London Council

There is little doubt that the severe flooding of London could be the greatest natural disaster this country is likely to experience.

More than a million people who live in London's low-lying areas could be at risk and there could be loss of life. More than a quarter of a million homes, factories and offices could also be in danger. Thousands of cars would be swamped.

Gas and electricity supplies could be in danger and water could become contaminated.

Transport could come to a standstill in central London. The Underground system could be paralysed for six months. Buses could operate only outside the flooded areas. Thames bridges and tunnels would be unusable.

Many areas of London might be under water for days. The Houses of Parliament could be under 3 feet of water.

The direct cost of a major flood in London could be around £3000 million, the indirect cost being many times greater.

Figure 17.2 Location of east coast flooded areas in 1953

Figure 17.3 The Thames barrier

Figure 17.4 Road signs marking flood evacuation routes on Canvey Island

What to take upstairs

Figure 17.5 'What to take upstairs'—advice given to residents of Canvey Island

The Thames barrier will protect London for many years to come, but the people who live further down the Thames are still at risk. Canvey Island is a small island joined to the north shore of the Thames estuary by a bridge. In 1953, Canvey was almost entirely flooded and fifty-eight people died. Many large housing estates have been built on Canvey Island, and today about 36 000 people live there.

If you visit Canvey Island, you will see strange road signs like those shown in Figure 17.4. They mean nothing to most visitors, but every resident knows that they mark the flood evacuation routes. Everyone who lives on Canvey Island is also given a booklet which includes the picture shown in Figure 17.5. The picture tells people 'what to take upstairs' if a flood is likely.

> 4 Discuss the picture in Figure 17.5 and decide the reason each item may be important. Compare the items that are thought to be important in England with items that would be important in your country if a flood threatened.

Wells-next-the-Sea is a small coastal town and port in North Norfolk. It was flooded in 1953 and again in 1978. On both occasions the sea wall was breached during a storm. Figure 17.6 shows the results of the storm that hit the town

Figure 17.6a The 1978 floods at Wells-next-the-Sea where the sea wall was breached

Figure 17.6b The coaster Function *was deposited on the quay when the water subsided*

in January 1978. Storm waters covered the quayside and flooded the shops. They also deposited a seagoing ship on the quayside and it took quite some time to remove it!

The reaction of the local council in 1978 was very similar to that in 1953. They rebuilt and strengthened the sea wall again and added a flood gate for the quayside to prevent water from spreading to the rest of the town.

> 5 The areas in danger from floods are approximately those below the 5 metre contour line. Make a copy of the map of Wells-next-the-Sea. Shade the sea in dark blue and the area likely to be flooded in lighter blue. Write a brief report on the risks of flooding in Wells-next-the-Sea in the future.
> 6 The possibility of flooding in this town is a matter of concern at both the local and the national levels. Here are two simulation activities to explore how people at the two levels may react to the problem.

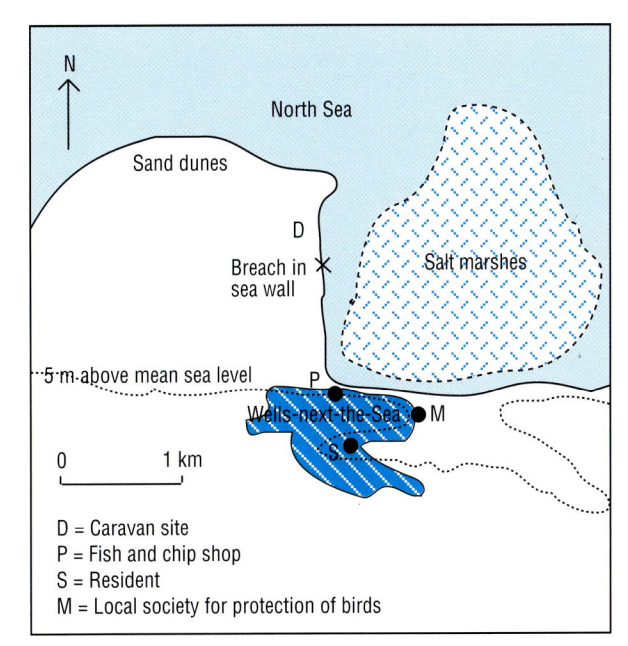

Figure 17.7 The site of Wells-next-the-Sea

D = Caravan site
P = Fish and chip shop
S = Resident
M = Local society for protection of birds

> **The Wells-next-the-Sea Flood Action Committee**
> - Dave runs a caravan site at D on the map. His livelihood is threatened by a flood. He is a member of the Tourist Committee.
> - Pat runs a fish and chip shop at P on the map. Her livelihood is also threatened by a flood and she is a member of the local Chamber of Trade.
> - Stef is a member of the Residents' Association and lives in the house marked S on the map. Maintaining a high quality of life and the value of houses is a priority for Stef's group.
> - Mike is retired and works as a volunteer for the Royal Society for the Protection of Birds. He 'keeps an eye' on the area to the north and east of his house at M on the map. This area is home to many local and migrating birds

> a For each of the four people mentioned above, discuss possible reasons why they chose to locate their activities in the places shown, and why each of those locations is threatened by potential floods.
> b Prepare a case for one of these people to argue at a Public Enquiry for future action. Should more money be spent on coastal defences or are there alternative actions that could be taken?
> c Divide the class into four and pool your suggestions on how the interests of each group listed above could be best served. Each class group should then appoint one person to represent them at a Public Enquiry.
> d Hold a Public Enquiry into future action in this area. Your teacher may chair the enquiry. The representatives of the four groups should present their cases to the Chair while the rest of the class represents the general public and may question the speakers.
> e At the end of the enquiry, prepare a petition to the local member of parliament. Present your conclusions on how best the town should be helped with its flooding problems.
> 7 The local member of parliament understands that the government wants to cut public spending, but also wants the people of Wells-next-the-Sea to vote for her at the next election. Draft a reply to the petition for her in which she explains why the government is unlikely to find enough money for the extra expenditure needed to make the town safe.

POSSIBLE RESULTS OF AN ENHANCED GREENHOUSE EFFECT

The Norfolk Broads form one of Britain's largest wetland areas. The Broads are a group of twenty-five freshwater lakes just to the north-west of Great Yarmouth (see Figure 17.2). They were once thought to be natural, but historical research has shown that peat diggers before AD 1300 removed 25.5 million cubic metres of peat for heating and cooking purposes. The holes left have filled with water. It is also possible that the rising sea level has helped in this process.

Today, the Broads and their old villages attract thousands of tourists each year and are important for their rare plants, birds, insects and mammals.

The Broads have experienced great problems from pressure of people. The water becomes polluted by wastes from motor cruisers as well as fertilisers and pesticides from the farms. There are no gates between the Broads and the sea

Table 17.2   Problems noted in the Broads Authority pamphlet

Today's problems	Today's solutions—Broads Authority answers
The Fens The problem: Loss of important wildlife habitats	
What's gone wrong? The Broadland fens are large open areas of reeds, sedges and other plants growing on a spongy peat soil. For hundreds of years they used to be cut regularly to provide thatching for roofs and food for cattle. This has declined over the last 50 years and the fens are reverting to woodland.	The Broads Authority is supporting conservation groups who own fens with grants and the loan of specialist machinery to encourage fen management. Many of the best fens are in private ownership and the Authority offers help as advice, grant aid, and a labour supply to manage their land.
Grazing marshes: The problem: One quarter of the broads' unique grazing marsh has been ploughed up for agriculture	
What's gone wrong? The European Union's common agricultural policy made cereal farming more profitable than dairy and beef cattle. Farmers were given grants to deep-drain and convert their grazing marsh to cropland.	Encourage the type of farming which has created this unique grazing marsh landscape. To do this, Halvergate marshes have been declared an Environmentally Sensitive Area under the Broads Grazing Marsh Conservation Scheme
Water quality: The problem: Cloudy, lifeless rivers and broads	
What's gone wrong? The delicate chemical balance of the water has been upset by pollution—phosphates from sewage effluent and nitrates from farm fertilisers	Isolate and mud-pump the Broads. This removes the pollution from the water and dumps it back on the banks where it forms very fertile soil. This treatment is only suitable for private broads with no rights of navigation. Also, remove phosphates from sewage effluent before the remainder is pumped into the broads.
Bank erosion: The problem: Banks along the broads are eroding up to 3 m in 10 years	
What's gone wrong? Poor water quality has made the banks more vulnerable to erosion as they are no longer naturally protected by water plants. The banks of both rivers and broads are being washed away by waves from motor cruisers.	Protect the banks either naturally or artificially. This may include reducing the wash from boats by imposing speed limits; and changing the design of boats so that the hull shape causes less wash (long, thin, boats produce less wash than the present generation of broads cruisers).
The Broads as a holiday area: The problem: The thriving holiday industry puts pressure on the quiet riverside villages	
What's gone wrong? Some of the broads villages have developed without sufficient care with ugly, out of character buildings, kiosks and amusement halls. Badly designed chalets and houseboats now line some river banks.	The Authority is improving facilities for visitors and landscaping heavily used riverside areas so that broads villages can cope with visitors and be attractive places for people to live in.

Figure 17.8a Filby Broad and Rollesby Broad—note the variety of vegetation and intensive farming in the Broads area

Figure 17.8b Oulton Broad is particularly popular with tourists who hire cruisers in the summer months

Figure 17.8c Many birds visit the Broads in the winter months—these ducks are resident at Filby Broad

to protect them from salt creeping upriver as a result of rising sea levels.

In a pamphlet entitled 'Last Enchanted Land' the Broads Authority listed five problems and five present-day solutions, but they did not even mention the enhanced greenhouse effect. The problems and solutions are summarised in Table 17.2.

> 8 *a* For each of the problems recognised by the Broads Authority, discuss ways in which the enhanced greenhouse effect may cause new problems. At the same time, consider what solutions could be adopted. Remember that the negative effects of the enhanced greenhouse effect may be to
> - increase the risk of flooding
> - increase the height and range of the tides
> - cause an influx of salt water further inland
> - result in tourists being less willing to visit a high-flood risk area.
>
> *b* There may be some advantages also if the climate becomes a little warmer and the rainfall of the area (currently about 650 millimetres per year) increases. How may these positive factors balance the negative factors mentioned above?

THE FUTURE

Human beings in the past have survived changes in sea level similar to those which are threatened now. However, the cost has often been very high. Money spent on sea defences cannot be spent on other projects, such as improving the quality of life for the many people in the world who live in poverty. Furthermore, we are not even sure whether the changes in temperature, carbon dioxide and sea levels that have been measured are linked.

If global warming does continue, then there will be changes in other aspects of the world's climate. The prairie provinces of Canada and central Australia, for example, may enjoy higher rainfalls than they receive at present, and may be able to grow more food. Plant growth all over the world would be helped by higher levels of carbon dioxide.

Whatever the outcome of the debate about the enhanced greenhouse effect, it will have encouraged many more people to think about how our lives are linked to one another and with nature. The scientific interest in the greenhouse effect also means that we know much more about the amounts of pollution that our actions create in the natural environment. We already know many of the damaging effects of such pollution. That in itself is enough to encourage us to treat the natural environment with respect, perhaps by changing our lifestyles.

CHAPTER 18

THE NETHERLANDS AND GLOBAL WARMING

Marga Terwindt

At the end of the last ice age (10 000 years ago) the ice at the poles and the glaciers in the mountains of the world began to melt. This resulted in a rise in sea level. During the same period, the land surface of the Netherlands has sunk due to compaction. The result is that over the last 10 000 years, sea level compared with the land of the Netherlands has risen by 100 metres. Although the greatest changes in sea level occurred up to 5000 years ago, the trend has continued. Figure 18.2 shows that sea level rose 20 centimetres in the last 100 years. In the next 100 years the sea may rise between 35 and 85 centimetres (say about 60 centimetres) because of the enhanced greenhouse effect. These estimates have not been proved, but this chapter will assume that a rise in sea level of about this amount will occur.

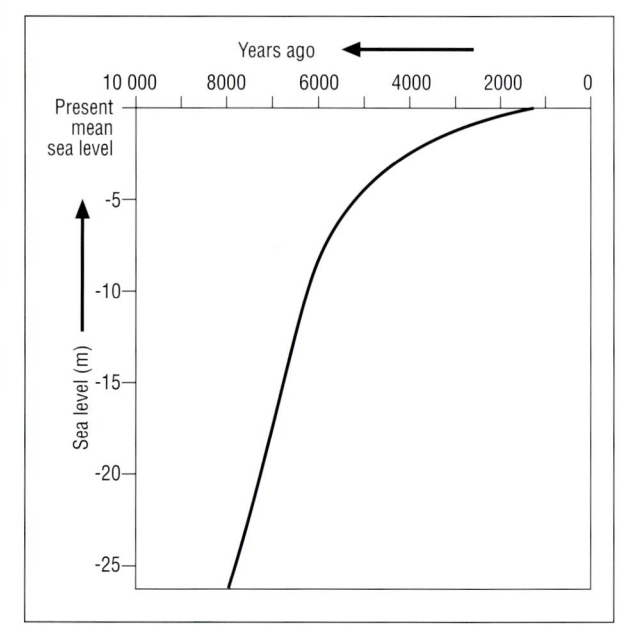

Figure 18.1 Melting polar ice and the sinking of the land in the Netherlands has resulted in a relative increase in sea level of about 100 metres in the past 10 000 years

The changes in relative sea level are due to several factors. From Table 18.1 you will notice that the expansion of sea water is likely to be the major contributor to rises in the future.

Table 18.1 The various factors that contribute to a rise in sea level

Cause	Today (%)	Future (%)
Melting glaciers	28	29
Melting polar ice	11	10
Expansion of sea water	28	49
Sinking land surface	33	12

Source: Natuur Museum, Groningen

THE NETHERLANDS AND GLOBAL WARMING

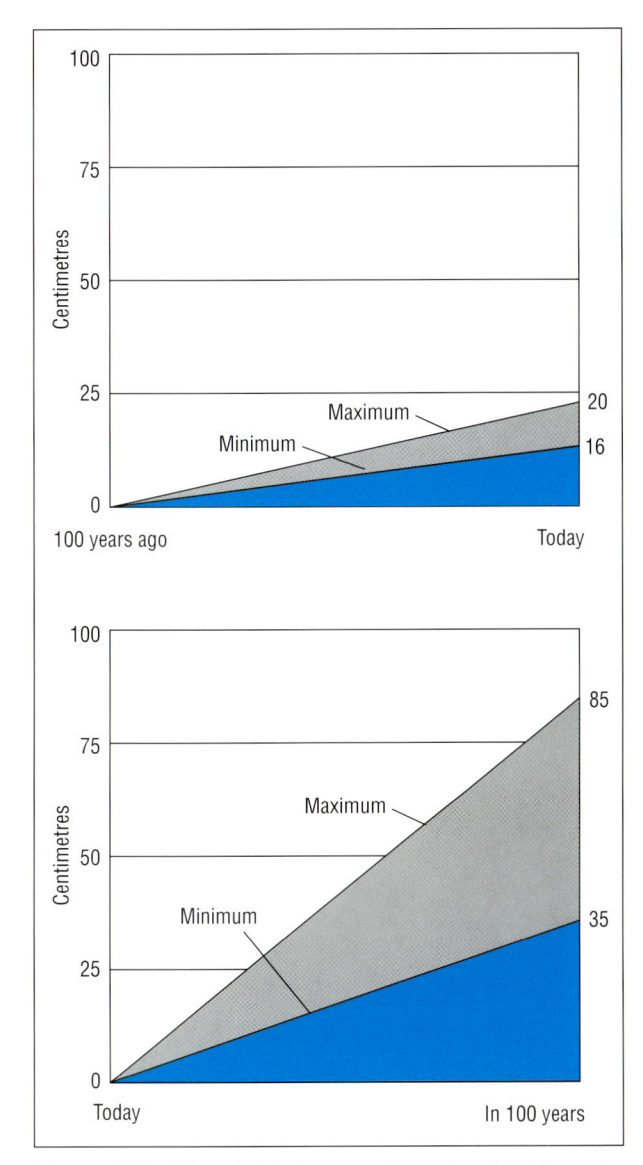

Figure 18.2 The relative increase in sea level in the past 100 years and the expectation for the next 100 years—in each graph, today's sea level is taken as 0, and a maximum and minimum possible change are given

Figure 18.3 shows that more than half of the Netherlands is situated below mean sea level. The Dutch have been fighting against the sea for more than a thousand years. In former days the land was only protected by sand dunes. Sometimes the sea water broke through the dunes and drowned the area behind. As a result, it became marshy and wet. About 500 BC the people started to build hills called **terpen** to live on.

Until about the year 1000 these terpen were safe enough but the rise in the sea level continued and new solutions had to be sought. The Dutch then started building dykes or walls around areas of alluvial deposition and so made the area fit for occupation. These reclaimed areas are called **polders**. The earliest polders were reclaimed in the northern part of the Netherlands. In the sixteenth century many of the lakes, some of which resulted from breaks in the dykes and others from the excavation of peat for heating, were also reclaimed. Today, most of the Netherlands is protected by dunes and dykes.

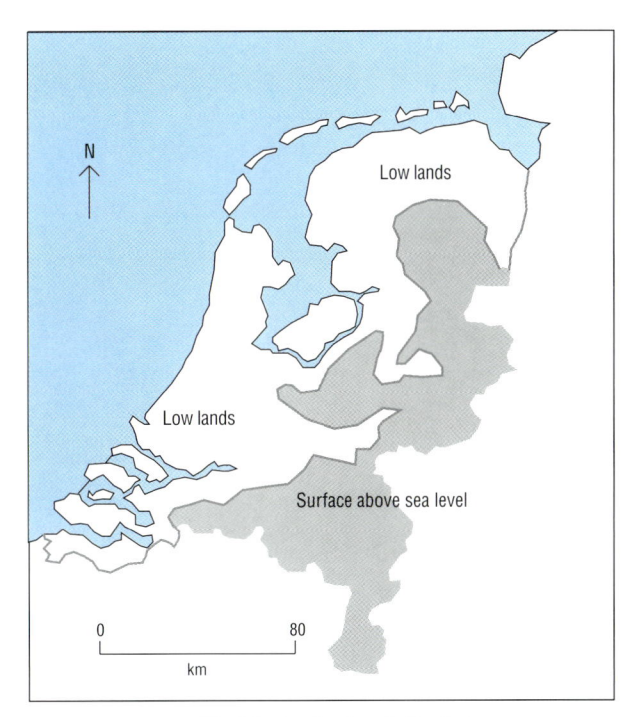

Figure 18.3 Half of the Netherlands lies below mean sea level

Figure 18.4 This house is built on a 'terp' or hill

Table 18.2 Land reclaimed from the sea per century

Date	sq km
1200–1300	350
1300–1400	350
1400–1500	425
1500–1600	710
1600–1700	1120
1700–1800	500
1800–1900	1170
1900–2000	2300

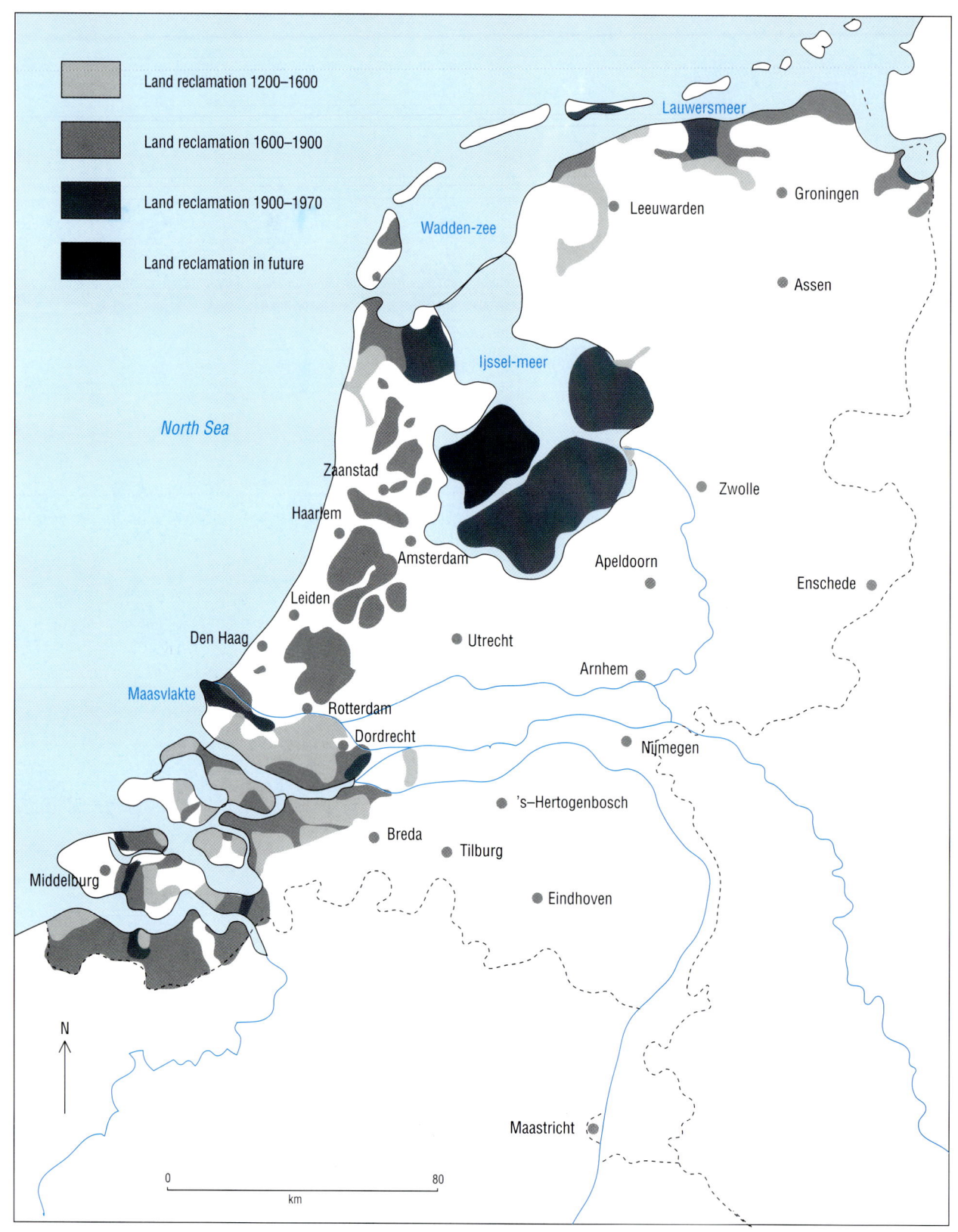

Figure 18.5 The progress in reclaiming and protecting land from the sea in the last 800 years

In 1930 the government took over the responsibility for the reclamation of future land and today the total reclaimed area has reached 6926 square kilometres. While the polders have traditionally been drained by windmills, the work was later taken on by steam and then diesel pumps and today is mainly electric.

Figure 18.6 Dutch windmills

During a severe storm surge on the night of 1 February 1953, many dykes broke and large areas were flooded. This disaster, in which more than 1800 people lost their lives, led to the execution of the Delta Project. This project involved closing several estuaries (see Figure 18.7). This shortened the coastline and created a modern sea defence system which can withstand storm surges with a frequency of occurrence of 1:10 000 years. It took thirty years to finish the project and the last dam was closed in 1986.

The total length of the Dutch North Sea coast is 353 kilometres of which about 75 per cent consists of sand dunes. The natural forces of waves, currents and winds are constantly working on the coastline, sometimes eroding and sometimes depositing.

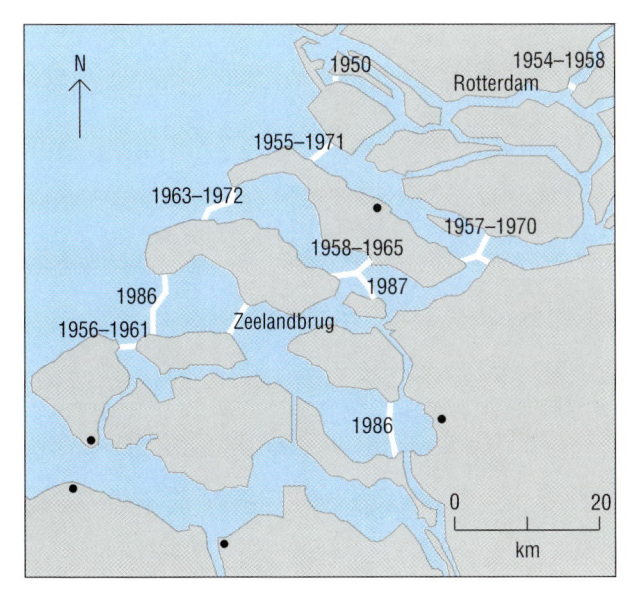

Figure 18.7 The Delta Project—dams were built across estuaries to reduce the exposed coastline from 800 to 30 kilometres

Figure 18.8 One of the dams across the estuaries in the Delta Project

1. The Dutch have been fighting the sea for a thousand years. Discuss the possible reasons why the early Dutch did not merely move further inland on to higher ground.
2. Use an atlas to prepare a map of the Netherlands locating the main towns and cities. Discuss the location of the Dutch population in relation to water.

THE NETHERLANDS AND A RISING SEA

Figure 18.2 shows the maximum and minimum likely rises in sea levels for the next 100 years. While there is no way of knowing precisely what will happen, there is strong evidence that the sea level will continue to rise.

There are three elements that protect the polder lands from flooding: the bank, the beach and the dune area. The landward boundary of the dune area is the polder line. The seaward boundary of the bank is the 20 metre deep contour.

In a normal situation the beach separates the dunes and the sea. During a storm, the sea can reach the dunes and erode them. This sand is then deposited on the bank. After a storm the seaward dunes are temporarily narrowed and the beach is wider for some time until eventually the dunes are re-formed.

Figure 18.9 Dunes are formed by windblown sand—these dunes have a pioneer vegetation of marram grass

On the other hand, if the eroded sand is transported away by waves or currents, then the dune erosion is permanent, in which case the coast is slowly retreating and we are dealing with coastal erosion.

Finally, a rising sea level will increase the coastal processes and the profile of the coast adapts itself to the higher sea level. This means that there is a narrower dune line to protect the polders and the effect of future storms may be to breach the dune line completely.

> 3 Describe the coastline near you. Is it natural or engineered? Is it being eroded or built up?

Already, nearly 50 per cent of the coastal dunes are being eroded. The immediate effect, as illustrated in Figure 18.10, is that the marram grass is killed and the dunes are then open to wind erosion and sea erosion. If sea level continues to rise, as expected, then these coastal erosion processes will be even more threatening. The erosion may not look dramatic on a map, but behind the dunes 50 per cent of the Netherlands already lies beneath mean sea level.

Fortunately, the Netherlands is not in immediate danger of drowning. In many places the dunes are wide and high enough and no dangerous situation will occur. However, 17 per cent of the dune coastline has less than 10 metres of dune width left. Of this 17 per cent, half lies in the south of the Netherlands where the polders are most densely settled.

WHAT SHOULD BE DONE IN THE FUTURE?

For much of the time that the Dutch have been fighting the sea they have adopted 'hard' approaches which involve coastal engineering measures. After the completion of the Delta Project, the dykes are safe for the present. However, the dunes are being weakened. The most common remedy at present is beach nourishment. This involves pumping large volumes of sand on to the beach and foredunes. Of course this sand may be eroded again, but that takes time and meanwhile the coast is safe. What further measures have to be taken depends on the rate of the rise of the sea level.

There is, however, a range of 'softer' options which involve changes in lifestyle. In areas which have not been settled for as long as the Netherlands, it may be desirable to accept the changes of the coastline and adjust human behaviour accordingly. However, in the Netherlands, where the people have reclaimed their land from the water over so many years, this is not possible. The future of the Netherlands could well depend on the rest of the world making lifestyle decisions. While it is likely that sea level will continue to rise, the rate of that rise appears to depend on the level of the enhanced greenhouse effect and global warming. This will in turn depend on lowering emissions of the greenhouse gases, in particular those of carbon dioxide.

Figure 18.10 Eroded dunes on the North Sea coast

> 4 Find out as many 'hard' engineering approaches to coastal management as you can. List the ways in which human beings affect the coastline. Where are such methods successful and where are they less successful?
> 5 List as many 'soft' approaches to meeting the problems of rising sea levels as you can. Discuss which of these techniques can be adopted by the Dutch on their own and which must be global in approach.
> 6 Do people in your country adopt 'hard' or 'soft' techniques when faced with problems on the coast?
> 7 Research greenhouse gases, the greenhouse effect and global warming. Write a report on current developments.
> 8 a Why is reducing the emission of greenhouse gases described as 'lifestyle choices'? Who has to make these decisions?
> b Why are techniques of managing coastal defence problems by influencing people's lifestyle choices sometimes known as 'soft approaches'?

CHAPTER 19

ENERGY: A PERSISTENT GLOBAL ISSUE

Joseph P. Stoltman

We all use energy in one form or another. It is used to cook food, to warm or cool houses, and as a substitute for human labour, powering machines that make manufacturing, transportation, and communications possible. These activities contribute to and signify economic development.

Energy also has another face. It is the face of environmental degradation. Environmental damage often results when energy is used. Sometimes it is the wastes that result from energy use. This is especially true in the extraction and consumption of the fossil fuels—coal, oil, peat, and natural gas. Some, such as coal, leave huge scars when they are extracted. They also contribute the majority of pollutants that affect the air. One consequence of fossil energy being burned is the release of greenhouse gases—mainly carbon dioxide—to the atmosphere. Greenhouse gases are believed to have an important effect on global climate change.

Non-fossil energy, such as hydro-electric, wind, and nuclear power, is not free from environmental consequences either. Nuclear power raises concerns about disposing of radioactive waste, and the risk of accidents. Figure 19.1 shows the areas of Europe that were affected when a fire occurred at the nuclear power station at Chernobyl in the Ukraine in 1986. Traces of radiation were also detected right across the globe.

Other sources of energy also present environmental risks. Large scale hydro-electric dams flood the landscape, changing habitats, and altering river biosystems. Hydro-electric projects have been cancelled due to their likely impacts upon threatened or endangered species. Dams constructed in areas subject to earthquakes require engineering safeguards that greatly increase costs. In the same way, windmills used to power electric generators stand out in the landscape, changing greatly the natural appearance of large areas. Figure 19.2 shows how our needs for all types of energy change the landscapes in which we live.

1 Discuss the photographs in Figure 19.2 with a classmate. What are the environmental consequences of each of these forms of gaining energy? (You may consider effects on the landscape, the atmosphere, safety and any other aspects of the environment that you can think of.)

Energy is something that everyone relies upon. It has a special place in any discussion of economic issues surrounding the use of global resources, environmental issues, including atmospheric pollution and global change, when considering the social wellbeing of people in different parts of the world.

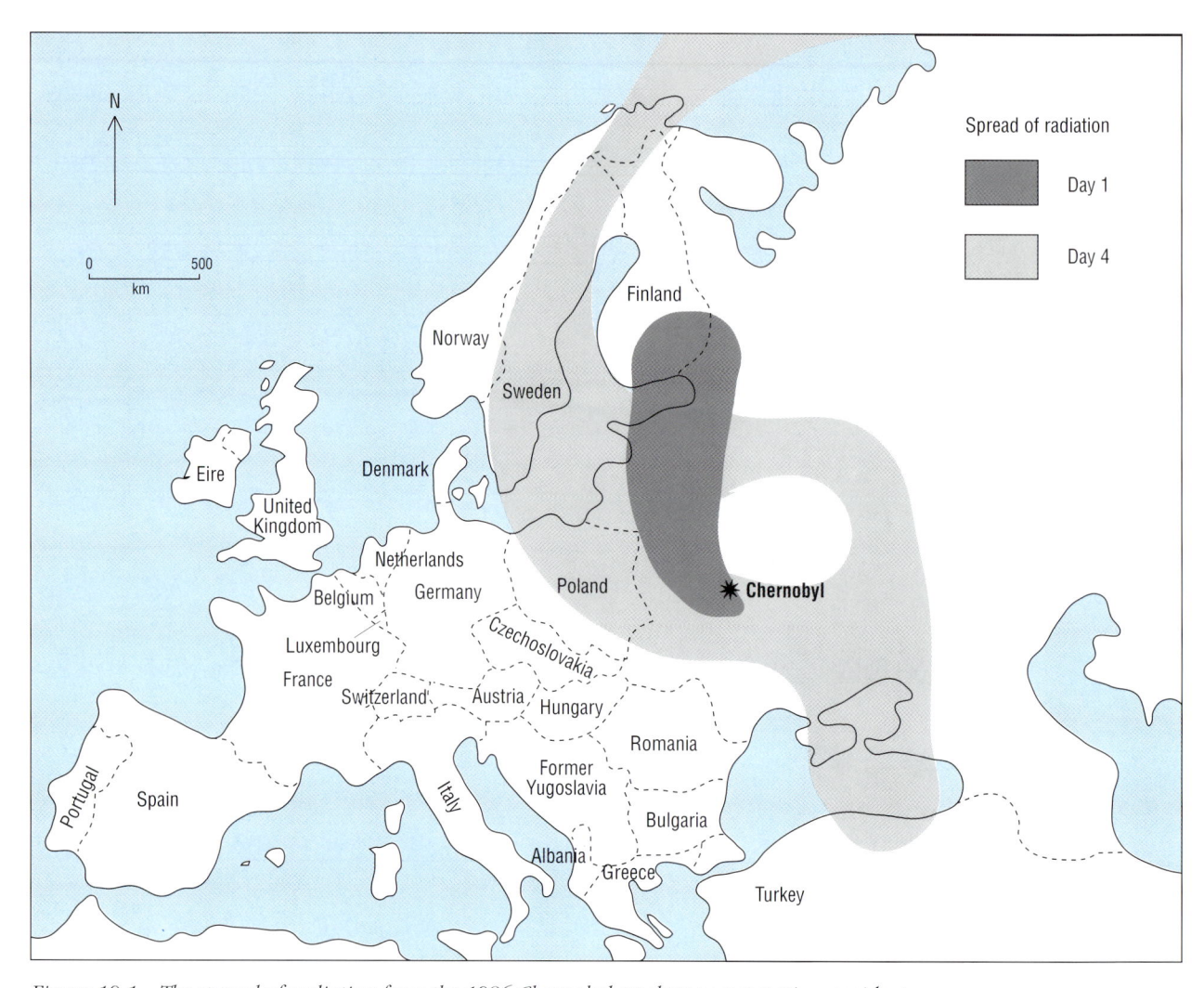

Figure 19.1 The spread of radiation from the 1986 Chernobyl nuclear power station accident

WORLD ENERGY PRODUCTION AND CONSUMPTION

Energy fuels the economies of countries and encourages the development of better living conditions, whether it is transportation or powering technologically-appropriate threshing machines. People respond to the benefits of energy use, but rarely do they predict the negative consequences of increased energy consumption.

There are two very basic questions that must be asked when studying the geography of energy. First, where does energy come from at the global scale? Second, what purpose does energy serve us as individuals and groups of

Figure 19.2a   An open pit coalmine in West Virginia

Figure 19.2b   A nuclear power station on Lake Michigan

Figure 19.2c   Solar panels on a private house in Michigan

people? This second question relates to the global consumption of, or demand for, energy. The production and consumption of and demands for energy vary from place to place and change with time. The geographic study of energy provides important information about both energy resources/production and consumption/demand patterns.

Sources of energy

Almost all the energy on earth has the sun as its origin. The energy elements based upon the sun that people use regularly include the following.

Energy sources related to sunlight
- **Fossil fuels**—Coal, oil, natural gas, and peat are based on carbon fuels made possible by plants and animals. Green plants use sunlight to produce energy, and animals consume plants. Both result in the storage of carbon.
- **Biomass**—The wood and grass vegetation that grows using sunlight to convert carbon dioxide and water into energy.
- **Wind**—The warming of earth and water and the mixing of warm and cool air results in the wind, which can be harnessed and converted to energy.
- **Sunlight**—The sunlight the earth receives warms the surface and the objects on it. Sunlight may also be used to produce electricity using photovoltaic cells.
- **Chemical processes**—Methanol and ethanol are chemically based alcohol products that may be used instead of oil, for example when alcohol (gasahol) replaces gasoline (petrol) used in cars and trucks. There is also a chemically based means to produce electricity using the hydrogen fuel cell. This experimental process uses oxygen and hydrogen to form water (H_2O) and in so doing releases an electrical charge that can be controlled.

Energy sources not related directly to sunlight
- **Nuclear**—Energy that comes from atomic particles that are split or joined to produce heat, a form of energy.
- **Tidal**—The effects of the moon and, to a much lesser extent, the sun, on the motion of the oceans and seas.

Figure 19.2d   A wind farm at Altamont Pass, California

- **Geothermal**—Residual energy in the form of heat from the core of the earth. This is most apparent when volcanoes erupt, but is also evident when geothermally heated water comes to or near the surface.

Energy from the sun

What is the amount of energy that comes from the sun? The sunlight that reaches the earth each year is equal to about 15 000 times the total energy supply of the earth from traditional sources such as coal and natural gas. This is a huge amount, but tapping it as a usable source is not so easy. First, about 30 per cent of the incoming sunlight is reflected back into space from snow, cloud, and water surfaces. About 50 per cent of the sunlight is absorbed by the earth, converted to heat, and re-radiated into the atmosphere and space. It takes about 20 per cent of the incoming energy from the sun to keep the water cycle working. Only a very small part (about 0.06 per cent) of the sunlight is used by plants in the process of photosynthesis.

The sun is the primary source of energy for earth. Most people are not seriously concerned with the sun's production of energy, although they may miss it if there are too many cloudy days. Few people realise how much they rely on the transformed energy from the sun that is made available for their consumption as electricity or petrol. They only become concerned when there is a disruption in the production of available energy because the flow of oil in world markets is reduced greatly, or a severe storm causes problems with the electrical power grid, leaving people in the dark.

The daily dependence on energy for cooking, heating, and lighting makes people concerned for its reliable delivery whether it is wood, charcoal, or electricity.

While the tropics receive the rays from the sun most directly, its energy is distributed predictably to the rest of the globe by the movements of the winds. Other types of energy, however, have patterns that result in uneven availability and uneven consumption. This necessitates the exchange, or trade, of energy around the world. Oil may be used as an example of this.

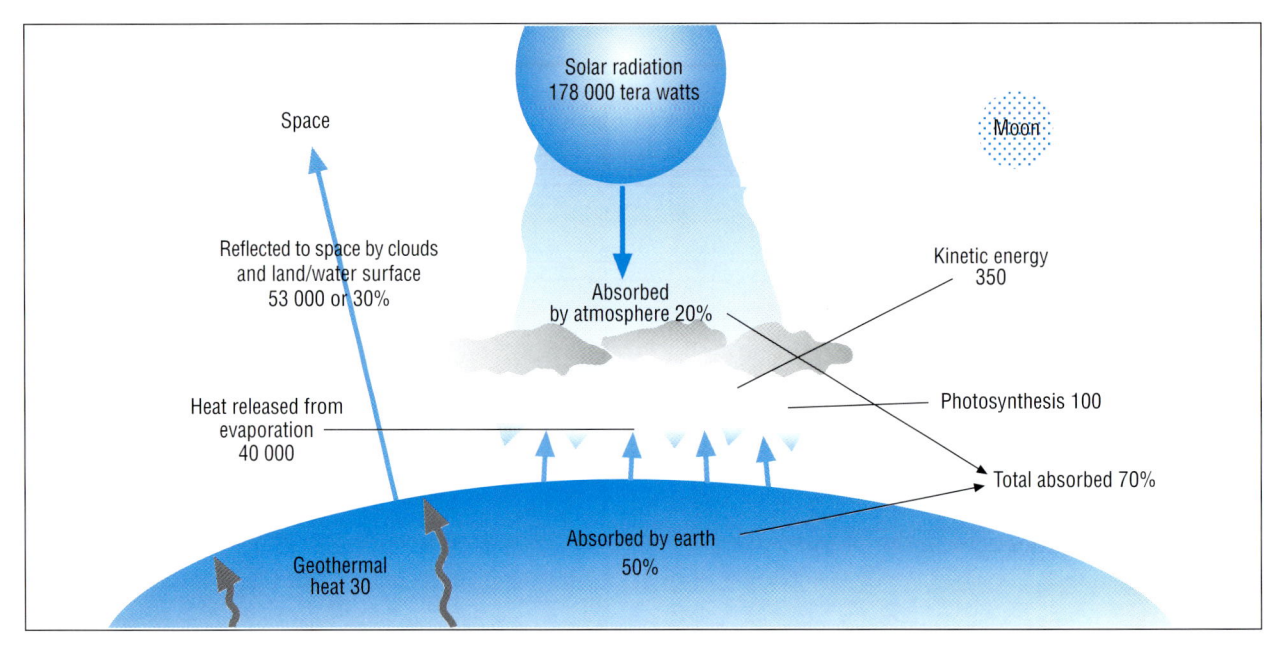

Figure 19.3 What happens to the sun's energy

The world flow of oil

Energy in the form of oil moves around the world in specific patterns between where it is produced and where it is consumed.

Figure 19.5 tells you two main things about the movement of oil. The first is about the direction, distance and quantity of oil being moved. The second is about the pattern of oil movements that develops across the earth.

> 2 *a* What region exports the largest amount of oil?
> *b* What three areas in the world consume most of the oil from major exporting regions?
> *c* What are the world's five major transportation routes for oil?
> 3 *a* Discuss possible reasons that might explain the large flow of energy to some regions, but not to others.
> *b* Why do some regions both import and export oil? (Hint: Some countries, such as the United States, produce large amounts of oil, but consume even greater amounts. Some oil products are very valuable for export and leave a country whereas others are in short supply and must be imported. Oil for jet fuel may be imported while heavy crude oil used in making road tar may be exported.)
> 4 Where does your home region fall in this global pattern of oil movement?

These flow patterns may also be explained by examining the crude oil production by region. Figure 19.4 shows the percentage of total crude oil produced in the world by major regions. Combining the information from Figures 19.4 and 19.5 makes it possible to produce additional knowledge about world oil flows.

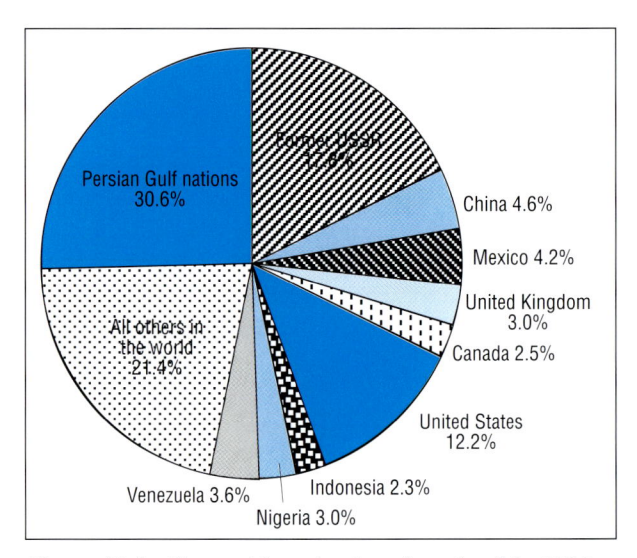

Figure 19.4 The world production of crude oil in 1990

> 5 *a* What information does Figure 19.4 present that supports the Persian Gulf region as a major oil producing area?
> *b* What countries are second and third after the Persian Gulf region in the total production of oil?
> *c* Compare the flow arrows on Figure 19.5 with the production levels on Figure 19.4. What major oil producing country also imported large amounts of oil from other regions of the world?

The world oil flow map shows both where oil is produced and where it is consumed. Countries and people at the destinations of the oil flows use the energy resource for a number of purposes. Some oil is used to generate electricity in huge cities, while some is burned in kerosene lamps

ENERGY: A PERSISTENT GLOBAL ISSUE

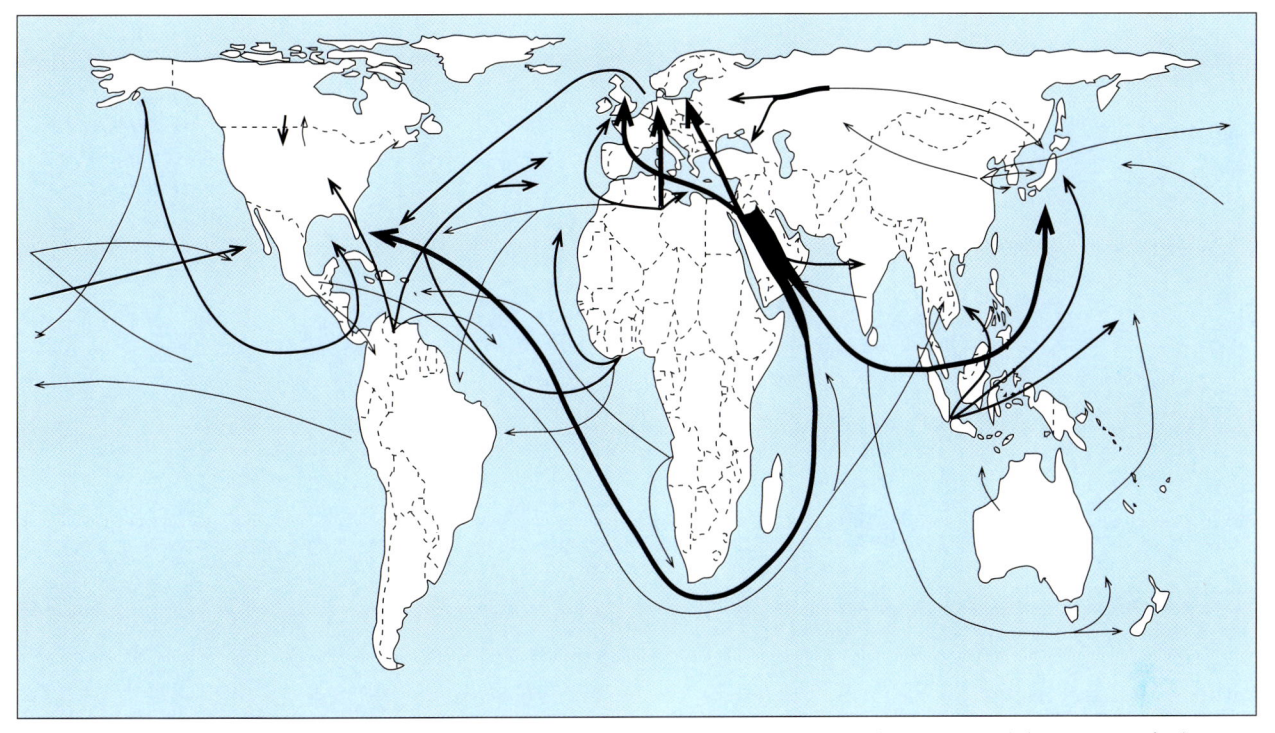

Figure 19.5 The movement of energy as oil around the world—the arrows indicate the origin and destination of oil transport, but not specific amounts or routes

in small mountain villages. Some is used for petrol and diesel fuel to power cars, trucks, aeroplanes and ships. Oil is also used for powering industry and in petrochemicals.

The measure that tells about the consumption of oil is the amount of energy used by each person in a country. It is called per capita energy use, or energy use per person (see Table 19.1). The energy use is measured in the equivalent of barrels of oil, even though some of the energy was produced from coal, natural gas, geothermal, and hydro-electricity. These four are called the primary sources of energy. The figures do not include traditional energy sources, such as wood, grass, or animal dung, which are also important in many places.

The yearly world average consumption of energy per head is approximately the equivalent of eight barrels of oil.

The data in Table 19.2 make it possible to extend generalisations and hypotheses regarding the global consumption of energy from the primary sources. For example, the information in Table 19.2 may be mapped to determine those

Table 19.1 Annual energy consumption per head of population in selected countries, 1988

Country	Barrels of oil equivalent
Canada	44
United States	41
Australia	37
Saudi Arabia	34
Sweden	30
Germany	27
Former USSR	23
United Kingdom	20
Japan	18
Italy	15
Spain	11
Zambia	8
Mexico	6
Brazil	5
Uruguay	4
China	3
Egypt	3
Nigeria	1
India	1

Table 19.2 Average annual energy consumption per head of population for world regions, 1988

World region	Barrels of oil equivalent
South America	4.3
Africa	1.7
Asia	3.0
Oceania	21.0
North America	28.0
Europe	18.5
Former USSR	28.0

Source: Energy Information Administration, *Annual Energy Review*, 1989

parts of the world that consume above average amounts and those that consume below average amounts of primary energy.

> 6 *a* Classify the regions of the world into two major categories—those regions that use more than the global annual per capita average of eight barrels equivalent of energy and those that use less than the average.
> *b* Draw a world map and locate the regions. Shade the two categories in different colours.
> *c* Study the categories on the map. Are they in distinct areas as groupings? What conclusions can you draw about the pattern of energy consumption on the map?
> 7 Use the information in Table 19.1 to test if the generalisation is true for all the countries in each region. Look specifically at Japan, Saudi Arabia, and Mexico. Do those countries differ from the dominant regional pattern? For each country, suggest reasons why it differs from its regional pattern.

ENERGY AND PUBLIC POLICY IN THE UNITED STATES

One of the common questions regarding energy focuses on demand, and how demand, or consumption, changes. Changes in energy production are generally in response to demand, although a country's national energy policy may also alter production. For example, the minimum distance standard legislated for new automobiles in the United States reduced petrol consumption in the 1980s. As a result, petrol prices decreased and the search for alternative sources of energy for powering cars was delayed.

The price of producing oil from oil shale would have been about US$25 per barrel. This was a viable economic activity if imported and domestic crude remained at a price above US$25 on the world market. However, if the price dropped below US$25, then the synthetic fuels would no longer be competitive. The question became: 'Why develop an alternative fuel at US$25 per barrel equivalent when US$17 per barrel petroleum is available on the world market?' In fact, that is exactly what happened. Short term prices of oil diminished the necessity to seek long term solutions in the form of alternative fuels. Many of the energy policies of the past in the United States have been based on production. This often meant that greater production was better.

In the future people will have more choices regarding the energy efficiency of the activities they pursue—such as more energy-efficient cars. In addition, urban and regional planning, which considers landuses that reduce dependence on long distance commuting by car, are policies being examined in the United States. New types of transportation networks and more efficient ways to select travel routes are reducing the amount of energy used. Refrigerators, recycling, and the heating and cooling of buildings are all receiving greater attention regarding energy efficiency.

The efficient use of energy has developed as a major policy issue in the United States. In some cases, as with petrol consumption, the higher fuel efficiency is partly the result of legislated public policy and partly the result of the manufacturer meeting consumer demands for more fuel-efficient cars.

While energy use in transport may be influenced by government action, the recycling of containers in the United States is often at the initiative of local citizens. The citizens establish a local policy and program for recycling centres or kerbside pick up of materials that are to be recycled. In some states, such as Oregon and Michigan, citizens have led initiatives to pass laws that result in the state-wide recycling of materials. The recycling of metal and glass contain-

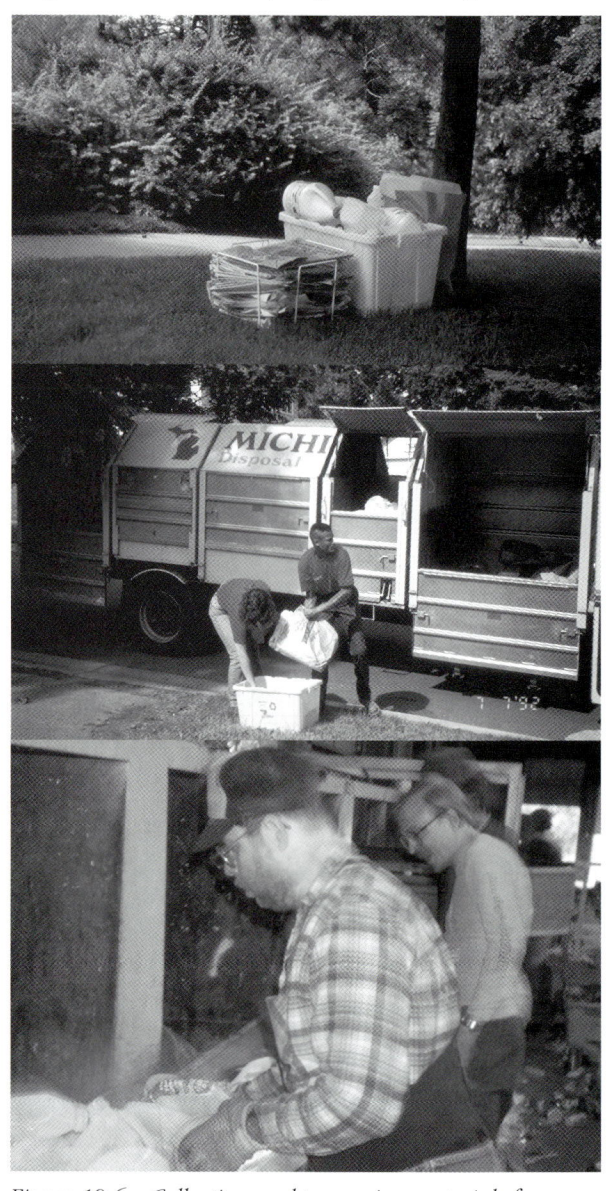

Figure 19.6 Collecting and processing materials for recycling in Kalamazoo, Michigan

ers is a program that reaches many people because they use those containers regularly.

In Kalamazoo, Michigan, a community-wide program of refuse separation and recycling began in 1991. The grassroots nature of the program may be witnessed during a schedule of alternate pick up days along residential streets. Figure 19.6 shows the process where the materials to be recycled are sorted into glass, paper and metal into recycling bins by the resident, collected into containers in the truck by type of material, and sorted for processing and recycling based on the type at a central facility.

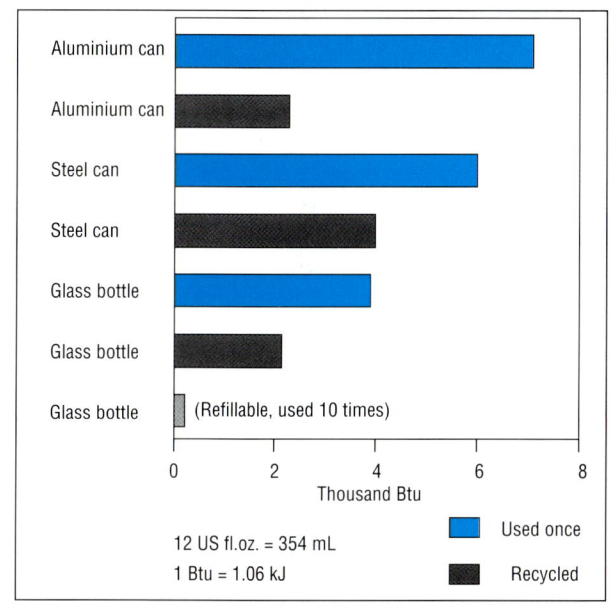

Figure 19.7 The amount of energy required to produce and reuse a 12 US ounce soft drink container

Community information regarding the collection schedule and drop-off locations for other recyclable items, such as coated papers and special plastics, as well as household hazardous wastes such as paints, solvents and pesticides, is published in the local newspaper. In this way, the project takes on community wide participation and results in a major change in public policy and the perception of recycling.

> 8 What facilities are there in your community for recycling household wastes? Compare them with the system operating in Kalamazoo. What could your community learn from the Kalamazoo system? How do you think the Kalamazoo system could be improved?

The energy used in the production of bottles and cans for drinks and other liquid products may be greatly reduced by recycling and reusing containers. It is also an excellent example of the effects that individual choices by people who consume bottled and canned drinks can have on energy use. Your decision to purchase products in reusable containers has an important energy saving function.

> 9 Imagine that you and two other students are members of the management board of a soft drink company in the United States. Your board has already decided that the company will have only two types of containers to market its soft drinks: cans and bottles. The company is concerned with holding costs down, and is looking for the most cost-effective way to produce and market soft drinks. The company is also concerned with a growing public recognition that recycling and energy conservation are good policies.
> *a* Based on the data in Figure 19.7, what containers will you recommend to the management board?
> *b* Discuss how the containers may affect the cost of marketing soft drinks, save valuable resources, and help protect the environment.
> *c* Develop a written company policy that addresses these issues.

Improvements in recycling in the United States

The United States is going through a major rethinking process on waste disposal. The recycling of materials is viewed as a local priority by many people. Customers are urged to return metal cans to devices such as can-pactors, which crush and compact as many as 10 000 cans in a machine about the size of a drink dispenser. Cash is often refunded by the number of cans or their weight.

The purchase of products made from recycled materials is also increasing. Plastic bottles now contain 25 per cent or more recycled plastics. Roofing shingles for buildings and outdoor furniture are being made from recycled plastics, glass, metal or paper. The means to use recycled materials in paper, metal and plastic products is essential.

How is petroleum used in the United States?

An important consideration when investigating how energy might be conserved is to ask how it is used. This is a particularly important question in the United States. Look at Table 19.1 again to discover where the United States ranks in terms of per capita consumption of energy. How is this huge appetite, or demand, for energy, met? Energy in the United States is supplied mainly from the primary sources—coal, petroleum and natural gas. Figure 19.8 shows the percentage of energy met from each of the primary energy sources from 1973 to 1990. These data can be used to develop an energy use profile for the United States.

> 10 Which primary sources contributed a greater percentage of the United States energy demand in 1990 than in 1973?
> 11 What was the percentage of change in reliance on petroleum and natural gas during the period shown

in Figure 19.8? What does this change mean since the graph shows the total amount of energy consumed as a constant from 1973 to 1990? (Note: The graph does not tell whether the total energy consumption for the United States increased or decreased.)

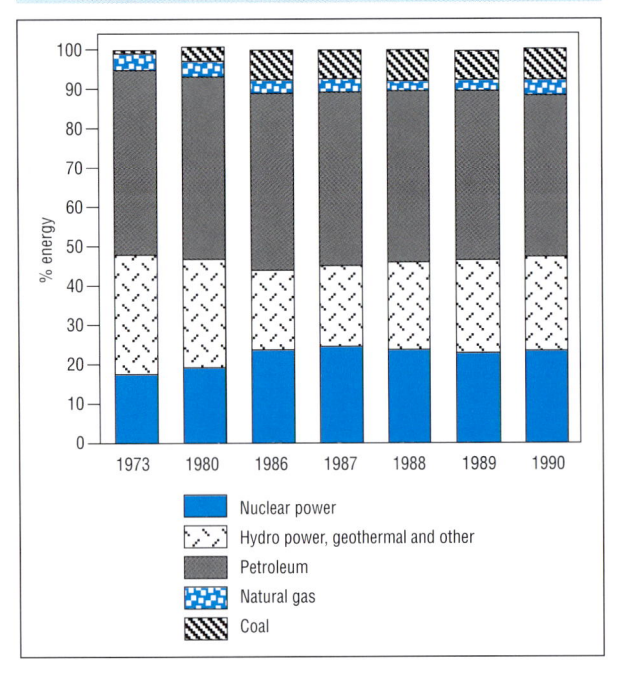

Figure 19.8 The percentage of United States energy supplied by each of the main primary sources, 1973–90

The data in Figure 19.8 show that the percentage of petroleum decreased each year following 1973. Can we use this information to suggest that the United States used less petroleum in 1990 than it did in 1980? Table 19.3 shows the absolute amounts of petroleum used in the United States from 1981 to 1989.

12 Explain how the information in Figure 19.8 and the information in Table 19.3 can both be true. (Note: Figure 19.8 shows that the United States reduced the percentage contribution of petroleum to its energy supply between 1973 and 1990. Table 19.3 shows that the consumption of petroleum increased from 16 060 000 barrels per day in 1981 to 17 240 000 barrels per day in 1989.)

13 Imagine you are sitting on an important policy making board in the United States and considering the question: 'How can the United States best reduce its overall consumption of petroleum?'
  a Using the information in Table 19.3, what would you recommend as a public policy to reduce petroleum consumption?
  b What other information might you need in order to build a case for your policy recommendations? (Hint: The information in Table 19.3 suggests that the trans-

Table 19.3 Petroleum use by sector, United States (million barrels per day)

Year	Residential and commercial	Industrial	Transportation	Electric utilities	Total
1981	1.33	4.27	9.49	0.96	16.06
1983	1.29	3.85	9.41	0.68	15.23
1985	1.35	4.03	9.87	0.48	15.73
1987	1.37	4.26	10.49	0.55	16.67
1989	1.40	4.26	10.85	0.74	17.24

Note: The figures may not total due to rounding
Source: Energy Information Administration, *Annual Energy Review*, 1989

portation sector is where the policy should be focused. Other useful information might include: price of petrol, consumption of petrol per head, average distance statistics for journeys to work, average distance driven per litre of petrol and the availability of mass transit.)

Research is underway in the United States to achieve lower emissions and larger distance substitutes for petrol, such as natural gas, electricity, ethanol, methanol, hydrogen, propane, diesel and reformulated petrol. Many companies already operate fleets of natural gas cars and trucks since developments have been rapid in natural and propane usage. Greater efficiency is also a positive effect, along with cleaner emissions. For example, cars using 45 litres of fuel travel 572 kilometres on natural gas, 363 kilometres on petrol and 275 kilometres on methanol.

The case for highly efficient electric cars is also being proved through the development of experimental models. All the major automobile manufacturers in the United States are committed to producing commercial electric vehicles.

Policies related to energy often have the effect of changing demand, which in turn alters consumption patterns. Slight changes in energy consumption patterns in the major industrial countries—those that are major consumers of energy—are generally further reaching than changes in energy consumption in the developing countries. This will change in the future as the population of developing countries and increased economic development put greater demands on energy.

FUTURE WORLD ENERGY DEMAND

Energy demand varies in different regions of the world. Perhaps the greatest and most obvious variations are between the developed and developing countries. Figure 19.10 shows the past energy demands and predicted future consumption for different groupings of countries in the world. These are the data that policy makers use. Guidelines for

ENERGY: A PERSISTENT GLOBAL ISSUE

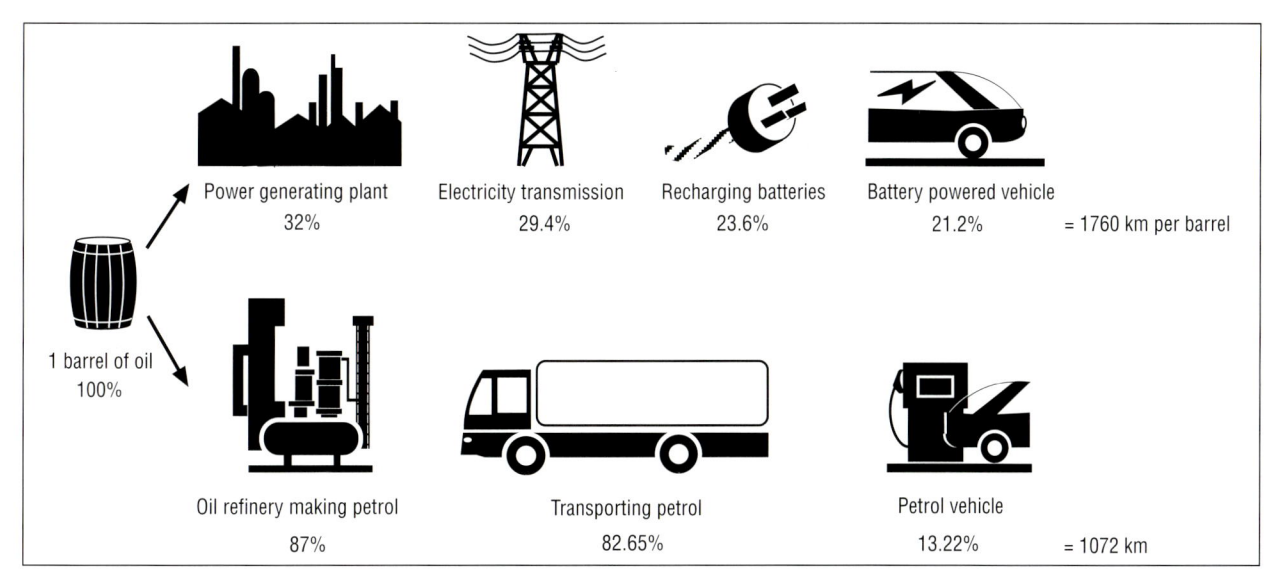

Figure 19.9 Comparing the efficiency of using one barrel of oil to power a petrol and a battery vehicle

national and international energy policy recommendations are often based on past trends, present practices, and predictions. The next activity is based on Figure 19.10 and will demonstrate how the data may be used.

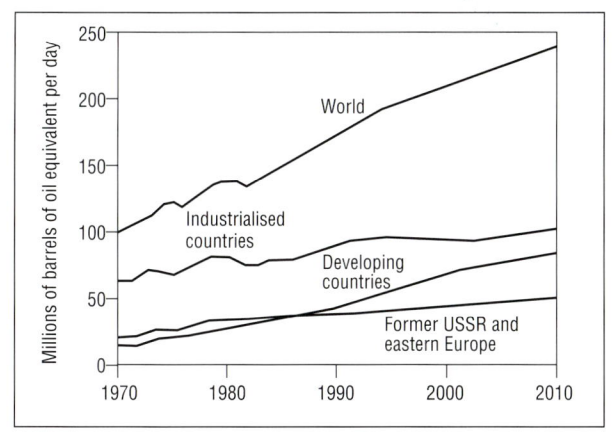

Figure 19.10 World energy demand, 1970–2010 (projected)

> 14 Follow these steps in using the information to develop predictions about world energy demands.
> *a* What has the trend for world energy demand been from 1970 to the present? (Consider the total trend over the whole period, and then look at variations within the period shown on the graph.) What were the effects of the oil embargo of 1973 and the global recession that began in the early 1980s?
> *b* How do the developing countries affect the predicted world energy demand after 1990? (Hint: The developing countries are building economies that both produce and consume energy. Agriculture with tractors uses more primary energy than does agriculture with draft animals. A steel mill uses more primary energy than a sawmill powered by a water wheel. In addition, the population of the developing countries is growing at rates that are greater than the developed countries. The larger the population of a country, the greater the potential demand for energy.)
> *c* Suppose that the world energy demand is to stabilise in the year 2000 so that from that time onward it flattens out, with no increase or decrease. (Remember that the developing countries will still be short of energy and the demand to meet their economic development and growing populations will continue at about the same rate.) What changes will have to occur in the industrialised countries, the former USSR, and eastern Europe for the world energy consumption trend to stabilise?

If the developing countries continue to demand energy at about the same levels and the eastern European countries remain below average in their demand, then the greatest responsibility for reduction will fall on the industrialised countries. They are also the best equipped to develop alternative energy sources. Experts predict the curve for the industrialised countries would have to be reduced by the equivalent of approximately 30 million barrels of oil per day between 2000 and 2010. This would permit a stable world demand, yet provide the developing countries with the energy they will need.

It is also important to test the changes in the future trends in energy demand by comparing your projections with predicted population changes.

> 15 Graph the data in Table 19.4 so it shows the population changes for the regions of the world. Remember that the change from 1985 to 2020 is a prediction, so draw that part of the graph in a different colour.

Table 19.4 Population of the world and major geographical regions from 1971 projected to 2020

Region	Population (millions)		
	1971	1985	2020
World	3 706	4 845	7 760
Industrialised countries	685	756	826
Former USSR and eastern European countries	373	416	521
Developing countries	2 648	3673	6413

Source: Population Reference Bureau, World Population Data Sheets, 1971, 1985, Washington, DC

16 Enter the population data in Table 19.4 on a copy of Figure 19.10 in the following ways.
  a Using a coloured pencil, write 1970 to correspond with 1970, 1985 with 1990, and 2020 with 2010. Next on the vertical axis, write 2 billion population to correspond with 50 million barrels of oil equivalent per day, 4 billion people at 100, 6 billion at 150, 8 billion at 200, and 10 billion at 250 millions barrels of oil equivalent per day.
  b Now, enter the data from Table 19.4 on your copy of Figure 19.10, connect the data entry points with lines, and label them world, developing countries, industrialised countries, and former USSR/eastern Europe.
17 Compare the lines on the graphs that show the geographical categories for countries. For example, compare the trend lines for world energy demand and world population change; the trend lines for energy demands in developing countries and population change in developing countries. Are the trends on each of the four sets of lines similar or different? What does this tell you about the relationship between population change and energy demand?
18 Compare the relative position for each pair of trend lines. For example, the population trend line for developing countries on the graph is higher on the scale than energy demand. The population trend for industrialised countries is lower on the scale than the energy demand line. What does this relationship of the trend lines for each category suggest about the share of world energy that is used by the industrialised countries?
19 Draw another graph to show what an equitable distribution of world energy would look like.

Changing scenarios of energy background

The twentieth century has been a period of huge increases in energy demand and consumption. Much of the world's easily obtainable oil and gas fuelled the growth. Those easily obtainable energy resources have been, or are being, used at a rapid rate.

At the same time, the world's population continues to increase. The demand for industrial energy per head of population increases with development. Economic development and improved standards of living are tied to available energy. In the twenty-first century the dependence on the most available or the least expensive traditional energy will no longer be possible. There will be more competition for the traditional energy that is available, especially for oil. Oil will probably remain the most available and transportable traditional source of energy for some time. How will the world's oil flows be altered in the future as demands for energy change? How might the map of oil flow appear as those changes are met in the year 2010?

The map of world oil flow (Figure 19.5) has many economic and development forces affecting it. Some of those are the result of industrial energy demand and others are mainly the consequence of population change.

20 Using the data presented earlier in Tables 19.1 and 19.2, make two predictions regarding what the world oil demand for the major regions of the world will be in the year 2010.
21 Draw a new world oil flow map to reflect the changes you expect. Summarise your ideas by writing a statement explaining why you believe the oil flow map will change as you suggest.

THE FUTURE

Energy is a resource that has many different forms and, depending on the kind of energy, it is distributed across the earth in a variety of geographical patterns. The most important patterns show where energy is produced and where it is consumed, as well as the kinds of movement that must occur when places of production are in different locations from places of consumption.

The way energy is used affects the lives of people and makes it an issue of political, economic, and social importance. Energy production and consumption are topics often heard in public policy discussions. World primary energy resources are diminishing. There is an increasing reliance on non-traditional sources of energy. These changes affect people in all parts of the world in many different ways. Participation by all citizens in public policy decisions is important when deciding how to use energy wisely—both for the present and in the future.

CHAPTER 20

CHANGING LIFESTYLES IN EUROPE: THE COAL AND STEEL INDUSTRIES

Hartmut Volkman

**Till 1985 our coal was dear to us.
Is it too expensive for us in 1987?**
From 1980 to 1985 we had to pay 90 billion DM annually for energy imports. Imported oil and gas were twice as much as our coal.
Now the oil price has come down. Should this make our coal too expensive for us? You cannot have insurance at no cost.

Our Coal

Figure 20.1 An advertisement published by the German coal industry, 17 November 1987

Größter Bergbauprotest seit Kohlekrise der 60er Jahre
140 000 demonstrieren in den Revieren gegen Möllemanns Politik

Figure 20.2 'Greatest miners' protest since coal crisis of the '60s: 140 000 demonstrate against the government's policies' is the headline from this German newspaper in 1991

Figures 20.1 and 20.2 are extracts from German newspapers published in November 1987 and late September 1991. They are concerned with the decline in the German coal mining industry and the probability of rises in unemployment among many coalminers in the future. Figure 20.3 is a translation of another newspaper article published earlier in 1991.

A map of global population density identifies three major concentrations of people—east Asia, south Asia and Europe. Within Europe, many of these people live in cities that grew on the coalfields as a result of the industrial revolution. Coal miners and their families all over Europe are facing worries similar to those of the German coal industry. Some of the highest rates of unemployment are in former coal mining and steel making communities in which the mines and steel works are now closed or reduced in size.

The cause of this disruption of life is not that the global community is using less coal or steel. Coal continues to be a major source of the electricity on which our lifestyles

> # German coal fears loss of 100 000 jobs by 1995
>
> *Coal industry misses energy-concept from Bonn and Brussels*
>
> The future of German coal mining remains uncertain, as the Association's General Secretary indicated yesterday. According to present plans, hardly more than 50 million tonnes of domestic coal are to be produced and sold in 1995, a decrease of 20 million tonnes as compared with the output in 1990. This would mean a loss of 40 000 jobs in coal mining alone and of 100 000 jobs overall. According to the Secretary General, the EEC [now the European Union] demands that Germany burns no more than 35 million tonnes of domestic coal in thermal power stations in 1995, instead of the 41 million tonnes that has already been agreed upon at the national level. Only if this level is reached will the EEC approve of the present rate of subsidies for German coal.

Figure 20.3 A translation of an article in the Ruhr Gazette, *7 September 1991*

depend and steel has continued to be an integral part of everyday living in the modern world. Despite the introduction of many new materials such as aluminium, glass and plastics, and the development of energy sources such as oil, gas, nuclear, solar and wind power, steel and coal are still produced in huge quantities. However, the importance of European coalfields and steel making has diminished internationally and such changes have affected the lives of many Europeans.

COAL: BLACK GOLD!

Coal is the fossilised remains of forest timber and other vegetation. The oldest and most efficient form of energy is the black, hard, bituminous coal. However, there are two other forms of coal that are used in various parts of the world. Brown coal (lignite) was formed much more recently than black coal. It has only about half the energy of black coal and is usually used for generating electricity in power stations near the open cast pits from which it is dug. Peat is the most recently formed type of coal. It is made from vegetation which has decomposed in water where there is little oxygen. It contains very little energy and is burned in only a few isolated houses in Europe today. Peat bogs are often preserved for the varieties of natural plants and animals that live in them.

Black coal was the most important source of energy in western countries in the nineteenth century. The availability of coal encouraged the use of steam engines and made possible the development of the blast furnaces on which the iron and, later, the steel industry was based. From about 1200 BC, when the iron age began, until the eighteenth century, iron (pig iron, cast iron and wrought iron) was the main industrial metal in Europe. Small quantities of steel were made, but the methods used were expensive and complex. In 1709, Abraham Darby, an Englishman, produced coke from coal so that finer pig iron could be made in large quantities. The nineteenth century industrial revolution, which changed the face of Europe and North America, was based on easy access to large quantities of coal, both for steam generation and for iron making.

Demand for steel (which is not brittle like cast iron nor soft like wrought iron) grew during the nineteenth century. Developments in steel manufacture were rapid.

- In 1846, an American, William Kelly, made steel by blowing air up through a molten mass of pig iron.
- In 1856, Henry Bessemer made the first Bessemer converter in England.
- In the same year, two German brothers, William and Friedrich Siemens, started to develop an open hearth furnace which could produce steel from both pig and scrap iron.
- In 1864, the French brothers, Pièrre and Émile Martin, modified the Siemens' furnace to produce the Siemens–Martin furnace which produced even better steel.
- In 1878, Siemens started the first electric steel furnace and by 1914, electric furnaces were used for all high quality steel making.

However, the electricity that was required was still generated mainly in coal-fired power stations. Within a decade, the open hearth and converter were being used by every major steel manufacturer and steel had become the main ingredient of industrialisation. The railways spread on their steel rails, and by 1880, even buildings were made of steel.

THE WORLD COAL INDUSTRY TODAY

Although coal is found throughout the world, the deposits vary in quality and amount as well as the ease with which it can be extracted and transported to its markets.

In the nineteenth century only a limited number of coal deposits in Europe and North America were exploited. In the early days, the seams that were mined had either to be close to the surface or had to be easily accessible from the sides of river valleys. Soon, however, the technology of deep mining was developed in Great Britain. The technology spread rapidly to other areas in Belgium, northern France, Germany and Poland.

Although it was then possible to mine coal that lay deep beneath the surface, the costs of transporting it once it was mined were high, and much of the industry which relied on it was located as close as possible to the mines. Fortunately for the early iron industry, both coal and iron ore were often found in the same areas.

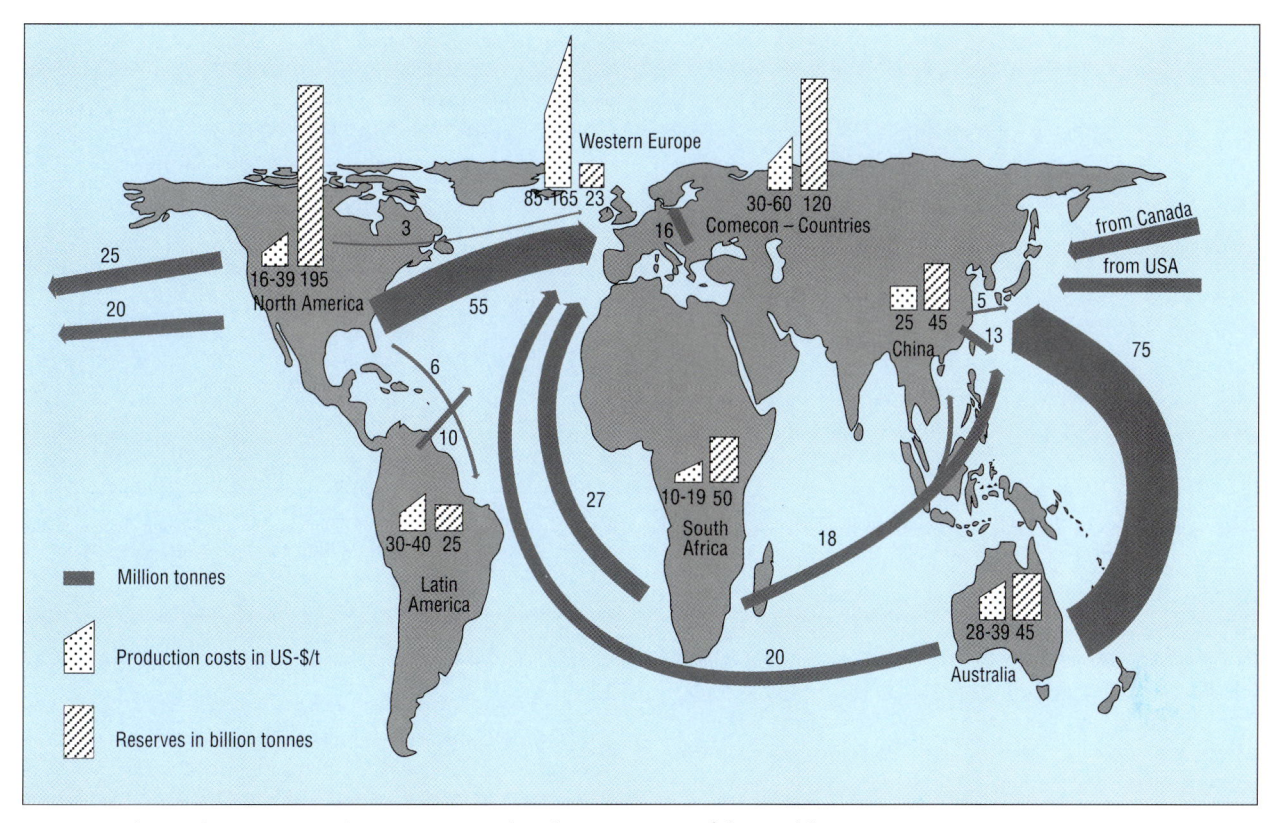

CHANGING LIFESTYLES IN EUROPE: THE COAL AND STEEL INDUSTRIES

Figure 20.4   Coal reserves, production costs and seaborne exports of the world, 1990

By the middle of the twentieth century, two major changes had occurred. First, technology had improved so that less and less coal was needed for each tonne of steel produced, and second, larger vessels and more efficient harbour facilities had reduced ocean transport costs, which allowed for the development of a worldwide seaborne trade in both iron ore and the energy sources needed to smelt it. High quality iron ore and coal could now be brought to Europe from wherever in the world it was cheapest to be smelted in large, modern steel works.

The change from a local market to a global market for

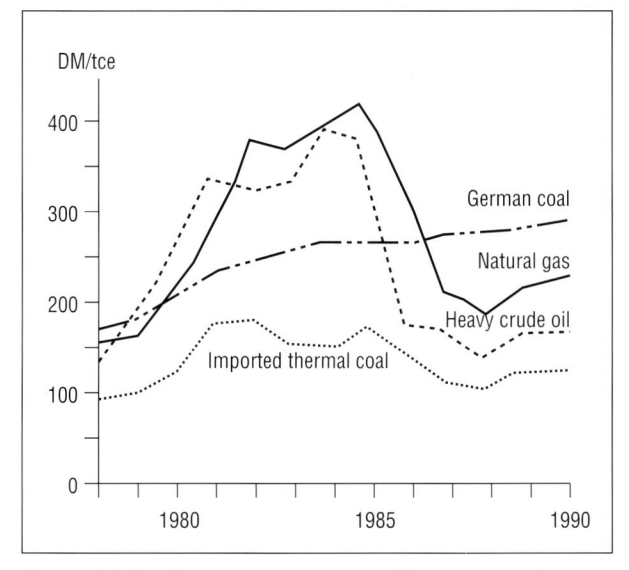

Figure 20.5   The average prices paid in Germany for various energy sources, 1978–90

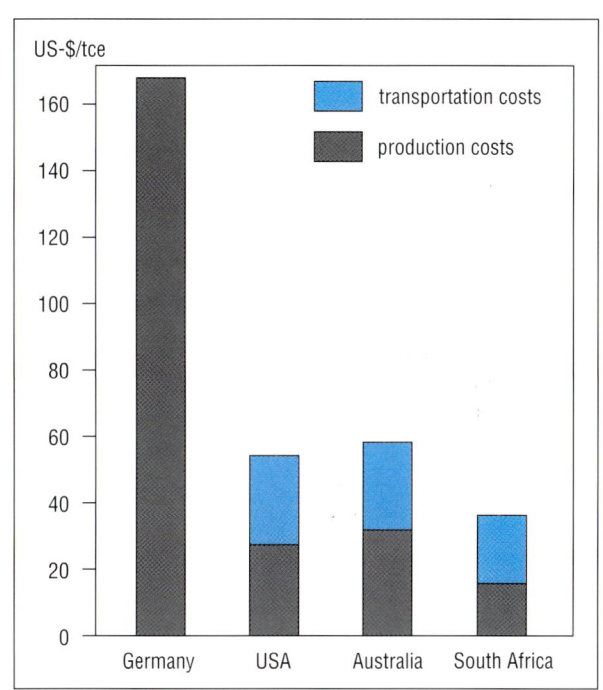

Figure 20.6   A comparison of the costs of German and overseas coal delivered to Amsterdam, Rotterdam or Antwerp, 1990

Table 20.1 The tonnage of coal produced in selected countries between 1950 and 1990

Year	Coal production per year in million tonnes							
	Germany	Great Britain	Poland	Australia	South Africa	USA	Canada	World
1950	125.8	219.7	78.0	16.8	26.5	508.7	15.4	1500.0
1955	148.1	225.7	96.0	19.6	32.1	445.3	13.4	1602.0
1960	142.3	196.8	104.4	22.9	38.2	394.0	8.0	1980.0
1965	135.1	191.6	118.8	27.8	48.5	474.1	8.6	2300.0
1970	111.3	144.6	140.1	48.4	54.2	541.6	11.7	2104.9
1975	92.4	128.7	171.6	70.2	69.5	568.0	21.7	2271.0
1980	86.6	128.3	193.1	82.9	112.6	719.1	33.5	2829.6
1985	81.8	90.8	191.6	136.0	173.1	740.9	34.1	3212.4
1990	69.8	89.3	147.7	155.6	174.8	861.6	37.7	3622.4

coal meant that the large scale open cut mines in Australia, Canada, the United States and South Africa competed against underground mines in Europe, which operated at considerably higher costs. At the same time, coal also had to compete with oil and gas which were being exploited in larger quantities, could also be transported in the new large bulk-handling ships, and were both cheaper and cleaner. For the whole of this period, the costs of mining German coal were higher than those of importing coal. Also, except during the oil and gas crisis of the early 1980s, German coal was more expensive than those fuels.

Table 20.1 shows the tonnage of coal produced in selected countries between 1950 and 1990. Figure 20.6 compares the costs of German and overseas coal delivered to Amsterdam, Rotterdam or Antwerp in 1990. The costs for German coal are given as f.o.b. (free on board) which means that they include the costs of mining the coal, delivering it to one of the ports and loading it on a ship. The costs for overseas coal are given as c.i.f. (cost, insurance, freight) which means that they include the costs of mining the coal overseas, delivering it to the ship, transporting it to Europe and insuring it on the way. It is then the responsibility of the importer to pay for unloading the coal at its destination.

1 Using Figures 20.4 and 20.6 and the information above, explain the main differences between the coal industries of the various producing countries in the world.
2 Calculate the percentage of world coal production contributed by
   a the three European countries
   b the United States and Canada
   c Australia and South Africa
   for the period 1950 to 1990. Present your figures as graphs and comment on the pattern shown.
3 The last Japanese coal mine was closed down in 1989. Between 1970 and 1989, the Japanese steel industry had become joint owner of many coal mines in Australia and Canada. What may have been the reasons and the effects of these changes?
4 Discuss the major changes in the industrial structure of your country that have occurred in the past twenty years. Have some communities suffered from the changes more than others? Which communities have lost and which have gained from the changes?

The inevitable consequence of this change in production patterns between the old and the new worlds was that many thousands of European miners lost their jobs. At the same time as these changes in coal mining and trade were occurring, similar changes were occurring in iron ore mining and steel making. These changes also led to the loss of thousands of jobs in the European steel industry. Across the whole of Europe, many major industrial regions with their huge populations found that their economic 'legs' were either weakened or broken.

COAL: THE TREASURE CHEST OF GERMANY

Black (bituminous) coal has been one of the mainstays of the German economy for many years. The main coalfields of the former West Germany are the Ruhr and the Saar, while the former East Germany has the coalfields of upper Silesia. Of these three coalfields, however, the largest and most productive has been the Ruhr.

The area between the rivers Ruhr and Lippe contains the main reserves of hard coal in Germany. The coal measures (the coal-bearing rock formations) reach the surface in the Ruhr valley and dip further beneath the surface towards the north-west. The rocks are heavily folded and faulted. The coal seams are thin—about 2 metres.

The first mines were either manholes or pits dug from the surface or were drift mines going horizontally into the valley sides. Later, underground mining began. Today, the coal seams that lie closer to the surface in the Ruhr Valley have been worked out and mining is currently carried out at about 1100 metres below the surface, using long-wall and continuous mining equipment. The mines are therefore highly capital intensive. Despite the high levels of

Figure 20.7a The surface buildings and associated infrastructure of a coal mine in the Ruhr coal field

Figure 20.7b The coal cutter at work on a long wall in a coal mine in the Ruhr

Figure 20.8 Modern coal operations in Queensland, Australia are on a huge scale, as shown by this open cut mine at Blackwater

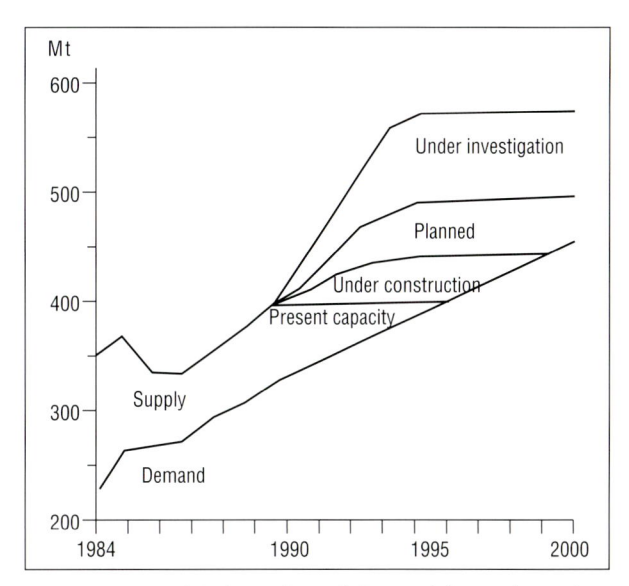

Figure 20.9 Global supply and demand for coal, 1984–2000

mechanisation, a miner in Germany produces only 640 kilograms of coal per hour. This compares with 534 kilograms in France, or five times as much in the United States or Australia.

5 Discuss the reasons why folding, faulting and thin coal seams decrease the amount of coal produced per miner and increase the costs of mining the coal.
6 Compare the photographs of coalmines in Germany and Australia (Figures 20.7 and 20.8). Why is the cost of extracting coal in Australia so much less than in Germany?

The graph, Figure 20.9, suggests that both supply and demand for coal will continue to increase across the world.

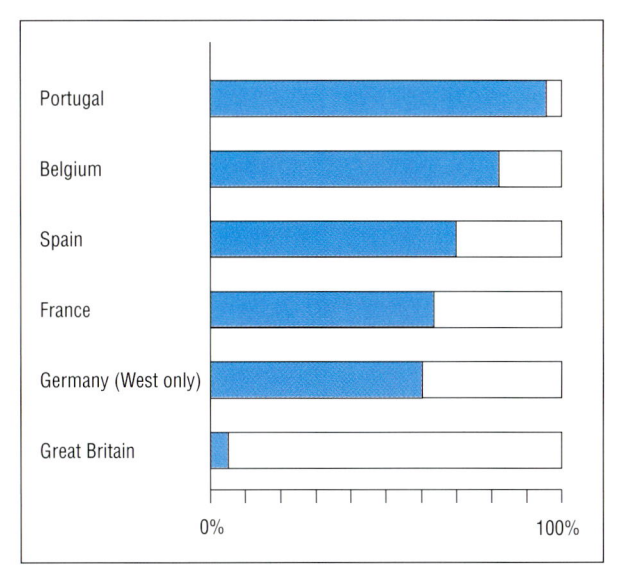

Figure 20.10 The percentage of total energy needs imported by selected European countries, 1990

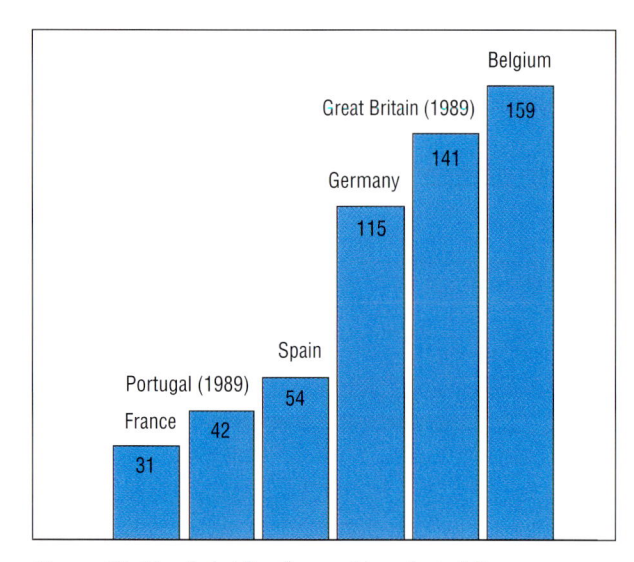

Figure 20.11 Subsidies for coal in selected European countries, 1990 (German Marks per t)

Values shown: France 31, Portugal (1989) 42, Spain 54, Germany 115, Great Britain (1989) 141, Belgium 159.

However, it seems likely that the amount of coal mined each year will increase faster than the demand and that this increase in supply will come from the countries of the new world rather than from European coalmines.

When supply is greater than demand for any commodity, the price usually falls, and since European coal is already more expensive than imported coal, more and more miners in Europe may lose their jobs.

In 1987, thermal power stations in Germany burned 34 million tonnes of domestic coal. Imported coal would have been about 8 billion DM cheaper. The difference was paid by the electricity customers. By paying more for their electricity, these customers supported 139 000 miners, 180 000 people in related industries and 500 000 family members.

Table 20.2 shows the effects of these changes in the world market on coal production and employment in the mining industry in Germany.

Table 20.2 Coal production and employed miners in Germany, 1957–90

Year	Coal production (million t)	Miners employed
1957	150	607 300
1965	135	377 000
1977	85	192 000
1987	75	156 500
1990	70	133 000

7 Illustrate the information in Table 20.2 as a graph showing changes in the German coal industry from 1957 to 1990.
8 Prepare a summary of the reasons why the German coal mining industry has met with economic difficulties.
9 Suggest reasons why Germany, Belgium and Great Britain subsidise their coal industries more than Spain, Portugal and France.
10 Discuss the two options available to the German government. Should they continue to subsidise coal mining in order to keep jobs for their coalminers and a secure domestic energy source or should they wind it down and buy coal from overseas at lower prices?

AN AGEING STEEL INDUSTRY

While coal is an important part of the economy of many countries, the steel industry is regarded as the key to the industrialisation of any country, since the construction of industrial plants and infrastructure requires a large amount of steel. The old industrialised countries in the northern hemisphere are proof of this relationship. However, the equation holds true only for the initial stages of industrial development. Once the basic infrastructure of railways, roads, bridges and buildings has been established, the demand for steel declines. The old steel producing areas of Europe and the United States succeeded in keeping high production levels for many years by exporting steel products—ships, cars and machines. A favourable precondition was that most of the iron ore was found in their countries and that they also owned coking coal for the furnaces.

Since the 1950s and 1960s, high grade iron ore deposits have been found and developed in the southern hemisphere, especially in Australia and Brazil.

At first, these new sources of iron ore were exported to the old steel producers who had usually invested technology and money in the new enterprises. Later, however, steel

Table 20.3 Employment in the steel industry, 1974–90

Country	Number of people employed ('000)		
	1974	1985	1990
Belgium	64	35	27
France	158	76	46
West Germany	232	151	127
Italy	96	67	56
Spain	89	54	36
United Kingdom	194	61	54
Canada	77	69	65
United States	521	238	204
Brazil	118	145	140
Australia	42	30	30
Japan	459	349	305
India	197	290	272
South Africa	100	110	112

Source: International Iron and Steel Institute, *World Steel in Figures*, 1991, Brussels 1991

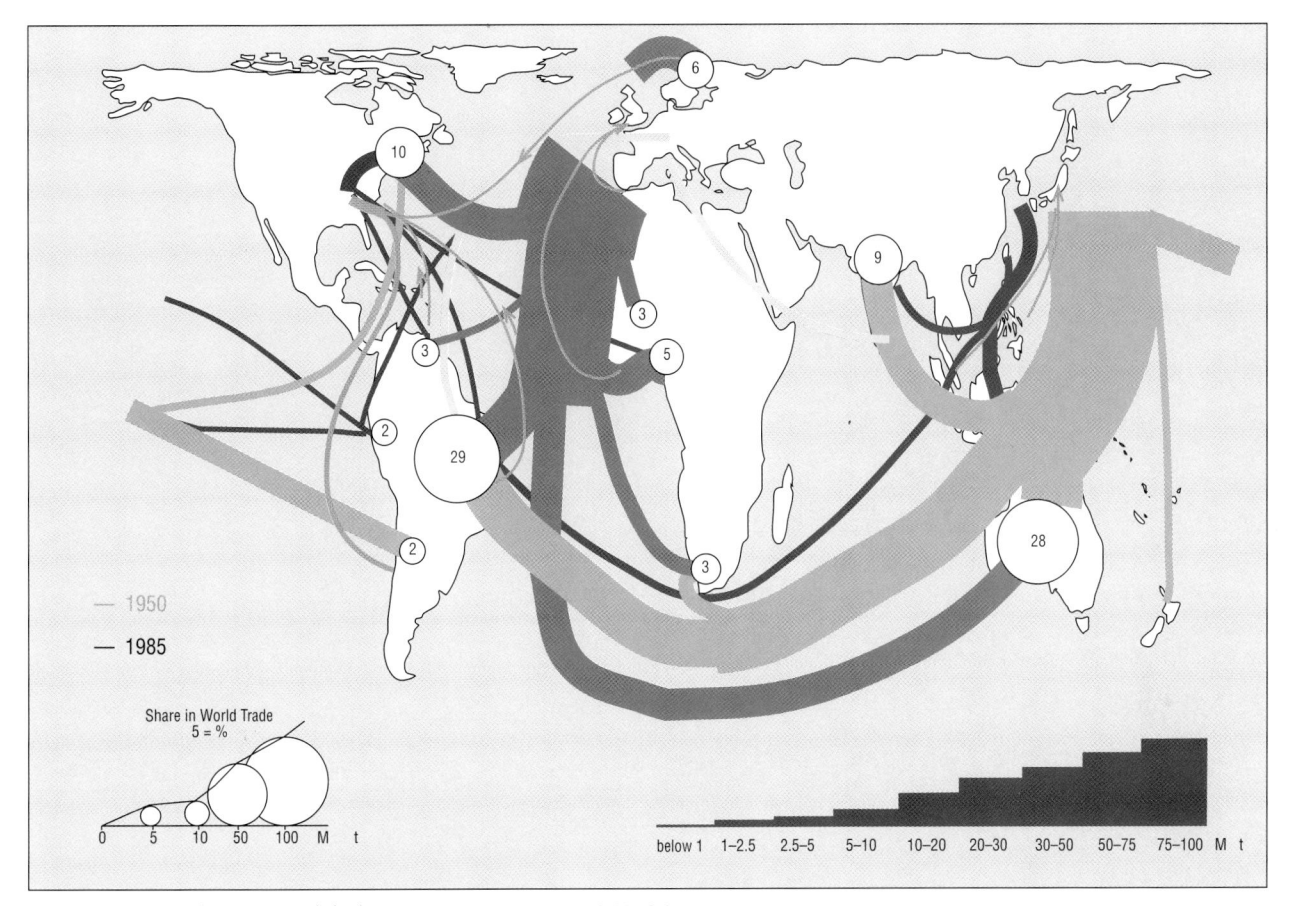

CHANGING LIFESTYLES IN EUROPE: THE COAL AND STEEL INDUSTRIES 165

Figure 20.12   Changes in global iron ore movements, 1950–85

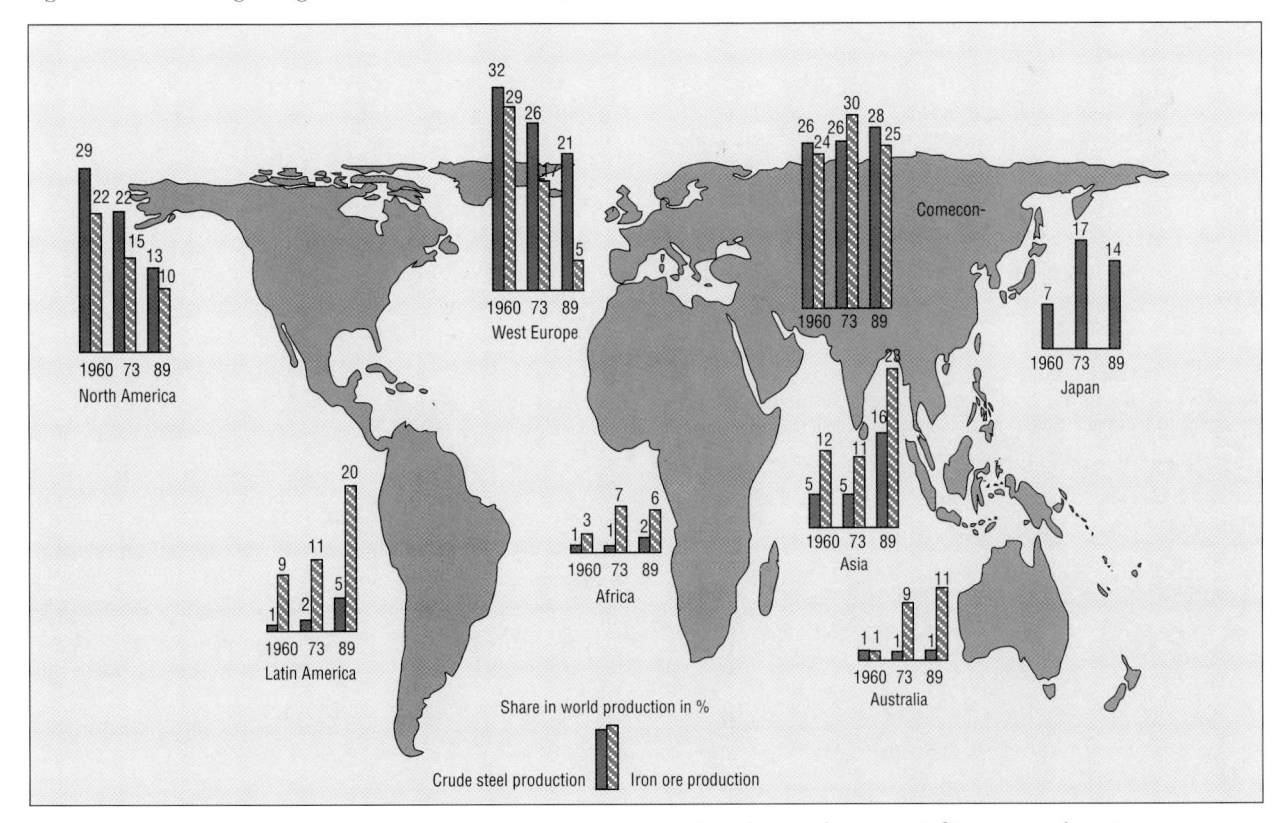

Figure 20.13   Changes in the pattern of iron ore mining and steel production between 1960, 1973 and 1989

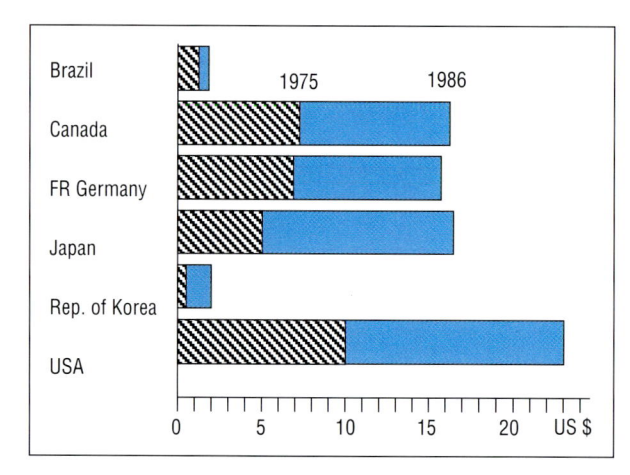

Figure 20.14 Comparison in the hourly labour costs in selected world steel making countries, 1975 and 1986

mills were established in the developing countries, too. These changes depended on the new technologies that had changed the steel making process, such as direct reduction, and the availability of coal anywhere on the globe at relatively low costs.

> 11 Describe the ways in which the pattern of global trade in iron ore changed between 1950 and 1985. Make a list of the factors which made these changes possible.
> 12 Discuss the changing roles of countries in each of the continents in the iron ore mining and steel manufacturing industries from 1950 to 1990. Comment on the ways in which various countries have changed their share of the global 'economic cake'.
> 13 Draw line graphs to illustrate the changes in the number of people employed in the steel industry in the selected countries. In which countries have the changes been greatest? Choose four countries and suggest reasons for the changes that have occurred.
> 14 List the factors that influence the ability of countries like Germany and the United States to compete with Brazil and Korea.

Your responses to the previous activities may suggest that the benefits of the iron and steel industry have become more evenly shared among the countries of the world. However, despite these changes, the apparent steel consumption per capita still differs greatly between countries in various regions of the world (see Figure 20.15).

> 15 *a* Compare the average amount of steel consumed by each person in Japan, the United States, countries of the European Community (EC on Figure 20.15, now the European Union) with the world average.
> *b* Compare patterns of steel use in western industrialised countries, western developing countries, and Japan with the world average. What conclusions can you draw about the distribution of steel consumption?

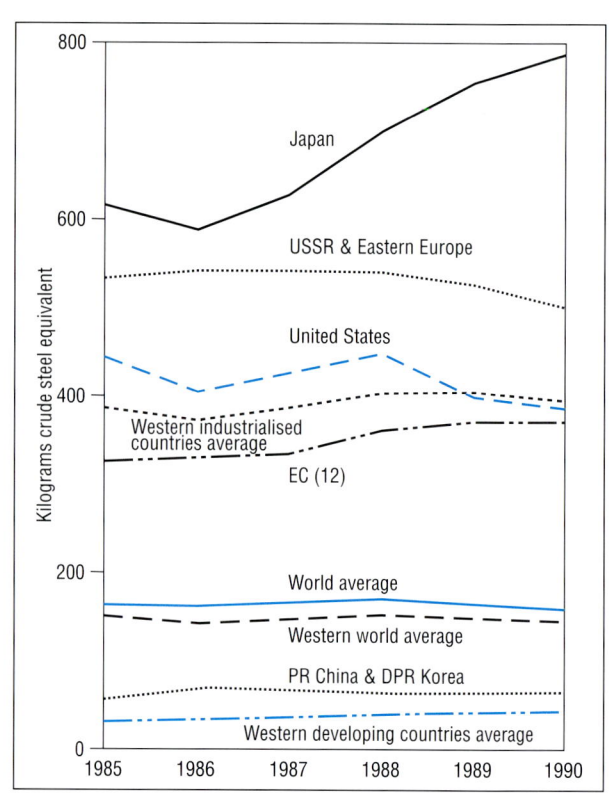

Figure 20.15 Apparent steel consumption per head in various regions of the world

> *c* Explain why the average consumption for the western world is less than the world average.
> *d* Which major group of countries is not represented on this graph? Where on the graph might the line for this group lie?

WORLD MARKETS: CHANGING CONTINUOUSLY

The global flow of commodities changes continuously depending on changes in consumption, production and transport. However, human beings generally seek continuity and security. At the very least, they want some assurance from one day to the next that they will not be sacked.

The miners in Germany appreciate that coal production will have to be reduced. All they are asking is that they get enough time for adjustment. Until now the number of

Table 20.4 Changes in the average age of German miners

Year	Average age of German miners
1970	40.16
1975	39.65
1980	38.75
1985	36.33
1991	35.29

miners has been reduced slowly by pre-retirement schemes which allowed them to retire at the age of fifty with little financial loss. However, the low average age in 1991 means that the majority of miners are too young for an early retirement. These people will have to find a new job or the task of reducing coal output in Germany must be slowed down.

In the steel industry the situation is similar. Steel making shops and rolling mills in industrialised countries work to meet the growing demands of their customers for high quality products. In Germany the production of galvanised and strip coated steel increases continuously while production of less elaborate materials, such as semi-finished and flat steel, is falling.

The consequences of these changes in world markets on traditional industrial areas are severe. Bergkamen, for example, is a town of 52 000 people in the eastern part of the Ruhr coalfield. Over half the 19 000 people employed in the town, including 679 apprentices, work in one of the two coalmines. The reduction of the mines removes the economic foundations of the town. Already the local employment office has 4000 people on its books, and only 400 vacancies. Three of these jobs are for two teachers and a clockmaker, hardly the kinds of jobs needed by unemployed miners. It will take a long time to change a town's economic structure. A haulage firm may bring in twelve jobs. A carpentry firm may bring in five jobs, but these are small numbers compared with the probable loss of 9800 jobs in the mines.

Similarly, when a steel mill closes, the 'job gap' cannot be filled easily. The effect is felt not only by the steel workers but also by other businesses where workers spend their wages.

One way in which people can be helped to come to terms with the changes is through subsidies. A way of cushioning the effects on a nation's economy is by investing money overseas. In November 1991, RWE, one of the major electricity producers in Germany, bought a 50 per cent share of the Consolidated Coal Company in Pittsburgh. This is the second largest coal company in the United States. Such ownership is another step on the way to accepting a global coal market and reducing the dependence on German coal. As demand for both coal and steel continues to grow worldwide, we may also consider that spreading the coal and steel industry worldwide is one way in which the older industrialised countries can assist the newly industrialising countries towards economic growth.

16 Would it be possible and advisable to close down the coal mines in Europe? Discuss the consequences for Europe and the world

17 People expect some degree of certainty in planning their lives. Rapid change is a feature of economic life. How can both be made to match?

18 Survey your class to discover how the grandparents of your colleagues earned their living. Make a list of all the jobs available to that generation that no longer exist in your area. Make a similar list of jobs in your area that have come into existence since your grandparents' day.

19 Discuss how far the changes that are taking place in the economic structure of the developed world may benefit people who live in the developing countries of the world. What opportunities for improving life in Europe can you see as a result of the changes in economic structure? (You may like to consider the improvements in environmental quality in the older industrial areas.)

20 The economies of western Europe need energy. Compare this chapter with Chapter 15 on acid rain in Finland and Chapter 19 on energy use in the United States. Prepare a report on the ways in which countries can obtain enough energy, maintain employment for their people *and* conserve their natural environments.

INDEX

acid rain 118–27
Africa 21–6, 113–17
agricultural products 13–15, 21, 22, 25, 31, 36, 39–43, 63, 69
agricultural programs 24, 39–43
agriculture 13, 15, 16, 30, 67, 68, 99–100, 102–3
aid organisations 26, 45, 68, 70
airport location 93–8
Amazon River, problems 10–11
Amazonia 10–18
    cattle ranching 16–17
    collecting produce 15–16
    eco-catastrophe 18
    features 11–13
    future challenges 17–18
    mining 13, 14–16
    people 13–15
    traditional lifestyles 14
Angola 114–15
asset distribution 24, 45, 50–1, 57
Australia 114, 115, 162, 164
    soil problems 71–80

Balkan Peninsula 107–10
Bangladesh 47–51
    problems 49–51
    recent growth 48–9
    urban distribution 48
    urbanisation, history 47–8
barley 123
beans 31
bee keeping 45
Belgium 111, 112, 114–17, 162, 163, 164
berry bushes 123
Bhutan 60–70
    achievements 62–3
    development (since 1961) 60–3
    impact of development 63–9
    planning 69–70
    problems 67–8
bio-diversity see genetic diversity
birth rates 27, 28, 33, 44
black market see informal economy
Brazil 10–18, 52–9, 114, 164, 166
    cities 54
    history of cities 52–3
    poverty 57–9
    problems in cities 55–6
    urban development 54–5
Britain see Great Britain
Broads, the 141–3
Bulgaria 104–10
    changes (since 1989) 109
    historical background 108–9

cadmium poisoning 103
Canada 164, 166
    dams as hazard 81–90
    Grand River Project 86–90
    politicking re dams 85–6
cars see roads; traffic; transport
cattle 16–17, 53, 64, 68, 69, 72, 75, 142
cereal see grain
chemical wastes 102–3
child mortality 56
China 27–35, 114
    economic development 29–30
    population issues 29–35
cities, migration to 2, 13–14, 21, 48–51, 52–9
coal 159–64
    reserves 161
coal industry 160–4
coastal protection 138, 145–8
coastline, changing 147
cocoa 21, 25
coffee 53
collecting produce 13, 14, 15–16, 36, 63
consumption levels 9
contributors iv–v, vi
Cornucopians 5–7, 9
cotton 21, 25, 38
countries and nations 105–7
crime 13, 20, 23, 58
crop failures 37
cultural assimilation 14–15

dams 25, 72, 81–90, 147, 150
De Beers 113–17
death rates 27, 28, 32, 33, 44, 56
demographic transition 27
development 24–6, 27, 29–30, 33–5, 43, 53, 60–70, 100–2
    damaging 18, 102–4
    managed 13, 28, 50–1, 62–3, 69–70
diamond trade 111, 113–17
diamonds 111–13, 114, 115
    cutting centres 114, 115–16
    price controls 114
diseases
    crops 38
    human 1, 14, 56
    of poverty 20
donkeys and mules 53
drought 37, 38, 71, 72
drug enforcement agencies 24
drug trafficking 23–4, 58
dunes 140
dust-bowl 83
dykes 138–40

eco-catastrophe, Amazonia 18
economic development see development
economic imbalance see rich and poor
education 7, 22, 24, 26, 35, 48, 61, 63, 70
electric cars 156, 157

electricity 38, 62, 100, 151, 152, 160, 164
employment programs 24, 25, 45
energy 149–58
    efficiency 156, 157
    per capita consumption 153
    public policy 154–7
    sources 151, 153, 160
entrepreneurship program 24
environmental planning 69
erosion see gully; soil; stream bank
Europe
    coal and steel 159–67
    geopolitics 104–10
    pollution 118–27
European Union 109–10
evapotranspiration 75–6
extinction see genetic diversity

Fair Price Shops 42, 44, 45, 59
family planning 29, 31–2, 34–5, 44
famine 29, 36–8
farm planning 78–9
farming see agriculture
farming, subsistence 13, 60, 61
fens 141–3
fertilisers 22, 25, 39, 40, 43, 123, 141
fertility rates 4, 33–5
Finland 118–27
fish 12, 15, 87, 90, 121, 124, 125
fishing 15, 91, 125
flood control 84
flooding and global warming 137–43
floods 37, 38, 83–4, 88, 137–43
food
    distribution 44
    increasing production 39–43
    preserving 36
    shortages 7, 15, 19–23, 29, 31, 36–45
    storage 36
    supply per capita 20, 42
forests 10–12, 14–15, 17, 36, 63, 64, 68, 69, 82, 87
    acid rain damage 120, 121, 123–4, 126
    clearing see vegetation
frosts 38

genetic diversity 12, 15, 69
geopolitical change 104–10
Germany 159–67
    coal industry 159–64
    steel industry 164–7
glaciers 87
global action needed 4–7, 9
global challenges iv–v, vi, 1–4, 7–8
global GNP per capita 3
global management approaches 5–6
global markets 152–4, 165, 166–7
global village vi
global warming 2, 137–43, 144–8
GNP per capita 3
grain 17, 31, 39–43, 63, 71, 83, 142

INDEX

grain consumption and poverty   41–2
Great Britain   138–43, 162, 163, 164
green revolution   39–43
greenhouse effect   137–43
greenhouse gases   128, 148
groundnuts   21, 25
groundwater acidification   125
gully erosion   73, 74

happiness   9, 67, 70
health care   13, 20, 49, 61
Hong Kong   91–8, 114
horses   53
human needs   19
human suffering *see* suffering
hunger *see* food shortages
hunter–gatherers   13–14, 36, 72, 89–90
hydro-electricity   16, 65, 88–90, 149, 150

ice   82, 86–7, 89, 123, 144
illiteracy   13
income distribution   57
income generation   44
India   36–45, 114–16, 164
    alleviating poverty   44–5
    economic and social indicators   43
    food production   39–43
    food shortages   36–45
    landscape   37
    poverty   38, 44–5
Indians, Amazonian   14–15
Indo-European languages   108
industrialisation   53–4, 67, 99–103
industry, categorised   100
informal economy   23, 25, 50
information sources   4
insect damage   38
instability, political   104–10
iron ore   160, 164–7
irrigation   38, 39, 40, 72, 76, 81, 82
    poisonous   102–3

job creation *see* employment programmes

land
    degradation *see* soil
    ownership   38, 45, 63
    protection from sea   144–8
    reclaimed   92, 93, 97, 145–8
    as resource   71
landslip   64, 66
Lapland   122
lichens   124
life expectancy   1, 3, 4, 7
lifestyle changes   14–15, 29, 60–2, 66–7,
    69, 159–67
livestock, damaging soil   64, 72
lobby groups   4–7

Malthusians   5–7, 9
migration   48, 50, 51, 66

mineral resources   36, 53, 64
mining   13, 14–16, 53, 64–5, 72, 159–64
multinational companies   17, 18, 113

nations and countries   105–7
Netherlands   114, 144–8, 162
Nigeria   19–26
    agriculture   21, 22, 25
    cities   21
    crime   23–4
    crops   21
    education   22, 26
    employment programs   24, 25
    job creation   24, 25
    oil production   21, 22
    rich and poor   21–6
non-government organisations   70
non-renewable resources   10, 19
North Sea   139–43, 144–8
nuclear power   149, 151

oats   123
offshore business ventures   103
oil
    crisis   22
    management   154, 156–8
    prices   22
    production   21, 22, 25, 152–4
    substitutes   156
optimism   1–9, 3–4, 18, 26, 45, 70, 98, 110,
    127, 136, 143
organisms, tolerances   76, 121
ozone depletion   2

packaging waste   9
palm oil   21, 25
pasture, degraded   71, 72
peas   123
peat   141, 145
permafrost   87
petroleum *see* oil
polders   145
political instability   104–10
pollution, *see also* acid rain   2, 49, 66, 101–
    3, 143
    air   119–20, 138, 149
    heavy metals   102–3
    industrial   99–103, 118–27
    traffic   118, 121, 125–7, 128–30
    water   10, 15, 119, 121, 124–6, 142
population   27–35
population control   27–33, 39, 43–4, 69
population density
    high   29, 91, 159
    low   11, 13, 63
population distribution, China   33
population pressure   31, 38, 48–50, 55–9
population pyramids   27–8, 32
positive approaches *see* optimism
poultry   43
poverty   1, 2, 7, 8, 10, 13, 19–26, 31, 36–45,

    47, 48–9, 55–9
    grain consumption and   41–2
prairies   82–3
price-fixing (minimums)   44

quality of life and suffering   7–8

rabbits   72
radiation, nuclear   149, 150
ragi   41
rainforest *see* forests
recycling   154–6
refugees   105–6
regional development   49, 51
religious teachings   9
resources   1, 20
rice   38, 39, 40, 42, 43, 44, 63, 102–3
rich and poor   10, 19–26, 58, 111–17
rill erosion   73, 74
rivers   10–18, 65, 82, 84–5, 86–90, 110, 114,
    124
road accidents   129
roads   13, 17–18, 24, 61, 66, 72, 128–36
rubber   16
rural migration *see* cities

salinity *see* soil
sanitation   48, 49, 55–6, 59
scientists   4–7
sea level, mean   143
sea levels, rising   137–43, 144–8
sewerage *see* sanitation
sheep   64, 72, 75
sheet erosion   73, 74
Singapore   128–36
slums   13, 45, 49, 50, 52, 56–8
smuggling   23
snow   82, 123, 124
social imbalance *see* rich and poor
social ladder   19
social stratification   19
soil
    acidification   123
    degradation   2, 71, 72, 73–8
    erosion   64, 71–80, 147–8
    fertility   13, 17, 36
    fragility   64, 66, 72, 73
    nutrient leaching   123
    restoration   78–80
    salinity   71, 72, 74–7, 79
sorghum   41
squatters *see* slums
starvation, *see also* famine; food, shortages
    38
steel   164–7
strativism   15, 16
stream bank erosion   49, 74, 75, 142
subsistence farming   13, 60, 61
suffering and quality of life   7–8
sugar   14, 44, 52–3
sulphur *see* acid rain; pollution

sun, energy source   151–2
sustainable use of resources   68

Taiwan   99–103
technology   2, 7
terpen   138
Thames, River   139–40
tidal range   138, 139
timber harvesting   14, 15
tolerances
    acidity   121
    salinity   76
topsoil   64, 71, 73, 83
tourism   66, 125, 141, 142
traditional lifestyles   14–15, 32
traffic, motor vehicles   128–36
traffic control measures   132–6
traffic problems   49, 130–2
transport systems   26, 37, 49, 51, 59, 128–36
tree-planting   69, 72, 78

unemployment   13, 24, 159
United States   154–7, 162, 164, 166
urban congestion   48–9, 91
urban planning   51, 59
urbanisation   13–14, 47–51, 52–9, 72

vegetation   10–12
    clearing   15, 17, 18, 65, 72, 73–4, 82
    protection for soil   73
volcanic rock   112–13

war   38, 46
waste disposal *see* sanitation
waste recycling *see* recycling
water, natural balance   81
water resources   2, 7, 12, 36, 49, 56, 62, 63, 65, 81–90, 118–27
water storage *see* dams
watertable *see* soil, salinity
wealth   1
weather, soil erosion   73, 147, 148
wheat   38, 39, 40, 41, 42, 43, 44, 63, 71
women's programmes   26, 45, 62, 70
women's role   29, 63, 70
wool   72
world *see* global

yams   31